GLOBAL BORDERLANDS

GLOBAL BORDERLANDS

Fantasy, Violence, and Empire
in Subic Bay, Philippines

VICTORIA REYES

STANFORD UNIVERSITY PRESS
STANFORD, CALIFORNIA

Stanford University Press
Stanford, California

Printed in the United States of America on acid-free, archival-quality paper

Library of Congress Cataloging-in-Publication Data

Names: Reyes, Victoria (Victoria Diane), author.

Title: Global borderlands : fantasy, violence, and empire in Subic Bay, Philippines / Victoria Reyes.

Description: Stanford, California : Stanford University Press, 2019. | Series: Culture and economic life | Includes bibliographical references and index.

Identifiers: LCCN 2019016327 (print) | LCCN 2019017646 (ebook) | ISBN 9781503609426 (electronic) | ISBN 9781503607996 (cloth : alk. paper) | ISBN 9781503609419 (pbk. : alk. paper)

Subjects: LCSH: Subic Bay Region (Philippines)—Social conditions. | Globalization—Social aspects—Philippines—Subic Bay Region. | Free ports and zones—Social aspects—Philippines—Subic Bay Region. | Subic Bay Naval Station (Philippines). | Philippines—Relations—United States. | United States—Relations—Philippines.

Classification: LCC HN720.S83 (ebook) | LCC HN720.S83 R49 2019 (print) | DDC 303.48/2599073—dc23

LC record available at https://lccn.loc.gov/2019016327

Typeset by Westchester Publishing Services in 10/14 Minion Pro

Cover design: Angela Moody

Contents

Preface

As scholars, we cannot help how our work is received. I and my work are often seen as either too critical or not critical enough. When pressed to say whether I think global borderlands, like overseas U.S. military bases or special economic zones, are "good" or "bad" for development, I never seem to give an answer that is quite satisfactory to the questioner. That's because, fundamentally, I think that is the wrong question to ask. As a researcher, I seek to understand social life. Although I may have inklings of what I may find in the field, the beauty of research is to be surprised—to be open to the people and places we encounter, not to go searching for the story we want to tell and suffering from confirmation bias.[1]

What I've found is that it's not the case that these highly controversial places are fundamentally good or bad. It depends on *who* you're talking about and the *topic* and *situation* at hand. We must focus on how contexts, interactions, and people come together within particular social structures and how their varying configurations produce very different understandings of what is going on.[2] That is the heart of sociology: to study how social structures, culture, and agency interact. It is not the case that we should, as Kieran Healy suggests, "fuck nuance" in order to go beyond producing fine-grain analysis, expanding conceptual frameworks, or self-boasting, all of which are "nuance" traps that hold back theoretical development.[3] Instead, as contemporary sociologists, we are likely Mertonian, midrange theorists that have rejected grand theoretical traditions that try to encompass our understandings of all social life. Noting the contours of theoretical constructs, when and under what conditions certain actions and understandings occur, is necessary for recognizing the *usefulness* of a particular theory, its specific contributions, and how it interacts with what we already know. Otherwise, we miss the conversations that others are having and fail to see research as a scholarly conversation from which we must build. In this project I'm writing for two very different audiences—historical/comparative sociologists and qualitative sociologists/ethnographers—all of whom have very different styles, conventions, and expectations for presenting data and book writing. It was important for me to tackle both audiences and sets of data, because contemporary Subic Bay cannot be understood without knowing its history and because I see history not as merely a descriptive backdrop but as an *explanation*. Equally important was the ethnographic and qualitative work I conducted on contemporary Subic Bay, because the historical tells us how and why we arrived here but not about how people on the ground make sense of this place, nor how they tie into its transformation from a military base to a Freeport Zone.

In this way, the book centers on the intersection of what Michael Burawoy calls structural versus transactional ethnography.[4] The former is attuned to theory and the broader social structures that shape society while the latter, he argues, is rooted in empirics and local life.[5] Yet, in focusing on sociology as the interplay among social structures, agency and culture, and uniting ethnographic with historical work, I argue that examining both structural inequalities *and* transactional relations is necessary to understand social life.[6] There are structural inequalities that fundamentally shape, for example, U.S.-Philippine relations. Yet, it is also the case that these same inequalities may look, are negotiated, and manifest themselves very differently across social relations and contexts. To be sure, Burawoy argues for a comparative logic, which centers on comparing differences across social contexts. Ethnographers like Leslie Salzinger,[7] a student of Burawoy's who has documented and theorized the differing gendered subjects and ideals found in her ethnography of four maquilas, epitomizes this approach, and my own work is indebted to hers and similar research. I differ in that I unite this comparative logic with an analysis that focuses on relationships and processes, which is rooted in Viviana Zelizer's[8] approach to studying economic life through what she calls "relational work" and is similar to what Matthew Desmond[9] calls for in a relational ethnography. Relationships are not static, they change, are enacted within, and are shaped by and shape broader social structures and contexts.

Another goal of mine was to make both theoretical and empirical contributions to the literature. In this book I argue that there is a new analytic space that I call "global borderlands," and I show how negotiations and imaginations within and around them are continually recreated and reproduce global inequality in surprising ways. In examining the role of culture, law, power, and stakes in global borderlands, this book also offers theoretical insight into their dynamics: how, why, and under which conditions social structures and differences in power are rigid and inflexible, as well as when they are porous and can be used to alter social life. That is, I explain why and how Filipino government officials, for example, are stymied by U.S. threats to pull aid in some situations, while in other contexts they are empowered to assert their will and sovereignty. It is only in focusing on relations, structures, and culture that we can understand U.S.-Philippine relations. Additionally, I strove to make the text accessible and readable to a wider audience. Part of making it more accessible was to frame the manuscript around narratives—that is, to tell the main argument through the stories of the people who, in the past and present, have lived, worked, and visited this place. Much of the research that I cite is in the endnotes so as to facilitate this narrative flow and accessibility.

This book departs from similar ethnographies and historical/comparative works in that I focus on a wide array of contexts (shopping, military agreements, and intimacies, among others) to develop both the contemporary and historical stories and to identify underlying mechanisms. It was important to examine each context to show how global borderland dynamics are not limited to one or two specific situations (e.g., high-profile crimes involving U.S. servicemen and Filipina women). Instead, they permeate many facets of life. As such, the book does not follow the same set of actors across chapters. Instead, each chapter tackles a different set of actors and situations, while still advancing the manuscript's main argument. This format, while untraditional, is central to both the argument itself and my goals with the book.

These contradictions and the stories that get lost when scholars only focus on whether global borderlands are "good" or "bad" for development also get at the heart of my own family's history: the stigma surrounding my grandmother's migration through marriage, her longing for a better life, the upward mobility of some (though not all) family members, and the origin of terrible family secrets that all tie back to everyday life in a neighborhood surrounding a U.S. base.

My grandmother Maria describes herself as the black sheep of the family. She was about seven or eight years old when her family moved to Subic, a *barangay* (neighborhood) of Olongapo City, which was home to the U.S. Subic Bay Naval Base. Her family home, eventually destroyed by the 1992 Mt. Pinatubo volcanic explosion, had no electricity. Instead, it had a communal water pump that was used for showering, laundering clothes, and washing dishes. These conditions stood in stark contrast to her visits to the base and seeing the ships up close and in person. When she was a teenager, she and her friends "went to the base and there was a lot of ship. Oh, so exciting to see a lot of big ship. You won't get tired of it to see it. I went to [the] ship and went inside. Oh, it's so big you won't believe it."

It was there that, on different occasions, she met three U.S. naval seamen. With one, she became pregnant with her first daughter and gave birth to her in 1967. However, she didn't love him and refused to marry him. They fought over custody until he committed suicide in his jail cell, where he was being held because he went AWOL (absence without official leave) from the U.S. Navy and stayed with her family. Later on she met another serviceman, whom she describes as the love of her life. The times they spent together were some of the happiest of her life. However, he could not yet commit to marriage and fulfill her dream of leaving the Philippines. She met her now ex-husband because he was friends with the love of her life. He became infatuated with Maria and proposed.

She was faced with a dilemma: to pursue a relationship with someone whom she loved dearly but who was unable or unwilling to make an immediate commitment to her, or to marry a man she liked but who promised to take her away from the Philippines and travel the world. He offered a whirlwind of global travel, marriage, and an immediate departure from the land she longed to disappear from, allowing her to fulfill her dream of changing her life.

She made her choice. Leaving her daughter with her mother to ensure her safety until she settled, Maria, at nineteen years old, embarked on her journey around the world, visiting Ireland, Morocco, and Hawaii, among other places. As she tells me, "I grab the opportunity. I get what I want. I travel the world, but I didn't get the person that I love. So . . . I got my dream. I went everywhere since I married my ex-husband, I went everywhere: cruising, see the world." However, she also laments what she lost because of her choice. "But I guess I'm not really happy because I didn't get the man that I love. It's my fault [*softly*]. I have to live with that. . . . It's my fault. But I have to see my dream first. OK. To see how, how's the other country look like, but I'm not happy. . . . I see the world, but I didn't get the person that I love [*pause*]. I guess you don't get everything."[10]

She lived in Ohio with his parents while he completed his tour of duty abroad, and she changed her name to Frances. There, his mother helped her learn to drive and to pass the U.S. citizenship test. A few years after she was settled, she brought her daughter from the Philippines to the United States, and her husband adopted her. It must have been a relatively short time before her fairy-tale story started to show cracks.

Frances and her husband remained married for over a decade, relocating to cities across the United States based on his military assignments. At the time of their divorce, she was around thirty years old, and he was serving a ten-year jail sentence for breaking and entering and threatening a police officer. He was released in three years, even though this was not his first time behind bars. They were living in Florida at the time of their divorce, and after he was arrested, she discovered that he had gambled away their money. During this time, the car he bought her was repossessed, and she lost touch with her family in the Philippines because she couldn't afford to keep in contact with them. With no income and no car, she took her five children on a bus to Cincinnati, where his family was from. They didn't live with her former in-laws, nor even in the same school district because it was too expensive. They moved into a small house in Blue Ash, Ohio. There, and alone, she raised her five children and her first granddaughter, whom her first daughter gave birth to when she was only fifteen years old. To survive, she worked at Prime N Wine (a steak and wine restaurant), at McDonald's, and as a domestic worker for a family. She slept on the couch in the living room, so her two sons could each have their own rooms, while her middle daughter, youngest daughter, and granddaughter shared the other room.

·   ·   ·

Frances is my grandmother,[11] and I am her first granddaughter, the one whom she raised. While I knew many parts of my family's history growing up, other details were revealed after I left for college. She was always wary of and hesitant about talking about her past, but because I knew bits and pieces of her migration story, I longed to know more about how she made sense of her life and convinced her to talk to me for an oral history assignment in an Asian American history class taught by Judy Tzu-Chun Wu that I was taking at the time.

Despite the sad turn her story later takes, the nostalgia she associated with the base and its personnel stuck with me. It puzzled me as I took classes as an undergraduate and learned about the U.S. empire in the Philippines and other countries. Yes, bases were demonstrations of military power and hegemony that brought with them worsening environmental conditions, prostitution, sexually transmitted infections, and unequal power in state-to-state dynamics and in the day-to-day relationships and interactions between Americans (often men) and Filipino/as. How did the goodwill and nostalgia of which my grandmother spoke fit in? Was she an anomaly? Is that why she always spoke about Filipinos being "stuck up"? She told me that she once tried visiting a Filipino American organization, but when all the women wanted to know who her husband was and what he did for a living, she told them he was a garbageman rather than a naval seaman. She did this, in part, I suspect, because she thought these first-generation Filipino immigrants—her peers—would look down on her marriage and the associated stigmas of being a "gold digger," who "used" a man to leave the Philippines. After her encounter, she ceased contact with those women and that organization.

For this book's research, I returned to the place that captivated me from my grandmother's stories: Subic Bay, Philippines. I often walked along the boardwalk around the bay, and the first time I saw a U.S. military ship docked there, the memory of my conversations with my grandmother, including her awe of the ships, came back to me full force. I also regularly visited my family and their home in Calapacuan, a *barangay* of Olongapo City. It is a family compound of sorts, with a central, shared concrete space and small, concrete-walled "apartments" surrounding it. In this open space, at a spot between my great-grandmother's place and the room for her granddaughter's family, was the spigot for well water. This one-handle pump was used for showering and getting buckets of water for household chores. There was no running water, not even for the toilet. I could only imagine how my grandmother felt growing up with such limited amenities—though this was and continues to be a commonplace scenario in the Philippines—and then being brought into a whole new world inside the military base, with buildings, structures, and amenities not available to her just outside its gates. Yet she was able to accomplish her dream of leaving the Philippines and traveling the world, though through the price of her ill-fated marriage.

Acknowledgments

My grandmother's story and my family's history more generally stayed with me as a budding academic. It shaped the theories that I gravitated to[12]—for one, the relational economic sociology approach pioneered by Viviana Zelizer. Her book *Purchase of Intimacy* was a text that transformed the way I viewed the world. That people's lives were rooted in cultural understandings and that we make efforts to "match" particular media and transactions with particular relationships spoke to me and sociologically explained what I had previously uncovered in my work on Filipina marriage migrants, the women "left behind," and how they understood their relationships with U.S. servicemembers. It also resonated with my personal family history—how my grandmother briefly lived out her fantasies of a life full of travel but at the expense of stigma, pain, and eventual poverty and how she navigated encounters with other Filipinos and Filipino Americans in each stage of her life.

So, too, did my work with Miguel Centeno help me bring together and understand how structural global forces of power and inequality, not only shaped people's lives in surprising ways but how power, structure, and states cannot be easily categorized. He pushed my thinking about U.S. empire and challenged my understanding of concepts I thought I knew, such as "informal empire" and "neocolonialism," and how contemporary U.S.-Philippine relations compared to previous classical and formal empire dynamics that shaped U.S.-Philippine relations for fifty years. He also pushed me to think about the different social actors at play and to understand their points of view. Very few people are villains in real life, and shedding light on people's complexity has become the foundation of my research.

This project could not have come to fruition without the guidance, mentorship, and assistance of several people, some of whom have already been mentioned. I'm grateful to Judy Tzu-Chun Wu, who sparked my interest in Asian American studies and whose class brought with it an opportunity to get to know my grandmother's story, and to Roland Sintos Coloma, an Ohio State University graduate student at the time who cultivated my interests in Filipino America and the Philippines. I'm also grateful to my initial sociology mentor, Rachel E. Dwyer, without whom I would not have become a sociologist. Miguel A. Centeno and Viviana A. Zelizer have given me thoughtful, kind, and expansive guidance and bestowed on me the intellectual tool kits I still use today. I am forever in their debt. I am also grateful to Douglas S. Massey for his generous feedback and guidance throughout this project. Mitch Duneier and Bob Wuthnow similarly provided helpful feedback. I am also grateful to members of my working group, Erin F. Johnston and Joanne Wang Golann. Erin, Joanne, and I encouraged and critiqued each other's work, praised our relative accomplishments, and empathized with the obstacles we all similarly encountered. I could not have gone through this process without them. Paul DiMaggio served as a critical figure in the development of my previous article on cultural wealth and influenced my approach on how to specify boundaries when creating a new concept, which helped shape this project. I also owe intellectual debts to the

2013–14 Princeton Center for the Study of Social Organization workshop led by Viviana A. Zelizer, and I am grateful to Donna DeFrancisco, Cindy Gibson, and Amanda Rowe for all of their administrative assistance. Additionally, Saskia Sassen provided important feedback on earlier versions of parts of the book, as did Annie Bunting and Sally Engle Merry. Additionally, conversations with Tanya Golash-Boza and Amy A. Quark proved to be invaluable. Chapter comments from Randol Contreras, Emmanuel David, Matthew Mahutga, and Rourke O'Brien were also helpful.

   I am indebted to many amazing colleagues at the University of Michigan's National Center for Institutional Diversity, particularly Tabbye Chavous, Charlotte Ezo, Bill Lopez, Marie Ting, and Shana Wright. At Michigan, I'm also grateful for Al Young, who provided me with office space and generously commented on my work. He is an inspirational mentor. I'd also like to thank Zaineb Al-Kalby, Jennifer Eshelman, Vicky Horvath, and Victoria McIntyre for their administrative support.

   I'm also indebted to Müge Göçek, Allen Hicken, Karen Lacy, Victor Mendoza, and George Steinmetz for their generous feedback, as well as Elizabeth Armstrong, Rob Jensen, Greta Krippner, Jacob Lederman, Jeremy Levine, Roi Livne, Karin Martin, and Alex Murphy for their comments on various chapters of the book. In April 2017 I held a book manuscript workshop and Julian Go, Rhacel Parreñas, and Fred Wherry each provided generous insights, comments, and direction, without which the manuscript would not be what it is today. Furthermore, I'd like to thank my editor at Stanford University Press, Marcela Cristina Maxfield, and the editors of the Culture and Economic Life series, Greta Hsu, Jennifer Lena, and Fred Wherry, for incredible guidance throughout this process. As a first-time book author, I appreciate the time and effort they put into the project and the confidence they had in me. The two anonymous reviewers of the book also provided wonderful guidance that sharpened the book's focus and argument. I'm also appreciative of the entire Stanford University Press team and all of their work in getting the book published.

   The research and writing for this project were supported by generous funds from the Department of Sociology, East Asian Studies Program, and the Center for Migration and Development at Princeton University; the Princeton Institute for International and Regional Studies; the American Sociological Association's Minority Fellowship Program; and the University of Michigan's National Center for Institutional Diversity. Funding from the National Science Foundation's Graduate Research Fellowship Program also proved invaluable. Early versions of some materials have been previously published in *Theory and Society*, *City & Community*, and a chapter in the edited volume *International Marriages and Marital Citizenship: Southeast Asian Women on the Move*. Expanded discussions regarding the "ethnographic tool kit" and transparency in ethnographic research that I mention in the methodological appendix have been published as separate articles in *Ethnography*. I thank the editors and anonymous reviewers of these materials for their generous feedback and comments.

This project would not be in existence without the people who allowed me a peek into their lives, the Subic Bay Metropolitan Authority officials whom I interviewed and who provided me access to materials, and the Subic Bay Metropolitan Authority chairman who granted me permission to do so. I'd also like to thank Harbor Point mall officials, specifically Derrick Manuel, who granted me permission to solicit interviews from workers and visitors and graciously answered my questions, and the officials from the various Olongapo City Regional Trial Courts for their assistance in obtaining local court documents. Additionally, I am grateful to the administration and my colleagues at Bryn Mawr College and at the University of California, Riverside. I also could not have accomplished my research without the support of my family still living in the Philippines, including but not limited to sina Lola, Tita Linda, Tita Olly, AiAi, Angie, at Maria, among many others.

Finally, I wouldn't be where I am today without my grandmother, whose life sparked my sociological imagination; Adam Arnett, my supportive husband who takes credit for my being a sociologist because he recommended that I take Rachel's class; and my daughter Olivia, who is such a delight and who taught me how to write more efficiently. Recently, my mother passed away after a short and intense battle with breast cancer, and I gave birth to my son, James, who had health issues while in the womb. Both of them permeated my thoughts as I neared the end of this process. This book is dedicated to them all.

Timeline of Key Events

1898	Treaty of Paris
1899–1902	Philippine-American War
1934	Tydings-McDuffie Act (Philippine Independence Act)
1946	Treaty of General Relations
1946	Bell Trade Act
1947	Military Bases Agreement
1947	Military Assistance Act
1951	Mutual Defense Treaty
1955	Laurel-Langley Agreement
1965	Ferdinand Marcos elected president
1966	Military Bases Agreement amendment: a change from a ninety-nine-year lease to a twenty-five-year lease
1972	Martial law declared
1979	Military Bases Agreement amendment: bases will now be under Philippine control
1986	People's Power Movement: ousting of Marcos and election of Corazon Aquino
1991	All facilities except Subic Bay Naval Base and Clark Air Force Base are handed over to the Philippines
1991	Mt. Pinatubo erupts; United States cedes Clark Air Force Base to the Philippines
1991	The Treaty of Friendship, Cooperation and Security is rejected by a 12–11 Senate vote
1992	Creation of the Subic Bay Freeport Zone
1992	Withdrawal of the U.S. military

GLOBAL BORDERLANDS

Introduction

"On Women's Day, we seek not only to end all violence perpetrated against women but also to address the primordial roots of violence in our country—the continued and intensifying foreign exploitation of our sovereignty and environment," proclaims Terry Ridon, president of the Kabataan Partylist, a youth-based political party in the Philippines. "Why do we say that violence emanates from foreign intervention and exploitation? Throughout history, violence has been perpetrated by invaders upon conquest of new lands. From the Spaniards to the continuing domination of the Americans, our nation has continuously been beaten and persecuted to the point of subjugation."[1] His words echo through the crowd gathered in Manila, the country's capital.

Bai Ali Indayla, a Muslim Filipina activist and Kabataan Partylist nominee, concurs, saying, "Where foreign troops go, lives are lost, women are abused, and our sovereignty is raped."[2]

Just a few hours away, on that very same day, a group of women stand in the middle of Magsaysay Drive, part of a thickening crowd. One shows her support by wearing a heart-shaped sign around her neck that says, "US Troops Out Now!" Speaking into a microphone, she calls for the U.S. military to leave the Philippines. Behind her, someone holds two signs that read, "Philippine Territory Off Limits to GI Joe!" and "We've Suffered Enough."[3]

This protest is held outside the gates of the Subic Bay Freeport Zone (SBFZ), a place dedicated to attracting foreign direct investment, or economic transactions through the partial or full foreign ownership of businesses located in host countries. Freeport Zones (FZs) like Subic Bay attract these businesses by being physical places where domestic economic laws are relaxed.[4] Protests like these, against foreign investment and intervention, are written into the fabric and history of the Philippines—from revolutionaries fighting against Spanish and U.S. colonialism, to the popular and nonviolent overthrow of a dictator who was seen as a puppet of the U.S. government, to demonstrations against the U.S. military in the Philippines.[5] Home to the former U.S. Subic Bay Naval Base, Subic Bay has long been a lightning rod for what it means to host a foreign power.

Yet, as these women chant and hold signs decrying the U.S. military presence in the Philippines, hundreds of people mill about. They go about their daily routines, paying no attention to what is occurring just a few feet away. Everyday life continues on. Informal food vendors still gather around the FZ's entrance, selling *pina* (pineapple), *pandasal* (bread), *mani* (peanuts), *suman* (a form of sticky rice), *saging* (bananas), *buko* (coconut) juice, gum, candies, and cigarettes. Workers and visitors continue to enter the FZ, and others pass by its entrance as they make their way to the rest of the day.

This protest and the mundane of everyday life occurring alongside it are emblematic of what it means to live within a *global borderland*,[6] a place controlled by foreigners and one where the rules that govern socioeconomic life differ from those that are outside its walls.[7] These places—whether an overseas military base, a special economic zone (SEZ),[8] an all-inclusive tourist resort, an embassy, a cruise ship, a port city, or a colonial trading fort—mean different things to different people. They elicit *multiple* meanings. For some, these places are symbols of imperialism, unequal power, and foreign penetration into domestic society, something to be protested and lobbied against so that their very presence is destroyed. For others, they represent the "good life" and are rooted in utopian imaginaries that provide status and something in which to belong and partake, whether through work or leisure. Both things are true, depending on who you ask and where you look.

This book is a cultural sociology of globalization, development, and inequality. It focuses on these seemingly contradictory claims by examining everyday experiences of people living in, working at, and visiting Subic Bay and the accompanying love, crimes, statuses, and meanings that they (re)create within it. Subic Bay is just one of many global borderlands around the world, like Acapulco, New York University Abu Dhabi, Cayman Enterprise City Special Economic Zone, and any of the 307 U.S. embassies, consulates, or diplomatic missions abroad.[9]

Global Borderlands

Global borderlands represent a new analytic, spatialized unit of globalization, whose activities have consequences far beyond their borders. They are not global centers of finance, although, like global cities,[10] they are places where the rich depend on relatively low-wage work. Instead, they are global centers of foreign-local encounters, whether for work and/or pleasure, that lay within, rather than alongside, geopolitical borders.[11] They are not "flat" spaces where global exchanges take place. Rather global borderlands are particular, spatialized configurations of inequalities that are based on differences in nationality and class. As such, inequalities are written into their very fabric. They are, by definition, spaces of high inequalities, and their physical location remains important.[12] Every time you step into a place that has different sets of rules governing it, is semiautonomous from domestic laws, and is based on the interaction between the foreign and the local, you enter a global borderland. So, too, do you enter one if you are a foreigner abroad who visits a place because of its familiarity to your home land.

Global borderlands are *legally plural*, places where two or more legal systems coexist.[13] That is, they are places where there are competing and intersecting jurisdictions over people, rules, norms, and expectations and where the rule of law increasingly depends on the context of the crime and the identities of individuals and governments.[14] In this respect, global borderlands are "unsettled"[15] places where sociocultural and legal strategies of action are continually negotiated and contested.

Here I use a law and society perspective that sees laws as cultural meaning-making systems[16] and recognize the difference between "law on the books" and "law in action," where the former are written laws and the latter are laws as they are understood, experienced, and enacted on the ground in everyday life.[17] These legally plural systems may be formal, informal, or somewhere in between. For example, if outside of these places, being gay, having uncovered hair, or wearing shorts are illegal, prohibited, or frowned upon, within them, these things may be accepted, welcomed, and/or pass unremarked on. In a similar way, international agreements governing U.S. military bases or visiting forces stipulate the when, where, why, and over whom U.S. versus domestic laws apply. So, too, are domestic economic laws relaxed in order to attract foreign businesses within SEZs like the Panama Pacifico Special Economic Area, South Korea's Yellow Sea Free Economic Zone, Egypt's North West Suez Special

Economic Zone (SEZONE), or Poland's SEZ EURO-PARK MIELEC (SSE Euro-Park Mielec).

Global borderlands provide a window into broader economic and political relations and the accompanying demonstrations of power they entail. Where the foreign and the local meet, inequalities serve as their foundation. As such, whether defined in the Weberian sense of the ability to assert your will despite resistance,[18] as state's infrastructural[19] or despotic[20] forms, as having relational, discursive, and performative dimensions,[21] or as stemming from ideology, economy, military, or politics,[22] differences in *power* shape the content and form of these global interactions. This is true if we regard global borderlands as sites where empire, "expansive, militarized, and multiethnic political organizations that significantly limit the sovereignty of the peoples and polities they conquer," and imperialism, "a strategy of political control over foreign lands that does not necessarily involve conquest, occupation, and durable rule by outside invaders,"[23] thrive and take hold,[24] such as when the International Monetary Fund, the World Bank, or the United States flex their muscles and demand that countries meet particular conditions before being granted aid,[25] or when the overt or subtle threat of military power and taking away military aid lies in the shadow of socioeconomic and political negotiations. Yet, even if you see global borderlands not as arms of empire but as the result of diplomacy, soft power, and/or hegemony in action,[26] power's influence seeps into these exchanges, shaping dynamics and underlying the actions and inactions taken within and about them.

Global borderlands can be examples of what Carl Schmitt calls a "state of exception,"[27] where norms are suspended and who is sovereign is the one who decides what is exceptional and what is not. They can also be representative of how Aihwa Ong describes "neoliberalism as exception"—where neoliberalism, as a political, economic, and ideological platform, has reconfigured definitions and experiences of citizenship and sovereignty around the world and where SEZs' autonomy "creates conditions of total market freedom but without . . . democratic rights."[28] Foreigners and accompanying socioeconomic and political policies enact undue influence within these places precisely because domestic actors are using these policies as a way to lure foreigners and their investments into their country. As such, domestic actors do not *solely* decide on who and what is "exceptional."

However, within these boundaries, I've also found that power is not a one-way demonstration of domination of the foreign over the domestic[29] or the rich over the poor. Rather, within the gates of these spaces, we can witness the inner workings of power as something that is relational and situational, even within places of stark structural inequality. For example, power shapes and is shaped by legal agreements: their writing and their use in resolving disputes. As Carruthers and Halliday note, "countries which appear relatively powerless over enactment nevertheless have some power to shape implementation. Groups within countries, which may be unable to block enactment, can (as in weapons of the weak) undermine or frustrate implementation" and locals have the ability to translate and adapt global laws.[30]

Power can also differ in degree or type and can be exercised using leverage, persuasion, and reciprocity and through social structures and arenas.[31] It is wielded by the elite and the nonelite, as well as foreign and domestic actors, alike. As such, and contrary to popular understanding, we can think of global borderlands not as sites where domestic actors fully cede sovereignty to foreigners. Rather, we need to see them as places where sovereignty is *contingent*. It is continually negotiated and contested, long after they've been created. When seen as arms of empires, global borderlands highlight their informal forms, which is when "international control is exercised through military, economic, and other means, but there is no conquest or permanent seizure of political sovereignty and therefore no possibility of systematically enforcing a rule of difference. Informal empire is more coercive than hegemony."[32] Informal empire is not about absolute control nor only about the appearance or facade of domestic sovereignty as a mask for foreign sovereignty, power, or control. Rather, I show how within these places, control is contingent; it is continually negotiated and contested by both the foreign and the local.

The notion that politics involve negotiations where the powerful may give some concessions to the less powerful is not new. Indeed, international politics, political sociology, and international law are just a few of the fields where these negotiations take center stage. Alexander Cooley,[33] for example, suggests that what he calls "base politics" over U.S. overseas military bases depends on the relative bargaining positions of host country leaders and the agreement's legitimacy. Similarly, Amy Austin Holmes[34] suggests that overseas military bases spark social unrest depending on two factors: whether outside threats to the host nation are high and whether they commit harm to the people they are supposed to protect. Depending on these factors, overseas U.S. military bases can provide "legitimate protection," "pernicious protection," "precautionary protection," or a "protection racket," and these roles can change across time.

Given these analyses that highlight the political negotiations between powerful and less powerful countries, what is new about the approach laid out in this book? By extending and connecting this analysis of negotiations to *multiple* facets of life, this examination goes beyond international politics or economic laws. Second, and following Julian Go's work,[35] I highlight the role of culture and meaning-making in international politics and laws, and bridge together insights from a wide array of fields that often are not in conversation with one another: from international politics and international law to scholarship on empire, economic sociology, urban sociology, and cultural sociology. Place and space are foregrounded as central aspects of these negotiations because they often revolve around global borderlands. To paint a nuanced picture of global borderlands, I offer different mechanisms—that of law, power, meaning-making, and stakes—for understanding them.

Global borderlands are sites where meanings and identities are continually reimagined and recreated.[36] Whether seen as a symbol of empire or as a facet of the "good life," these places attract attention and demand explanations for their existence. Here, people draw on imaginaries of the past and present to work out their own understanding of how these sites fit into daily life.[37] These understandings touch upon global, national, community, place, family, and personal issues, where legacies of the past, whether "good" or "bad," continue to reverberate and shape contemporary social life.[38] Within Subic Bay, I've discovered how sovereignty, status, meanings, and place are experiential, contingent, and remade. They are not things that are taken for granted; rather, they are *enacted* in, around, and concerning global borderlands in everyday interactions. Uniting people's imaginations and their behavior, alongside the broader social structures that shape their lives,[39] this book shows how in these spaces, power, culture, and agency do not negate one another. Rather, they are entwined and come together to reinforce existing inequalities. Focusing on how power, law, and meanings interact and operate across a wide array of contexts is one purpose of the book. Yet they are not the only mechanisms shaping the terms and outcomes of negotiations. So, too, do we have to pay attention to the role of *stakes*.[40] That is, the relative importance of a situation to government officials is a key determinate of understanding when, where, and how negotiations play out within and around global borderlands.

One important device used to shape the stakes of a situation is the media. Traditional media (newspapers), social media (like Twitter and Facebook), and their coverage are important to study because they frame our understanding of events and the world around us.[41] However, we also know that newspaper coverage is not absolute and depends on conflict, intensity of the conflict, geography, audience, day of the week, and organizational sponsors, among other factors,[42] and that newspaper organizations and journalists themselves play a role in what Marilyn Lester calls "generating newsworthiness."[43] Organizers use cultural artifacts (such as documentaries) to shape public debates,[44] and we know that similar social problems are framed and discussed differently across countries.[45] Yet not all framing efforts by social movement organizations are successful, as their relative effectiveness depends on the larger political and cultural context in which they occur,[46] and whether their events are covered in the news depends on organizations' geographic proximity to news outlets, organizational capacity, and their use of demonstrations.[47] Christopher Bail,[48] for example, has shown how "fringe" organizations can use appeals to negative emotions—in the case he examines, fear and anger—to enter into national media dialogue and cultivate cultural change.

However, social movement organizations are not the only ones to rely on and use media attention strategically. Research in international law shows that not only do court actions shape, and are shaped by, their political environment[49] but that court systems around the world use the media to selectively promote cases and also use public oral hearings as a way to increase awareness about particular cases, about legitimacy and public awareness of the court, and about transparency in the judicial branch.[50] Drawing on a rational-actor model, for example, Guzman[51] also argues that international law has the most influence "when stakes are relatively modest" rather than those that "receive the most attention." Here, we see that scholars define stakes, or importance, a priori.[52] Yet, by definition, this approach presumes that we can hypothesize when something will be high or low stakes before it occurs. It does not account for fluidity in importance and how matters may become important from the ground up. As we'll see in the following pages, this fluidity of stakes is most visible in global borderlands. Uniting the sociology of media with work in international law, we can see how the stakes of a situation can be identified a priori as well as from the ground up, and we can interrogate the role it plays in global borderlands.

· · ·

Global borderlands represent new analytic spaces of global exchanges. Yet they also existed prior to the twentieth century. We see these same dynamics of semi-autonomy and legal pluralism, windows into political and economic

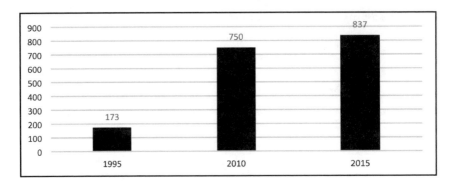

Figure I.1. Number of Overseas U.S. Military Bases in 1995, 2010, and 2015
NOTE: Overseas includes bases in foreign countries and U.S. territories.
SOURCES: Evinger 1995; United States Department of Defense 2010, 2015.

relations, and competing claims to meanings and identities in colonial trading forts. In the Great Lakes region of the United States, for example, sexual
activity, political alliances, and fur trades reflected the "meanings these goods
and their exchange(s) had for both the Algonquians and the French."[53] These
legally plural and semi-autonomous dynamics also occur in precolonial port
cities, for example, when "thousands of borderlanders [living in nineteenth-
century Alexandria] from Greek, Maltese, Levantine, and Egyptian backgrounds
sought the legal and economic protection that larger powers like France,
Britain, Austria, and Russia could provide"[54] vis-à-vis consulate protection
and/or protégé status.

A key difference today, however, is the increasing number of these places
and their ever-changing forms. For example, the number of U.S. overseas military
bases grew from 173 in 32 countries in 1995 to 750 in 45 countries in 2010 to
over 837 in 2015[55] (see figure I.1), and export processing zones (EPZs), one of
many types of SEZs, grew from 93 in 25 countries in 1997 to 3,500 in 130 countries
in 2006 (see figure I.2).[56]

Likewise, tourism has been called the "world's biggest business" and affects
gross domestic product, employment rates, exports, imports, and national images.[57] In September 2014, the company RCI alone operated 271 resort/vacation
exchanges in Africa and the Middle East, 593 in Asia, 234 in Australia and the
South Pacific, 114 in Canada, 281 in the Caribbean and Bermuda, 62 in Central America, 1,037 in Europe, 476 in Mexico, and 375 in South America (see
figure I.3).[58]

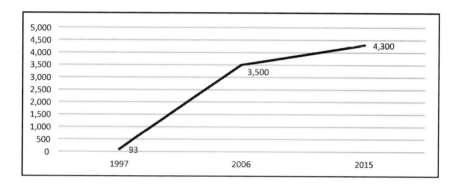

Figure I.2. Number of Export Processing Zones in 1997, 2006, and 2015
SOURCES: Boyenge 2007; *Economist* 2015.

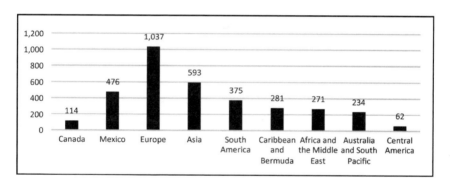

Figure I.3. Number of Non-U.S. RCI Resort/Vacation Exchanges in 2014
SOURCE: RCI online resort directory, http://www.rci.com/resort-directory/landing (accessed September 15, 2014).

Global borderlands play an important socioeconomic role in local communities. Each has its own infrastructure, workers, and consumers. They also represent a microcosm of the relationship between the host and guest nations and have important political ramifications. Formal agreements related to embassies, military bases, and international branch campuses have the most visible and direct connection between micro-interactions and international relationships, as we can see in popular news accounts of, for example, the 2012 attacks on the U.S. diplomatic compound in Benghazi, Libya, and its political aftermath[59] or in threats to academic freedom when it concerns a professor[60] or graduate student[61] blocked from a U.S. university's Middle Eastern international branch campus for writing critically about labor conditions there.

Yet time-shares and all-inclusive resorts also share such a connection by shaping local markets and structuring the interactions among different groups of people. Their very success depends on successful short-term relationships being built across nationalities. For example, in 2013, news that six tourists were raped in Acapulco, Mexico—a center of foreign tourism—made global news precisely because the rapists crossed certain boundaries.[62] Government travel warnings, such as those issued by the U.S. Department of State, lead tourists to choose certain destinations over others, and cartel violence that lines Acapulco's tourist resorts result in a decrease in international tourism, which is then redirected to "safer" tourist locations elsewhere in Mexico.[63] Global borderlands are supposed to be "safe" and "cosmopolitan,"[64] and when crimes or expectations of behavior are violated, it makes international news.

This book offers four insights into how the ever-increasing number of global borderlands affect public policy. First, it helps us understand global borderlands as critical spaces where tensions among global actors arise. Second, it accounts for how international diplomacy operates in action and on the ground. Third, it highlights how and why these places continue to proliferate around the world despite demonstrations against their presence: through both the encouragement of foreigners and the consent and enthusiasm of some locals. Finally, it reveals how these sites are often where informal empire continues to hold sway.

Why Subic Bay, Philippines?

In the wave of post–World War II decolonization, national leaders had to re-configure their relationships not only with their former colonial overlords but also with foreigners from other sovereign nation-states and with their own people. With these transformations, former colonies, like the Philippines, had a chance to reimagine their communities.[65] Who is a citizen? How will they be ruled? What are the rights of Americans? Of other non-Filipinos? How will people respond to and understand these transformations?

The Philippines provides a strategic research site[66] to investigate global borderlands because of its long colonial history and the continued presence and proliferation of these spaces there today. A common saying is that the Philippines spent four hundred years in the convent and fifty years in Hollywood, referring to Spanish and U.S. colonialism respectively. It also was colonized by the Japanese for a short period during World War II. Spanish rule over the

Philippines[67] began in 1521 with the arrival of Ferdinand Magellan and concluded in 1898 with the signing of the Treaty of Paris, which marked the end of the Spanish-American War and resulted in the Spanish ceding the Philippines, and other territories, to the United States. Spanish colonial rule in the Philippines blended indigenous and Spanish traditions in a way that resulted in the current patron-client system, implemented feudal land holding, and left educational instruction to the religious orders who educated very few natives and taught in local tongues rather than in Spanish to discourage rebellion.[68] Although the Spanish unified the islands under Catholicism and as a single political unit under the monarchy, they also kept indigenous political units and factions intact.

Six years after conquest, the city of Manila was established.[69] As a key port in the Manila-Acapulco trade route, Manila became a site of significant international exchange.[70] However, it was also economically vulnerable,[71] and the wealth it generated was unevenly distributed. Poverty was rampant, and the country's wealth and infrastructure were concentrated within this single city. Intermarriage was a means of social and economic mobility available to rich Filipinos, and many married lighter-skinned Spaniards and Chinese—who controlled most aspects of the retail, agricultural, and industrial markets. The resulting interwoven racial, class, and urban-rural distinctions continue today with high-status, light-skinned urban families from Spanish descent at the top, followed by those of Filipino-Chinese descent, and indigenous, dark-skinned rural Filipinos at the very bottom of the hierarchy.[72] A simple walk from Olongapo City to the SBFZ, which directly and indirectly excludes the poor, can give insight into these legacies of Spanish colonialism.

When Americans asserted sovereignty over the Philippines, U.S. officials and civilians alike initially debated the value of controlling the islands.[73] Imperialists saw overseas colonies as the next viable step in the Manifest Destiny doctrine and the Philippines as a strategic and commercial island where U.S. values and institutions could be spread, while anti-imperialists argued that they were an unimportant outpost in the Pacific that would make the United States vulnerable.[74] The imperialists ultimately won. During the colonial era, Americans enforced a policy of "benevolent assimilation" and of Filipinazation— placing day-to-day rule of the Philippines in the hands of Filipinos.[75] Their goal was to Americanize Filipinos. One way to do this was to institute English as the lingua franca, with teachers called "Thomasites" immigrating to the Philippines to teach English and with select Filipinos, called *pensionados*, traveling to the United States to study at U.S. universities.[76] The United States' empire in the Philippines also created additional labor and professional pathways of migration for Filipinos to the United States.[77]

Another key element of U.S. colonialism was the racialization of Filipinos.[78] U.S. colonial officers conceptualized Filipinos as their "little brown brothers" and as inferior subjects who would become civilized under U.S. rule, because Americans would teach them the so-called correct style of government, practices and tools needed for self-governance,[79] and particular hygienic practices that would transform their bodies into ones healthy and fit enough to eventually lead their nation.[80] Yet, according to Paul Kramer, this racialization was both inclusionary and bifurcated, as U.S. colonial officials divided Christian and "Hispanicized Filipino elites" who were civilized from non-Christian Filipinos who were "savages" and tribal peoples, and this differentiation "both invited and delimited Filipino political agency in colonial state-building."[81] Although rooted in legacies of Spanish colonialism, racial formation in U.S. colonial Philippines was not just a U.S. export or homogenous colonial discourse imposed on the Philippines context.[82] Instead, it was negotiated, contingent, and contested by both Americans and Filipinos on the ground and in policies, and its initial formation during the Philippine-American War relied on the simultaneous racialization of Americans as "'Anglo-Saxons' whose overseas conquests were legitimated by racial-historical ties to the British Empire" and the Philippines as a "tribal" nation.[83]

However, the policies promoting Filipino rule remained limited and a benevolent myth.[84] U.S. officials backed the elite oligarchy instituted by the Spanish, failed to implement promised land reform, widened the gaps between the rich and the poor,[85] and restructured the Philippine economy in order to export cheap, duty-free goods—such as sugar, coconut oil, and various fibers—to the United States and import U.S. goods, including cigarettes, galvanized iron, steel sheets, paints, canned milk, and soap. For example, in 1934, the Philippines was the ninth largest market for U.S. goods, and in 1935 U.S. investments in the Philippines were worth over $200 million.[86] However, it was this very policy of cheap Philippine exports to the United States, Kramer[87] argues, that was key in securing the Philippines their independence.

The popular saying that the Philippines spent four hundred years in the convent and fifty years in Hollywood is particularly applicable for Subic Bay, which serves as a water entrance to the South China Sea. Originally a small fishing village, Subic Bay was initially transformed into a minor, unorganized garrison under Spanish colonialism. The Spanish first scouted Subic Bay in 1572 and in 1884 built an armory there.[88] With infrequent use and poorly planned and ill-equipped facilities, the small subset of the Spanish navy that was stationed at Subic during the Spanish-American War was easily defeated.[89] With the U.S. takeover, Subic Bay's journey into Hollywood began.

At its height, Subic Bay was one of the largest U.S. overseas military bases in the world. It was a logistical and maintenance hub that held strategic importance because of its location in the South China Sea. However, contrary to popular perception, the U.S. bases in the Philippines have never been seen as necessary at all costs. Rather, Americans questioned their presence and use at almost every stage of development. For example, despite later assertions of the importance of Subic Bay by both U.S. and Philippine officials, the choice of where to locate the U.S. military fleet was not obvious. At least five other sea entrances were initially seen as viable alternatives,[90] and local officers serving on the ground saw Subic as a "rat trap," vulnerable to land attack, and too far away from Manila—the capital city that some argued was a better, more strategic site for the main base—for the fleets to support one another.[91] However, due to Admiral George Dewey's influence,[92] in 1900 the Navy's general board chose Subic as its primary location in the Philippines.[93]

Within the first five years of U.S. use,[94] Subic Bay became the largest training ground for the U.S. Marines, and it was built up during World War I. However, in the mid-1930s, there were simultaneously orders to increase the security at Subic Bay to counter a Japanese attack and plans for gradual withdrawal. Yet the U.S. and Filipino forces were ultimately ill prepared for the Japanese attacks on December 8, 11, and 13, 1941. The Japanese ruled over Subic Bay for three years, and after Japan's defeat, the Philippines became a sovereign republic in 1946.[95] During this time, issues regarding the importance and possible withdrawal of the bases were again brought to U.S. attention, this time by General Dwight D. Eisenhower.[96]

With the 1947 Military Bases Agreement between the Philippines and the U.S., the city and the base remained linked, and this relationship was evident in the physical structures and cultural meanings attached to the city.[97] It was only in 1966—twenty years after Philippine independence—that Olongapo officially became a Philippine city.[98] Like Manila, its rebuilt architecture and physical development reflected two kinds of spaces: "first, an abstract space of [U.S.] ideals and intentions; second, a 'real' or physical space shaped by its inhabitants"—U.S. and Filipino military and civilians alike.[99]

To some, the U.S. military facilities in the Philippines symbolized a continuation of this unequal relationship between the two countries, and the creation of the SBFZ following their 1992 withdrawal represented the real beginning of Philippine sovereignty. Currently, Subic Bay continues to house the SBFZ, a tourism and business destination that is home to a wide array of complexes: a tiger zoo, a water park, tourist resorts, universities, an international high school, shipping and manufacturing facilities, an upscale mall, and three gated residential communities. Part of its land is shared with the Aetas (an indigenous people of the Philippines), some of whom help run the tiger zoo and perform cultural dances for tourists. The SBFZ also serves as a popular dock for foreign ships—evangelical and U.S. military ships alike. However, with the 2014 Enhanced Defense Cooperation Agreement, the Philippines has once again become a quasi-permanent home to the U.S. military.

Yet Subic Bay is not only a story about the U.S. military abroad. It also encapsulates the rise of the East Asian tigers, attracts European and British Commonwealth businesses, and tells the tale of the Philippines' efforts to attain socioeconomic ascendency and the obstacles in its path. For example, according to 2012 Subic Bay Metropolitan Authority (SBMA) raw statistics given to me, there are 1,069 companies in the SBFZ: 25 percent (264 of 1,069) are foreign-owned, 58 percent (624 of 1,069) are Filipino-owned, 16 percent (174 of 1,069) are owned by a joint company that has at least one Filipino partner, and .01 percent (7 of 1069) are owned by a joint company among various foreign partners. Among foreign-owned SBFZ companies, Korean (119 companies, or 45.08 percent) companies make up the largest share, and their presence is growing.

For example, in recent months, SBMA signed an agreement for a P20 billion ($4.44 billion[100]) resort project with Korean-owned Resom Resort and a memorandum of understanding with Daejeon TechnoPark, the "second biggest center of Administration and Science and Technology" in Korea.[101] Forty-seven Taiwanese companies (17.80 percent), thirty-one Japanese companies (11.74 percent), and twenty-five U.S. companies (9.47 percent) make up the next largest share of foreign direct investment. The rest are relatively negligible and range from five (British) businesses to one (e.g., Qatari) (see figure I.4). The transformation of the SBFZ since the withdrawal of U.S. military facilities has resulted in the cultivation of East Asian companies, which now dominate the market in the sheer number of businesses operating there.[102]

An analysis of life in Subic Bay reveals how people in a former colony articulate their understandings of what it means to be a rich or poor Filipino and

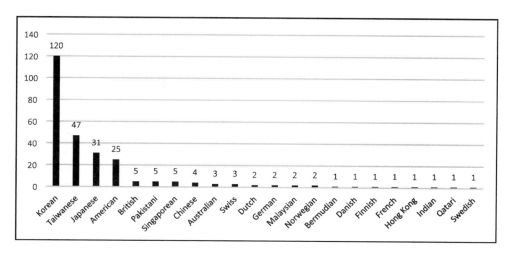

Figure I.4. Number of SBFZ Businesses by Nationality, 2012
SOURCE: Subic Bay Metropolitan Authority.

what it means to be foreign, and what kind of foreign, and how these compare with foreigners' conceptions of the same. I examine Subic Bay as a global borderland because these are new analytic spaces to study how globalization and inequality are experienced on the ground in places that are built on a foundation of competing jurisdictions and inequalities between foreigners and locals, the rich and the poor.

Subic Bay also serves as a Mertonian strategic research site for two more reasons. First, by studying Subic Bay historically and ethnographically, it allows me to examine the cultural dynamics of global borderlands in two forms: an overseas military base and an SEZ. Second, given its history as a former U.S. colony, its siting as a former U.S. military base that continues to host U.S. military personnel, and its geopolitical status as a part of a less developing and less powerful Southeast Asia country, we would expect the negotiations that take place to be relatively lopsided and stable (in favor of foreigners, particularly Americans) compared to global borderlands located elsewhere in the world. Yet even here, at a site of such stark inequality, we find sovereignty, meanings, and power continually negotiated, contingent, and contested by locals and foreigners alike in a way that reproduces global inequality on the ground in often surprising ways. In these spaces, the powerful can use ambiguities to assert their will and shape cultural understandings, but who has power, status, and authority is relational, depending on who is involved, the context, and the content of interactions. Foreigners are not the only ones to exert their will. Filipinos do as well, over conationals and foreigners alike.

Data and Methods

In this book, I examine the experiential of globalization by focusing on one global borderland—the Subic Bay, Philippines—and show how everyday people make meaning of this space and consciously and unconsciously reproduce the difference between it and the city of Olongapo, right outside its gate. The FZ is not just a site of contestation; nor is it a successful development strategy that eliminated Olongapo's poverty. Rather, it is a site of contradictions and complexities.[103] It is a place where globalization and global inequality are experienced and reproduced in everyday life and where power, meanings, and identities are enacted on the ground. Dynamics within can symbolize the United States' continued power in the Philippines and inequalities that are rooted in differences in nationality, gender, and class. Yet these continued inequalities are also recreated by Filipinos themselves. Some Filipinos hold a sense of nostalgia and goodwill for the SBFZ precisely because it is a place where the U.S. can be and was experienced.

To examine these lived experiences of Subic Bay, I relied on multiple methods: nine months of fieldwork in 2012–13; forty-seven formal interviews with Filipino SBFZ workers, Filipino SBFZ visitors, and SBFZ foreigners; informal interviews with government officials and people I encountered during my daily routines; and archival research, including over 429 legal cases and a number of international treaties, government writings, and laws. I also drew on a wide array of Filipino activist and academic writings, memoirs, oral histories, and research and analyzed them as data related to cultural understandings of Subic Bay. My knowledge of the Philippines and Subic Bay is also complemented by my time as a 2005 participant in a heritage program at the University of Philippines, Diliman campus in Quezon City, my research as a 2006–7 Fulbright Scholar to the Philippines, my shorter visits to Subic Bay and Clark since my extended fieldwork, and familial-based cultural knowledge and ties.

In incorporating multiple methods, this book straddles ethnography and historical/comparative research.[104] Ethnography allows us to get at the "definition of the situation"[105] through the eyes of everyday individuals and includes multiple methods: from participant observation and interviews to videos, photographs, and the like.[106] Ethnographic methods allow us to compare "what people say" to "what people do"[107] and provide the sights, sounds, and smells of places by just "being there," highlighting the texture, richness, and meanings behind life on the ground that can only be known through experience. It also allows researchers to interact with people, asking follow-up questions and clarifications, which we're often unable to do with the authors of primary sources. Talk is not always "cheap," as Jerolmack and Khan suggest; it can reveal insights into how people think about themselves and others.[108] Like many urban scholars,[109] I've approached writing about the people I've come to know from a framework based on empathy, seeing them holistically, showcasing their humanity and morality and how they operate within broader social structures. The physicality of being there—seeing firsthand the differences between inside and outside the SBFZ, how people acted, and how they talked—was also central to my understanding of the SBFZ's multifaceted role in everyday Olongapo life.

Historical and comparative[110] methodological approaches allow us to understand the role of *time*[111] and, as such, allow us to move beyond snapshots of life and its meanings to get at the causal mechanisms and explanations for social life. Communities are not created in a vacuum; nor do they operate ahistorically. Rather, they are formed through events that are sequential, contingent, path dependent, and/or singular[112] As Larry Griffin explains, historical sociology uses "the narrative mode to examine and exploit the temporality of social action and historical events."[113] In analyzing a wide array of documents, I do not read these documents as "natural" or "objective" works. Rather, I seek to understand these texts as byproducts of actors that are shaped by social structures, cultural understandings, and power relations. It is important to think about *who* (author) is writing to *whom* (audience) and *why* (the purpose or reason for the text) and the social position of actors, their relations, and the broader social and global field[114] in which the text takes place.

One set of documents I examine are legal agreements or treaties, which are the basis of international law.[115] These documents are important to examine because the ways in which they were written shed light on the process of power. How they are enacted—for example, in legal cases (another set of documents I examine)—also informs our understandings of power relations and their evolution. Both sets of documents are important to examine because why states ratify and comply with these agreements is a central question of the field,[116] and we know that who makes treaties and who consents are shaped by more powerful nation-states, though multilateral treaties provide opportunities for less powerful nation-states to form alliances to block certain positions or clauses.[117] Their respective usefulness, specific commitments, motivations,[118] and countries' reputation for keeping commitments[119] all matter for forming, maintaining, and ending alliances, and alliances are key because they signal that countries share common interests and intentions.[120]

Whether an agreement is bi- or multilateral and their level of formality—that is, whether a formal treaty or an "executive agreement"—also matters since these decisions are used as signaling devices for reliability and compliance.[121] We'll also see how this distinction between formal treaties and executive agreements is at the center of many legal debates in and around Subic Bay. I focus on another central aspect of treaties that helps us understand the role that these agreements play in geopolitics: the level of ambiguity in their writing. Ambiguity in wording matters because, as we can see in the U.S.-Philippine case, the interpretation of language is closely debated in crafting agreements and their use in resolving disputes.[122]

These differences in the ambiguity and precision of language reflect differences between "hard" and "soft" law. While legal agreements may fall anywhere on the spectrum between these two poles, hard laws are agreements written in precise language around the responsibilities of each signatory. Soft law, on the other hand, is characterized by more ambiguous language regarding the trifecta of legal agreements: "obligation, precision and delegation."[123] Some scholars suggest that an increasing reliance on international law, which tends to be soft, opens up opportunities for a handful of states to impose their will on others, and it is only hard law "that comes between the weak and the mighty to protect and deliver."[124] Kenneth Abbott and Duncan Snidal,[125] on the other hand, focus on the advantages and disadvantages of both sets of laws and argue that states may pursue hard laws because these types of laws "reduce transaction costs, strengthen the credibility of their commitments, expand their available political strategies and resolve problems of incomplete contracting . . . [though it also] restricts actors' behaviors and even their sovereignty." In contrast, "international actors often deliberately choose softer forms of legalization as superior institutional arrangements"[126] because soft laws lower the costs of coming to an agreement and allow for more and less powerful states to compromise both at a single point in time and across time. How state and nonstate actors choose to use hard and soft laws ultimately depends, among other aspects, on each actor's power and the presence of conflict between them.[127] However, whether an agreement is hard or soft does not necessarily determine who will exert power over its interpretation or implementation. What's also needed is the importance of the situational context, or whether something is of high or low stakes to each country, and the meanings people associate with the laws and the related social life it deals with.

It might be said that looking at legal agreements and legal cases, which by definition are based on conflict, is an odd if not impractical way to analyze everyday life, sovereignty, status, and meaning. However, in examining documents, I highlight how these documents were written by specific people in a specific period; they did not emerge in a vacuum. I also did not search for terms related to sovereignty, status, or meaning. Instead, I focused on the place itself by searching for "Subic Bay" and "Subic." Discussions around these topics arose inductively and in often surprising contexts: from intimate relations and taxes to high-profile cases involving U.S. service members and Filipinas.

Ethnography and historical/comparative research are complementary methods.[128] They each offer particular ways to analyze social life, whether by focusing on meanings or mechanisms, or whether by witnessing behavior and talk or analyzing written or visual mediums. Relying on both allows me to incorporate both "from above" and "from below" perspectives, interrogate multiple points of view, and observe historical (dis)continuities.

In highlighting Subic Bay as a global borderland, I'll take you on a tour of six arenas of social life where these cultural contestations, negotiations, and imaginations[129] are most visible. Following Rogers Brubaker and colleagues,[130] none of these chapters are labeled "nationalism," "identity," "status," "sovereignty," or "foreign/foreignness" because these things cannot be disentangled. They are entwined in social life. Instead, I focus on how people interpret and make meaning in these situations. As such, I highlight the ways in which they emerge (or fail to emerge) in everyday life, in multiple arenas, and from varied social actors. In doing so, I show how global borderlands revolve around negotiations over sovereignty, power, and culture, and I heed the warning from Andreas Wimmer[131] and Rogers Brubaker and colleagues[132] that it is important not to take a particular lens of analysis—for example, a "sovereignty" lens, where I see sovereignty in every encounter.[133]

In each of the following chapters, what we see are the visible and invisible contestations and negotiations about what it means to be a rich or poor Filipino, what it means to be foreign, and the varied places within which they take place: from courtrooms to shopping malls to private lives at home. These local, everyday dynamics connect to global forces through cultural, cogitative boundary-making[134] processes that link the local and the global, and the strategic adaptation and use of foreign and local products, discourses, and practices. They are also entwined at the level of the nation-state, as on-the-ground conflicts have direct influence on relationships among countries. Here, we'll see how global borderlands are specific spatial locations of globalization whose consequences reverberate beyond their geographic confines, how they also provide windows into broader political and economic relations between countries, and how being legally plural places with competing jurisdictions shapes social life.

In chapter 1, "Money and Authority," I examine the foundations of Subic Bay through an analysis of military agreements, tax law, and tax disputes. The chapter focuses on how inequality is written into the foundation of these places through legal negotiations and the conflicts they spark on the ground. However, it also shows how Filipinos have increasingly found ways to exploit the language of these documents to assert sovereignty, though they do so with varying levels of success. In these negotiations, we see how sovereignty is negotiated in the minutia of who has control over *territory* versus who has control in the *administration* over people and facilities, allowing Filipinos and foreigners alike to stake a claim and view these negotiations through a lens of success.

In chapter 2, "Rape and Murder," I lay out the stakes involved in global borderlands by examining two high-profile crimes: a rape and a murder, both of which were committed by U.S. servicemen and both of which were against Filipinas. In these two cases, we see how activists, judges, lawyers, and reporters use these cases to critique the continued unequal power of the United States and its military in the Philippines, and the inability of Filipinos to fully punish these men for the crimes they committed. In chapter 3, "Sex and Romance," I juxtapose two competing understandings of the relationships between U.S. servicemen and Filipinas: as being wrought with violence, inequality, and exploitative sex versus being imagined in romance and seen through a lens of a heroic love myth. In chapter 4, "Born in the Shadows of Bases," I'll focus on Amerasians, the children of these pairs, their place in Philippine and U.S. societies, and under which conditions they thrive versus barely survive. In each of these three chapters, we see how international relations are worked out in everyday lives and how Filipinos and Americans negotiate the "definition of the situation"[135] in places and relationships built on a foundation of inequality.

Chapter 5, "Labor and Imagined Identities," shows how experiences and the reputation of employers and customers recreate utopian imaginaries and other imaginaries based on human rights violations, hell, and poverty—and how people link them to their understandings of what it means to be a foreigner of a particular nationality. In chapter 6, "Buying Inequality," I turn to how inequality is continually reproduced through imagining and consuming Subic Bay as a utopian-like place where modernity, dreams, and status are within reach and can be realized. Both chapters show how economic systems are moralized.[136] Finally, the conclusion takes a step back, reflecting on what these dynamics mean for global inequality and the future of global borderlands in the face of increasing ethnonationalism and a possible return to more insular economies around the world.

Money and Authority

1

On Sunday, August 21, 1983,[1] crowds of people gathered along Roxas Boulevard and at Manila's international airport to welcome home former senator Benigno "Ninoy" Aquino, an outspoken opponent of dictator Ferdinand Marcos. He was finally returning home after spending three years in the United States, where he had lived in self-imposed exile. He knew the dangers he faced in the Philippines. After Marcos declared martial law, Aquino was tried and found guilty by the military for murder, subversion, and illegal possession of firearms. He was sentenced to die, though the sentence was never carried out because of an international outcry.[2] Despite the dangers, Ninoy decided to return to the Philippines in an effort to restore democracy. Although his dreams of a democracy would come to fruition, it would do so only because of his death. As he was escorted off the plane and to a military van that would whisk him away to jail, he was shot in the back of the head, assassinated after taking just a few steps back in his homeland. Ninoy's assassination started a chain reaction that changed the course of Philippine history.[3]

Ninoy's wife was Corazon "Cory" Aquino, and his family accompanied him to the United States. They remained in Boston as Ninoy made what would be his final journey back to his homeland. After Ninoy's death, Cory returned to the Philippines and became the face of the nonviolent People Power Revolution and the continued fight for democracy in the face of authoritative leadership.[4] Using the corruption of the Marcos regime—including its alleged part in Ninoy's assassination—and the anti–U.S. military bases movements, she united a broad base of support. Two and a half years after Ninoy's assassination, the revolution ousted Marcos from power and ushered Cory into Malacañang.[5]

Cory is widely seen in popular and scholarly accounts as kicking out the U.S. bases since the U.S. military withdrew from the Philippines during her reign. However, it was actually under her watchful eye that U.S and Philippine officials negotiated and signed the Treaty of Friendship, Cooperation and Security on August 27, 1991, which would have extended the lease of the bases. This agreement sparked controversy. Opponents to the treaty framed it in terms of further institutionalizing the United States' undue power in the Philippines, while advocates noted the benefits the Philippines would receive. Despite Cory's backing, less than one month after it was signed, the Philippine Senate rejected the treaty by a vote of 12 to 11, five votes shy of ratification. The ballot was in: the U.S. military had a deadline before which they must leave the Philippines.

Six months later, in one of her final acts as president, Cory Aquino approved Republic Act (RA) 7227 on March 13, 1992. On the heels of the U.S. military withdrawal, RA 7227's presidential approval ushered in a new era in the Philippines. This act officially transformed the former U.S. military bases into special economic zones (SEZs), places aimed at attracting foreign direct investments through tax-free incentives. These changes were intended to promote Philippine development. Ninoy Aquino's death sparked the flame that would eventually lead to the U.S. military's withdrawal, and it was during Cory's administration that Subic Bay transformed from a military base into a Freeport Zone (FZ).

.   .   .

Both military agreements and tax laws form social contracts to which people and countries agree. They also both weave inequalities into the very foundations of the places over which they rule.[6] Examining Subic Bay's military agreements, tax laws, and tax disputes uncovers the negotiations that occur over property and land ownership, the placement of flags, and *who* and *what materials* are taxed, among other things. Delving into these small and seemingly minute details shows the precise circumstances of *when* and *under what conditions* power is asserted or contested and under what conditions it fails. Importantly, particular facets of power are sought after by certain officials, and parsing these out further helps define the parameters of these agreements.

If we focus only on particular clauses of these documents, such as businesses' tax-free status, or selective outcomes, such as how the U.S. military continued to

have a presence in the Philippines after their 1992 withdrawal, we miss the push
and pull of political negotiations. We would miss the concessions that Philippine
officials were able to get from the United States, the ways in which and under
what circumstances they are able to assert authority over foreigners, and when
they are unable to do so. We would miss the everyday decisions and negotiations
that shape the how and why Philippine national identity and sovereignty can
be asserted in the face of foreign power and within foreign-controlled places.
These dynamics also highlight how and why the U.S. military continues to hold
a strong presence in the Philippines, as well as how and why SEZs became an
important development strategy. Cases that showcase individuals negotiating
the agreements' terms demonstrate how Filipino officials are able to push back
against foreign power and achieve some level of success, despite the durable inequality[7] between nations. Their sovereignty is not forsaken.

That political agreements about a foreign presence involve negotiations and
compromises is not surprising. Indeed, political scientist Alexander Cooley
"develops a theory of base politics to explain when and why bilateral military
basing agreements become accepted, politicized, or challenged by host countries"[8] based on the relative bargaining position of host country leaders and
the agreement's legitimacy. He also recognizes how people in countries that
host overseas military bases often see bases as symbolic of broader relations
between the two nation-states. Nor is it surprising that government officials
extract taxes on imported goods and services and from foreigners living and
working within a sovereign nation-state. Taxes constitute a key characteristic of
a nation-state, both its creation and its development.[9]

Nevertheless, much of sociological research pays more attention to the exploitation of rich countries over the poor in these legally plural and semiautonomous zones and less attention to the more nuanced ways in which power
and sovereignty are negotiated and enacted. This chapter sheds sociological
light on these processes that have been less focused on. It provides a glimpse
into both the breadth and depth of the types of negotiations that take place and
the similarities between base politics and taxes. While taxes are a part of base
politics, research does not often connect the two. It also provides alternative
mechanisms for how we can understand both base and tax politics through the
role of law, power, stakes, and cultural meanings. Cooley[10] highlights the role
of bargaining power in base politics as it pertains to countries' regime type—
authoritarian, democratizing, or consolidated democracy—and the credibility
of the agreements and related institutions. Yet his work doesn't account for how

power, high or low stakes, and meanings can all be differently enacted and used even within the same regime type, for example, under the Marcos dictatorship. Similarly, the mundane understandings and contestations around tax-free incentives reveal the frustrations of foreigners over working and living within tax-free zones and the ability of the Philippine government to assert sovereignty over a place traditionally seen as catering to foreigners at the expense of Philippine sovereignty and people.

In both taxes and military agreements, we also see negotiations over who has authority over what and whom, with carefully delineated claims between territorial sovereignty[11] and what I call administrative sovereignty,[12] or authority and power by a government or organization that extends over people.[13] This term draws on scholars of empire and law and society,[14] as well as scholars of migration and human rights,[15] to focus on sovereignty as a *process* in which rules are negotiated and highlight the rights and interests of multiple social actors.[16] It allows us to differentiate between, for example, the United States exerting control over the Philippines' policies, people, resources, and territory versus exerting control over their own citizens within the Philippines' geographic boundaries. This is important because it distinguishes when control is over full members of a nation's "imagined community"[17] from when it is exerted over non- or partial members. It also allows for us to see how sovereignty is multidimensional and negotiated, rather than a characteristic that a nation-state possesses and something government officials may choose to partially cede to maintain order.[18]

Negotiating Military Agreements

Manuel A. Roxas was born to a father who served in the military during Spanish colonial rule in the Philippines. A graduate of the University of Philippines Diliman Law, Roxas entered into politics at the age of twenty-seven, when he would become the youngest person ever to be elected as governor of Capiz, a province in the middle of the Philippines.[19] He would become the president of the Commonwealth of the Philippines and the Philippines' first president. His descendants would follow in his political footsteps, and members of his family would form one of the major business families in contemporary Philippines—the founders of the Ayala Corporation. Paul V. McNutt's life had a similar, though less grand, trajectory. A graduate of Harvard Law School, McNutt was born in Indiana in 1891 to a mother who was a schoolteacher and a father who was a former schoolteacher-turned-lawyer and eventual Indiana Supreme Court librarian.[20] After law school, he became an assistant professor at Indiana University's School of Law, and although he left the academy to join the U.S. military, he later returned after finishing his tour of duty. In 1933, he was sworn in as governor of Indiana, formally entering what would be a long political career, including positions as U.S. high commissioner to the Philippines and the first U.S. ambassador to the Philippines.[21]

On July 4, 1946, Roxas and McNutt signed a long-anticipated, historic document: the Treaty of General Relations, which formally recognized the Philippines as a sovereign nation.[22] In doing so, they ushered in a new era of U.S.-Philippine relations. No longer would they officially be in a relationship defined by colonialism. Moving forward, they would be two sovereign nations working together and maintaining their "close and long friendship"[23] with one another. However, the agreement contained an important caveat. Although the United States would "withdraw" and "surrender" the Philippines, it would do so "except the use of such bases,"[24] ensuring initial sovereignty of the Philippines was limited and did not extend over the bases.

Remnants of the colonial era, U.S.-Philippine basing and military agreements dictated the rights and responsibilities of the U.S. military and the Philippine government and further institutionalized inequalities between the two nations.[25] We know that law on the books, as law and society scholars describe written laws, does not translate into how people experience law in action.[26] However, written laws are important to examine because they provide the foundation and terms of agreement from which officials operate. They outline *who* has power in *what* circumstances, over *which* conditions, and as it relates to *who* is involved. Yet these agreements are not just the terms that dictate behavior and who has what power in future situations; they are also the very product of said differences in power since the inequality between the two nation-states shapes who is able to agree on which terms and why. These agreements are written out of sight, and their terms often only become publicly scrutinized after high-profile events. Yet they are also *living* documents, subject to change and negotiation. Indeed, these military agreements are *continually* negotiated, contingent, and contested. The changes[27] we'll see in the following pages reflect Filipinos' evolving claims of sovereignty and national identity over their land, the people within it, and their former colonial overlord.[28]

1947 Military Bases Agreement and Its Amendments

The 1947 Military Bases Agreement (MBA) signed by Roxas and McNutt set the parameters of U.S. rights over the bases in the Philippines, and it was negotiated "with a view to insuring the territorial integrity of the Philippines, the mutual protection of the United States of America and the Philippines, and the maintenance of peace in the Pacific."[29] From the beginning, the *appearance* of Philippine national sovereignty was of utmost importance, as was the framing of the bases as having mutual benefit for both countries. In the MBA, the Philippines grants the United States the right to retain sixteen bases of varying sizes and purposes and the right to use an additional seven bases throughout the country.[30] Those listed in both annexes were considered bases in the MBA, and as such, the Philippine government granted the U.S. military particular rights and responsibilities over them, such as rights over water, air, and land and the right to construct, maintain, and control transportation, facilities, and vehicles, among other rights. The United States' base rights also extended over the administrative flow of goods and services and even included the right to enter private property and improve health and sanitation in nearby areas outside the base,[31] the ability to import and export goods tax-free,[32] and the right to maintain U.S. and U.S.-Philippine joint cemeteries and memorials. The inequality and power of the United States over the Philippines is evident in this expansive declaration of rights. Yet important amendments to this agreement can be seen as curtailing U.S. power.

A law graduate from the University of the Philippines, Elpidio Quirino[33] served as the Philippines' vice president and foreign affairs secretary from 1946 to 1948.[34] A graduate of Yale University and the University of Louisville Law School, Emmet O'Neal was a white American who was a former U.S. representative from Kentucky and the U.S. ambassador to the Philippines from June 20, 1947, to January 20, 1949.[35] Between the two of them, important amendments[36] were immediately negotiated after the MBA's signing through embassy notes. These notes shed additional light on how sovereignty and inequality were disentangled and negotiated between the two nations. For example, one of the five amendments that occurred later that same year transferred the Leyte-Samar Naval Base from Annex A to Annex B, which moved the base from one where the United States was able "to retain the use of the bases" to one in which the Philippine government grants or "permit[s]" the United States use of the base. Although both sets of bases in Annex A and Annex B were controlled by the

United States, the former are retained U.S. bases and are a *continuation* of U.S. control of the land, while the latter is an agreement where the Philippines have given permission for the United States to take control and use. The latter recognizes the Philippines' sovereign rights to land and territory, and Philippine officials give permission to the United States to use their land.

These changes are significant because they represent particular shifts in the sovereignty—or the rights and responsibilities—of each government. Take, for example, another set of 1947 notes regarding the Fort William McKinley Military Reservation.[37] In O'Neal's December 23, 1947, embassy note to Quirino, he states that there are portions of Fort McKinley "in excess to military requirements," and he acknowledges Philippine officials' interests in using it as an international commercial airport. As such, O'Neal "authorize(s) the Philippine Government to enter into temporary use and custody of the area in question," but in doing so, he sets precise parameters regarding the land in question. For example, although he states that water and electric power will continue to be supplied, they both "will be limited to existing systems,"[38] and the Philippine government will be charged for their use. Electric power would only be supplied until February 28, 1948, after which the Philippines must establish their own source. Furthermore, any "supplies, personal property, stocks, goods, wares and merchandise"[39] on the land would remain U.S. property and the United States would maintain temporary rights to use and enter areas marked on an attached map for security purposes as long as the aforementioned property remained in the area and/or under U.S. control. He dictated that any transfer of ownership would have to be negotiated in a separate agreement and that the United States would also retain "free use" of facilities along water, sewage, and power lines and the right of entry of said facilities for maintenance purposes. Referring to an attached map regarding U.S. rights to use particular access roads, O'Neal outlines the United States' rights to use particular access roads and "aircraft runway and airport facilities"[40] and its associated activities, such as take-off, landing, and parking facilities.[41]

Yet, on December 24, 1947, Quirino replies that his government understands the transfer of said property as "a further implementation of the transfer and surrender of possession, supervision, control, and sovereignty of Philippine territory already made by the United States in favor of the Philippines in the Treaty of General Relations."[42] In this set of exchanges, we see the differences regarding what types of rights are associated with what kind of land title. Whether it was for Philippine *use* or a *transfer* of ownership had very different implications for both governments and who had which rights of access and what kinds of activities could be pursued and who ultimately owned which facilities and materials.

Yet, even with these different implications, the U.S. military was still able to limit Philippine sovereignty in cases where they transferred over ownership. For example, one of the 1947 amendments concerned the aforementioned transfer of Corregidor Island (Fort Mills) and Pettit Barracks to the Philippines. In doing so O'Neal asked Quirino that Philippine officials hold the United States free of any liability or claims in connection with the two military installations, maintain a U.S. cemetery at Pettit Barracks, house U.S. civilian agencies at Pettit Barracks rent-free, and that the Philippine government demilitarize any remaining ammunition. Corregidor Island and Pettit Barracks would be placed back within the territorial sovereignty of the Philippines but only if the United States could dictate key terms of the transfer. So, while the Philippines officially had sovereignty over this land, in practice, their abilities to assert administrative sovereignty, impose taxes or rents, and determine the location of services were limited.

Within the MBA and its subsequent amendments, we also see a delineation between *who* had control over *what* and *under what conditions* in articles over criminal jurisdiction. The MBA states that "the Philippines shall have the right to exercise jurisdiction over . . . offenses committed outside the bases by any member of the armed forces of the United States,"[43] except in three situations, when the United States would have jurisdiction. The first situation relates to any offense within the base except when both parties are Philippine citizens or the crime is against the national security of the Philippines. This clause reflects both the U.S. military's territorial sovereignty because the United States has jurisdiction over crimes committed within the base and the sovereignty of the Philippines because when both parties of a criminal incident are Philippine citizens who are not a part of the U.S. armed forces, the Philippines has jurisdiction. Similarly, the second caveat is when U.S. military personnel commit crimes outside the base that do not include Filipinos or other foreign nationals. Here, the United States is able to rule over their people regardless of the territory in which they are located. Finally, the third situation relates to crimes outside the base against U.S. national security, a vague concept that can be stretched to encompass many different incidents, institutionalizing ambiguity in jurisdictional oversight. Each of these three clauses reflect the reach of U.S. power and influence in the Philippines.[44]

A slim man, with a law degree from the University of the Philippines, Ferdinand Marcos was politically ambitious. During his tenure as the president of the Philippines, from 1965 to 1986, he instituted martial law—rule through the military. He is often remembered as a corrupt dictator who colluded with U.S. officials and was ousted by the people in the nonviolent protests that are commonly referred to as the People Power Revolution. Yet Marcos was not a passive puppet of the United States. He was also very good at manipulating the meanings and uses of the bases for his own political gain, including for more U.S. aid, by saying one thing to his constituents in public and another to U.S. officials in private. Several MBA amendments that asserted Philippine sovereignty were instituted under his regime.[45]

Under Marcos, a 1966 amendment changed the lease of the base from ninety-nine years to twenty-five years, which allowed for the renegotiation and possible oust of the bases within a single generation—something that ultimately occurred just twenty-six years later. Similarly, a 1979 amendment stipulated that the U.S. flag was prohibited from being flown by itself over the base, and when both flags were flown together, the Philippine flag would now take the first spot, thus symbolizing *Philippine*, not U.S., sovereignty over the base. This 1979 amendment is often overlooked in analyses of U.S.-Philippine military agreements. Yet it is arguably one of the most important ones because it also transformed the bases from U.S. to *Philippine* bases that were subject to control by a Philippine base commander. In this instance, the territory of the bases was now under Philippine sovereignty and control. In the media, Marcos emphasized both the symbolic and practical changes these amendments brought to the MBA and declared them proof of Philippine sovereignty over the United States. Yet this amendment also stipulated that U.S. officials continued to rule over their *personnel* and *facilities*. So, while this amendment was a victory for Philippine sovereignty, it was severely limited by not extending Philippine power over U.S. military personnel.

During this time, conflict often erupted between Americans and Filipinos, and Marcos was also able to negotiate amendments related to having Filipino guards monitor the bases' perimeters and give Filipinos the right to organize, voluntarily enlist in the U.S. military, obtain training, and receive preferential hiring within the bases.[46] Furthermore, U.S. Department of State telegrams from the mid-1970s show how Philippine officials made an agreement with the Japanese firm Kawasaki Heavy Industries to have a presence in Subic Bay alongside the U.S. Navy and, in doing so, asserted Philippine sovereign rights over the area.[47]

Although Cory Aquino toppled Marcos from leadership and succeeded him as president, on antibase rhetoric she soon changed her position and wanted to let the people decide whether to keep or remove the bases.[48] She also continued in Marcos's footsteps regarding amendments that expanded Philippine sovereignty and control, such as a 1988 amendment that started a "Buy Philippines Program," which required that the U.S. military buy as many goods and services as possible in the Philippines, limiting the United States' purchasing decisions for their personnel, and a 1991 amendment that turned over all but the two largest U.S.-operated bases (Subic Bay Naval Base and Clark Air Force Base) to the Philippines on January 31, 1991, just a few months shy of the Mt. Pinatubo eruption.

As we can see, the MBA reflects the United States' undue power in the Philippines. Yet that does not tell the whole story. Filipinos did not let U.S. power go unfettered. Rather, Philippine officials—including Ferdinand Marcos, who is often seen as a U.S. puppet, and Cory Aquino, who is often seen as an antibase advocate—continually exerted increasing power to change the terms of the agreement. The bases and U.S.-Philippine military relations were of utmost importance to the U.S. government and its national security. As such, Philippine officials were relatively successful in their increasing claims to territorial sovereignty in the MBA; however, their administrative claims over U.S. personnel and facilities were constrained. The United States retained administrative sovereignty, or control, over them.

1991 Treaty of Friendship, Cooperation and Security

June 15, 1991, started off like any other day. By 2:00 P.M.,[49] however, the course of U.S.-Philippine military relations would be forever altered. That afternoon, ash exploded twenty-eight miles into the air, and magma and mudslides poured into valleys, as the sleeping giant that was Mt. Pinatubo erupted.[50] Typhoon Yunya, with winds as high as 120 miles per hour, blew in at the same time, from just east of Samar Island in the Eastern Visayas and from the Philippine Sea.[51] White-gray clouds of ash filled the sky and darkened the sun. Together, the heavy winds, ash, rain, mud, and magma destroyed thousands of buildings; the damage left in their wake reached as far as the Indian Ocean and claimed over 840 lives.[52] The U.S. Geological Survey called it the "second-largest volcanic eruption of this [twentieth] century."[53] These events destroyed Clark Air Force Base, damaged the Subic Bay Naval Base, and drastically altered the U.S.-Philippine base negotiations that were occurring just prior to the disaster.

Although U.S. officials no longer wanted Clark because it had been destroyed, Philippine officials asked for the same compensation for Subic as they had originally negotiated for both bases.[54] Turned down, they went to the media, declaring that the United States' refusal was evidence of their strong-arming the Philippine government.

Nonetheless, under Cory Aquino's guidance, U.S military and Philippine officials came to an agreement and signed the Treaty of Friendship, Cooperation and Security (TFCS) on August 27, 1991, which opens stating that the countries "desir[e] to recast their historic ties of friendship . . . in the context of full recognition of and respect for each other's independence, sovereignty and territorial integrity."[55] Its first article frames the treaty as being "maintained and developed on the basis of sovereignty equality . . . and concerns of Filipino war veterans."[56] While these words do not negate long-standing historical and structural inequalities between the two nations, they are powerfully symbolic and skillfully used by Filipinos to assert their rights in the face of the United States' unequal power. Here, historic ties of colonialism are rewritten to affirm each other's standing as sovereign nation-states.

In addition to provisions related to the relationships between U.S. and Philippine military commands and how each country's flag should be flown in relation to the other,[57] the TFCS introduces the importance of scientific and technological,[58] cultural and educational,[59] and health[60] cooperation and addresses contested issues between the two nation-states, including the denial of benefits to Filipino World War II veterans who served in the U.S. military.[61] It also includes important environmental stipulations[62] that outlined how U.S. and Philippine commanders would establish "an environmental program and formulate substantive environmental protection standards governing the disposal of hazardous or toxic waste . . . [and] would also have empowered the Philippine government to monitor and verify U.S. adherence to the substantive standards."[63] All of these additional clauses signal the increasing ability of Philippine officials to assert power to set the agenda and terms of discussion by including these two contentious issues in the treaty[64] and to assert administrative control over their own citizens enlisted within the U.S. military and the hazardous materials that seeped into the land.

Less than a month after its signing, on September 16, 1991, the Philippine Senate rejected the TFCS by a vote of 12 to 11, five votes shy of the two-thirds majority required for ratification. To say that this vote was politically fraught is an understatement. Opponents saw the treaty as an affront to Philippine sovereignty, while advocates emphasized the economic benefits of the base and the additional terms Philippine officials were able to negotiate. Initially pushing for a national referendum so the public could vote on the issue, Cory Aquino ended up not pursuing it,[65] and because the treaty was rejected, the United States was not held accountable to any of the agreements in the failed treaty, including the hazardous and toxic waste that were left behind.[66]

The Visiting Forces Agreement

The end of the permanent U.S. military presence marked the beginnings of Subic Bay's transformation into a FZ. Yet the U.S. military never really left the Philippines. Other military agreements between the two nations,[67] including but not limited to the 1998 Visiting Forces Agreement (VFA), ensured that they remained.

With a master's in public administration from Harvard's Kennedy School of Government, Domingo L. Siazon Jr. was a Filipino career diplomat who served as the director general of the United Nations Industrial Development Organization (1985–93), the Philippine ambassador to Japan (1993–95),[68] and the Philippine secretary of foreign affairs (1995–2001).[69] A graduate of the University of Alabama, Thomas C. Hubbard joined the U.S. Foreign Service in 1965, and from 1996 until 2000 he served as the U.S. ambassador to the Philippines.[70] Together, Hubbard and Siazon negotiated and signed the VFA,[71] which in many ways is similar to the MBA, except there are no clauses related to a *permanent* presence, such as differentiating rights, crimes, or activities based on whether it was within or outside a base.[72]

In the VFA's article 5, which details criminal jurisdiction, authority over U.S. personnel in the Philippines is carefully delineated.[73] The Philippines has authority when U.S. personnel violate Philippine laws—particularly those that are also not U.S. laws—and commit crimes against Philippine national security. In contrast, the U.S. military has jurisdiction when the personnel commit crimes that violate U.S. military law, U.S. national security, property or security of U.S. property or people, and crimes that fall under U.S. laws but not Philippine laws and those that are committed "in performance of official duty."[74]

The document also specifies that either government may request the other to waive their right to jurisdiction, and a particular clause states, "Recognizing the responsibility of the United States military authorities to maintain good order and discipline among their forces, Philippine authorities will, upon request by the United States, waive their primary right to exercise jurisdiction *except in cases of particular importance to the Philippines.*" It further states that "in extraordinary cases, the Philippine government shall present its position to the United States Government regarding custody, which the United States Government *shall take into full account.*"[75] Yet, in a 2006 trial, where Lance Corporal Daniel Smith was accused—and found guilty—of raping a Filipina named Nicole, he was kept in U.S. custody despite Philippine repeated requests for transfer. Here, we see how in practice this clause did not mean that the United States would *agree* with the Philippine request for jurisdiction—only that they would "take [it] into account." Another clause says, "The custody of any United States personnel over whom the Philippines is to exercise jurisdiction shall immediately reside with United States military authorities, if they so request . . . until completion of all judicial proceedings."[76] Yet, in Smith's trial, the United States did not request custody before taking him in and ignored Philippine attempts to obtain custody. Written ambiguities allowed for differing interpretations and implementations, and whose prevailed depended on who had the power to enforce or ignore the other's requests.[77]

Before being implemented, the VFA successfully passed through official channels. First, Philippine president Joseph Estrada ratified it and presented it to the Senate. Next, the Senate held public hearings on the issue, and their Committee on Foreign Relations and Committee on National Defense and Security both recommended its approval. Nonetheless, its signing renewed controversy over the U.S. military's presence in the Philippines. On October 10, 2000, five different petitions led by left-wing coalitions, organizations, and individuals regarding the VFA's constitutionality and its alleged violation of Philippine sovereignty were heard before the Philippine Supreme Court.[78]

Arguments centered on a close reading of the Philippine Constitution and under which clause the VFA fell: the clause that states, "Foreign military bases, troops, or facilities shall not be allowed in the Philippines except under a treaty duly concurred in by the senate and, when the Congress so requires, ratified by a majority of the votes cast by the people in a national referendum held for that purpose, and recognized as a treaty by the other contracting State,"[79] or the clause that states, "No treaty or international agreement shall be valid and effective unless concurred in by at least two-thirds of all the Members of the Senate."[80] Whereas the latter is a broader clause, the former is specifically related to the presence of foreign militaries in the Philippines, and this seemingly minute difference was important because it determined the how, why, and whether the VFA was constitutional and thus should be implemented.

Relying on close readings of the Constitution, the VFA, speeches from the 1986 Constitutional Commission—whose participants penned the Constitution—and the Vienna Convention on the Law of Treaties, the Honorable Judge Buena[81] asserts that both clauses are to be read concurrently and are complementary, and after noting that the Philippine Senate ratified the VFA, Buena focuses on whether the VFA is recognized as a treaty by the United States. Since Hubbard, as U.S. ambassador, said that the United States would comply with the VFA, Buena found that since the United States accepted the VFA as a treaty and would meet its stipulations, it was constitutional. Buena rejects petitioners' arguments that the VFA was not put before the U.S. Senate, and, therefore, the U.S. does not consider it a *treaty*. Instead, Buena ruled that "it is inconsequential whether the United States treats the VFA only as an executive agreement because, under international law, an executive agreement is as binding as a treaty." Turning next to petitioners' arguments that the president committed "grave abuse of discretion" in ratifying the treaty, Buena delineates the differing rights and responsibilities of the president and Senate and dismisses the petition,[82] ultimately declaring the constitutionality of the VFA. The VFA continues to govern visiting U.S. troops in the Philippines. However, the U.S. military has recently returned to semipermanent locations in the Philippines, not just a temporary, visiting location through a 2014 agreement that reignited controversy about the role of the United States in the Philippines.

Enhanced Defense Cooperation Agreement

With a bachelor's degree from the University of the Philippines, Voltaire Gazmin had extensive experience in the military, serving as the fortieth commanding general of the Philippine army for a year, and in diplomacy, when he was the Philippine ambassador to Cambodia from 2002 to 2004.[83] Appointed by Philippine president Benigno Aquino III, Gazmin served as the Philippine secretary of national defense from 2010 to 2016. A graduate of Boston University, Philip Seth Goldberg had extensive experience in government work and diplomacy before his 2013–16 term as the U.S. ambassador to the Philippines.[84] Together, Voltaire Gazmin and Philip Goldberg signed the 2014 Enhanced Defense Cooperation Agreement (EDCA).[85]

The EDCA begins with a preamble that sets a foundation that both governments "share an understanding for the United States not to establish a permanent military presence of base in the territory of the Philippines." This is because the 1987 Philippine Constitution states that foreign military bases—as well as troops or facilities, which are covered under the VFA—are not allowed in the Philippines except by a treaty that has been ratified by a majority of Philippine voters in a national referendum "held for that purpose."[86] That is, a basing issue has to stand on its own and cannot be folded into another issue. Additionally, a proposed bases treaty must be "recognized as a treaty by the other contracting State" since one historical point of contention about the MBA and the VFA was that they were considered executive agreements, not treaties, within the United States, and thus could be seen as being less important for the United States than the Philippines.

The EDCA's main prerogative is that it allows the U.S. military to have "access to Agreed Locations"[87] within the Philippines, for "security cooperation exercises; joint and combined training activities; humanitarian assistance and disaster relief activities; and such other activities as may be agreed upon by the Parties," stipulating which activities would be permitted, though leaving it open-ended concerning what the U.S. military could do while in the country.[88] These locations are facilities and areas that the United States would use rent-free, though they would pay for operational expenses. Philippine authorities have rights to access to all areas within these locations that is prompt and "consistent with operational safety and security requirements,"[89] and the Philippines would retain title and ownership. Buildings constructed or improved by the United States are *Philippine* property that the U.S. military uses, though the U.S. retains title to all "moveable property,"[90] such as equipment or supplies. The EDCA also stipulates that the U.S. has no restriction on which contractors they could use, though they "shall strive to use Philippine suppliers . . . to the greatest extent practicable,"[91] and addresses environmental protections, including the intentional and unintentional "release [of] any hazardous materials or hazardous waste"[92] and the actions that must be taken when spills occur. However, these articles are under a caveat regarding the availability of funds to implement them.[93] While the buildings are physically Philippine property and part of Philippine sovereignty, the United States controls the people, moveable property, and actions within them.

Despite the fact that the U.S. military never really left the Philippines, the April 28, 2014, signing of the EDCA renewed controversy over their presence. Two coalitions of left-wing activists led the charge.[94] Separately, these two groups filed a lawsuit, arguing that the EDCA was unconstitutional because it allowed foreign troops on Philippine soil but did not go before the Senate for a vote, as required by the 1987 Constitution. Aware of these legal proceedings, on November 10, 2015, the Senate adopted a resolution stating that "the RP-US EDCA treaty requires senate concurrence, in order to be valid and effective," indirectly—though not explicitly—supporting both coalitions.[95]

The cases were heard jointly before the Philippine Supreme Court. Drawing on previous case law around U.S.-Philippine military agreements, close readings of speeches from the 1986 Constitutional Commissioners who drafted the current 1987 Philippine Constitution[96] and referencing the dissenting opinions written by her fellow justices,[97] Chief Justice Maria Lourdes P. A. Sereno[98] dismissed the petitions. Her January 2016 opinion outlined discussions regarding the differences between executive agreements and treaties, the duties and powers of the president (who is to conduct foreign affairs without being undermined), the thirteen ways the EDCA differs from the original MBA, and how the EDCA relates to the 1987 Constitution's clause that states, "Foreign military bases, troops, or facilities shall not be allowed in the Philippines except under a treaty duly concurred in by the Senate."[99] Here, she takes a holistic and historical view of U.S.-Philippine military agreements and rests their decision on the "three legal standards that were articulated by the Constitutional Commission Members . . . : independence from foreign control, sovereignty and applicable law, and national security and territorial integrity." In the course of her close reading of the "plain language" and intentional ambiguity of the various agreements, Sereno determined that the EDCA does not qualify as a new agreement; rather, it builds and extends on already existing and enacted agreements, such as the 1951 Mutual Defense Treaty and the VFA.[100] Affirming the constitutionality of the EDCA, she ends the legal opinion with a note that acknowledges a shared desire by all parties to have an independent Philippines, saying, "The fear that EDCA is a reincarnation of the U.S. bases so zealously protested by noted personalities in Philippine history arises not so much from xenophobia, but from a genuine desire for self-determination, nationalism, and above all a commitment to ensure the independence of the Philippine Republic from any foreign domination."[101]

In documenting the evolution of U.S.-Philippine military agreements, we can see how and why the EDCA contains particular clauses (e.g., those related to the environment), as well as how its signing and its controversy represent a continuation of a complicated and often contested relationship between the U.S. military and the Philippines. Yet military agreements are not the only place where inequality is institutionalized or where debates between who has territorial and administrative control are enacted. So, too, do the tax-free incentives of SEZs create an unequal playing field between locals and foreigners and follow similar debates. Yet, like military agreements, these policies are not uncontested, and foreign and Filipino officials alike use these agreements to make claims about particular types of sovereignty, inequality, and rights.

Regulating Taxes

Republic Act (RA) 7227, which created the Subic Bay Freeport Zone (SBFZ), declared that it would be "a separate customs territory ensuring free flow or movement of goods and capital" that provided tax-free incentives, with a goal of "attract[ing] and promot[ing] productive foreign investments." Within the FZ's walls "no taxes, local and national, [would] be imposed," except for a blanket 5 percent[102] of gross income earned: 3 percent of which goes to the national government and 2 percent to the SBFZ for distribution to local governments affected by it. These tax-free incentives make it cheaper for business to import and export products, and because the SBFZ, like many other SEZs, is located in a less developed country, businesses also profit from cheaper labor. Focusing on taxes and their repercussions is important because taxation is central to the creation of states and their development.[103] They are part and parcel of citizenship and daily life through the resources states provide and the payments extracted from work. As Isaac Martin, Ajay Mehrotra, and Monica Prasad argue, "taxes formalize our obligations to each other. They define the inequalities we accept and those we collectively seek to redress. . . . In the modern world, taxation *is* the social contract."[104]

It is precisely because states are unable to fully extract taxes from businesses within SEZs that they are a mechanism of inequality.[105] These inequalities were written into the tax foundations of the SBFZ to benefit foreigners. Businesses can have up to 100 percent foreign ownership—that is, they do not have to have domestic partnerships. There is no control over foreign exchange, and expatriates are able to obtain special visas if they invest $250,000, circumventing the Philippine Bureau of Immigration and Deportation and allowing foreign individuals, not just businesses, to become members of this exclusive community.[106] These are parts of the Philippines' administrative sovereignty that are ceded within SEZs.

These tax foundations also benefited rich Filipinos who were able to live within its boundaries. In the original document outlining SBFZ's purpose and stipulating the Subic Bay Metropolitan Authority's power and authority, rules also centered on *whom* can purchase *what* and *how much* before being charged tax, or, in other words, who is able to partake in tax-free incentives. For example, SBFZ residents were able to import an unlimited (but in noncommercial quantities) quantity of duty-, tax-, and customs-free goods and freely consume, purchase, or lease duty- and customs-free goods from other SBFZ residents and businesses while within the area but were also subject to Philippine income tax. In contrast, while non-SBFZ residents could freely consume items within the SBFZ, they could only bring customs-free goods outside the FZ once a month. There were also limits on what they could buy; for example, the total cost of goods they bought could not exceed $200. If it did, the items would be taxed. However, these limitations were soon removed, so SBFZ businesses could become more profitable.

Yet, even after this change in policy, the SBFZ was not an unfettered tax-free haven, as scholars critical of these zones often suggest. Tax-free privileges are not unilateral, given to all businesses or people within the zone. Rather, its incentives, *who* is able to partake in them, and *what* they cover are meticulously tracked and highly contested by both individuals and organizations because of competing understandings of Philippine administrative and territorial sovereignty over the area. I'll show how the SBFZ's very foundations left room for negotiations that allow local governments to draw on their sovereignty to exert power over foreigners in often surprising and overlooked ways that reproduce this inequality on the ground and in the courts.

· · ·

Jaime A. Cotero is a U.S. citizen working at Coastal Subic Bay Terminal Inc. On April 5, 2001, he filed for a refund for income taxes with the Philippine Bureau of Internal Revenue and the next day filed a petition to the Court of Tax Appeals, which is located outside the SBFZ.[107] In his petitions, Jamie argued that because the SBFZ is a tax-free territory, income derived from within it is also tax-free, and since SBFZ businesses are only taxed at a 5 percent rate on gross tax, their employees are not subject to taxes. That is, Jamie claims that by virtue of working in a SEZ, individuals are entitled to the same tax-free privileges as businesses.

The commissioner of Internal Revenue disagreed with Cotero. In the official response, he argued that since Jamie is not a business, he is not entitled to the same incentives given to registered SBFZ businesses. The commissioner also argued that Jamie did not prove that the amount he was claiming was "erroneously paid," and he—not the Bureau of Internal Revenue—has the burden of proof to show that he's entitled to a refund and that he complied with the law. Discussing the creation of the law and its roots in transforming the former military base into civilian use, Judge Ernesto D. Acosta[108] finds that Jamie Cotero's interpretation expands "the coverage provided by the law" and that "tax exemptions cannot be granted by mere implication." In response to Cotero's claim that his income comes from within the SBFZ—a specific tax-free territory—and thus is not subject to Philippine tax laws nor is it Philippine-derived income in the traditional sense, Judge Acosta asserts that the SBFZ "is not a tax[-]free territory in the full sense of the word, i.e., no tax at all. . . . It is a tax in another form." That is, he declared that the SBFZ is not foreign land but part of the territory of the Philippines and subject to Philippine rule. On September 12, 2002, Judge Acosta ruled that SBFZ matters are subject to the national government's jurisdiction and rejected any understanding of the SBFZ as a foreign land, outside the court's control.

At the heart of the disagreement is whether foreigners who work in the SBFZ must pay income taxes and are subject to Philippine tax laws—more specifically, whether Jamie is eligible for a refund or tax credit from income taxes he paid from his work inside the SBFZ and whether the RA 7227's statement that "no taxes, local and national, shall be imposed within the Subic Special Economic Zone" applies to individuals, not just businesses. What we see is how Acosta draws on understandings of what sovereignty is to reject American individuals' claims to tax-free status. He asserts Philippine sovereignty over the area *and* over the people within it and rejects understandings that see the SBFZ as a foreign land that is not under Philippine jurisdiction. Here, the court also makes clear that tax-free incentives are for businesses, not individuals, and that foreigners—just by virtue of being a foreigner or an individual working within the SBFZ—do not enjoy unlimited privileges but are subject to domestic laws and both Philippine territorial and administrative sovereignty.[109]

Businesses themselves are also not unfettered. Rather, they too are regulated as to whether they can enjoy the SBFZ's tax-free privileges. Take, for instance, the two PureGold grocery stores located within the FZ, which are not subject to the same regulations. Whereas Duty Free PureGold is a tax-free entity, the PureGold at Harbor Point mall is not.[110] These differences reflect the two types of businesses allowed within the SBFZ: *locators* that are entitled to these economic incentives and *nonlocators* that are not. Locators must apply for tax exemptions and meet certain requirements before being granted economic privileges. One of these requirements is being a separate SBFZ entity. Registration is overseen by one of the Subic Bay Metropolitan Authority (SBMA) Business and Investment Departments; it is a fourteen-day, two-stage process, and businesses are subject to additional requirements postcertification. The other type of business is a nonlocator. Nonlocators are overseen by the Accreditation Department, not by the Business and Investment Departments. They operate within the SBFZ and may be branches of other business but are not separate SBFZ entities and, therefore, are ineligible for the same incentives.

In my fieldwork, confusions regarding tax-incentives plagued foreigners and Filipinos alike, because both shared a misperception that all SBFZ goods and services are tax-free. For example, Tim, a white foreign businessman married to a Filipina, refers to being subject to income taxes as being "ripped off." Giving me an example of FZ gas stations including value-added tax (VAT) in their prices, Tim derides having to manually deduct the VAT in his business expenses rather than this tax being automatically deducted when he or his employees fill up gas in their vehicles. When I told him that not all SBFZ companies receive the same tax exemptions, he was surprised. Even as a current businessman hiring and firing Filipino employees and purchasing and selling materials, Tim—like many others—wrongly assumed all SBFZ businesses and their accompanying goods and services are VAT-free.

Locators themselves are also not unilaterally given access to these incentives for all of their materials. For example, Contex Corporation is a Taiwanese company specializing in manufacturing hospital supplies[111] and is eligible for the tax incentives befitting SBFZ-registered entities. Yet these tax incentives are not always guaranteed. From January 1997 to December 1998, Contex Corporation officials argued, when they purchased necessary materials for their work, the vendors shifted the 10 percent VAT onto them, despite their being exempt from local and national taxes and their products exported. They sought a credit or refund of the VAT for ₱1,011,467.04 ($22,477.05[112]), the total VAT they paid in 1997 and 1998, from the commissioner of Internal Revenue.

Their first application to the SBMA Bureau of Internal Revenue was denied, and their second application was ignored. Contex officials then filed an appeal with the Court of Tax Appeals on June 29, 1999, and made two claims. First, they claimed that they are exempt because their goods were exported and thus eligible for 0 percent rates. Their second claim is based on RA 7227, the SBFZ's founding document, which outlines that they are not subject to local or national taxes, aside from the required SBFZ tax. In response, Bureau of Internal Revenue officials asserted that Contex's claims were subject to their

investigations—not the Court of Tax Appeals—Contex had the burden of proof
to show that they had a right to a refund, that they complied with tax-related
rules, and finally that "rudimentary is the rule that claims for refund is [*sic*]
construed in *strictissimi juris* [strictest letter of the law] against the taxpayer for
they partake the nature of exemption from tax."

On October 13, 2000, Judge Ernesto D. Acosta ruled on these three issues:
whether Contex Corporation was entitled to a refund claim, if they are exempt from VAT on supplies and materials, and if they had enough evidence
to support their claim for refund.[113] Acosta disagreed with Contex's first claim
because the 0 percent rate is for businesses registered with the Bureau of Internal Revenue as a VAT taxpayer. Here, he differentiates among the type of
incentives available to business. However, he agreed with their second claim.
Acosta delineates further, saying that only the *raw materials* bought are exempt
from VAT and, of those, only those that were used to manufacture the product
and weren't taken off their SBFZ premises. He also found that claims for refunds are valid for only up to two years, so despite first filing an application on
December 29, 1998, with the Bureau of Internal Revenue, Acosta ruled, Contex
Corporation was not eligible for refunds on purchases made prior to June 29,
1997, because they filed their Court of Tax Appeals petition on June 29, 1999. As
such, Acosta[114] ordered the commissioner of Internal Revenue to refund or give
credit to Contex in the amount of P683,061.90, calculating the sum from a table
that delineated which taxes were (dis)allowable.

In 2001, the Court of Appeals overturned the Court of Tax Appeal's ruling
because it agreed with the commissioner of Internal Revenue that tax exemption "was limited only to direct taxes and not to indirect taxes such as the input
component of the [Court of Tax Appeals]."[115] Four years later, Contex Corporation's appeal on the Court of Appeals' reversal was brought before the Supreme
Court. Contex officials claim that the tax-free stipulations of RA 7227 were
"clearly" and "unambiguously" mandated, while the commissioner of Internal
Revenue argues that the tax-free incentives are not a catch-all category for taxes
(aside from the mandated 3 percent). Rather, they are limited to only direct
taxes; therefore, indirect taxes are not exempt.

In his ruling, Judge Quisumbing clarified "that the VAT is an indirect tax . . .
[which] is a tax on consumption of goods, services or certain transactions
involving the same." He also further disentangled indirect taxes into two categories. There are what he calls "the liability for the tax" and "the burden of
the tax." When taxes are shifted onto the seller, they shift the burden, not the

liability, of taxes, and this is what Contex officials are claiming happened and why they had a right to a refund. Quisumbing gives an example of this difference between liability and burden: "Stated differently, a seller who is directly and legally liable for payment of an indirect tax, such as the VAT on goods or services is not necessarily the person who ultimately bears the burden of the same tax." That is, "it is the final purchaser or consumer of such goods or services who, although not directly and legally liable for the payment thereof, ultimately bears the burden of the tax." He also discusses how the differences between a VAT exemption and zero-rated sales are at the heart of the matter. Whereas a VAT "exemption means that the sale of goods or properties and/or services and the use or lease of properties is not subject to VAT (output tax) and the seller is not allowed any tax credit on VAT (input tax) previously paid," zero-rated sales "are sales by VAT-registered persons which are subject to 0% rate, meaning the tax burden is not passed on to the purchaser." While it is undisputed that Contex Corporation is exempted from VAT, they also assert that they are "exempt from VAT on all its sales and importations of goods and services."

What's at stake is "whether or not [Contex Corporation] may claim a refund on the input VAT erroneously passed on to it by its suppliers." Judge Quisumbing[116] agrees that Contex should not have had taxes imposed by their supplier but claims that the *suppliers*, not Contex, are the ones to claim a VAT refund. What should happen is their suppliers seek tax credits or a refund that they then would pass on to Contex Corporation. As a VAT-exempt organization, they are not entitled to tax credits on input VAT. What we see here is how the SBFZ's socioeconomic incentives are not unilaterally granted; nor is the SBFZ a place outside Philippine jurisdiction, where foreign businesses have unfettered privileges. Instead, the tax-free incentives companies are granted are based on the *types* of item at hand (raw materials or not), what *kinds* of privileges they are eligible for (VAT exempt, zero-rated sales), and *who* can make claims for refunds when these rights are erroneously overlooked (main company or suppliers).[117] Privileges, like sovereignty, are contingent.

Regulations, negotiations, and conflicts over socioeconomic privileges and the VAT also take place when calculating foreign exchange rates. On March 17, 2006, Judge Juanito C. Castañeda Jr. in the Court of Tax Appeals ruled on the case of a Taiwanese SBFZ business, *Taian (Subic) Electric, Inc. v. The Commissioner of Internal Revenue*. The commissioner of Internal Revenue sought payment from Taian Electric for "deficiency income taxes," amounting to

P2,430,308.87 ($54,006.86) in undeclared sales and documentary stamp tax.[118] Taian received a notice from the commissioner and sent a letter requesting reconsideration, which was denied because the commissioner stated that they "fail[ed] to disprove the deficiency internal revenue tax findings of the Revenue Officer."

Taian asked the Court of Tax Appeals to review their appeal on two grounds: first, because the assessments "are void for they failed to state the factual and legal bases for the assessments, in violation of Section 228 of the Tax Code," and second, because they claimed that the discrepancies seen were due to fluctuations in foreign exchange rates. In response, the commissioner submitted tables that documented sales, undeclared revenue, unexplained payables, allowable deductions, undeclared sales, and the like. At the heart of the case were whether the revenue officer's assessment was in line with law and what were the explanations for the monetary discrepancies. Judge Castañeda[119] found that the assessments were lawful. Section 228 says that "the taxpayer shall be informed in writing of the law and the facts on which the assessment is made, otherwise the assessment shall be void," and in the finding Castañeda focuses on how writing consists of more than just words. It also includes numbers and electronic recordings, and it can be hand-written or typed. As such, the assessments that the commissioner gave to Taian were lawful.

Castañeda also agreed that the discrepancies were due to foreign exchange rates, where the agreed upon rate was collected from one exchange rate (P39.495 to US$1.00), which was subject to change when the transaction is completed (currently at P40.116 to US$1.00). Since the amount hadn't been collected, there was no increased revenue that hadn't been taxed. The court also hired an independent certified public accountant to examine both Taian's and the commissioner of Internal Revenue's related documents, which confirmed that the transactions weren't yet closed out and completed.

Another set of discrepancies were related to the section "Accounts Receivable—Others," which is composed of deposits paid, advances to employees and officers, and prepaid expenses. Only 0.58 percent (P17,000/P2,911,438.57) of these expenses had official receipts as supporting documents, while others had photocopied—not original—receipts and vouchers. As such, Castañeda ruled that P2,945,887.53 ($73,647.19) "is a proper adjustment to petitioner's taxable income." The certified public accountant went through this process for all of the discrepancies, clarifying what constituted "unexplained" expenses, what had the appropriate documentation, which discrepancies Taian officials attributed to "cash advances" from their parent company, which were "based in Taiwan, and how these advances related to changes in foreign exchange rates." In all, Castañeda ruled in partial favor of Taian. He found that part of the gain was due to money that was not yet collected and resulted from fluctuations in the foreign exchange rate, while another part was due to money infused by the parent company in Taiwan. Yet because some of the discrepancies did not have sufficient documentation and others were the result of actual deficiencies, Taian was also ordered to pay P752,501.67 ($18,812.54) for 1997, with a 20 percent delinquency interest. What we see here is how SBFZ transactions are rigorously tracked by the SBMA local government. SBFZ businesses are not given a blanket exemption from taxes; nor are the 5 percent taxes they are required to pay uncontested. Rather, SBFZ businesses need to maintain strict accounting of their expenses and the foreign exchange rates at the time of contract and time of purchase; otherwise, they may be subject to increased fines and payments.

Taxes represent a social contract between governments and their associated citizens and businesses. They also are a key part of a state's administrative sovereignty. We know that the reception of taxes and citizens' sacrifices relate to social boundaries between groups and morality, where taxes are more readily accepted if benefits are perceived to be used toward a group to which we belong (an "us" group) and less readily accepted if they are perceived to benefit a group to which we do not belong (a "them" group).[120] The creation of SEZs attracts foreign businesses and individuals precisely because they are assumed to be places where those entities are not obligated to pay the same level of taxes or make the same level of sacrifices as they would to their own country. Yet, even in the SBFZ, we can see the centrality of taxes in the construction of state and nonstate actors and how tax conflicts reflect battles related to what the SBFZ is to the Philippines, what it is to foreign and domestic businesses, and who and what the people who inhabit, visit, work, and live in the zone are subject to: the Philippines as a sovereign nation-state or an ambiguous zone that is designed only for foreigners' monetary and administrative benefits.

Inequality in Global Borderlands

Military agreements and taxes define the stakes involved in global borderlands. But instead of the stakes being plastered on headlines, as we'll see in high-profile criminal cases, these stakes are sorted out and worked through within the walls of bureaucracies and courts through discussion of the most seemingly mundane of details: Who owns which properties, and why? Who is entitled to which privileges? These questions ultimately come down to who has territorial and administrative sovereignty over the area—the Philippines or foreign businesses and people?

Inequality is written into the very foundation of these special zones. Whether in military agreements that provide preferential treatment to the U.S. military or SEZs that allow foreigners tax incentives, Subic Bay is built on a foundation of inequality in access to resources. Yet this chapter also provides a counternarrative to the prevailing sentiments that stop at documenting this inequality. Rather than seeing global borderlands—overseas military bases, SEZs, and the like—as places of neoliberal "exception"[121] where domestic governments cede sovereignty to foreigners or foreigners get free reign, what I've found is that sovereignty is both a negotiated and contingent process. Filipinos have been and continue to be deliberate about which parts of their sovereignty they cede and have also made ever evolving and increasing claims to exert their sovereignty since the very beginning.

That Filipinos have made increasing claims to sovereignty in military agreements does not mean there is equality between the United States and the Philippines. Instead, it shows that while inequality is institutionalized in the U.S.-Philippine relationship, it is also not static. Rather, inequality between the two is surprisingly flexible and fluid, and the disparate inequality between the two has not stopped Filipinos from trying to exert their will in the face of U.S. power. So, too, are sovereignty and inequality surprisingly flexible and fluid in SEZs, despite popular notions suggesting that foreigners more or less have free reign. Yes, these places are set on a foundation of tax-free incentives for foreigners. They also provide these incentives for rich Filipinos who are able to meet the standards required to live, work, and visit the SBFZ. Yet both tax policies and related legal court cases show how these incentives are not unfettered. They are strictly regulated, and Filipinos draw on Philippine sovereignty and their national identity to assert their will in the face of foreign businesses and people.

In all, examining military agreements and taxes reveals how sovereignty is not a catch-all term or concept used to encompass all associated activities within a place. It is highly differentiated. Important distinctions are made concerning who has sovereign claims over which territory, people, and materials (or administration). This allows all parties to "save face"[122] and proclaim they've "won" in negotiations. Filipino officials continue to assert sovereignty, though often a particular type of territorial sovereignty, in the face of foreign control, while foreigners simultaneously continue to be afforded special privileges, including administrative privileges or sovereignty, though these are also often constrained.

But the minute terms of the military agreements I've uncovered here, while high stakes to governments, are often negotiated within closed walls. What happens when these agreements are put into action? When the consequences of U.S. servicemen's actions prove to be damaging and lethal for Filipina women? Who is able to exert their power when these decisions are put under the microscope of intense media attention and are subject to strong public opinion: the Philippines or the U.S. military?

Rape and Murder

2

The case lasted four years.

It all began on a seemingly regular October day in 2005. Twenty-two-year-old Filipina college graduate "Nicole"[1] and her sister "AA" were invited by two U.S. servicemen to visit the Subic Bay Freeport Zone (SBFZ). They accepted, in part, because they knew these men from how often they frequented their family's canteen, which was located at a military base in Mindanao.

For two nights in a row, the four of them went barhopping around the SBFZ, and on October 31, Nicole met Lance Corporal (LCpl) Daniel Smith, a U.S. Marine she described as "heart-shaped, white, pointed nose and tall,"[2] at the Neptune Club. They spent the night drinking and dancing, and after a while, they went outside. There, in a white van with three other servicemen in the back, Nicole and Smith had sexual intercourse—rape as alleged by Nicole, consensual sex as countered by Smith. Although later challenged, witness reports initially described the men escorting Nicole out of the white van "like a pig"[3]—each person holding one of her limbs—and placing her on the side of the road.

The Subic Bay Metropolitan Authority (SBMA) police eventually arrived and took Nicole to the hospital for a check-up, where a doctor asked her if she was raped, adding, "*Baka ginusto mo?*"[4] (Maybe you liked it?). Upon leaving the hospital, Nicole headed straight to the police station to file a report. By all accounts, the four men returned to the ship, carrying on the rest of the night and the next day as normal—that is, until the early hours of November 3. When they were awakened they were interrogated by U.S. Navy Criminal Investigative

Service (NCIS) officer Guy Papageorge and later taken to a U.S. embassy–run safe house.

In 2006, after one of the most publicized trials in the history of U.S. and Philippine relations, the three men in the back of the van when the incident occurred were acquitted. Smith, however, was found guilty beyond a reasonable doubt. Despite a win at the trial, Nicole was unable to return to her home in Zamboanga because the national media "portrayed her as a bad girl,"[5] which had lasting effects on her reputation.

During the Philippine trial and in the years following Smith's conviction, the location of his detainment—whether in a Philippine or U.S. jail—was contested. Leftist activists and academics condemned U.S. custody of Smith as a clear challenge by the U.S. military to the Philippines' independence from its former colonial power, and Nicole took this argument to the Philippine Supreme Court to argue for Philippine custody of him. Smith, on the other hand, argued for U.S. custody in the Philippine Court of Appeals. Before his case was decided, however, Smith was transferred to U.S. custody, per the Visiting Forces Agreement (VFA). The 1998 VFA was an agreement between the United States and the Philippines that was signed six years after the U.S. military withdrew from the permanent military bases in the Philippines. It stipulated the rules that governed U.S. service personnel visiting the Philippines on a temporary basis. One of its provisions states that U.S. and Philippine officials will agree on where a U.S. servicemember will be detained, and the U.S. ambassador and the Philippine secretary of foreign affairs used this clause to transfer Smith out of Philippine, and into U.S., custody.

In 2009, a Philippine Court of Appeals overturned Smith's guilty verdict, but before they did so, Nicole recanted her accusation. After her statement, U.S. government officials granted her a visa, and she permanently left the Philippines to reside in the United States.

.   .   .

Almost eight years later, another violent case from the SBFZ exploded across the U.S.-Philippine media. Jennifer Laude, a twenty-six-year-old transgender Filipina, was killed in the late hours of October 11, 2014. Her body was found by an employee of Celzone Lodge, a hotel that she, LCpl Joseph Pemberton (a U.S. Marine), and Jennifer's transgender Filipina friend Barbie Gelviro checked into around 10:55 P.M. that night.[6] Jennifer and Barbie were two sex workers who met Pemberton at Ambyanz Night Life, a bar and dance club located on Magsaysay

Drive in Olongapo City. Shortly after meeting each other, the three checked into Celzone Lodge.[7] After negotiating payment, Jennifer and Barbie individually performed oral sex on Pemberton, and afterward, Jennifer took Barbie to the side and asked her to leave. Jennifer feared Pemberton's reaction to Barbie if they became more intimate, since Barbie did not have augmented breasts like her and so did not visibly present as a woman to the same degree as Jennifer.

After Jennifer's death, Pemberton returned to the ship, the HSV WESTPAC Express docked at the SBFZ, and confided to LCpl Jairn Michael Rose, "I think I killed a he/she,"[8] reflecting his transphobia. Rose thought Pemberton was joking and asked Pemberton "if he was serious. LCpl Pemberton replied that he was serious."[9] Pemberton also spoke to Corporal Christopher Miller and told Miller that "'[he] fucked up bad' because '[he] got into a fight [and] when [he] left, [Laude] was unconscious."[10]

On December 1, 2015, Pemberton was found guilty of homicide—a reduced charge from murder. Although the judge sentenced Pemberton to a local Philippine jail, there was a two-hour standoff because Pemberton's U.S. security escorts refused to turn him over to the Philippine local police.[11] After negotiations between the Philippine Department of Foreign Affairs and U.S. embassy, a judge ordered Pemberton to be transferred to the Joint United States Military Advisory Group (JUSMAG) facility located at Camp Aguinaldo, a Philippine military base where he had been detained while he awaited trial. As in Nicole's trial, leftist activists critiqued the unequal and special treatment of Pemberton and the U.S. military more broadly. Like Smith, Pemberton appealed his case. Yet, in this case, the court affirmed Pemberton's guilty verdict but counterintuitively reduced his sentence from a maximum of twelve years in prison to a maximum of ten years.

. . .

Nicole's and Jennifer's cases represent moments where the very identity of what it means to be a "nation," imagined political communities that are limited and sovereign,[12] becomes contested and embodied in global borderlands. Alongside colonial and contemporary international politics, nations themselves are gendered, racialized, and intertwined with intimate relations,[13] which is evident whenever rape is used as a tool of war, statehood, and nationality,[14] when national policies encourage births of certain populations over others, when everyday discourses relate understandings of motherhood to citizenship and community,[15] and, historically, when masculinity defined the European colonial project.[16] In their cases, both Nicole and Jennifer embodied a gendered idea of the Philippine nation, one where whether and when the Philippines or the United States asserted authority and jurisdiction over the accused spoke to Philippine officials' ability, or lack thereof, to protect Filipinas from violence caused by citizens of their former colonial overlord and to prosecute the men who violated these daughters of the nation.

Yet the fact that a rape or murder case would become an internationally covered news story or be linked to the broader global political economy, national identities, and issues over sovereignty is not obvious. To understand why and how it became so, the negotiations at the heart of each trial, and their outcomes, we need to understand the relationship between law, power, meanings, and stakes. In these cases, competing claims over custody, detention, and jail conditions were infused with meanings of sovereignty, violations thereof, nationality, and continuing U.S. power in the Philippines. These claims also revolved around particular conceptions of class, nationality, and gender-based discrimination. Agreements made by Philippine and U.S. military officials concerning Smith's and Pemberton's detention and conditions were also subject to public scrutiny and critique. In these cases, the dynamics of Subic Bay as a global borderland that serves as a temporary home to U.S. servicemembers exceeded its spatial boundaries and provided a window into broader political and economic relations between the U.S. and the Philippines. These negotiations over the competing legal jurisdictions of these two nation-states and the ways in which ambiguously worded military agreements affected them were worked out on the ground and through differences in power and influence. So, too, do we see how sexual violence became a vehicle and proxy for making broader sociopolitical critiques about the relationship between the United States and the Philippines and the effect it has on the Philippines as a sovereign nation-state.

I examine both cases to undercover these negotiations over where and under what conditions the culprits are held, who controls access to them, and who stipulates the terms of their detention. These small, seemingly minute details are where power dynamics between the United States and the Philippines are most visible. If we focus only on selective case outcomes—Smith's guilty verdict was overturned, and the U.S. dictated the conditions under which Pemberton is held in the Armed Forces of the Philippines (AFP) headquarters—we miss the push and pull of political negotiations. We would miss which officials are able to get their way, why, under what circumstances, and when they are overruled, and we would miss the ways in which power is constructed, asserted, and railed against. These dynamics highlight how and why the U.S. military continues to hold a strong presence in the Philippines, because they demonstrate how Filipino officials push back against U.S. power to achieve some level of success, no matter how small, despite the inequality between the two nations. They also allow us to recognize that the ability to punish criminals and the negotiations over who has authority go beyond the verdict that is reached. They also include who is able to maintain custody before and during trial, who maintains custody after subsequent guilty verdicts, and who is able to dictate the conditions of detainment.

Understanding the Importance of Both Cases

Both trials were of the utmost importance to U.S. and Philippine officials, in part due to the role that the media[17] played in heightening their stakes, framing them as evidence of the United States' undue power and influence in the Philippines, and bringing issues of power and inequality to a broader audience, all of which contributed to widespread, or at least extremely vocal, opposition to the U.S. military and threatened their presence in the country. This opposition also threatened domestic incumbent politicians if they were widely seen as kowtowing to the United States and if it caused their power and effectiveness to be questioned by the masses. However, it is only in Jennifer's case that we see relative constraints on the United States' willingness to exert their power and U.S. officials working less antagonistically with Philippine authorities on these issues. Why did Jennifer's case elicit more compromise from the United States?

First, Jennifer's death occurred only six months after the Enhanced Defense Cooperation Agreement (EDCA) was signed by the United States and the Philippines, which allowed the U.S. military to return to the Philippines on a quasi-permanent basis through their use of "agreed locations." After the U.S. military withdrew from the bases in 1992, it continued to return to the Philippines; however, it was on a *visiting* basis. The EDCA allowed the U.S. military to once again assert control over particular locations in the Philippines. This agreement raised the stakes even higher for Jennifer's case and how Pemberton's trial would unfold, precisely because its signing was controversial and caused widespread media discussion, protests, and ultimately a Supreme Court case over its validity. Contributing to the controversy was the fact that the EDCA had not been put before a Philippine Senate vote for approval, something required by the 1987 Philippine Constitution for the establishment or presence of any foreign military base, facilities, or troops. It was also controversial for what it symbolically meant to have the U.S. military and U.S. power return on a quasi-permanent basis: a violation or limitation of Philippine sovereignty. As such, the U.S. military was more cognizant of the consequences of violating agreements and the importance of maintaining good relations with the Philippine government so as to not endanger the EDCA, granting the Philippines leverage in negotiations in Pemberton's detainment and custody.

Second, although the Philippine media and to a much lesser extent the U.S. media have long played a role in critiquing U.S. involvement in the Philippines,[18] the more rapid diffusion of news stories covering Jennifer's case and the explicit comparison of her case with Nicole's case and Smith's overturned guilty verdict allowed these critiques to reach an immediate, more widespread audience, including international popular news media outlets like BuzzFeed. It also put more pressure on both governments—though especially the United States—to adhere to domestic laws and the VFA more strictly than before,[19] precisely because this was a contentious time when the EDCA's validity was being publicly questioned. Noting the role of the media matters because, while reporting and coverage are highly selective,[20] it frames our understanding of events and the world around us.[21] Activists and social movement organizations have long used the media to mobilize others and validate their concerns,[22] though their effectiveness in doing so depends on the larger sociopolitical and cultural context,[23] and so-called fringe organizations in particular can tap into negative emotions to promote cultural change in our understandings and framing of issues.[24] The activists engaging with Nicole's and Jennifer's cases were no different, using the media as tools to pressure the Philippine and U.S. governments and to highlight the inequalities between the two nations as they played out in the courtroom.

Pretrial Custody and Detention

In both Nicole's and Jennifer's trials, the pretrial custody and detention of the accused became a locus of anti-U.S. rhetoric because of the perceived special treatment of U.S. servicemen. In Nicole's case, the accused remained in U.S. custody and was not handed over to Philippine officials. In Jennifer's case, the handover of the defendant to Philippine authorities was delayed, and when he was in their custody, he stayed at the AFP headquarters, where he was treated to special amenities like air-conditioning. He was not, in other words, detained in a regular Philippine jail. Here, we see how many different types of people—U.S. and Philippine government officials, lawyers, judges, justices, and activists—contested and negotiated *who* had *which* rights (or jurisdiction) to custody, detention, and jail conditions.[25] They questioned what the men's unequal and preferential treatment by virtue of their U.S. nationality meant for Philippine sovereignty more generally.

Nicole's Case

Nicole met Smith while at the Neptune Club inside the SBFZ, and shortly thereafter they had intercourse in a white van outside—rape as alleged by Nicole and consensual sex as countered by Smith. Afterward, she was placed down on the pavement. Crying on the ground, she was found by two bystanders who noticed that she couldn't pull up "her pants properly because the front part was at the back."[26] After a bike patrol was hailed and SBMA police arrived, they took Nicole to a local hospital for a checkup.

Around 2:00 or 3:00 A.M. on November 3, U.S. NCIS special agent Guy Papageorge interviewed Smith, and a few hours later he and the other servicemen in the van "were taken to a safe house run by the US Embassy until the time the Embassy got a room for them."[27]

On November 16, 2005, the Philippine Department of Foreign Affairs sent an embassy note to U.S. officials that requested they turn over Smith.[28] Citing the VFA clauses related to the nonreceipt of a formal request for U.S. custody and the "extraordinary" and "heinous" nature of the case, the secretary of foreign affairs, Alberto Romulo, asserted that custody was to be decided among U.S. and Philippine authorities. Officials in the U.S. embassy did not respond to the note until a follow-up exchange almost two months later, an act that can be seen as a "symbolic display of degradation . . . implying that [the Philippines'] time is quite worthless."[29]

On January 16, 2006, the United States responded, saying that although they took into account the Philippines' request, they would nevertheless maintain custody of Smith. Taking into account the Philippines' desire to have custody of the accused did not translate into U.S. officials deferring to or abiding by their request. In their immediate reply, Philippine Department of Foreign Affairs officials stated their concern over the United States' refusal to hand over custody and linked what was known as "the Subic Rape Case" to similar cases in other countries—criminal cases where U.S. military personnel received special treatment over custody issues.[30]

In this set of exchanges, U.S. officials drew on a particular, ambiguous VFA clause, devoid of context, to willingly exert their power and resources to maintain custody of Smith and ignore Philippine requests.[31] In contrast, the Philippine Department of Foreign Affairs officials relied on multiple VFA clauses that grant the Philippines power in determining custody issues, which were ignored, and raised concerns over the unequal treatment of U.S. personnel around the world to frame both their request and subsequent critiques of the United States as an issue of Philippine sovereignty and unequal U.S. power.

Philippine officials were not the only ones critiquing the behavior of U.S. personnel and their seeming disregard or disrespect for Philippine authority. In protests during and after the trial, we see this same issue of disparate treatment based on nationality raised. Smith's identity as a white U.S. military serviceman goes hand in hand with discussions of Philippine sovereignty and jurisdiction. During the November 1, 2006, protest, for example, activists shouted, "US band of rapists, guilty, *ikulong, parusahan* [jail them, punish them]," while Nicole, who helped lead the protest, questioned, "Why can't our government do anything to stop the Americans from coming here? [We need] to avoid another rape [of Filipinas]." Both sentiments indicated a sense that the Philippine government was incapable of protecting its women from U.S. servicemen or of punishing those who hurt their citizens. Nicole also expressed dismay at the sight of U.S. ships in Subic Bay again "as if nothing happened, as if it is business as usual,"[32] which further signified the inability of the Philippine government to do anything significant in curtailing the U.S. military presence in Subic, holding them accountable for the alleged rape, or in moving forward with the criminal case. Likewise, during a November 21, 2006, rally, a protester, Joms Salvador, referring to the VFA and the United States having custody of Smith, told a newspaper that the Philippine government "has long been subservient to the US,"[33] tying U.S. custody of Smith to the lasting power the United States has had in the Philippines even after they relinquished colonial control and recognized the Philippines as a sovereign nation.

Jennifer's Case

There are key differences between Jennifer's and Nicole's cases, including the severity of them, with one leading to death. Another difference is that Jennifer's case ignited debate around lesbian, gay, bisexual, and transgender (LGBT) rights in the Philippines. LGBT and human rights activists staged protests around the trial and called her murder a hate crime.[34] Despite these important

differences, in many ways Jennifer's case parallels Nicole's in how it sparked debates around sovereignty, U.S.-Philippine relations, and the presence of the U.S.
military in the Philippines. One way these similarities can be seen is through
debates around U.S. custody of Pemberton prior to trial.

Jennifer Laude[35] was killed in the late hours of October 11, 2014, after check-
ing into the Celzone Lodge to have sex with Pemberton. A few days later, shortly
after Jennifer's friend Barbie positively identified Pemberton, the United States
placed Pemberton "in detention, inside a brig on board the USS Peleliu,"[36] and
the U.S. military also put their personnel on restricted liberty—also known as
short-term, authorized leave—which included restrictions on bars and night-
clubs and an earlier, 10:00 P.M., curfew. Although the restricted policy started
soon after Pemberton was accused of murdering Jennifer, there were reports
that it "isn't just about the Laude slaying but is only the latest tension point
between the former U.S. colony and the U.S. military,"[37] referring to the mass
protests and anti-U.S. sentiment that led to the U.S. military withdrawing from
the bases in the Philippines in 1992 and the possibility of lingering resentment
from their quasi-permanent return.

On December 16, 2014, the Regional Trial Court, Branch 74 in Olongapo
City, issued an arrest warrant for Pemberton. He appeared before the court
on December 19, 2014. On that same day he was transferred to the JUSMAG
compound in Camp Aguinaldo, located in Quezon City, which is part of metro
Manila.[38] Camp Aguinaldo is a Philippine military base run by the AFP, and
upon his arrival Pemberton was detained at the JUSMAG facility within it.

During the six days between Barbie positively identifying Pemberton and
his transfer to Camp Aguinaldo, Philippine activists argued that U.S. custody of
Pemberton constituted an affront to Philippine sovereignty by the U.S. military.
Protest rallies were held in front of the U.S. embassy in Manila by such groups
as Bagong Alyansang Makabayan (BAYAN), a leftist alliance of organizations
with members in Congress dedicated to eradicating poverty and critiquing
power structures that reproduce inequality within the Philippines. In response
to Pemberton being held by the United States and calling to mind the U.S. colonial era in the Philippines, Bayan secretary general Renato Reyes Jr. declared
that "the US refusal to surrender Pemberton to Philippine authorities shows
how it regards our country. The US doesn't look at us on an equal footing. The
entire Visiting Forces Agreement (VFA) is premised on unequal relations.
There is no mutuality in our relations."[39] He linked U.S. custody of Pemberton
to violations of sovereignty and continued inequality between the United States

and the Philippines. In the same article, he also used U.S. custody of Pemberton as grounds to terminate the VFA and the recently signed EDCA, calling for the permanent removal of the U.S. military in the Philippines, whether of "visiting" or "permanent" status.

The Presidential Commission on the Visiting Forces Agreement, or VFA commission, was created on January 17, 2000.[40] An advisory body to the president, composed of high-ranking government officials and two appointed nongovernmental representatives, it is charged with monitoring and assessing VFA activities and ensuring the U.S. military's compliance with existing Philippine and VFA rules, among other responsibilities. In response to outrage over U.S. custody of Pemberton prior to his transfer to Camp Aguinaldo, Eduardo Oban, the executive director of the VFA commission, stated that an appropriate time for the Philippine government to request custody is after an arrest warrant is issued.[41] Oban argued that since the Philippine courts had not yet issued an arrest warrant, requesting custody of Pemberton did not seem like a "good" or feasible option, as Pemberton had not yet been charged with a crime. Oban relied on selective technicalities and readings of the VFA. Although there are particular VFA clauses that reference the *arrest* of U.S. personnel and others that reference jurisdiction over the *detention* of U.S. personnel, many clauses reference both processes of arrest and detention. Oban pays particular attention to the technicality of whether Pemberton was arrested to argue that the VFA is being adhered to, the Philippines is not subordinate to the United States, and the United States is not exerting undue power over the Philippines to keep Pemberton in their custody.

Within a week after Barbie's positive identification of him, Pemberton was transferred to Camp Aguinaldo.[42] The negotiations between U.S. and Philippine officials and the subsequent transfer were the results of "huge public pressure for [Pemberton] to be handed over to local authorities. . . . [It] was in response to . . . demands to the United States, as it sought to assuage angry critics."[43] Yet, although Pemberton was now detained in a Philippine military facility, his transfer did not alleviate politicians', lawyers', and activists' concerns about Philippine sovereignty or calls to dismantle or at least review the VFA and EDCA as U.S. and Philippine officials hoped it would. This was because Pemberton continued to receive special treatment. U.S. military personnel were stationed directly outside the air-conditioned freight container where Pemberton was held, while Philippine military police were posted outside the JUSMAG facility.[44] He remained technically in U.S. custody since U.S. guards directly surrounded him and within a Philippine facility and military base.

Senator Miriam Defensor Santiago chaired a Senate pretrial hearing on the case and questioned why U.S., and not Philippine, guards surrounded him when he was being held in the Philippines, which was its own sovereign nation-state, and not in the United States.[45] The compromise over Pemberton's detainment was, Santiago asserted, "VIP treatment . . . I don't consider that full custody because the Americans are guarding him and the Filipinos are guarding the Americans. . . . If the Philippines has primary jurisdiction, then it follows that the Philippines should have custody. But this logic is spurned by the VFA."[46]

Terry Ridon, a Kabataan representative, said that this compromise "is akin to not granting custody of Pemberton to Philippine authorities at all. . . . The Aquino administration must still demand clear, unequivocal surrender of Pemberton's custody."[47] These critics demanded that, instead of being held at Camp Aguinaldo, Pemberton not be given "special treatment," and the Laude family even petitioned the court to reconsider its decision and transfer him to a Philippine jail instead of Camp Aguinaldo, though they were unsuccessful. Being held at a Philippine jail alongside Filipinos would have been the only way to show that the Philippines was able to assert control and authority over Pemberton. Otherwise, where he was held—whether in a Philippine or U.S. facility—didn't matter if he continued to be surrounded and protected by U.S. guards. In placing guards outside Pemberton's detention center, the U.S. both served as a physical barrier between Pemberton and Philippine authorities and presented bureaucratic obstacles for them to meet face-to-face.

However, at least outwardly, the Philippine government did not agree. President Aquino said "critics were 'jumping the gun' on the government by alleging special treatment" and that Pemberton was receiving a type of "negative special treatment" since he had not been afforded the same rights as a Filipino.[48] In public, Aquino asserted that Pemberton "is not being treated with kid gloves." Instead, he defended both the judicial process thus far and the location in which Pemberton was detained, and emphasized three things: the VFA was being adhered to, Philippine officials had been granted access to Pemberton, and importance was being given to protecting both the victim's and the accused's rights.[49] Similarly, Philippine defense secretary Voltaire Gazmin defended the choice of Camp Aguinaldo as the location of Pemberton's detainment because it "will pass US custodial standards," in essence, implying that Philippine jails would not because they were inferior.[50]

After the transfer of Pemberton and the repeated request Philippine officials made for custody of Pemberton, foreign affairs spokesperson Charles Jose said, "We will not request anymore. We will just wait for the court to advise us when the trial starts and where we expect Pemberton to appear." Agreeing that this situation where the U.S. had technical custody while the Philippines had criminal jurisdiction fell within the bounds of the VFA, he then shifted his focus to achieving justice in Jennifer's specific case and ensuring that Pemberton would serve time in the Philippines—if found guilty—and not be taken back to the United States.[51]

Similarly, U.S. representatives—including U.S. ambassador to the Philippines Philip Goldberg, U.S. secretary of state John Kerry, and U.S. Marine Corps Pacific spokesperson Col. Brad Bartelt—emphasized the United States' compliance with the terms of the VFA, their cooperation with Philippine officials, and the protection of Pemberton's rights.[52] They each emphasized that they were abiding by the legal code governing U.S. military relations in the Philippines. Denying accusations of Pemberton receiving "special" rights during this process, they instead asserted that the negotiations over detainment and custody were about safeguarding Pemberton's right to be presumed innocent before a court of law.

Both Philippine and U.S. officials also drew on the language of the VFA and its stipulations regarding U.S. custody of an accused defendant "until the completion of all judicial proceedings."[53] Both sets of officials focused on the seventh point in the VFA's article on criminal jurisdiction that stipulates that both U.S. and Philippine authorities assist one another and the ninth point that states that U.S. and Philippine officials would agree on where an accused would be held. Yet the VFA also says that "custody of any United States personnel over whom the Philippines is to exercise jurisdiction shall immediately reside with United States military authorities, if they so request, from the commission of the offense until completion of all judicial proceedings."[54] In declassified embassy exchanges, the clause "if they so request" was also repeatedly a source of contestation between U.S. and Philippine officials in Smith's trial because the U.S. never requested Smith's custody, and Philippine officials argued that this clause—and the extraordinary nature of the crime—meant that the Philippines had legal custody rights over Smith.[55] In response to the custody and detention issues over Pemberton, Justice Secretary Leila de Lima attributed the VFA's vagueness and these jurisdictional problems that seem to keep occurring to different interpretations of these clauses.[56]

Both vague and specific stipulations regarding criminal jurisdiction coexist within the VFA, and the vague wording often results in outcomes shaped by the unequal power between U.S. and Philippine officials. Although the intention of the specific stipulations is likely to ensure the fair treatment of accused individuals since being afforded certain rights—such as the right to a speedy and fair trial, access to an interpreter, and regular visits by U.S. officials—are woven into the VFA, the implementation and strict adherence to certain guidelines can hamper the Philippine legal system. The VFA has a clause, for example, that stipulates that if a trial lasts more than one year, the United States does not have to make their personnel available to Philippine officials.[57] Philippine officials accused U.S. authorities of intentional delays in both trials, indicating that they thought the United States used these trial delays as a tactic to not be held accountable for their personnel's crimes.

What we see in the pretrial custody of both Smith and Pemberton is how in these high-stake court settings, differences in power become a point of contention. What started as intimate encounters between U.S. servicemen and Filipinas in Subic Bay extended to issues beyond its spatial boundaries. In both cases, differences in power became linked to cultural understandings of Philippine national identity and sovereignty that highlighted the continued Philippine dependence on the United States and the United States' continued power in their former colony.

While anti-U.S. activists used anti-U.S. rhetoric in both trials, we do see a shift in formal government relations. With Smith's custody, we see that the United States refused to turn him over and exerted power to keep him in custody by not replying to Philippine officials' requests for custody. In response, both Philippine officials, through embassy notes, and activists leveled accusations of unequal power against the United States. Yet with Pemberton's custody we see a shift in formal relations. High-ranking government officials from both nation-states—including the Philippine president—framed pretrial custody and detention in terms of both governments adhering to the VFA. For the United States, that meant handing over Pemberton after a Philippine court issued an arrest warrant. For the Philippines, that meant Pemberton being physically held inside the AFP headquarters, even though he was held in a JUSMAG facility and was surrounded by members of the U.S. military. But strides in Philippine authority did not mean that the Philippines and the United States were now on equal ground. Instead, in Pemberton's case, the United States used informal power, or influence, to determine the conditions of his detention under Philippine custody, thereby limiting Philippine authority.

Posttrial Custody and Detention

Differences in power led to U.S. custody of Smith pretrial and during the proceedings and to the special circumstances of Pemberton's detention, despite
Philippine national critiques. Yet both trials were held in Philippine courts and
overseen by Philippine judges and justices, and both Smith and Pemberton
were found guilty. These facts are not insignificant. They are important avenues
in which Philippine authorities exercised judgment, control, and sovereignty
over foreign, American men and the U.S. military.

In this section, we'll see the possible evolution of the Philippine legal system's power, as well as its limits, and the accompanying debates, negotiations,
and contestations around Smith's and Pemberton's postconviction custody and
detention. Although Philippine judges and justices found the men guilty, this
does not mean that Philippine sovereignty prevailed. Indeed, Philippine power
and authority is not unfettered. Instead, we see the extent to which U.S. formal
and informal power also molds posttrial custody, jail conditions, and even the
overturn of the guilty verdict.

Nicole's Case and Smith's Conviction

Although Smith's conviction was seen as a victory of Philippine independence,
the controversy over postconviction custody and detention refueled the discourse of U.S. power and Philippine dependency. Smith was sentenced to a
Makati City jail until, per the VFA, U.S. and Philippine authorities could work
out an appropriate detention facility.

Smith filed two appeals, one of which was a request to be transferred to U.S.
custody, and a temporary restraining order. In his ruling on Smith's petition,
Justice Bruselas outlines why and how custody relates to Philippine sovereignty
and continued dependence on the United States. He states, "At the core of the
controversy is the basic question of who gets to keep a person who has been
charged, tried and convicted of committing a crime, or stated differently, who
should punish persons who commit crimes in a given territory."[58] He frames
the issue of custody in terms of sovereignty and territorial supremacy when
he says that being able to punish people for the crimes committed within their
boundaries is the sign of a sovereign state[59] and points out that jurisdiction and
custody go hand in hand—the one is an essential part of the other. The VFA is
and should be about protecting the people of the host nation, not the visiting
foreign soldiers.

Justice Bruselas dissected all ten paragraphs of the VFA article that delineates criminal jurisdiction. He concludes that the single paragraph that states that "custody of any United States personnel over whom the Philippines is to exercise jurisdiction *shall immediately reside* with United States military authorities, *if they so request*, from the commission of the offense until completion of all judicial proceedings" (emphasis is the court's[60]) is far outweighed by the other nine paragraphs regarding Philippine jurisdiction and, thus, custody. In the original draft of his opinion, Justice Bruselas dismissed Smith's petition based on lack of merit.

However, by the time the official decision was filed, the petition was dismissed for another reason: Smith had already been transferred to U.S. authorities because of an agreement reached between the Philippine foreign affairs secretary Alberto Romulo and Kristie Kenney, the U.S. ambassador to the Philippines. This agreement became known as the Romulo-Kenney Agreements of December 19 and 22, which were made between the two state officials vis-á-vis embassy notes. These writings detailed the return of Smith to U.S. military custody, his detainment at the U.S. embassy compound—guarded by U.S. personnel—and the access Philippine authorities would have to Smith. They were also written at the same time the United States canceled the Balikatan (which means "shoulder to shoulder" in Tagalog) U.S.-Philippine joint military exercise scheduled for February 2007. These exercises are held on an annual basis and provide the foundation for cooperation between the U.S. military and the Philippine armed forces. They are important to maintain not only for training purposes but also because the Philippine armed forces are heavily reliant on the U.S. military for defense of the Philippines more generally and aid. The canceling of such an event signals an uneasy relationship between the United States and the Philippines and can threaten Philippine national security. Its cancelation was a display of U.S. power and served as a not-so-subtle threat to the Philippines since it was canceled as an explicit response to Smith remaining in Philippine custody.[61]

In the original and published versions of his decision, Justice Bruselas discusses how courts are unable to intervene in diplomatic matters. Although the original draft of the decision follows this with a declaration of safeguarding state sovereignty and assertion that the VFA recognized this sovereignty, the official decision ended in a dismissal, rendered moot because Smith had already been transferred.[62] Smith's transfer instigated renewed debate on Philippine sovereignty and continued dependence on the United States. Evalyn Ursua,

Nicole's lawyer, said that U.S. efforts concerning the transfer amounted to "arm-twisting" the Philippine government and that Philippine president Gloria Macapagal-Arroyo could be impeached for allowing this "violation of our sovereignty" and "clear foreign intervention."[63] Similarly, the Akbayan party list representative Risa Hontiveros said that Malacañang's[64] role in facilitating Smith's transfer to U.S. custody "lacked gender sensitivity and nationalism and [was] an insult to our nation."[65] Here again, we see how what could be seen as a seemingly trivial matter over custody becomes entwined with a gendered nationalism and what it means to be a sovereign nation.

In addition to the anti-U.S. discourse of protestors and governmental officials, Nicole filed a petition,[66] which was decided in conjunction with two other cases concerning related issues.[67] First, she argued that the VFA was unconstitutional, and therefore, the Philippines should have custody of Smith after his guilty verdict. Second, she argued that U.S. custody of the accused during trial violated the Constitution's equal protection clause because it allowed different rules for the accused based on nationality. The court disagreed with Nicole. First, they found that the issue of whether or not the VFA was unconstitutional had already been addressed in a previous case, *Bayan v. Zamora*.

The question regarding the VFA's unconstitutionality stems from the present 1987 Philippine Constitution, which states that foreign military bases require a treaty ratified by both nations. The main argument for its unconstitutionality is that the VFA was not presented to the U.S. Senate for approval. However, the court found that since it was approved by the Philippine Senate and recognized by the United States as a treaty—a binding international agreement—it was a treaty per the Philippine Constitution. Additionally, since it was signed as an implementing factor of the 1951 Mutual Defense Treaty between the United States and the Philippines—which continues to be in effect—it was not necessary for the U.S. Senate to approve it, merely for the U.S. Congress to recognize it, which it did.

A second issue raised in this petition was on the differential treatment of Smith based on his nationality—for example, U.S. custody of him during trial—which Nicole argued violated the Constitution's equal protection clause. The Court did not agree because they linked U.S. custody of Smith to international law and a limited immunity from jurisdiction, which is bounded by the terms of treaties that are signed. Elaborating, Justice Azcuna likened jurisdiction of U.S. military personnel to officials like diplomats and heads of states who also enjoy immunity.[68]

Although not addressed in the appeal, the court then turned its attention to the detention of Smith, postconviction, at the U.S. embassy compound, and the justice found that there *was* illegal, differential treatment. Zoning in on the language of the VFA concerning U.S. and Philippine agreements on detention facilities, the court asserted that there was a clear difference between custody during trial and after conviction. In addition, the aforementioned Romulo-Kenney Agreements violated the VFA because Smith was not being held "by Philippine authorities." The court then moved for Philippine and U.S. officials to negotiate an appropriate detention facility and for the court of appeals to resolve Smith's second appeal.

In separate dissenting opinions, two justices premised their dissent of the precedent case, *Bayan v. Zamora*, arguing that the VFA is unconstitutional because it is not considered a treaty but rather an executive agreement by the U.S. While the agreements created an obligation to international law, it was not binding in U.S. domestic law, and the disparity between being enforceable within the Philippines but not the U.S. "would render our sovereignty in tatters."[69] Justice Antonio T. Carpio concurred with the dissention. In a separate opinion, he stated that "the Philippines is a sovereign and independent State. It is no longer a colony of the United States. This Court should not countenance an unequal treaty that is not only contrary to the express mandate of the Philippine Constitution, but also an affront to the sovereignty, dignity and independence of the Philippine State."[70] In these words, he suggests that the VFA is another way in which Philippine independence and sovereignty is hampered by the United States.

Despite the anti-U.S. rhetoric and Smith's original guilty verdict, in 2009, and in answer to another of Smith's appeal, a Philippine court of appeals acquitted him, ruling that there was insufficient evidence of rape. Activists and Philippine government officials used this decision to condemn the United States. The Bayan Muna party list representative, Satur Ocampo, called this reversal "a major blow to our national sovereignty and dignity, and to Philippine jurisprudence."[71] In practice, Ocampo suggested that this decision abetted the sustained, historical abuses of U.S. military forces, whether they were "visiting" or stationed at the permanent Subic Bay Naval Base. The court's acquittal of Smith also raised questions on probable political pressures on the justices coming from the U.S. government and the executive branch. In the decision to overturn Smith's conviction, the justice specifically stated that they did not take into account Nicole's recantation, which was made public prior to the court's decision.

Yet it is difficult to imagine that Nicole's recantation had no effect, even indirect, on the decision. In it, she admitted that she was attracted to Smith. She also said that she "was so drunk when the incident happened,"[72] thereby raising doubts about her ability to recall the rape. The widespread reporting of Nicole's recantation also perpetuates a gendered narrative of what constitutes rape, where rape is not a crime but an accident and where consent refers to attraction rather than consensual affirmation of sex. There is also significant circumstantial evidence that her admission was a result of U.S. intimidation and informal power. Shortly after her recantation, she permanently left the Philippines to reside in the United States, something she could have only been able to do with the proper authorization and documents, which can be difficult and time consuming to obtain.

In both Nicole's and Smith's posttrial appeals, the court was tasked with addressing questions of the constitutionality of the VFA, delving into the minute details of the ten paragraphs of the VFA that deal with criminal jurisdiction and custody, and interpreting diplomacy in action through the agreements between the U.S. ambassador to the Philippines and the Philippine secretary of foreign affairs. In their rulings, the judges and justices, along with newspaper accounts, protests, and activist writings, imbued these decisions with symbolism related to sovereignty, respect, and independence/dependence among nations. These issues of sovereignty and how it relates to the presence of the U.S. military in the Philippines were not resolved. They came up again almost eight years later, in Jennifer's case.

Jennifer's Case and Pemberton's Conviction

Like Nicole in her own case and the protests that surrounded it, Marilou Laude, Jennifer's sister, called for U.S. military personnel to be held accountable for their actions. Yet, despite Pemberton's conviction by a Philippine court, Jennifer was ultimately thought not to have received justice, in part, because he was guilty of homicide, and not murder. This reduction in charges was due to the court's ruling that passion and obfuscation were mitigating circumstances in the case because Pemberton testified that he choked her in direct relation to his discovery of her male-presenting genitalia. LGBT and anti–U.S. military advocates see this as evidence that Jennifer's murder was a hate crime. Yet there are no national laws against hate crimes or against LGBTQ discrimination.[73] Although some Philippine cities have laws that prohibit discrimination, Olongapo does not.[74] LGBT and anti–U.S. military activists also argue that the court's reduction of Pemberton's sentence because of his discovery of Jennifer's genitalia suggests that Pemberton's "passion" and "obfuscation" were understandable, as was her subsequent murder, and their words spread internationally.

As Jamille, Jennifer's former roommate, said, "If Jennifer were a real girl, the conviction would automatically be murder."[75] Indeed, Pemberton's defense tried to argue that Pemberton did not have "superior strength" over Laude precisely because Laude was a man. One of the ways they did this was by referring to Jennifer as "Jeffrey," the male name she was given when she was born, rather than the name she went by, a practice commonly referred to as "dead-naming." They did so as a way to emphasize that her physical body and its associated strength was male and used this as evidence that the prosecution failed to offer proof that Pemberton had "physically superior strength," which is one of the necessary requirements to be found guilty of murder.[76]

They also framed Pemberton's action in terms of defense against his honor—in this case, a particular masculine conceptualization of honor that was accosted when he engaged in intimate acts with a transgender Filipina who had both female- and male-presenting physical characteristics (breasts and genitals). Sovereignty becomes gendered when people link violations of a nation's sovereignty to, in this case, the Philippines' inability to protect those most disenfranchised—cis and transgender women—and when court rulings uphold a masculine honor that is predicated on heterosexual acts and "protecting" men against sexual activity with transgender women and that takes on a particular racialized form, where white U.S. men violently harm Filipinas.

Jennifer was also thought not to have received justice by her family, friends, and activists for a second reason: Pemberton's special treatment postconviction. In Nicole's case, from almost the beginning, the court systems and other professionals dissected the VFA, its ramifications, and how it related to Smith's custody and Philippine sovereignty. Likewise, the judge in Jennifer's case evoked the VFA twice in her finding that Pemberton was guilty of homicide: first, in awarding exemplary damages and second, in discussing custody.[77]

Although Judge Roline M. Ginez-Jabalde acknowledged that exemplary damages are usually reserved for "aggravating circumstances" and the court did not find any, she awarded these damages "to set a public example, to serve as deterrent to all military and civilian personnel of the United States of America . . . to respect every Filipino citizen regardless of his/her sexual orientation and also the laws of the Republic of the Philippines."[78] She awarded Jennifer's family P30,000 (US$750[79])—not the P100 million (US$2.5 million) they originally requested—as a symbolic rebuke of the U.S. military, to hold Pemberton up as an example of someone who, despite his U.S. nationality, would be held accountable to Philippine laws and to assert that all Filipino citizens have equal rights of protection and respect.

Like the judges and justices before her, Judge Ginez-Jabalde, in her decision, quotes article 5, section 10 of the VFA. She also draws on the language in U.S. embassy note 2332 dated November 12, 2015. Both of these documents focus on U.S. and Philippine authorities' agreeing to detention facilities. Highlighting the VFA's "by Philippine authorities" clause, she orders Pemberton to be temporarily committed to the New Bilibid Prison in Muntinlupa City, where national prisoners who are found guilty of similar crimes and sentenced to serve similar amounts of time are held.[80] To order Pemberton to be held at New Bilibid Prison, Judge Ginez-Jabalde draws on national law regarding detainment. Comparable to activists and lawyers who critiqued Philippine and U.S. officials regarding U.S. custody of Pemberton during his trial, Judge Ginez-Jabalde likens Pemberton to other national prisoners and asserts that his nationality does not grant him special rights as to where he is held, at least initially. Pemberton would be detained with Filipinos convicted and sentenced to an equivalent amount of time, all of which are hallmarks of Philippine sovereignty in effect—being able to punish people convicted of crimes within their territory and without leniency because of his different nationality.

After Pemberton was found guilty, however, he did not immediately reside in a Philippine jail as the judge ordered nor as Smith originally did. Instead, there was a two-hour standoff because Pemberton's U.S. security escorts refused to turn him over to the Philippine local police,[81] another demonstration of U.S. power in the face of Philippine requests. The standoff ended when Judge Ginez-Jabalde received a motion from the defense lawyers regarding clarification on his detainment and communication from Eduardo Oban Jr., executive director of the Presidential Commission on the Visiting Forces Agreement, that stated there was a prior agreement with Philippine authorities that Pemberton would be temporarily held at the AFP custodial center in Camp Aguinaldo until a decision was reached on where he would be permanently detained. Pemberton was then brought to the JUSMAG facility at Camp Aguinaldo, where he was kept during trial. Drawing on the authority of the Philippine court system and emphasizing that Philippine courts ultimately had authority and jurisdiction, Harry Roque Jr., the Laude family lead counsel, "asked the court to cite Eduardo Oban Jr., executive director of the PCVFA, and the 11 American soldiers in indirect contempt for refusing to turn Pemberton over to local authorities after his conviction on Dec 1," because they were in "indirect contempt for 'violating and refusing to obey' the court's original commitment order."[82]

Yet no one was held in contempt of court, and Pemberton remained in Camp Aguinaldo, drawing similar critiques to those leveled against U.S. and Philippine officials regarding his detainment at Camp Aguinaldo during the trial and the special treatment he received. This special treatment included renovating the facility, for which the Philippines was tasked with paying.[83] The activist Liza Maza, an International League of Peoples' Struggles representative and a former representative of GABRIELA, a radical leftist women's organization, expressed her dismay at the situation, saying, "The Philippine government is spending to renovate and construct a special jail for Pemberton who committed murder and giving him special treatment, special food, 18 policemen guarding his cell and in all the comforts and you call that punishing a person?" As she points out, "that's not how you punish a person that has committed a crime. . . . That's how lopsided our government is."[84]

She called Pemberton "Daniel Smith part 2" and linked Jennifer's case to Nicole's, where Smith remained in U.S. custody and his guilty verdict was eventually overturned. She argued that the VFA and EDCA were unequal agreements that disproportionately benefited the U.S. and its military personnel who rape and murder Filipinas. As such, Philippine "sovereignty is [also] getting raped and killed, because of the connivance between US and Philippine officials. . . . As long as there is collussion [sic] with the US and whoever is in power, who is subservient to America, we will not attain our rights as individuals and as a free nation."[85] Renato Reyes concurred, saying he was appalled at how President Aquino and the Department of Justice responded to Pemberton's trial. He stated, "Our own officials are spineless. They did not even stand up to US arrogance. They did not assert our national sovereignty."[86] Both Maza and Reyes critiqued the inability of the Philippine government to assert their will regarding Pemberton's detention and equated VFA provisions that specify detention facilities must be mutually agreed upon to the United States strong-arming the Philippine government to acquiesce to their demands.

In a similar response that they gave regarding his pretrial detainment, the Department of Justice and President Aquino emphasized that he was detained within Philippine—not U.S.—territory and within a Philippine-controlled facility under the guard of Bureau of Corrections personnel. He used this as evidence that the United States and the Philippines were on equal standing and that the Philippines adhered to the rule of law.[87] The fact that Pemberton was held within a Philippine facility mattered and represented an important growth in U.S.-Philippine relations precisely because Smith was not similarly detained within a Philippine facility.

In the midst of these public critiques, Pemberton filed a motion for the court to overturn his conviction or, if not overturn the conviction, then grant him bail and reduce his sentence. In contrast to Smith's verdict, the court upheld Pemberton's conviction and denied him bail. However, because of the mitigating circumstances in the case—intoxication and passion and obfuscation—his sentence was reduced from a maximum of twelve years to a maximum of ten years.

In response to the news of Pemberton's maximum-sentence reduction, many politicians and activists rushed to the media to denounce the ruling. The Kabataan Partylist representative Terry Ridon detailed the issue at hand when he said, "First, Pemberton was allowed to stay, not in a regular prison facility, but in Camp Aguinaldo. Then we have the court affirming his conviction yet reducing his jail time. All these speak of preferential treatment only accorded to US servicemen—the hallmark of unjustifiable subservience of our government to Washington."[88] Walden Bello, a professor of sociology at the University of Philippines, former member of the Philippine House of Representatives, and a candidate to the Philippine Senate during Pemberton's trial and appeal, chimed in and agreed with Ridon's critique. He said, "This decision does not deliver complete justice because Pemberton continues to enjoy the privilege of serving his sentence in a 'jail' where only the US has control. This is a mockery of our judicial and legal system; it further underscores why [military] agreements . . . , which allow such a mockery to happen, must be abrogated."[89]

Younger Filipino activists agreed. Sarah Elago, a representative of the group Youth Party, said that Pemberton's sentence reduction "speaks volumes about our nation's continued subservience to the U.S. . . . We cannot accept the fact that a convicted murderer has been able to easily sway the court in his favor just because he is a U.S. citizen."[90] Renato Reyes also suggested, "If we allow Pemberton's conviction to be reversed or reduce his sentence, this will send a wrong message to U.S. soldiers: That they can commit crimes and get away with it."[91] So, too, did Jennifer's former roommate say that this was evidence that "America is still the favorite" and linked the court's finding that there were mitigating circumstances in the case to discrimination against LGBT individuals, because "if Jennifer were a real girl, the conviction would automatically be murder."[92]

Yet, according to Meredith Talusan, a transgender Filipina American BuzzFeed news reporter, some locals were "eager to move past the Laude incident altogether . . . [while other] locals have even accused the Laudes of being selfish by not settling the case early."[93] She gave the example of Olongapo City councilor Aquilino Cortez Jr., who focused not on how Jennifer's death symbolized continued U.S. power in the Philippines. Rather, he was worried about the economic impact of Jennifer's case on Olongapo City's economy. The restricted liberty policy of the U.S. military following Pemberton's arrest affected the livelihoods of thousands of people who relied on the money U.S. military brought into their businesses. Yet this didn't mean he was immune to seeing the broader symbolism of Jennifer's case. Instead, and in contrast to anti–U.S. military activists and government officials, Cortez emphasized that Pemberton was found guilty. Focusing on the gains made by the Philippine nation over the U.S. military since Smith's trial, he suggested that this "will be the first time that a U.S. service member would be successfully convicted of a crime against a Filipino citizen in a Philippine court."[94]

Yet Smith was convicted of the rape against Nicole. Michael Butler, an African American naval seaman, was also convicted of murdering Filipina Gina Barrios in 1975. A more appropriate and accurate observation is whether U.S. servicemen *stay* convicted and are required to adhere to the original punishments handed down by Philippine courts. Although time will tell if Pemberton will serve his full sentence, Smith's conviction was overturned three years later, and Butler's case was dismissed by the Philippine Supreme Court after six years for good behavior and rehabilitation.[95] Both instances suggest that the problem lies not with the initial conviction of U.S. servicemen. Rather, the problem is whether they stay convicted and serve the punishment that Philippine courts hand down.

Gains and Losses in Global Borderland Negotiations

Why focus on the rape and murder of Filipina women by U.S. servicemen? These two cases showcase the stakes involved in global borderlands. The minutiae of legal language—who gets custody, where someone is detained, how and under what circumstances they are detained before, during, and after trial— matter. These are not trivial details that should be glossed over for the big-picture argument that the United States ultimately asserts undue power and influence in these types of criminal cases. Doing so loses sight of the gains and loses made by both Philippine and U.S. officials. That these cases were tried in Philippine courts, without question, matters. It showcases how Philippine jurisdictional authority was not questioned and each set of officials subjected themselves to the authority of the Philippine court system.

That Pemberton was not held in a U.S. facility but in the AFP headquarters also matters. It's a distinct gain for Philippine officials and the Philippine nation to be able to hold the accused within a place where there is no question in whose territory they are held. Yet it also matters that the United States dictated the conditions of his detention facilities and placed armed guards directly outside of his cell. It highlights continued U.S. power and influence in the Philippines. It is this back-and-forth, the losses and gains, and the processes in which they are enacted or constrained that are important.

These cases also highlight how these issues of stakes and power are entwined with meanings. Nicole and Jennifer came to be seen as embodying the Philippine nation, and the lack of justice in each of their cases—to their lawyers, families, and activists—is directly tied to Philippine dependence and subservience to the United States, something that has been ongoing, they argue, since the colonial era. Similarly, differences in Jennifer's case were seen as a win for Philippine authorities. That Pemberton was held in a Philippine facility showed the nation and the world, President Aquino argued, that the Philippines is a sovereign state and of equal standing to the United States. In each of these, we see competing understandings of the symbolism of these cases and what should be the focus of attention: continued subservience or the gains made and promising signs of an evolving, and not stagnant, relationship between the two countries. It is these competing understandings that make possible the continued existence of the U.S. military in the Philippines and also allow the foothold of the accompanying inequalities that follow.

Nicole's and Jennifer's cases were wrought with violence, and this violence was indicative of stark power differences between the two countries and the bloody history that defines the U.S. colonial period in the Philippines. Yet not all intimacies between U.S. servicemen and Filipina women are defined by violence. Nor do they always garner national and international attention. Instead, other types of intimacies between U.S. servicemen and Filipinas are found in everyday life in global borderlands like Subic Bay. Given how much more common they are than violent cases that make headline news, we need to understand the ways in which these less sensationalized relationships play a role in the enactment of global borderlands and the accompanying reproduction of inequalities.

Sex and Romance

3

Susan did not set out to be a sex worker.[1] Instead, she went to Olongapo to escape her brother-in-law, who had hurt and abused her. She arrived on a rainy day. Exhausted, with no food and no money, she approached owners of the bars that peppered Olongapo's streets, trying to find a place to sleep. She faced constant rejection. Finally, one woman took her in and allowed her to stay in exchange for washing clothes and cleaning their house. Eventually, however, she grew resentful of the women sex workers she was surrounded by. They always had money—and not just Philippine pesos but U.S. dollars, which went much further in the economy. Although she also found a job as a manicurist, she was always trying to make ends meet. She finally decided that the women's jobs weren't so bad, and in 1983 she began her journey as a sex worker. Her first client was a Mexican American serviceman who was in town for three months. During this time he paid her steady bar fine, the payment that frees a woman from the day-to-day work at the bar, though she continued to live there.

In contrast, Danielle did not work in a bar. However, she loved to dance. She would sneak out of her parents' house to go to a local bar to dance the night away with her friends. It was during one of these times that she met Tim, an Italian American U.S. serviceman. He asked her to dance. She responded that she was "not a bar girl," making it clear that she was in the bar having fun and wasn't trying to meet with any men nor looking for clients. He insisted that he knew she wasn't a bar girl. He could tell from how she dressed. That's why he liked her and wanted to approach her. His directness surprised Danielle and was contrary to everything she expected because she was used to the Filipino way of courting, which she describes as taking a long time. Instead, she and Tim hit it off and began dating immediately. He would tell her of his plans to marry her, to take her to the United States with him. She fell in love though wasn't quite ready to get married just yet, and she thought he fell in love with her too. Even their first fight sticks out in her mind. "It's like a movie, with rain and the fighting; we're arguing." Afterward, she received flowers and an apology, another step that followed in the footsteps of the romances she saw on screen.

·   ·   ·

The global borderlands of active and decommissioned overseas U.S. military bases often conjure up images and sexual fantasies of local women at the beck and call of men, ready to indulge their every desire. Olongapo, the city surrounding the former U.S. Subic Bay Naval Base, was no different. Vendors sold souvenirs that reflected these fantasies. One shirt pictured a Filipina with long hair sitting seductively in an oversized alcoholic drink alongside the label "little brown fucking machines powered by rice."[2] Sex and desire were packaged together, often crudely, ready for the taking in any of the many bars lining Olongapo's streets. These sexual "global imaginaries"[3] flourished, as did the sex industry, during the Vietnam War and beyond. In 1987, for example, an estimated 700 bars and clubs, 9,053 registered entertainers, and 6,000 unregistered sex workers thrived in Olongapo City.[4] Even today, if you take one of the blue jeepneys from the heart of Olongapo toward Baloy Road, you'll see many of these clubs as you pass through Barrio Barretto, where they sit alongside the winding RH5 National Highway and beach coastline of Subic Bay.

This landscape of global sex work, or what Denise Brennan calls a sexscape,[5] is rooted in power differences based on racial, gender, class, and nationality differences between the sex workers in less developed worlds and sex consumers from more developed countries. When aligned with former or active military bases, they are also what Emmanuel David[6] refers to as the "sexual fields of empire." These hotspots of desire serve as important conduits connecting the global political economy.[7] They were also created for the U.S. servicemen stationed and visiting the Subic Bay Naval Base. They represent the appeal of these places for these men and the mythical subservient women ready to welcome them in the hot, tropical country to which they are sent. They say nothing of the appeal nor sexual myths of military bases for Filipina women who live and work in and around the streets surrounding it.

Both Susan's and Danielle's stories speak to two types of global imaginations that shape how intimate relations between U.S. servicemen and Filipina women are seen and how they play out on the ground. Yet they tell different versions, different from the cultivated fantasies for U.S. servicemen, as well as from one another. How can there be so many competing sex-based imaginaries within this place? Because how we think about sex, desire, and love is not self-evident. Rather, they are rooted in particular cultural frameworks and entwined with our notions about race and nationhood.[8] This chapter uncovers how we understand the sexual relationships between Filipinas and U.S. servicemen through two prevalent myths—what I call the exploitative sex myth and the heroic love myth—and the ways in which these myths contribute to the sustained presence of global borderlands and their accompanying inequality.

Activists make sense of these interracial intimacies through the particular lens of an exploitative sex myth that links these encounters to the broader political economy and unequal relationship between the United States and the Philippines and narrates sexual relationships between U.S. servicemen and Filipinas—including but not limited to those that emerge out of sex work—as necessarily bad and exploitative.[9] These understandings are centered around gendered identities that become symbolic of the nation; that is, Filipina women serve as a representative for the Philippine nation while U.S. servicemen represent the United States. In doing so, they use gendered symbolism of the nation to critique international politics and the unequal power the United States continues to hold over the Philippines. These understandings also orient their strategies of action, or "the patterns into which action is routinely organized,"[10] concerning their activism work, which focuses on trying to oust the U.S. military and reduce poverty and inequality in the Philippines.[11] Susan's entry into sex work occurred after she fled from home and the abuse that she had endured there and after she had tried to start over in Olongapo City as a domestic worker and manicurist. Her story can be seen as representing the exploitative sex myth and used to demonstrate the evils perpetuated by the institutionalization of sex work, the dollar resources sex work provides, and the limited opportunities that can be found elsewhere.

Yet, as Danielle's story suggests, there's another alternative framework from which to understand relationships between U.S. servicemen and Filipina women and how Filipina women make sense of their relatively subordinated position—that of a particular type of "love myth,"[12] or narrative of romance and love. I call this framework the heroic love myth, which is rooted in seeing the other as a savior, lifting Filipina women up from poverty and opening up a new world for them. For Danielle, this took the form of potential marriage and migration to the United States and later, after her daughter with Tim was diagnosed with epilepsy, of saving them from poverty and providing them with the medical care their daughter needed. These myths orient these women's own strategies of action and general understandings and attitudes of their relationships and the world around them. It is precisely because these two myths are both prevalent and at odds with one another that these relationships both continue to flourish while simultaneously being used by activists as examples of exploitation and abuse of power.

In the pages that follow, I unpack these two myths and how they contribute to the staying power of global borderlands. As I do so, I also show how underneath the fantasies of an unfettered sexual playground for the U.S. military that underlie much—but not all—of the exploitative sex myth lies a highly regulated and variegated system put in place for the safeguard of the men. That system, regulated by both the U.S. military and the Olongapo City government, policed Filipina women's bodies but not American men's. They did so through mandatory health checkups and registrations for sex workers, which were of utmost concern. However, eradicating sex work or even regulating the *content* of the daily interactions between Filipinas and U.S. servicemen was of *comparatively* low stakes or not of interest to either government. That is, the Philippine and U.S. governments did not interfere with the meanings ascribed to these relationships; nor did they want to rid Olongapo of the institutionalized sex work; rather, they wanted to only enforce regulations that would ensure hygiene, which would have far-reaching consequences for both the United States and the Philippines. In contrast, however, the U.S. military did rely on the exploitative sex myth when it concerned legal marriages with Filipinas, though they flip the myth and caution men against exploitation by Filipina women.

The desire for love and marriage that is evoked in the form of the heroic love myth is also regulated, though through informal systems that policed Filipina women's motivations and were used to make a distinction between those women who are "deserving" of being saved versus those who are not. This informal system often revolves around gossip, where Filipina women involved in intimate relationships with U.S. military men were often seen as sex workers, "gold diggers," or as using men to migrate; they were viewed in these ways by their families, by other Filipina women, and by the families of the men they were involved with. Here, different types of people draw on moral boundaries to differentiate "real" relationships from those they perceived as fake.

Exploitative Sex Myth

In 1987, as thousands of servicemen stationed at the U.S. Subic Bay Naval Base were consuming these images of desire and sexuality by frequenting local bars and engaging in intimate encounters with Filipinas, another set of actors were working to abolish these same foreign military men from Philippine soil. The National Council of Churches in the Philippines (NCCP, a network of Protestant churches across the Philippines that tie religion to social justice efforts) and GABRIELA (a leftist alliance of organizations, grassroots efforts, and institutions coming together to fight for women's issues), among others, hosted a conference "National Consultation on Prostitution" (NCP) to confront the issue of the exploitation of women in sex work. Together, they represented a powerful alliance that harkened back to the coalitions that organized the mass peaceful protests that ousted the dictator Ferdinand Marcos from power the previous year,[13] and speakers included current and former sex workers, as well as a consultant from UNICEF, academics, the minister of social services and development and the deputy minister of the Ministry of Justice. The conference set a national agenda on what sex work was in the Philippines and how it related to the military base. What was this agenda centered on? The exploitative sex myth.

Sr. Mary John Mananzan was the chairperson of GABRIELA and director of the Center for Women's Resources. In her conference address, she linked sex work to international tourism through the promotion of "mail-order brides; the entertainers; and the migrant workers"[14] and cited an unsourced statistic saying that 85 percent of tourists to the Philippines are men and that "we can be fairly certain we know what these 85% are after"—sexual encounters with Filipinas. Describing the Filipino/a sex workers at home and abroad as a moral problem that has an economic foundation, she advocated a two-pronged approach: transforming tourism from sex-based to one of cultural exchange and rehabilitating children and older sex workers, because "for the adult women prostitutes, I'm sorry to say there is no possibility of rehabilitation. There is a law that the only thing we can do is to make things easier for them, so they are not exploited too much: not victims of sadism etc."[15]

As we see, in the Philippines and elsewhere, activists, organizations, and others rely on an *exploitative sex myth* to understand intimate relations between

Filipina women and U.S. servicemen. Within this myth, the creation, regulation, and growth of military-based sex work and sex work more generally are framed as a fundamentally moral problem.[16] Philippine organizations, in particular, see the sex work surrounding overseas military bases as evidence of the United States' continual exploitation of the Philippine nation and see relationships between Filipina women and U.S. servicemen as defined by and symbolic of this broader and unequal political economy.

In the conference, particularly in Sr. Mary John's address, we can see how (im)morality is threefold. First, there is an assumption that any type of sex work—particularly that which is associated with military bases—is immoral, exploitative, and forced and that these women are in need of saving. The following story echoes this assumption of exploitation, showing how these understandings of military-based sex work may hold a grain of truth.

When Alma was in high school she moved to Olongapo City, where her brother was a manager of a bar, the 9,000 Club. Her brother financially supported their parents, and although he was unable to help Alma go to college, he did send her to vocational school. However, he also constantly encouraged her to date Americans and to find an American husband. In response, she ran away. She didn't want to be with an American. Years later, after she had two children with a Filipino, she ran into her brother again. He said that "since [she] was no longer a virgin, then [she] could already work in the bar," and she entered into the peripheries of the sex industry by becoming a waitress. But soon, she found out pay was not based on a salary. Instead, it was based on tips and a small five-peso allowance; she says, "There comes a time when you really need money, like when my son was sick I was desperate for money, so I had no choice but to go out with an American."[17] The first few times, however, she backed out of going on a date with them. But when she was told by the bar managers that she would have to leave if she continued to do that, she began going out with Americans.

However, she describes these so-called dates as performances. "When you see a bar, all the women will be smiling, but inside we feel like we are almost being raped. When we are cursed, we smile. Most of the women are on drugs just to forget, to be able to swallow what is happening. . . . Frowning will not help you get the money."[18] She also describes the exploitation of the system, where it is impossible to save money, particularly when two-thirds of the bar fine a man pays to take her out goes to the bar, leaving her with only a third of the pay. She stopped being a sex worker when Buklod, a nonprofit women's organization made up of former sex workers and dedicated to helping the urban poor and sex workers in Subic Bay and Angeles, approached her. She now heads Buklod and tries to "raise [sex workers'] self esteem. When you work in the bar, you think you are trapped, that people will always look at you and treat you like a slut."[19] Her narration echoes these themes of the exploitation of sex workers and the immorality of the industry.

A second aspect of the (im)morality surrounding the exploitative sex myth is that there is a delineation between those who can be "saved" from a life of sex work and those who cannot. This categorization of sex workers is often framed around choice—whereas adult women enter into sex work by choice, children and older women have little to no choice. Sr. Mary John described a telling encounter that frames this rationale: "The most pathetic thing I saw was on the staircase going to the Penthouse [of Haven, a brothel]. They were about 40 to 35 [sic] years old and very haggard. I said, 'What is going to happen to them?' They no longer have any prospect of doing the trade. They are very ready and open to whatever rehabilitation work you can give them. I think that is the chance." Both the industry as a whole and adult sex workers are dismissed as immoral. Although activists try to work on bettering conditions so the women are "not exploited too much," their primary focus is on children and older women—those whom they think they can help the most because they can convince them to leave the sex industry.

Arsenia is one such sex worker who is seen by the NCCP and GABRIELA as deserving of being saved.[20] She was the second youngest of twelve children. Her father didn't have a job, and any money he could scrounge up, whether through temporary jobs or something else, was spent "on cockfights and women."[21] He died when her younger sister was only two years old. Neither Arnesia nor any of her eleven siblings finished elementary school. Because of their poverty, her oldest sister became a sex worker in Olongapo and later recruited the next oldest girl into the industry. Her youngest sister also entered the sex industry, though in her case it was through their mother, who was her pimp. Arnesia, however, was adopted when she was three years old, to a woman physician and her husband. Although her adoption could have been Arnesia's chance to escape poverty and a life of sex work, that's not what happened. Instead, her adopted father molested her. At eleven years old she stopped going to school and started hanging around people who used drugs. She also became a sex worker. She was taken off the streets and put into a correctional institute where she stayed for three years.

At fourteen years old she got out, and her mother sent her to live with extended family, where she was sexually abused by her male cousins. Her mother then brought her into the fold of the formal sex industry and took the money Arnesia earned for herself. After escaping that situation, Arnesia worked as a "high class call girl" and lived with "several men."[22] One of her "live-ins" "ripped off a half-million peso hold-up. They used the money for their getaway that sent [him] to prison."[23] Afterward, she went back to working at a bar. This time, however, her sister, rather than her mother, was her pimp. From the family she was born into to the molestation that shattered her dreams of escaping poverty through adoption, Arnesia's pathway represents just one among the many ways young sex workers enter into the industry, workers whom the NCCP and GABRIELA hope to help change their lives and exit sex work.

Finally, another aspect of the (im)morality found alongside the exploitative sex myth revolves around the men who are clients of sex workers. These men who visit the Philippines and other less developed countries in Southeast Asia are classified as immoral, only traveling to these places to pay for sex. Framing the foreign men in this way disallows for any other understanding of the intimate relations that occur between Filipina women and foreigners except as exploitative relationships and disregards other reasons for temporary migration.[24]

Violy[25] was taken from her family home in Bicol when she was six years old, for example, and given to a foster family in Cavite. While in high school, she reunited with her biological family, who thought she was long dead. When she was sixteen she wanted to start working at a bar in Angeles City to help financially support her Bicol family. She had a classmate whose mother worked at a bar there, and she visited it with her classmate. She began working at a bar in Angeles in 1980 and was at first a "stay-in counter girl" who "did not go out with [customers]."[26] After three months, she began to give massages to clients at a hotel and would masturbate clients if they requested, for an additional P150, though "sex was not part of the deal."[27] Here, she differentiated masturbating a client from "real" sex.

She met Richard Green, an Australian tourist, after he was mugged and she took him to a hospital.[28] Afterward, he paid her steady bar fine for three months. Before he returned to Australia, they had intercourse after drinking wine. She was unaware of the sex until after she woke up and had pain in her genitals, and she was "annoyed because she could not ask him to pay the price for her virginity: P5,000."[29] Richard told Violy that he wanted to marry her and would return. As he was leaving, he gave her an envelope with P37,000; she used it to buy her

Bicol family farmland. After he left, she waited for Richard in Angeles and did not see other clients. She remained sexually committed to him.

Later, his brother, Ryan, returned and told her that Richard had committed suicide. Violy "felt frustrated and angry that she had been made to wait with high expectations. She decided to become a full-fledged bar woman. Ryan became [her] first customer. He was violent."[30] He also promised to marry her, but he "always embarrassed her."[31] She had other clients while she was with Ryan because her relationship with him was not like the one she had had with Richard. Over the next seven years, she worked inside the bar intermittently as she had clients who would pay steady fines to the bar in which she worked, which meant that Violy did not have to work each night and could live with the client.

She eventually moved to Olongapo and was working as a dancer during the U.S. military's 1991 withdrawal. In Olongapo, she and other entertainers were recruited to be dancers in Cyprus, showing how the movement of women around global borderlands includes both internal migration—in this case, within and around Subic and Clark—and across national boundaries. In Cyprus she worked at a brothel and was supposed to entertain at least ten men each night. However, the bar was raided by the police and Violy and one other entertainer jumped out a window and made their escape by swimming out to sea, where they were rescued by an oil tanker. Later Violy stayed with the captain of the oil tanker for a week until he "gave Violy to another friend" for sex.[32] She stayed with the ship captain's friend for a month, after which he "also discarded her. He gave her US$150 and she went back to Olongapo."[33] She stayed in Olongapo until 1994, when she returned to Angeles. Eventually she worked at a food stall, though she still had foreign boyfriends, including one who started off as a pen pal in Canada.[34] She continues to work at bars to make money when she needs it. During her stint as an entertainer, she says that she always encountered men she describes as sadists, those who were violent with her. These sadists she meets—her first encounter with Richard, where she did not remember consenting to sex, and her relationship with Richard's brother, Ryan—all echo the ways in which the NCCP, GABRIELA, and Sr. Mary John describe the foreign men who visit the Philippines for sex as exploiting Filipinas and immoral.

Despite emphasizing an exploitative sex myth where encounters between Filipinas and foreign men were inherently immoral and harmful, the men and women of the National Consultation on Prostitution (NCP) and GABRIELA also work to dispel common myths about Olongapo sex workers—namely, that these women migrate "out of lust or a desire for sex . . . that women become rich from their work, or that they are in need of a conversion of faith, after which they would recognize their sin and leave their work."[35] Indeed, Violeta A. Marasigan, the chairperson of the Ad-hoc Committee for the NCP conference, said in the conference's closing remarks that "prostitution is more than a moral problem [related to individuals]—so our approaches and programs should also go beyond morality. . . . [Sex workers] are no different from any of us—only in circumstances and conditions perpetuated by oppressive economic, political, and social structures."[36] We can see how these broader structures have shaped the lives of Alma, Arnesia, and Violy.

Despite noting that these issues should "go beyond morality," sex work continued to be drawn around moral boundaries in both Violeta's closing address and throughout the conference proceedings. Morality continued to be framed as an individual problem—this time, however, by delineating who can be "saved" from those who cannot. Morality was also redefined to indict the broader structural conditions and organizations that facilitate sex work—such as overseas military bases—and the ill-fated lives of the women and children in this industry, who are seen as working in a dehumanizing industry, regardless of the actual conditions of their place of employment, and who face shame and ostracization from family and others who know about their occupation.[37] In tying women's and men's identities to national identities and broader power relations, activists, academics, and former sex workers critiqued Philippine dependence on the United States and how the United States continued to exert undue power in a country that had been independent for, at the time, forty years. In doing so, they showed how Philippine sovereignty and independence was limited and dependent on the U.S. military, which exploits Filipina women.

Yet Filipinos are not the only people who critique military-based sex work and link sex workers' exploitation to international relations. Father Shay Cullen, for example, is an Irish missionary priest who cofounded the prominent and internationally award-winning Olongapo-based nonprofit for sexually exploited women and children, People's Recovery Empowerment Development Assistance (PREDA).[38] He describes Olongapo's sex industry as filled with "thousands of young Filipinas have been lured away from their homes with cash payments to parents and promises of well-paid jobs as maids and food-servers, instead they are sold into slavery and prostitution. . . . [They] frequently end up beaten or even killed by customers of the bars and clubs where the women are forced to live and work in awful inhuman conditions."[39]

To Cullen, the entertainment industry during the base's era was a place where U.S. servicemembers' "failures on the battlefield were assuaged in drug induced amnesia and the haze of drunken orgies."[40] Whereas the base and its servicemembers were the low point of the city's history, the U.S. military's 1992 departure signaled a "great hope for a moral regeneration and spiritual renewal . . . when . . . the Philippines would move on from this sordid abuse of women and children to an economic life that would bring work with dignity and pride."[41] Later he describes his understanding about "why Subic was such as great loss [to the U.S. military]. Here they had the free run of the city. They were the blue-eyed gods of plenty that showered their money on the bar owners as they bought the women and sometimes children for sex and worked off their frustrations."[42] In 1997 Father Shay condemned the negotiations of what would become the 1998 Visiting Forces Agreement because it signaled the imminent return of the U.S. military and the devolution of any so-called moral and spiritual progress that had been made since they left. Racializing the U.S. military in a particular way, he also describes U.S. servicemen as whites, with Aryan-like features. Evoking the image of a predator in nature, he suggests that these men are ready to devour the poor and destitute for their own pleasurable consumption.[43]

Indeed, many of the stories told about Olongapo and Angeles and their respective bases, Subic and Clark—whether from the National Consultation on Prostitution conference, Father Cullen/PREDA, or other activists or academics, Filipino/a or non-Filipino/a alike—fall alongside an antimilitarization worldview that critiques the network of U.S. overseas military bases and sees them as arms of a U.S. informal empire.[44] Pre-Spanish Philippines, in contrast, is evoked as an idealized model of gender relations, a Philippine past when women and men held equal roles—as seen through the Filipino mythical origin story, where a man and a woman arise simultaneously from a split bamboo stick.[45] To many activists and academics, it is only with the advent of Spanish colonialism that women's place in Philippine society began a decline,[46] and the sex work that is currently found in Olongapo City and elsewhere in the Philippines is a direct consequence of the U.S. Subic Bay Naval Base and the capitalist system, which exploits poor countries at the expense of rich ones.[47]

Yet underneath the fantasies of an unfettered sexual playground for white U.S. military men that Father Shay describes lay a highly regulated system that policed Filipina women's bodies but not U.S. servicemen's. This system was regulated by both the U.S. military and the local city government. Being a registered, or legal, sex worker in Olongapo, for example, meant that a woman like Susan applied for and received a permit from the mayor and had an entertainer ID. Without a permit or registration with the mayor's office, sex workers could be arrested and charged, since city laws "regulate[d] the solicitation of customers in the streets."[48] Other laws "prohibit[ed] the operation of cabarets or dancing within the city limits except in the districts of Barreto and Cabalan"[49] and "require[d] the club owners to issue out passes to prostitutes who go out with their customers,"[50] effectively allowing any Filipina walking with an American to be stopped by the police. If she was unable to show the police officer her "night-off pass, she [could] be arrested as a streetwalker, whether or not she is employed in a club."[51] In enacting these laws, government officials tried to spatialize sex work and keep entertainers hidden from public view by moving the sex industry indoors and to particular *mga barangay* (neighborhoods) in the city. However, punishing visible street sex workers who worked outside the registered establishments did not diminish their demand. Instead, they made the women more vulnerable to intimate and structural (police, government) mistreatment and harassment.

Being registered also meant that Susan and women like her were required to undergo regular checkups and tests at a Social Hygiene Clinic, which was run by the Olongapo City Health Department and cofunded by the U.S. military. After each checkup she would receive a card indicating that she did not have any sexually transmitted infections; if tested positive she couldn't work until she was cleared.[52] In requiring registration and mandatory health checks, the U.S. military and Olongapo City government joined forces to scrutinize and keep Filipina women's, but not American men's, bodies and diseases under surveillance. However, as we'll see, both the U.S. military and the Olongapo City government were less concerned with the meanings people attached to these relationships or the *content* of their daily interactions.

For some activists, this regulation by both the Philippine government and U.S. military legitimized the dehumanization of Filipinos and provided more evidence of Philippine dependence on the United States and the United States' undue power in the Philippines. Indeed, many claimed that any benefits derived from it were funneled to the rich, and the sex industry was responsible for other "severe social and moral problems . . . [such as] STD, drug addiction, abortion and unwanted pregnancies, racket, extortion, gambling, illicit dollar trading, smuggling of PX [post exchange] goods, broken homes, neglected and abandoned children, illegitimate children, marginalized Amerasians [children of Filipina and American descent], graft and corruption, deteriorating moral and sexual values, etc."[53] And it seemed that neither the Philippine government nor U.S. military cared. Even the U.S. military's shore patrol,[54] which regulated and monitored on- and off-duty U.S. servicemembers' behavior so as to maintain relatively friendly and peaceful relations with the Philippines, was critiqued because it institutionalized "the expectation that sailors will use the women as part of a military system that encourages the belief that women are commodities. A sailor learns to use women . . . as part of his rights and pleasures as a serviceman."[55]

In addition to critiquing any so-called regulation of the sex industry and revealing its underbelly, where Filipina women but not U.S. servicemembers are heavily surveilled, many activists and academics also used scientific research as a way to validate their claims about the immorality of the bases. For example, describing 1983-era Angeles City and Olongapo City as having the largest incidences of reported gonorrhea in the entire country (29 percent [3,819 of 13,359] and 23 percent [3,117 of 13,359], respectively)[56] offered proof of the immorality of the U.S. bases and the servicemen they bring into the Philippines.

In 1990, a prominent Philippine nonprofit organization, Women's Education, Development, Productivity and Research Organization (WeDpro) conducted a survey of 300 Filipina sex workers and similarly used the results to critique the broader structural conditions brought on by the U.S. military. Virginia Miralao, Celia Carlos, and Aida Santos were the lead authors of the study. Dividing sex workers into two groups—registered entertainers and unregistered streetwalkers—their team interviewed 150 in Olongapo City[57] and found that almost two-thirds of these women were migrants to the city,[58] only 16 percent had graduated elementary school,[59] and over half of both registered and unregistered women sent remittances to help support their families,[60] despite an irregular income that is dependent on the number of clients per night and the number of ships and accompanying men docked in the former base.

As a self-proclaimed feminist organization founded on the principle to support "those with unheard voices, the disadvantaged and those in the fringes of our communities,"[61] much of the writing in their published report takes on a particular moral perspective of the lives of women sex workers living in the shadow of the bases. For instance, Miralao, Carlos, and Santos describe the women they interviewed in their report as having "to perform other revolting sexual acts," implying that certain sexual acts are moral or appropriate while other sex acts are necessarily demeaning and assuming that sex workers are necessarily exploited.[62]

There are many grains of truth to the myth, as we can see in the lives of Alma, Arnesia, and Violy and the survey results from within and around the former military bases. Yet framing these relationships and the sex worker job as exploitative dismisses women's agency in their labor choices. It hides differences related to labor conditions and what the women themselves think should be done to better their livelihood.[63] Sex work does not *necessarily* have to involve these things, and sex workers can be active agents in their labor choices. Seeing sex workers as active agents allows us to see how they are subject to different conditions, such as their registration status, their clientele, their coworkers, and how they use their work as part of their advancement strategies to marry, migrate, and/or increase their socioeconomic standing.[64] It also allows us to interrogate whether what Rhacel Parreñas identifies as workers' moral boundaries and clubs' moral regimes[65] are well matched[66] or mismatched—and how all of these factors make the women more or less vulnerable to abuse and unhappiness.

During their two-day June 1986 meeting, for example, the NCP held open forums, where audience members could ask current sex workers questions. Deborah, a manager of an Olongapo bar, was one such woman who came to speak with the audience. During one of the open forums she described her work and said that neither she nor anyone else working in her bar was forced into sex work. Her bar, she declared, did not admit young women, and she pointed out how the women who are employed there, despite many not having finished their education, see bar work as bettering their future. She also described how the women entertainers made more money than was often reported by activists; for example, "from P1000 [bar fine], P600 goes to the woman, only P400 to us— P350 to the owner and P50 to me. . . . [In Olongapo] it is not like here in Manila where the women are not free [after they leave the bar for the night]. They have their own houses. They are renting. They don't stay in the bar except those who want to save money for their children. It is up to them."[67] Here Deborah pointed to how many women entered sex work as a way to save money for their children. Her bar, she asserted, did not financially exploit the women, although they had few other opportunities available to them. The women in Olongapo made more money than she did as a bar manager and were not confined to the bar after hours.

These moral understandings and economic accounting that she described as occurring between bar managers and registered workers echoes Rhacel

Parreñas's[68] work that documents how women reconfigure and reimagine moralities, both alternative ones they create and ones that adhere to broader contemporary societal understandings of morality, and the relative absence of Filipinas who are forced to engage in sex work in Tokyo. Deborah's account also calls to mind Kimberly Kay Hoang's[69] findings on the moral orders of Vietnamese sex industries, which rely on women choosing to enter the entertainment industry to better their lives and refusing to force others into this line of work.

Susan, the sex worker from the beginning of the chapter, also attended the conference's open forums to describe her work at the bar and her moral understandings of it. According to Susan the bar fine system was unfair. Susan only received about a third of the pay, while the rest went to the bar (which was similar to Alma's sex work experience). Instead, she would have rather been directly paid by clients, so she wouldn't have to give up such a substantial part of her income. Describing how and when she got paid and linking it to the U.S. servicemen she met, her own moral stance, and dilemmas she faced when customers did not pay her bar fine, she declared, "It is better if he pays the bar fine, than if he doesn't. But if he doesn't, well, that is a part of getting along; getting along with the Americans. If our way with people is good, we get something. That is beautiful. But it is not because . . . we are assured bar fines will be paid." Clarifying a common—to her—misperception, she elaborated, "It also doesn't mean that if they don't pay our bar fines, the Americans are bad. For us, no one don't see it that way. We also respect them. We try to show each other what is good even though we are just lowly beings." She described her approach and understanding of the American men she encountered in her work and how "we also see and choose the Americans who have good attitudes because there are also Americans who are really bad, especially the Marines. Like what happened with my life." She clarified, "But I am not saying I hate Marines, that I hate all Americans. I don't say that. I just mentioned that because I am angry but deep within me I don't hate (the Americans). It's like gambling for me, sometimes I win, sometimes I lose. Simple is that. You just cry it out. What can I do? Our life is like this."[70]

Instead of condemning the U.S. servicemen who are the bar's patrons, she found that it was the owners who took advantage of her, because of the percentage of money they took. She would have preferred no middle manager, because the small portion of earnings she received went into keeping herself attractive through makeup, perfume, clothes, and the like. She described how the women workers cleaned all day in the bar, left to get ready for the night, and returned to work to meet with the men. Yet she did not passively accept clients.

Neither did she allow herself to be taken for granted or degraded. Instead, she stood up for herself and tied her own empathy to the men who said they could not afford her bar fine and whom she pitied because of that.

Recounting one experience, she said, "So, here come the Americans—those weird Americans—acting high and mighty—some say 'bitch.' Now I will fight for my rights, 'I'm not a bitch, you know, maybe your mother is.' So the American says, 'Wow, I'm sorry.'" She was not a doormat, nor did she let people talk to her in a degrading manner.[71] She clarified, "But I don't always do that because it is from them that we earn. It is from their taking me out that I keep my child alive, that I rent my house. Those who take an American home with no bar fine have a reason. The reason is like this: the American says, 'I can't pay a bar fine, I can't afford it. I will just give you some money.'" She explained her reasoning concerning being intimate with an American who could not pay her fine: "I am humane. I have a heart and feelings. I feel sorry for this American. I take him home. I give him my address. We ride a tricycle. They understand. They also respect us. I said earlier, not all Americans are abusive."[72]

Rather than seeing herself as a passive victim or as unable to say no to a customer,[73] Susan drew on her and many Americans' humanity to understand her work. She was guided by respect—for herself and for her clients. She rejected a view of sex work that hid her agency, her humanity, the humanity of her clients, and the relatively more positive aspects of her work. Her account does not negate the structural critiques of activists, but it does complicate them by showing how lived experiences can differ and shed insight into why such a system remains intact. It shows how the institutionalized inequality of global borderlands depends on these conflicting meanings regarding why some women enter and stay in the sex industry. If women see every sexual act, every American, and every choice they make as exploitative, dangerous, and perpetuating inhumane conditions, then global borderlands and any surrounding sex industries would collapse.

Heroic Love Myth

Activists and academics railed against the U.S. military, using survey instruments, interviews, and health statistics to demonstrate their undue power and influence in the Philippines and how they exploit and harm Filipina women. Yet, circling back to those very same reports, I uncover additional patterns and show how sex workers themselves differentiate work and clients in moral ways and link them to ideas of romance, love, and marriage.[74] For example, one way they earn money is by the number of drinks customers by for them. Some of the men, who are there for a relatively longer period of time, pay "steady" bar fines, so the woman doesn't have to work at the bar but, instead, can focus on the relationships with the men. Even according to the WeDpro authors, Miralao, Carlos, and Santos, a registered entertainer "welcomes the respite from nightly hustling for customers and fantasizes that her 'boyfriend' just might decide to make permanent their temporary arrangements. The fantasy usually does not become reality but the few that do, keep the hopes of many women entertainers burning."[75]

Indeed, in their survey, 26 percent of the women they interviewed "have gone into wishful thinking, fantasizing of marrying an American and having American kids. For many prostituted women, marriage to an American serviceman is the surest passport out of prostitution. They believe . . . Americans are more understanding and will not flaunt in their faces their prostituted past."[76] The women categorize these men who pay their bar fines not as clients but as boyfriends and dream of marrying Americans and having American children. One-third (33 percent) of the women described their jobs as "light and fun"; 27 percent said "they like dancing, entertaining and dressing up"; and 26 percent said "it gives them the opportunity to marry an American."[77] Even Brenda Stoltzfus, a representative of the Mennonite Central Committee to the NCP conference, provides a similar description in her work with Filipina women whose "main hope is marriage to an American sailor who will take them away from the hell of Olongapo, or at least support them so they no longer need to work in a bar. Most women desire a genuine love relationship rather than a continual change of customers who are sometimes abusive."[78]

However, WeDpro and Stoltzfus both ultimately dismiss these constructions of marriages to Americans as ill-fated fantasies and view the U.S. military in the Philippines as necessarily harming Filipinas. In contrast, I find that these imaginaries are rooted in interlocking cultural frameworks. First, the women understand marriage as a sexual—not legal—commitment.[79] Seeing marriage as a *sexual* commitment likely stems from national policies as the Philippines is one of two states[80] where divorce is illegal and legal marriages can only be dissolved through death, annulment, or, if you are married to a foreigner, your foreign spouse filing for a divorce in their home country.[81] Here, sexual exclusivity and intimacy stand in for legal commitments as a way to demonstrate love to one another, and this was something I witnessed not just in foreigner-Filipina pairings but also in those intimacies between Filipino/as.

Second, these imaginaries take the form of particular love myths that these women use to describe their relationships with these men. Similar to the middle-class, white Americans in Ann Swidler's[82] research who simultaneously and contradictorily drew on one love myth that was all encompassing and one that was a choice that required commitment and work, these Filipina women drew on competing conceptions of love as destiny and explicit choice. They also drew on another one that I call the *heroic love myth*. Similar to what Nicole Constable[83] refers to as an imagined "fairy tale" that Filipina and Chinese women use to describe possible relationships with U.S. men and what Denise Brennan describes as Dominican Republic sex workers' fantasy of escape, where "European men 'rescu[e]' them from a lifetime of poverty and foreclosed opportunities,"[84] this heroic myth is rooted in the notion of a savior. In the women's construction of love, the men play a very specific role, one on which these women pin their hopes and dreams of being taken out of poverty and being provided a better life in the United States, "the land of opportunity."

Yet, to understand these hopes and dreams of life in the United States, we have to understand that they stem from particular and competing understandings of the role that the U.S. military played in their lives, above and beyond U.S. colonialism in the Philippines (1898–1946) and its sociocultural and structural legacies. On one hand, the U.S. military invested over $2.199 billion in removable and nonremovable facilities[85] and served as the second largest employer in the Philippines; it is estimated that "some $500 million was pumped into the Philippine economy every year by the Clark and Subic Bases," and over 80,000 people in Central Luzon made their living from the bases.[86] In 1979, Subic alone employed 5,000 U.S. civilians and 14,490 Filipinos, with an additional 8,600 Filipinos under contract, for example, as domestic employees in individual U.S. households.[87] Many local Filipinos also describe the former base in nostalgic terms and describe Americans as "good" employers and customers when compared to those of other nationalities, echoing the enticements of what Brennan calls the "opportunity myth" that attracts local migrants to sex tourist locations in the Dominican Republic.[88] On the other hand, sex work did and continues to proliferate in these places, as does sexually transmitted infections and varied kinds of abuse. Both understandings of Subic and the U.S. military coexist. And it is precisely this coexistence of competing imaginaries—where national identities become entwined with understandings of power, whether the power to exploit or the power to save—that allows global borderlands like Subic to take hold and flourish.

Violy, for example, did not just meet sadists over the course of her career as a sex worker. She also found romantic partners. She also neither remembered her first sexual encounter with Richard as rape; nor did she see Richard as another person who exploited her. In describing the difference between a boyfriend and a client, for example, she linked these differences to how she felt about Richard: "Of course there's a difference between a customer and a boyfriend. With a customer, it's just all about body, no feeling involved. But with a boyfriend, *siyempre* [always], *mas feel ko* [I have a lot of feelings]." She elaborated, "It is also different because I can say 'I love you' to a customer a million times and not mean it. It is hard to say that to a boyfriend. I just show it by taking care of him. I prepare his things, do his laundry, everything. But I have never told a person that I love him and really mean it. Yet in my situation, who would still take me seriously? I am not hoping anymore."[89] She also described how angry she would get at her boyfriends, whom she trusted. "I also do not like men who are just good at making promises, making you wait forever. When Richard broke his promise to come back and marry me, I became angry. I felt there was nothing for me. . . . I started to throw my life away." Still, she described how "there are times when I still believe their sweet promises and I still hope. Then again, I think it is hard to believe them."[90] Violy drew moral boundaries between boyfriends and clients. While there are many overlaps, regarding financial and intimate support, she engaged in what Viviana Zelizer calls relational work[91] to demarcate the particular discourses, practices, and exchanges that differentiate these two different types of men. She also revealed her dreams and desires of being saved and loved—the heroic love myth—as well as skepticism due to broken promises that come bundled with her relationships with foreign men.

So, too, did Maria[92] dream of being loved and saved, though her dreams were also shattered. Initially, Maria worked as a cashier at a bar and was not a sex worker, when a friend of hers, who thought she was an entertainer, introduced her to a U.S. airman stationed at Clark Air Force Base. She subsequently became pregnant and told me that she felt as though she was trapped and forced into an abortion by the father. Afterward, she actively chose to continue working at the bar, this time as a more official sex worker, meeting U.S. servicemen from both Subic and Clark. In the hotel where she worked, she and the other women would line up in front of the foreign men who were new to the area, and these men would choose a woman from the lineup.

Maria became pregnant again. This time, however, she refused to have an abortion. Two weeks after her daughter was born, her daughter got sick, and Maria chose to return to sex work. The American man she went out with was a doctor, and she says he told her that "you're not supposed to do that, at least two months, because you just had a baby." She responded that she's "'gotta work, my little girl sick' and he just give me some money," which she used to take her daughter to a doctor. She worked for about four years at that bar before working in Olongapo, where she met another American, this time from the U.S. Navy, whom she describes as "even he's been coming to the Philippines since 1967, he's really nice. And I just stay with him the whole time. Then he said, you just go back home, and when I come back here, I'll just call you . . . he just send me money every month." She says the relationship didn't work out and tells her daughter that he is her father. Maria "told her [daughter] to go search in the internet. Maybe we can find him, or maybe he can help us out [*laughter*]. . . . He's nice. Even though he's old, I like him, he treat me nice. But most guys hurt me and don't treat me very nice."

Shortly after this relationship was over, she met a U.S. Air Force serviceman and got pregnant again. She lost the baby during childbirth, and afterward she tells me that she "work[s] at my sister's house or sometimes at the neighbor's, for food, when I don't have anyone to help me . . . I cry all the time! I did not like my luck." She attributes her life circumstances not to the U.S. military as an institution nor the poverty in which she was born but rather luck. She describes how "sometimes, some guys they thought that you just, that they just use you something like that. They have sex just like that. That's what they think . . . Maybe most of them. Only few that they want to be in a deep relationship."

However, she also told me that she's had four men ask for her hand in marriage and described one "marriage" she had with a U.S. Marine. "We got um . . . like marriage ceremony in Olongapo, and everything, I got wedding ring. All of the sudden, he's seeing another Filipino, and then he's cheating on me. And I don't like that, and I say 'no marry anymore!'" When I ask for clarification on whether they were married or planning on getting married, she tells me, "Yeah, we're planning. Because I always trying, his relatives in the States know me already, and we are working on our paper work [to migrate to the United States]. And then all of the sudden, we're not married yet, and he's cheating on me. And he's lying to me too!" She explains how one day, "He said he's gotta go [on tour of duty, outside the Philippines] and then I said, 'OK.' I took him to the airport, but he's still here! . . . That night, I went out with my friends. . . . And we go out to this one bar that we always go. And then he was there—with another girl! I was mad! I said no more marriage. I don't want to marry you anymore!"

That was the end of her marriage to that Marine. While she saw their sexual commitment to one another as a type of marriage, he presumably did not see their relationship in the same way, as he lied to her and continued to go out with other women. That was the final straw for Maria. Yet she also describes this instance as one of many times U.S. military men asked her to marry them, and she doesn't currently want a relationship with a Filipino because, as she tells me, "I don't want to get married anymore, I have enough heartache." Marriage, to her and others, is one way to describe these sexual relationships. Sometimes they are short-term encounters, but they can be relatively longer-term and sustaining for as long as the man is in the Philippines—whether weeks, months, or years at a time. It encompasses a *sexual commitment* or exclusivity for the duration of the relationship. Marriage is described as a choice and commitment, not as a legal relationship.

Danielle, in her forties, is a former entertainment dancer in Clark and in Japan with one Amerasian daughter and one Filipina daughter. She also weaved the bourgeois love myth of Swidler's work with the stigma that accompanied her relationship with her boyfriend Tim. She described to me her feelings regarding the failure of the hero and bourgeois myths: "The only thing that got me hurt was . . . when he came back to the Philippines he told something about me in his family and . . . the one thing that got me hurt was, his *lola* [grandmother] . . . don't want him to marry a Filipina."

Explaining why the grandmother was against their future marriage, she tells me "'cause you know . . . Americans, not all Americans, they think that Filipina just use American to go to the States. But that's always they think, about Filipinas who marry American. . . . His *lola* told him if he's gonna marry me . . . [she'll] disown him . . . If he chose me." Although Danielle and Tim continued their relationship, what his grandmother said to him haunted Danielle. "It's in my mind, what he say about his family about me . . . But I never told him, never asked him to marry me." If he really loved her, she thought, he would have known how troubled she was by those comments, and "if he wants to marry me, he'll marry me, right. But . . . I just found out later, when I got pregnant, that he left the Philippines then. He doesn't really love me at all. If he really loves me, he'll fight for me, right?"

Tim's grandmother's opposition to the relationship—which mimicked a common stereotype that Filipinas used the U.S. men they married to migrate abroad and did not love them—left a deep impression on Danielle. It permeated her thoughts and, from Danielle's point of view, continued to shape their relationship long after the incident occurred. For example, she tells me, "When he left the Philippines . . . we already broke up two months before. The reason why we broke up was that, um, for, maybe for six months or one year . . . for almost one year of the relationship, we always have a fight. . . . I remember . . . the last fight we had, the last time we had a fight he say, ah . . . he . . . he say a word that I don't like. Like a 'cunt/fuck' like that. I don't like that, I don't want to hear that, because I don't deserve that. I don't deserve that kind of word. So I get mad."

The fight, described in the opening of this chapter as like a movie, is a vivid memory. She tells me, "I-It's raining when we fight, you know. It's like a movie! [*laughter*]. It's like a movie, with rain and the fighting, we're arguing. We're, ah, outside the house of my friends. He told me that kind of word; then I run. I don't want to talk to him. For a week. Until . . . one day I receive a flower from him, saying sorry for the word that he said, he told to me." After that, they began talking again, but "he told me that . . . ah . . . he 'don't wanna have a fight like that. So if we had another fight like that, I will go to another place.' So we had another fight."

What they fought about was not what bothered Danielle; instead, she felt hurt and betrayed when he called her a name, and when he did that, it brought back a flood of insecurity "because if all these things reminding me about what his *lola* told him. Always in my mind. So when, every time, it's in my mind. I keep on silent, and not talk to him. He don't like that." Danielle felt as though she could not tell Tim that his grandmother's comments hurt her. She wanted to believe in the power of the bourgeois love that she and Tim shared but also felt as though she had to hide her true feelings and hurt about his grandmother. In the end, all they did was fight, and when Tim left, he never returned or fulfilled his promises, even after finding out about his daughter.

Tim did not know she was pregnant when their relationship dissolved. Eager to go to Japan and not wanting an abortion, Danielle hid her pregnancy while she worked as a dancer there, but she returned after a month because her manager found out. She returned to Japan when her daughter was nine months old to financially support her daughter, whom she left with her parents. There, she met a Japanese man who was younger than she was and asked her to marry him. She "told him my situation, I have a daughter. And he accept, and he accept it. So we got married, and so I came to Japan with him, stayed with him for three months, six months. And that was nice." Danielle soon became pregnant with her son. She tells me of how she initially missed Tim, and when she found out she was pregnant with his daughter, she "used to go to the church, and pray a lot. Pray that Tim will come back again and realize that he loves me. Always. Every night. But it never came."

Eventually, five years later, Tim did contact her, but by then Danielle had married the Japanese man,[93] and she thought, "It's too late, right?" But when they reconnected, she told him that she "asked for you, to God, I said. I always go to bed every night, keep on praying . . . hoping come back to me. That you still love me. It never happen. And I met a guy that marry me. Who accepted me." In their conversation, he discussed meeting his daughter and spoke with her on the phone, making promises to be in her life. But he never came, and despite many attempts, her daughter cannot find him online.

When she was younger and lived with Tim for a while, she didn't want to get married because what that meant to her—a change in lifestyle where she would have to stay at home. She rejected the societal expectations of married women's behaviors by staying single. She says, "That makes me crazy. I know, they don't know what I'm doing, like living with him! I don't know what-what to say, I said. Then my friend said 'Crazy. . . . Go on and grab it, the opportunity,' they told me." She told them, "No, I'm not ready to get married. I'm still going to my teenage years." She describes how, when she was twenty-two, her friends would always tell her, to any man she met, to marry them. But she was put off by their suggestions. "Why should I get married when I'm [not ready?] Why should I get married if I still go out? So I always told, the American guy I always ask me to dance, go out with them; I always tell them that, that. If I get married, I don't want to go to disco. I don't want to go out anymore. I just want to stay in the house. So that's why I don't wanna get married at my age."

She told me that now, to her friends, she makes jokes about eventually meeting someone to marry, someone to provide and "save" her, but she thinks that it's too late.[94] Like the previously described women who spoke of their childhood nostalgia for the former base and linked this to their desire to marry a U.S. serviceman and/or have American children, Danielle lost faith in the bourgeois and heroic love myths that she previously craved.[95]

Yet, although the heroic love myth ultimately failed for Violy, Maria, and Danielle, for those women who migrated to the U.S. through marriage to U.S. servicemen, it came true.

Aileen and Angie, both in their sixties, were two of the four wives I interviewed together. They are married to U.S. naval seamen and moved wherever
their husbands were stationed. At the time of the interview, both lived in Seattle, which had a small community of similar couples—Filipina women married
to U.S. servicemen—because of the domestic military bases stationed there.
Although they, like many other marriage migrants to the United States I spoke
with, did not always explicitly frame their marriages in heroic terms, they
evoked a particular construction of gratitude when describing Filipina–U.S.
servicemen marriages. They engaged in distinct moral boundary-making[96] that
differentiated themselves from "those women"—the women who remain in the
Philippines and are assumed to be sex workers and those who used Americans
to migrate to the U.S. and do not show enough gratitude to their husbands.
They used gossip about these women to draw moral boundaries among themselves and others and as an informal means of control and judgment about
women's motivations to be in these interracial intimacies.

Aileen explains to me, "This, this this, I will tell you; that, those women who
are doing such a thing, you know where they associate from. Because I know
them, I've been around those kind of women." Who are these women? She describes, "Those kind of women, they come over here and they are grateful. But
some of them, they are used to the lifestyle in the Philippines, that they can't
help it. They keep on doing it," linking ingratitude to their "lifestyle" back in the
Philippines, where lifestyle is a coded word for sex work and partying.

Elaborating how she can tell who "these women" are, Aileen tells me,
"Cause we're military people, we know. Whether the civilians, we don't know,
but military women, most of them, 99 percent of them, where did they come
from? Out of the bar, Olongapo or the bars from Clark Field. . . . Some of them
have a little bit of a decent background, not all of them."

Angie agrees but wants to clarify how they differentiate "those women"
from military women like them. "It all depends on what kind of helping," she
says. Giving an example of a woman they know, Angie says that this woman
"doesn't know how to drive, [and] I taught her how to drive and get her driver's
license. After she gets her driver's license, she cheating on her husband." That
woman's selfish behavior, in Angie's eyes, led to disaster as "the husband killed
himself, but before he did it, before he shot himself, he go in the house; got
three children. But still, she got the insurance. She was doing well after the husband pass away. But that's no way how to return the kindness of your husband."
Blaming the woman for her husband's suicide, Angie links cheating to Filipinas

who meet their future husbands in the bars of Clark and Subic and who are too selfish to change their behavior after migrating to the United States.

To outsiders, these women presumably also have a stigma of sex work clinging to their relationships. Yet they judged women, who unlike themselves, had to "use" the men to migrate to the United States. They maintain that, unlike "those" women, they could have migrated to the United States without their husbands. "Those" women are of questionable moral character. For the particular woman they referenced, they judged her for going out to clubs, cheating on her husband, and not showing him proper gratitude. Imee, who lives in the Midwest and is not part of a military community like the women I interviewed in Seattle, similarly asserts that "those women" "come here married somebody, take their husband for granted and if they are navy and are assigned to different places, the girl go[es] barhopping [while her husband is away]." This moral boundary-making between these Filipina women and others in seemingly similar relations reflects a common stereotype or myth about Filipina marriage migrants as "gold diggers," using men of non-Filipino nationality to leave the Philippines and improve their standing in life,[97] and is the stereotype that haunted Danielle in her relationship with Tim. This is a perversion of the heroic love myth, where some Filipina women are seen as using the men and not being sufficiently grateful for the opportunities the men they married provided.[98]

Revisiting the Exploitative Sex Myth

If Filipina marriage migrants' gossip about "gold diggers" is a perversion of the heroic love myth, so, too, do U.S. military regulations on marriage when its personnel are based overseas represent a version of the exploitative sex myth. In these cases, however, we see how U.S. servicemen have to be saved from exploitation by Filipina women.

Herbert Levinsky, an private first class in the U.S. Marine Corps, knew that he didn't have authorization, but he did it anyway. Marrying Anita S. Hernandez, a Filipina[99] living in Olongapo City, Philippines, could not wait, and on March 15, 1960, they pledged themselves to one another. A week later, on March 22, a special court-martial at the U.S. Subic Bay Naval Base found Levinsky guilty of two seemingly unrelated offenses: "failure to obey a named lawful general regulation by marrying without permission" from the commander of the U.S. Naval Forces, Philippines, and "conspiracy to steal a $457.43 moving picture film from the Government." He was demoted to private, sentenced to six months of forced labor, and fined $240 (about $2,036 in 2019), which would be taken from his monthly salary over the course of six months.[100]

Levinsky appealed the charge regarding marrying without his commander's permission because, he argued, this particular regulation was "not a lawful one." Indeed, he suggested that neither the U.S. Congress nor the U.S. Navy Department had any moral or legal rights to regulate his private affairs, especially when it had no bearing on his work duties. Instead, he was exercising his natural right to join his hand in marriage to a woman of his choice—in this case, Anita, whom he met during his tour of duty in the Philippines. In making these arguments, Levinsky draws distinct moral delineations between what the U.S. Navy, as his employer, can require of him and his private rights as an American citizen to marry.

Yet the U.S. military disagreed, and continues to disagree since its servicemembers were not and are not allowed to marry a foreign national overseas without their commander's permission; otherwise, they may be subject to a court-martial.[101] For example, in the 1950s and 1960s any marriage in the Philippines that involved a U.S. servicemember—with another U.S. citizen or with a Filipino—required permission from their commander, who would provide the "guidance and assistance [that] is necessary in order to prevent hasty and ill-considered unions followed by abandonment of wife or children who thereupon may become public charges . . . [which] has had an adverse effect on relations between the Philippine and United States Governments." Although two U.S. citizens wanting to get married can request a waiver, when it involved a Filipino/a national—like that of Levinsky and Anita—further requirements had to be met before they were allowed to wed.[102]

Such requirements included a statement from the U.S. servicemember that he was counselled on immigration laws and to simultaneously acknowledge that he intended "to exercise his right to gain such entry [to the United States] for his spouse,"[103] while also recognizing that marriage would not guarantee that his future spouse was eligible to migrate.[104] Before endorsing (or not) the marriage, the commander would request a naval intelligence report regarding "the existence or absence of derogatory information of a criminal or subversive nature which would affect the entry of the [prospective spouse] into the United States."

In these regulations, the U.S. military recognizes that what happens on the ground between their servicemembers and local Filipino/as has direct implications for broader U.S.-Philippines relations. The micro directly influences the macro. And because it does, the U.S. military delineates who is able to marry whom in order to safeguard international relations. These regulations are based on moral assumptions about the causes and consequences of interracial marriages between U.S. servicemen and local women.

Indeed, these policies are meant not only to regulate the marriages themselves but also "related problems such as immigration of alien spouses, children, step-children and adopted children." The offspring of such relationships are seen as social problems to be dealt with. These relationships are seen along a moral continuum based on time (fears of so-called hasty marriages, which are to be avoided), location (the marriage is taking place outside the United States), nationality and race (of a non-U.S. citizen "alien" who is Filipina and not white), and fears of the "criminal or subversive nature" of prospective spouses. Instead of such structural factors as the mostly young, male demographic in the military, tour of duty rotations, and stereotypes about Filipino/a nationals, the marriages and the women themselves are framed as the cause of abandonment and issues related to migration, citizenship, financial support. These problems can be avoided, according to the U.S. military, if only the marriage, and implicitly the fiancée, can pass moral inspection.

Levinsky's appeal was reviewed by the U.S. Navy Board of Review on August 8, 1960, and in their review of their marriage, Judges Edward J. Taylor and H. H. Brandenburg relied on case law—in particular, the U.S. Court of Military Appeals' decision in the 1958 case of *United States v. Nation*,[105] which had striking parallels with Levinsky's.

Unlike Levinsky, Paul S. Nation Jr. followed what was required of him. On July 16, 1956, Nation, a seaman apprentice, submitted an application to his commander for permission to marry his fiancée, an unnamed Filipina national whom he had known for about eleven months. Yet he was denied permission because the commander required that Nation wait an additional six months "in order to prevent ill-considered marriages between U. S. military personnel and aliens."[106]

Nation waited patiently, but when he still did not receive permission three days after the six-month mark had passed, he and his fiancée married, and on a cool January day, they pledged their love for one another. The consequences meted out to Nation were similar to those given to Levinsky. Nation was soon "convicted by special court-martial . . . [and] sentenced to a bad-conduct discharge, partial forfeitures, confinement at hard labor for six months and reduction in rank to seaman recruit."[107] In a retrial Nation was again found guilty.[108] However, the Judge Advocate General's Corps office conducted a review of his case and "set aside the conviction and ordered the charge dismissed, having decided the regulation in question [the six-month waiting period for marriage] was not a lawful order."[109] Nation's case was next put forth to the United States Court of Military Appeals, and on October 3, 1958, the Honorable George W. Latimer upheld the setting aside of Nation's conviction.

In the written opinion Latimer specifically sidesteps the question of whether permission to marry represents "reasonable control and regulation by appropriate military commanders."[110] Instead he focuses on the six-month waiting period, which "is sought to be justified under the theory that it is a 'cooling-off' period which will 'prevent ill-considered marriages between U. S. military personnel and aliens.' Without arguing against such paternalistic motivation, we conclude that an arbitrary selection of a six-month period before an application will be considered is unreasonable."[111]

This requirement was unreasonable for Nation's relationship because, as Judge Latimer writes, Nation knew "his intended spouse for almost a year before he applied for permission to marry her. . . . His decision, then, cannot reasonably be made to appear hasty." He then clarifies that point: "If a waiting period is believed needful to discourage youthful servicemen from entering into improvident marriage contracts, its length ought to have some reasonable relationship to the maturity of the persons involved and purposes to be accomplished." Finally, Latimer writes, "For a commander to restrain the free exercise of a serviceman's right to marry the woman of his choice for six months just so he might better reconsider his decision is an arbitrary and unreasonable interference with the latter's personal affairs which cannot be supported by the claim that the morale, discipline, and good order of the command require control of overseas marriages."[112] Here again, we see the role of time as an indicator of a "good" match or marriage. Nation's marriage was not a decision made rashly, which, according to Latimer, would have been an acceptable reason to delay a marriage for Nation's own good. In highlighting the extent to which he knew his bride, Latimer frames their relationship as *exceptional*. Nation and his fiancée did not need a waiting period because their relationship was cultivated over time—as it should be, in Latimer's eyes.

The corollary, of course, is that a shorter period between meeting and marrying a local woman is a rash and unacceptable decision, and a required waiting period can be seen as necessary to save the servicemember and the nation from a mistake. Here, we see a moral judgment around the causes and consequences of short-term intimate relations, which are set against the backdrop of the racialization and hypersexualization of Asian and Asian American women.[113] In framing short-term marriages as "ill-considered," "impetuous," and requiring moral supervision, we see an underlying fear of U.S. servicemen being "taken advantage of" by suspicious Filipinas.

In Levinsky's case, however, the U.S. Navy Board of Review found that it did not have the same elements that were present in the *Nation* decision, including the six-month wait. As such, Judges Taylor and Brandenburg denied his appeal and, in doing so, affirmed the U.S. military's right to interfere in servicemembers' domestic life. In a concurring opinion on Levinsky's case, the Honorable Donald Griffin framed the issue as revolving around the required "pre-marital counseling" before a servicemember could marry in the Philippines. He sidesteps moral claims of rights to marry by emphasizing logistical processes and the role of the commander for whom the servicemembers must request permission. According to Griffin, the commander serves as a moral gatekeeper, whose decisions are meant to uphold the morale and mission of the men he oversees. As such, what may initially appear to be a seemingly private matter on whom to marry and one's own domestic life is, in actuality, subject to the commander's discretion.

Judge Griffin also describes the case as related to adhering to domestic laws and draws a parallel to marriage in the United States, where people travel to other states if their state laws prevent their marriage, and gives the example of whether a state requires a blood test for a marriage license. As such, requiring a commander's permission is "reasonable," and, he claims, Levinsky "was not denied the right to marry the woman of his choice, he was only denied the right to marry in the Philippines without compliance with the commander's order." Similar to Levinsky's appeal, where Levinsky draws on seemingly "race-neutral"[114] language, framing his appeal in terms of marriage more generally and his constitutional rights regarding his private life, Judge Griffin uses a seemingly innocuous blood test—the origin of which has to do with public health concerns and strategies to prevent the spread of syphilis[115]—as an example of differences between state laws.

Yet this 1960 opinion was written during a time when anti-miscegenation laws in the United States were legal, including those against intermarriages involving Filipinos.[116] In the United States, the relationships between Filipino men and white women were part of a racialized moral panic, which sometimes turned violent, that centered on Filipino men "deceiving" white women, because they were "morally suspect" and diseased, and these interracial relationships threatened to pollute the white race.[117] It was only with the 1967 Supreme Court decision in *Loving v. Virginia* that these laws were ruled unconstitutional. *Loving v. Virginia* involved the marriage of Mildred Loving, a black woman, and Richard Loving, a white man. After Mildred became pregnant, she and Richard married in Washington, DC, before returning to their home in Virginia, where their union was prohibited by anti-miscegenation laws. However, "in the early morning hours of July 11, 1958, Sheriff Garnett Brooks and two deputies, acting on an anonymous tip that the Lovings were in violation of the law, stormed into the couple's bedroom"[118] and arrested them. The case eventually went to the Supreme Court, whose judges voted in favor of the Lovings and ruled that Virginia's anti-miscegenation laws violated the Constitution's Fourteenth Amendment's equal protection and due process clauses because marriage was a basic civil right for all.

As such, the U.S. military's legal and moral claims about military members' overseas marriages to local women are set against a backdrop of legal prohibitions against interracial marriages, which, by definition, are racialized regulations of private life. This is not surprising, since so-called private moral decisions have been and are regulated by the government, more generally. The history of the United States "at home" and "abroad" is a history of drawing racial and gendered moral boundaries around citizenship, nationhood, and intimate claims. In the case of the U.S. military, moral claims about families and marriage are not based in explicitly racial terms but rather based on time, location, and eligibility for migration. However, these writings rely on coded language about gender and race relations. This is especially true for relationships involving Filipino/as, who have long been racialized and sexualized,[119] set against a backdrop of what Emmanuel David calls the sexual fields of empire.[120] They are framed as saving the empire's men from being exploited by the local women who may seduce them, women whom they see as acceptable for sexual exploits but with whom caution must be taken if men wanted to marry them.[121]

Allure and Condemnation in Global Borderlands

Why focus on the exploitative sex myth and the heroic love myth? If the rape and murder of Filipina women by U.S. servicemen showed the stakes involved in global borderlands, sex and romance among everyday people is about the juxtaposition of the allure and moral condemnation that provides the foundation in which these everyday intimacies are formed. It tells us the contradictions that define these places, how they serve to simultaneously reproduce inequality and contribute to the lasting presence of global borderlands precisely because these places elicit multiple meanings. They are not solely condemned as exploitative by all Filipinos. Otherwise, Subic Bay as a military base would have never existed if it was subject to constant protests and the military had difficulty finding people to work there in a civilian capacity. Neither are they paragons of development, a type of savior organization that pumps money into the economy and lifts people out of poverty. Global borderlands are defined by this very juxtaposition of allure and condemnation, of providing hopes for marriage and the exploitation of local women.

However, these intimate encounters do not end when U.S. servicemen leave the Philippines and return home; nor do they only affect the minds and actions of the women involved. The U.S. military institutes strict regulations regarding who can marry and migrate to the United States based on moral understandings of these sexual relationships. So, too, do these pairings often result in children of Filipina and American descent and thus create *families*. What happens to these children? Those who are similarly left behind by U.S. servicemen and also those who may maintain, even haphazardly, some kind of physical, emotional, and/or symbolic connection with these men? Who is entitled to what parental rights and responsibilities and who, when, and why are these determined?

Born in the Shadows of Bases　　4

Born to an African American U.S. airman and a Filipina mother in Angeles City, home of the former U.S. Clark Air Force Base in the Philippines, Allan Pineda Lindo is what's known as a black Amerasian: a child of a black U.S. serviceman and an Asian mother. Shortly after Allan was born, his biological father deserted his family. When he was just two years old he became part of the U.S.-based Pearl S. Buck Foundation, a nonprofit organization founded by Pulitzer Prize and Nobel Prize in Literature winner Pearl S. Buck.[1] The foundation's work is dedicated to humanitarian aid for children, including Amerasian children like Allan who were abandoned by their U.S. servicemen fathers.[2] Through the foundation's dollar-a-day program,[3] Allan became a sponsored child. This meant that he was matched with a specific sponsor who committed to sending him one dollar a day to help alleviate the poverty in which he lived and provide for his basic needs.

However, a dollar a day was not nearly enough. Growing up, Allan spent his childhood working to help financially support his mother and six younger siblings. This included filling bottles with water and collecting sacks of charcoal to sell to those living in surrounding communities,[4] packing "salt, pepper, oil and vinegar, and sugar into little plastic bags that [were] sealed with candles,"[5] so his mother could sell them at her *sari-sari* store, and helping his grandfather farm and sell sweet potatoes and rice at the *palengke* (local market).

When Allan went to school he wore thick glasses and always sat in the front of the classroom so that he could see the chalkboard. His eyesight was so poor from untreated nystagmus,[6] an eye disease that causes the eye to vibrate, that although sitting up front helped him read his teacher's writing, he "could not see [his] classmates on the other side of the room. They looked fuzzy and blurry. [He] felt like [he] was looking at them through a very dirty window or a puddle of muddy tears."[7] When he tried to play basketball he couldn't even see the ball, and when he tried watching his peers play sports he could only make out "faded figures,"[8] not their faces.

He didn't receive medical treatment in time to save his eyesight, so Allan became legally blind at a very young age. He confessed to Joe Hudgens, his American Pearl S. Buck sponsor, about the problems he was having with his vision and the difficulties it caused in school. In response, Joe, with Allan's mother's permission, flew him to the United States for a medical consultation. Once there, in addition to the consultation, Allan visited Disneyland, which is where he "fell in love with the USA," and "upon returning home . . . he told his sponsor that he would love to live in the States."[9] Afterward he sat down with his mother to explain his reasoning for the move. At fourteen years old, with his mother's permission, Allan returned to the United States and was formally adopted by Hudgens,[10] which meant that Allan no longer had legal ties to his mother. Alongside his friend will.i.am, he would go on to form the American hip hop–turned–pop music group the Black Eyed Peas[11] and become known as apl.de.ap.[12]

apl.de.ap's life story is extraordinary. He is the epitome of a success story for the Pearl S. Buck Foundation and embodies the myths that the United States is a land of unlimited opportunity that rewards people who can pull themselves up by their so-called bootstraps, that anyone can rise up and better their life if they only try. But precisely because his life is extraordinary, he is exceptional.

Amerasian children like apl.de.ap are one of the Vietnam War's continuing legacies.[13] In the Philippines alone, there are an estimated 30,000 to 52,000 of them.[14] Born in the shadow of overseas U.S. bases, these children often face discrimination and stigma, because having an American father, in the mind of many, means that their mother was a sex worker. They also have a legally and socially ambiguous status in many societies due to their ties to the U.S. military and U.S. servicemen. Many are illegitimate because their biological fathers do not legally recognize them or may not even know of their existence. Given the stigma of sex work that surrounds them, how do Amerasian children grow up in the shadows of Subic Bay? How do they and their mothers understand the role of the U.S. servicemen who are their fathers? How do U.S. and Philippine authorities understand these children's place in society?

Amerasian children and their mothers make moral claims about paternity and the rights and responsibilities of the men who fathered and often abandoned them. Yet U.S. laws do not recognize Philippine Amerasians' claims, despite recognizing the claims of Amerasians born elsewhere in Southeast Asia. This is because place matters. Subic Bay was a logistic and maintenance hub, as well as a popular rest and relaxation location. It was not in direct combat nor contiguous with the countries most affected by the Vietnam War. The Filipino children from these relations are not legally recognized by the United States. Instead, these children only became a concern for the United States after a class action suit on their behalf was brought to U.S. courts and damages were filed against the U.S. military. Prior to this, they—and the U.S. rights and responsibilities toward these children and any claims to U.S. citizenship they should or should not have—were of little concern to the United States. When brought before the U.S. courts, the U.S. government stepped in to regulate whether these children are granted U.S. rights and aid precisely because the vast number of these children meant that the outcomes of these trials had high-stakes socioeconomic and political consequences for the U.S. government.

For the Philippine government, there was less concern about the marriages themselves and the legal and economic matters brought before U.S. courts over the Amerasian children. Instead, the Philippine legal system was concerned about the cases that came before their own courts. Here, within their walls, we see how Filipino judges drew particular moral boundaries around biological parents' and nation-states' rights and responsibilities to children who were the result of intimate relations between U.S. servicemen and Filipina women. Even when fathers wanted to recognize their children by signing the birth certificate or wanted to adopt the children of their Filipina wives, Philippine judges blocked their attempts. They exerted power over these families, particularly when these familial issues were of little to no concern to the U.S. military, and drew on two moral reasons to prevent adoptions: first, whether the child was legitimate or not, even when paternity was not questioned; and second, they emphasized the man's foreigner status and the possibility that the child would be denied protection from their homeland if they were adopted. Finally, for the women and children themselves, the type of relationship the women had with the father was of utmost importance. The birth certificate and whether the father legally recognized his offspring as his own serve as proof of a relationship that went beyond sex work and was one steeped in love. Despite not being legally married, acknowledgment vis-à-vis a signed birth certificate provided an aura of legitimacy for the offspring.

What we see here, then, is that the intimate sphere of the family and home is not immune to the differences in political and economic power or influence between countries. Indeed, what these stories show is how familial intimacy is ruled through multiple and competing laws and understandings around morality and imaginaries of belonging[15] that regulate the relationships that are created in and move beyond Subic Bay as a global borderland. Yet, even concerning familial relations, global borderlands do not operate in the same way. Rather, overseas U.S. military bases vary regarding familial laws and policies because place—its geography, sociocultural meanings, and use—matters.[16] The consequences of place, whether intended or otherwise, have important implications for thousands, if not millions, of children around the world.

Race and Status in the Philippines

Cecilia Gastardo-Conaco and Carolyn Sobritchea are two Filipina academics whose research examines the experiences of Amerasians. In a two-hour focus group with six other Amerasian young men, Larry describes his upbringing: "My mother left me at home . . . like trash. She never came back. I cried for three days. . . . Our neighbor found me, alone, and took me to her house. She advertised in the newspapers and television stations appealing to my mother to come back."[17] Abandoned by his mother, Larry felt lucky that their neighbor found and rescued him. Bill, who grew up with his *lola* (grandmother), chimes in to say, "When I am with my half brothers, it is like this . . . some of us are *tisoy* (white Amerasian), some are *negro* (black Amerasian). I do not mind but some people . . . many are against me. They would say: 'Oy! Boy *Negro*! Do not join in our game, you cannot join us', just because I do not know my father." He explains, "That's how it is. Life is difficult. It is like I am a bad person. Why do people treat me this way? Whenever this happens, I go to a corner and cry."[18] As a black Amerasian, Bill was isolated from his peers, made to feel worthless and alone. Even though his other brothers were Amerasian, like him, he never felt like he could relate to them. Peers also rejected him. As a result, he continues to question himself and whether or not he was a bad person because of his heritage, something over which he had no control.

Unlike Larry and Bill, Paul grew up with his mother. However, he, too, experienced similar feelings of worthlessness. He feels that family "is like a wound, a certain kind of loneliness. I know my mother is there for me and will always support me, but there are times when I feel some kind of emptiness, something lacking,"[19] due to his Amerasian heritage. Even with a supportive mother, he felt isolated and like he did not belong. It is not just Larry, Bill, and Paul who feel this way. Amerasian children across Southeast Asia often face all kinds of social discrimination, be it from friends, neighbors, or even their own mothers, because of their association with sex work and the accompanying stigma that surrounds their very presence.

As Bill notes, being a black or white Amerasian matters. While some white Amerasians benefit from their light skin and American features, black Amerasians face additional discrimination based on the color of their skin.[20] Tessa, a black Amerasian who attended a different three-hour focus group led by Gastardo-Conaco and Sobritchea,[21] shares her too common experience of discrimination among peers and superiors and being sexualized by men: "It is truly insulting if we are called 'tisay' (half white) even if we are black. Others would say 'tisay na baliktad' (half white in reverse), kulot (kinky-haired), or 'baluga' (black)." She describes particular class activities in elementary school where her teacher would ask the class to choose their partners for a dance activity. She was always left alone. No one wanted to be her partner. Elaborating, she describes how her teachers also often separated students based on the color of their skin. Now she faces difficulties in finding employment. Even though she often gets to the interview stage, she never is able to secure a job after they've talked with her in person. She thinks it is because of her skin color and the association with sex work, saying, "They look at me, a black person, and right away they ask about my father. They are not supposed to ask that, right? I know it is hard to find a good job if you are black." Like many her age, Tessa loves dancing and dressing up for a night out. So occasionally, she goes out to bars with her boyfriend. Yet, when she's there—even when she's with her boyfriend—she encounters men who think that because she's dressed provocatively and is an Amerasian, she is a "'loose woman.' They would stare at my body, comment on how sexy I looked, how they like my buttocks, and so on. Sometimes my boyfriend gets into trouble with them. He would parry their advances."[22]

However, Anna, a white Amerasian, disagrees that black Amerasians are treated worse than white Amerasians. "Even if I am white, people sometimes treat me badly. Some would tell me 'if not for your fair skin, you are just as ugly as the others.' Others would call me '*mestisang bangus*'" (a slur for an Amerasian, literally translated "mixed milkfish"). However, being seen as ugly is not the worst of it. She says, "But what is most hurting is the way men would ogle at me; they would look at me from head to toe in a very insulting way." Giving an example, she explains, "One time, when I was in third year in high school, my classmate and I were standing in a corner when a guy suddenly embraced me from the back. I was so angry but I could not do anything but cry. Men think that because we are white, they have the right to touch us and treat us like bar girls."[23] From a young age, Amerasian women and girls—whether black or white—do not only face discrimination due to the stigma of sex work associated with the mothers of Amerasian children, as their male counterparts do, but are also sexualized everywhere they go. The illicit sexuality these young women embody is marked by physical features from which they are unable to hide.

Across Southeast Asia, Amerasians are often born into poverty, have little to no financial support, and do not have ties to their biological fathers; many are abandoned by their families.[24] As we can see, Filipino Amerasians are no exception. Yet, despite similar circumstances, Filipino Amerasians occupy a different status in the eyes of the U.S. government than those born elsewhere in Southeast Asia.

U.S. Legal Recognition, Morality, and the Role of Place

On October 1, 1981, Jeremiah Denton, a Republican U.S. senator from Alabama, introduced the Amerasian Act to Congress.[25] This act would provide an immigration pathway for Amerasian children born in East and Southeast Asia during the Korean and Vietnam Wars.[26] Eight months later a congressional hearing was held about the status of Amerasian children, with their fate in U.S. officials' hands.[27] Among the witnesses that testified before Congress were a U.S. senator, a U.S. representative, representatives from the Department of State and Immigration and Naturalization Services, a lawyer, and directors of nonprofit organizations that advocate for Amerasian children, such as St. Vincent's Home for Amerasians and the Pearl S. Buck Foundation. Among the issues at stake in the hearing included the plight of Amerasian children in Southeast Asia, the necessity for the United States to take responsibility and provide for the children of U.S. fathers, the undue burden placed on Asian (but not European) Amerasian children to prove paternity, the validity of local marriages between their fathers and mothers (which would confer U.S. citizenship on the child), and how to identify Amerasians, such as what age limit, if any, to enact and their legitimate or illegitimate status concerning who would qualify for any migration preference. Concerns also revolved around whether they would assimilate in the United States if they migrated and whether they would be a burden on taxpayers.

Yet one topic that did not receive the same in-depth discussion in these hearings was that of Amerasians' nationality or race. This may not be surprising since the 1960s saw the enactment of laws that prohibited discrimination based on race or nationality in the United States. Yet the backdrop of the United States is one of racism and discrimination, and it was only a few decades prior to this congressional hearing that Filipinos were racialized as a menace to society, whose migration to the United States was objected against by lawmakers and others, in part because of fears of racial mixing and the possibility of a large number of mixed-race children with full citizenship rights, whose presence would dilute white blood.[28]

Although the Pearl S. Buck Foundation advocated for an inclusive law that took into account all countries where Amerasians were found, government officials made only veiled references to coming to an agreement with one another to restrict the countries to which any Amerasian-related law would apply. The original Senate proposal 1698 included references to Amerasian children born in Korea, Vietnam, Laos, Thailand, Japan, the Philippines, and Taiwan. However, the final version, which was enacted as Public Law 97-359, specified its applicability to only Amerasian children born in Korea, Vietnam, Cambodia, Laos, and Thailand. The Philippines, Japan, and Taiwan were purposefully excluded.

On June 16, 1993, a little over ten years after the Amerasian Act was signed into law, another attempt was made to include the Philippines and recognize Filipino Amerasians in U.S. law. Representative Lucien E. Blackwell, a black congressman and army veteran, introduced House Resolution 2429 to Congress. This amendment would have incorporated Filipino Amerasians into the 1982 Amerasian Act. However, two days after it was introduced, it was referred to a subcommittee, where it died and would not be signed into law. Blackwell is just one of many who have tried but ultimately failed to get Filipino Amerasians legally recognized after their erasure from the Amerasian Act.[29]

Thus, despite such similar circumstances as discrimination and poverty that other Amerasians across Southeast Asia experience,[30] Filipino Amerasians have a distinct U.S. status, or nonstatus.[31] Although not discussed in the hearings, one key difference is that the military bases in the Philippines, unlike those in other Southeast Asian countries, were not in the combat zone of the Vietnam War. Instead, they were maintenance and logistic hubs, as well as popular rest and relaxation destinations for military personnel on leave. It was a place to escape the horrors of war. Its lands were not ravaged. The South China Sea provided a barrier that separated the Philippines from the Southeast Asian landmass of Vietnam, Laos, Cambodia, and Thailand.

Amerasian children born in the Philippines are not afforded the same rights of migration and economic assistance as those born in Vietnam, Thailand, Laos, and Cambodia, where U.S. service personnel encountered the direct threats of war. Instead, the men who fathered Filipino Amerasian children were provided a respite from war when they served, either fully or on rotation, in the Philippines. The United States recognizes only the rights of children who were born in the direct, not indirect, countries that saw the horrors of war firsthand. In the case of the Philippines, the financial and emotional responsibilities that fathers or the U.S. military have toward these children are brushed over due to its bases serving as logistic and maintenance hubs and places for rest and relaxation. The lack of valid, legal marriage and the fathers' activities—whether in direct or indirect combat—and physical location trumped the children's blood relation and moral claims to these men. We see this most clearly in the legal case of Christopher Acebedo.

On March 4, 1993, Joseph W. Cotchett, of the San Francisco–based law firm Cotchet, Illston & Pitre, filed a class action lawsuit on behalf of an estimated 8,600 Amerasian children in Olongapo, the city surrounding Subic Bay.[32] Cotchett named, in particular, four Filipinos in the lawsuit: three Amerasian children and one Amerasian mother. First was Christopher Acebedo, who was fifteen years old when Cotchett filed the lawsuit. Christopher was the son of a U.S. sailor stationed at the U.S. Subic Bay Naval Base and was born after his mother's failed and illegal abortion attempt.[33] His mother had sought help from a *hilot*, or midwife, who uses "rough strokes and pincer-like grips on [a] belly . . . [or] pounding the lower abdomen to trigger a miscarriage."[34] This practice is referred to colloquially as a massage and is a common abortifacient for poor, often rural, Filipina women. His mother's massage "ruptured [Christopher's] spine, and he was born with one leg shorter than the other and a curved spinal column that has stunted his growth . . . [and] gives him the appearance of being younger than his younger sisters and brothers."[35] After being abandoned by his mother, his grandmother raised him. At the time that

Cotchett filed the lawsuit, Christopher was living at the PREDA Center, the Olongapo-based nonprofit for sexually exploited women and children founded and run by Father Shay Cullen, an Irish missionary priest.

Ruby Acebedo is Christopher's sister and the second named plaintiff in the lawsuit. She was a ten-year-old Amerasian at the time of filing and lived with her grandmother, a *labandara* (someone who washes clothes for a living) who raised Christopher, Ruby, and their other brothers and sisters after their mother abandoned them.[36] The next two named plaintiffs were mother and son. Brenda David is an Amerasian herself, born to her Filipina mother and a U.S. airman who "was stationed at the Clark Air Force Base in the 1950s."[37] Tyson David, a second-generation Amerasian, was five years old at the time of filing. Tyson is Brenda's son, and Brenda met his father, a U.S. Navy first class petty officer, while working at an Olongapo City club.

Christopher, Ruby, Tyson, and Brenda's case relied on the U.S. Tucker Act (28 U.S.C. §1491), which states that a contract, whether written or implied, with the U.S. military is a contract, more generally, with the United States. Cotchett traced the beginning of this contract to 1974, when the then U.S. chief of naval operations and mayor of Olongapo City entered into a series of memorandums of understanding, which created Olongapo's health and educational center: the Social Health Clinic.

The establishment of the Social Health Clinic solved one of the U.S. military's problems: the prevalence and treatment of sexually transmitted infections that follow overseas military servicemen and spread through the accompanying sex industry that arises to meet their carnal needs. This clinic's primary audience was Olongapo's sex workers. Cofunded by the U.S. military, the clinic required women to be registered with the mayor's office and to have regular checkups and HIV testing; it also provided educational classes. The clinic also required women to carry official documents from the bar or club at which they worked. Any Filipina woman accompanied by a U.S. serviceman could be stopped by the Olongapo City police and asked for these documents. The U.S. military and Olongapo City government both exerted tight control over the women, their activities, and the sex industry more broadly.[38]

Cotchett argued that because the United States helped fund the clinic, regulated the sexual health of sex workers surrounding the Subic Bay Naval Base, and entered into memorandums of understanding with the Olongapo City government, they engaged in an implied contract with the women themselves. The U.S. military, then, shared "a joint legal responsibility with those who fathered these children left behind with the withdrawal of the Naval personnel."[39] As such, Cotchett asserted, the Amerasian children of Olongapo City were entitled to damages.

Cotchett quoted President Bill Clinton's speech of February 17, 1993, where he said, "It is time to demand that people take responsibility for the children they bring into this world. Each day we delay really making a commitment to our children carries a dear cost." Cotchett declared that this lawsuit was about "the children of all Americans, brought into this world by our servicemen."[40] Existing laws around Amerasian children in Southeast Asia, he stated, were insufficient because they excluded Filipino Amerasian children, and "little, if any," of the money covered in related laws went to them precisely because the laws about Amerasian children did not specify nationality. Cotchett sought $68 million for education and medical expenses—which was "less than one-third the cost of a *single* Navy jet fighter airplane"[41]—for the estimated 8,600 Filipino Amerasian children living in the shadow of the former U.S. Subic Bay Naval Base. The damages he sought would cover these children until they reached the age of eighteen.

Joan Bernott represented the United States as the defendant and countered Cotchett's claims on three grounds. First, she said, the United States did not agree to a waiver of its sovereign immunity, so it could not be brought before the court as a defendant of a lawsuit. Second, there was no evidence of a contract, implied or otherwise. In order for there to be a contract, there must be an offer and acceptance of said offer. At the heart of this case, Bernott asserted, were details about a presumed contract, but the details and terms provided by the plaintiffs were ambiguous, unknown, and only guessed at. Finally, while Bernott acknowledged that at the center of the case was concern about the health and education of Amerasian children fathered by U.S. servicemen,[42] she argued that this issue was a political, not judicial, one and noted that the complainants' demands bypassed the U.S. legislative and executive branches, under whose purview these issues fell. Pointing to the U.S. Code's Foreign Assistance chapters that recognize the plight of these children, Bernott asserted that the United States already recognized and allowed for negotiations over assistance given to Amerasian children. In doing so, the United States was fulfilling its legal, and perhaps moral, obligations to these children. However, since these laws often contained no direct list of countries and what kind or what amount of financial assistance they should receive,[43] financial allocations by country for these children were inconsistent and subject to administrative discretion.

The Honorable Judge Hodges dismissed Christopher's case and agreed with the U.S. government that there was no evidence of an implied contract between the U.S. military and the Olongapo City sex workers and their children. Furthermore, even if there was evidence presented to support Christopher, Ruby, Tyson, and Brenda's claims, Hodges asserted that the court would not have had jurisdiction because it would have been an illegal contract, and thus nonbinding and unenforceable.

This dismissal raises critical questions regarding what responsibilities— if any—the United States has toward the often-inadvertent families it helps create and then abandons: Amerasian children and the socioeconomic and cultural difficulties they face in their home society. It shows how continuing moral boundary-making claims are tied to which and what kind of families are allowed to be created in overseas military bases and how these relate to the importance of place—where the military base is located and the activities in which they engage. Because claims based on paternity and blood were not sufficient to legally recognize the Filipino Amerasian children or their mothers who U.S. servicemen left behind, many of these children and women also made moral and financial claims based on institutional support of the sex industry out of which many of these children were born. In doing so, they linked legal recognition and financial assistance to contracts and the moral responsibilities provided by them. Yet, like the claims based on blood, moral claims based on contracts were denied by the court.

Philippine Courts, Adoption, and Power

Because they are often born out of wedlock, many Amerasian children are considered illegitimate, a status that continues to be enshrined in Philippine laws and one where children are not afforded the same rights as legitimate or legitimized natural children.[44] Yet when U.S. servicemen do try and claim Amerasian children, whether adopted or biological, they may run into legal obstacles. However, this time, the obstacles they face are those set forth by Philippine courts.

On an October day in 1958, Gilbert R. Brehm, a U.S. serviceman on temporary assignment at the Subic Bay Naval Base, married Ester Mira, a Filipina. After marrying, Gilbert and Ester moved to Manila. With them was Elizabeth, Ester's daughter by another U.S. serviceman who was no longer a part of their lives. By all accounts, Gilbert supported and cared for Elizabeth. Three and a half months after they wed, on January 28, 1959, Gilbert and Ester filed a petition for Gilbert to officially adopt Elizabeth. Both of them wanted Gilbert to adopt Elizabeth so as to provide her with legitimacy, cut any legal obligations Elizabeth had regarding her biological father, and for her own "best interest and well-being."[45] They wanted her to officially, not just informally, be Gilbert's daughter and to make a legal space for her within their family.

However, an unnamed representative of the Philippines opposed the petition because Gilbert's residence was temporary. Instead, they argued that according to Philippine law, Gilbert was disqualified from adopting, and the court did not have jurisdiction over him because he was a nonresident alien. In their response, Gilbert and Ester argued that the law used to oppose them did not apply because the law also allows for the adoption of a stepchild, and they pointed out that Gilbert, Ester, and Elizabeth all lived together in Manila. Furthermore, despite Gilbert's job being located in Subic Bay, he was always home during the weekends and intended to stay in Manila after his tour of duty was completed. Citing Gilbert's intention to become a permanent resident and Elizabeth's welfare and best interests in their decision, the Juvenile and Domestic Relations Court sided with Gilbert and Ester and allowed Gilbert to adopt Elizabeth.

The solicitor general disputed the verdict and claimed that the court erred in allowing Gilbert to adopt his stepdaughter Elizabeth because Gilbert was a nonresident alien. The Honorable Judge Paredes[46] drew on case law in his ruling, first from the 1963 Supreme Court case *Ellis and Ellis v. Republic of the Philippines*. In this case, Marvin and Gloria Ellis, a married couple who had been living in Angeles, Philippines, for three years due to Marvin's position as staff sergeant at the U.S. Clark Air Force Base, wanted to adopt an infant nicknamed "Baby Rose." Baby Rose was left at the "Heart of Mary Villa—an institution for unwed mothers and their babies" when she was only four or five days old, because the mother, according to her statement, "could not take care of Rose without bringing disgrace upon her (the mother's family)." In this case, the Honorable Judge Concepcion ruled that despite good intentions by Marvin and Gloria Ellis, the law was clear. Article 335 of the Philippine Civil Code states that a nonresident alien cannot adopt, so the judge denied their request. The Honorable Judge Paredes also drew on a second case in their ruling—that of Ricardo Caraballo, an American staff sergeant at the U.S. Clark Air Force Base, and his wife, Graciela Caraballo. Both Ricardo and Graciela wanted to adopt five-day-old newborn Norma Lee Caber, with her biological mother's consent. Again, however, the Philippine courts ruled against the adoption on the same grounds as Marvin and Gloria's case: Caraballo was a nonresident alien.

Quoting the Caraballo decision, which cautioned against the perils of a foreigner adopting a Filipino citizen, including the minor being "placed beyond the reach and protection of the country of his birth," Judge Paredes agreed with the solicitor general. Ruling that although stepparents may be allowed to adopt, nonresident aliens cannot, Judge Paredes voided Gilbert's adoption of Elizabeth. Despite being married and intending to stay in Manila with his wife, Gilbert could not adopt his stepdaughter because he was a military foreigner, no matter his desire to do so.

The case of Janalita Rapada, a Filipina, and Joel Dempsey, a U.S. serviceman, reveals additional complications regarding legal recognition of Amerasian children. Janalita and Joel were unmarried but cohabiting when their daughter, Christina Marie, was born on October 1, 1984, at the St. Jude's Family Clinic in Olongapo City. Joel is listed as her father on the birth certificate and also signed an affidavit of acknowledgment that she was his daughter. He never disputed his paternity and provided $150 in monthly child support to Janalita. Janalita also claimed that Joel promised that he would legally declare Christina Marie as his dependent, which is important because it would allow her to obtain his citizenship and, thus, "all the benefits and privileges extended to dependents of American US Navy servicemen like free medical check-up."[47] According to court documents, someone at the Naval Legal Service Office at Subic Bay tried to get Joel to follow through with his promises of citizenship to Christina Marie, though to no avail.

Janalita simultaneously filed two separate charges, one criminal and one civil, arguing that Joel abandoned his child and failed to give adequate financial support to Christina Marie. Joel pleaded guilty. For the criminal charge, the court sentenced him to three months and eleven days to four months of prison, a fine of P300 ($7.65[48]) for each charge, and the legal costs. For the civil charge, the court ordered Joel to continue his monthly $150 ($3.82) in child support until Christina Maria is eighteen, legally recognize her as his natural child, pay Christina Maria exemplary damages, and pay for Janalita's legal fees.

Joel appealed, requesting that the civil award be set aside and that the prison sentence be reduced to a fine. After reviewing his case, the regional trial court (RTC) reversed the municipal trial court's (MTC) decision. However, it was on grounds not found in Joel's appeal. Here, the court ruled that paternal authority and obligations are only for legitimate and adopted children, not illegitimate ones, and child abandonment is under the purview of the Department of Social Welfare. Furthermore, they found that "a person could not be held criminally liable for failure to support a minor child" and that the previous court had no authority to make their judgment. Because of the lack of marriage between the couple, the RTC found that he had no obligations. The lack of a marital bond trumped children's blood rights.

Next, Janalita took the case before the Philippine Supreme Court. On August 15, 1988, Justice Gutierrez Jr.[49] reversed the RTC's decision and reinstated the previous court's ruling. Gutierrez did so, in part, because Joel pleaded guilty. That Joel asked only to change the imprisonment to a fine—and already recognized Christina Marie as his child—suggested to the court that the MTC's guilty verdict was valid. Additionally, Gutierrez argued that, contrary to the RTC reason for overruling the original decision based on legitimacy of the child, all children are entitled to the same rights, regardless of whether they are legitimate or illegitimate. In this ruling, blood and marriage were seen as equally important in determining a child's welfare.

However, Justice Gutierrez disagreed with the MTC on two accounts. First, Christina Maria was an abandoned child. She was not, according to Gutierrez, because her mother took care of her. Second, Gutierrez ruled that the MTC had no jurisdiction to order Joel to recognize Christina Marie as his daughter, since parental recognition is a civil, not criminal, matter. Gutierrez also agreed with the RTC that the award in damages and attorney fees were erroneous, and the court could not grant exemplary damages without aggravating circumstances. In sum, Gutierrez reinstated the MTC's verdict; however, he also reduced Joel's sentence to one month in prison and a fine of P300 ($7.64) and acquitted Joel of the other charges and awards. What we see here is how despite Joel not contesting the paternity of Christina Maria nor his parental responsibilities, different Philippine courts made competing arguments about child support and legal recognition into one about morality, (il)legitimate status, and the benefits, rights, and privileges that accompany them.

The women and Amerasian children the U.S. men left behind are at the mercy of the father's whims regarding whether he wants to grant recognition and support, as we see when Larry, Bill, Paul, Liza, Anna, and Tessa retell their lives. We also see in the case of Christina Marie that this recognition is tenuous, even when fathers did not dispute paternity. One of the benefits of this recognition is that it serves as a pathway of migration and U.S. citizenship. If the father is willing to apply for a Consular Report of Birth Abroad of a Citizen of the United States of America, a document used to provide proof of U.S. citizenship, the Amerasian child will be a legal U.S. citizen and benefit from all the rights it confers, including a U.S. passport and entry into the United States. Furthermore, since family reunification is one major avenue of immigration, it opens up possibilities for their mother's migration.

Migration to the United States is one reason why Eden, the forty-two-year-old adoptive mother of Chad, a white Filipino Amerasian, continues to try and locate his biological father. We sat outside, by a small *sari-sari* store near where she lived, and on a bench alongside the adobo and *sinigang* (soup) put out for display. Right behind us was a group of three boys—one of whom was her son Chad—singing to a videoke (a form of karaoke), and twenty minutes later, they started to play basketball on the concrete in front of us. It was a hot day, loud with sounds, with trikes (motorized tricycles, or a motorcycle with an attached sidecar) riding past us and people talking all around us. Eden looked at me and, with a soft voice, told me how Chad was abandoned as a baby, and when the unnamed people brought him to her, he was naked, sick with the measles, and dying. Twenty-three years old and single, Eden informally and without any documentation adopted and cared for him from that moment on and enrolled him in a nonprofit organization for Amerasian children.

Chad was not Eden's first experience with the U.S. military, as her father worked for the former U.S. Clark Air Force Base, and after she adopted Chad, she was able to secure a job inside Clark for herself. In fact, she tells me, "It's [the base] a big help to the Filipinos who [are] living near Clark. All of, everybody here, they are all working inside [the] Air Force. I think it's a big help and they give a big salary, not like now. Even [now] you will work twenty-four hours [inside the Clark Freeport Zone], the salary is only going to pay for your food. That's why they miss Clark." Here, the base workers' salaries provided more than enough to help her and her family sustain and thrive, and she missed the base and the opportunities it provided to her friends, family, and herself.

In 2002, Eden found out she had the first of two cancers she would be diagnosed with. In 2006, at the time of our interview, she had to forgo her medication—which costs P20,000 (or about US$500) a month—to make sure Chad can have three meals every day. The foundation promised her that they would provide Chad a scholarship that would pay for his schooling and that they would help him find his biological father. However, Chad's allowance from the nonprofit does little to offset the costs needed to provide for a child. After he graduated high school, with the foundation's help, little to no support is given to Eden or Chad to make sure he can continue in his second year of college. Neither have they helped find his biological father. In Eden's eyes, they have not fulfilled either promise to her family.

Eden told me that Chad belongs in the United States because he is Amerasian. According to her, he's an *American* and should be there, not in Angeles City, where he's taunted and made fun of by his peers and their families, saying that he "*iniwan ng barko*" (was left by the ship) because of his Amerasian heritage. Instead, Eden thinks that Chad looks like he belongs in the United States because "[Americans] will not notice that he's half American and half Filipino." If he found his biological father, surely his father would give Chad access to resources and a chance for a better life in the United States. There's a sense of urgency in her voice as she tells me how she constantly worries what will happen to him when she passes away, something she feels will be soon. Yet this mythic American dream and image of the United States as the land of milk and honey and a meritocracy, where one only has to work hard to succeed, does not reflect reality.

In 2015, Filipinos were the fourth largest immigrant group to the United States,[50] and their migration is rooted in U.S. colonialism. Filipinos have long been racialized and discriminated against, both within the Philippines and in the United States. They were seen as the United States' "little brown brothers" during U.S. colonial rule, and President William McKinley described Filipinos as "a people redeemed from savage indolence and habits"[51] because of U.S. intervention. They have historically also been excluded from neighborhoods, jobs, and stores in the United States, where many displayed signs that said "Positively No Filipinos or Dogs Allowed" or "Get Rid of All Filipinos or We'll Burn This Town Down."[52] If he ever migrated, Chad, who knows very few English words and is dark-skinned, would likely face a different kind of discrimination in the United States than what he receives in the Philippines.

Legal Recognition and the Role of the Birth Certificate

The previous sections mainly focused how U.S. and Philippine courts dealt with the legally ambiguous status of Filipino Amerasian children. But how do the women involved with these U.S. servicemen understand these men's parental responsibilities and their Amerasian children? Legal recognition—whether the man signed the birth certificate and acknowledged his paternity—is one signal mothers of Amerasian children use to delineate moral boundaries between themselves and others seemingly like them. It serves as physical proof that the men cared about their children and that their relationships with the women were not merely based on sex work. Christine, who has one Amerasian daughter and two Filipino children, met Hugh, a black American, in 1977. It's nighttime when I talk with her, outside the home of the person I am staying with. We sit across from one another at a table with a yellow tablecloth. The table across from us is filled with two women and one man who are talking with one another. It is loud outside, though the noise fades to a constant hum in the background as we eat chicken feet while Christine talks.

Hugh was the love of her life and signed her daughter's birth certificate, giving "her all of the credential[s] that she needs," she asserts. In doing so he demonstrated the depth of their relationship. Although they couldn't legally wed because he was already married, their relationship was not a one-time occurrence. In Christine's eyes, the signed birth certificate served as outside proof of their relationship status. Together, a family of three, she and their daughter lived inside the base with him, where they went bowling and played bingo. She reports that he even authorized her on his credit card, so she could shop for things at the base commissary, and that he always took care of his daughter.

Yet, while they were together, Christine encountered friends and others who questioned her choices of being with a black, not white, American. Echoing the experiences of Amerasian children themselves, she faced a double stigma—both perceptions of her relationship as rooted in sex work and judgments about her relationship with a black American. Since Maria, her daughter, is light-skinned, these very same people also questioned whether Hugh was really Maria's father.

Telling her not to worry about what others were saying, Hugh pointed out that his own father was black and his mother was white. He also had sisters that appeared white. He used his family's spectrum of color to account for the discrepancy between the skin color of their daughter and himself. Skin color was not an issue for him. Hugh said to her, "I'm not stupid to sign and give her all my credential when I know that's not my daughter." He was willing to sign the birth certificate because he did not question whether he was the father. Christine tells me, nodding with a bit of pride, that she "never forced him to sign anything. . . . [She] was just lucky that he sign it." The birth certificate is a legal document that proved paternity, and a man's willingness to sign it is used as evidence of a meaningful relationship and his kindness and concern for his children. To Christine, Hugh fulfilled his paternal duty to Maria by legally recognizing her as his own.

I first talked with Danielle, a forty-something-year-old former entertainment dancer in Clark and in Japan,[53] over lunch in the sterile, florescent lighting at Chowking, a popular Chinese fast food chain. In contrast to Christine's story, Danielle told me that Tim, her American military boyfriend, didn't know she was pregnant when they broke up and he left the Philippines. They lost contact until her daughter Nancy was three years old. Maura, a Filipina friend of hers who married her American boyfriend and migrated to the United States, serendipitously ran into Tim in Las Vegas. She tells me, in between bites of food, that Maura wrote her a letter, saying that she told Tim that Danielle was pregnant and gave Tim her phone number—so Danielle should expect a call. One day, she received his call, and he asked her, "How come you did not— how come I did not tell him I was pregnant? . . . I told him, 'I don't know.' I don't know I'm pregnant, right? It's my first time to get pregnant, so how do I know! Until I just found out when I get bigger! [*laughter*]. 'You never left your address where you're going, so how can I get in touch with you?'" she asked.

As they reconnected, he asked Danielle if Nancy was his daughter, to which she replied of course. She understood his doubts and offered to do a DNA test to establish paternity. But the offer of a paternity test was not enough. Tim pushed her further, asking why Nancy didn't have his last name. Danielle explained to him the Philippine rules regarding the birth certificate. The civil code of the Philippines[54] states that a child conceived out of wedlock can only receive a parent's surname if that child is recognized by that parent. Tim wasn't in the Philippines when Nancy was born. Therefore, Danielle could not put him down as Nancy's father nor give her his family name because she didn't have Tim's acknowledgment and approval of Nancy's paternity.

After learning about Nancy, he called them every Saturday, for a month, telling Danielle that he was going to go back to the Philippines and meet his daughter, asking her why she didn't tell Nancy that Tim was her father. Danielle tells me, "How can I tell . . . how can I tell Nancy that her father's fine, he's live, but nowhere to come [get her]? My daughter is gonna get hurt. I understand that the feelings of having no father. Of having no father support everything you need. My family is the only one who help us. How can I tell my daughter that you're the father?" She says, "Every time he called, he asked to talk to Nancy. I let him talk to Nancy." In these talks, Tim "promised to come, that he's going to visit us by October. And October came and he did not come."

They haven't heard from him since.

What we see in contrasting Danielle's and Christine's stories is the importance of the birth certificate in forming families. They provide physical proof of the father fulfilling his paternal responsibility. A father's and mother's legal recognition of their children comes with very specific legal rights for the child, including their surnames and financial support. However, there are no ways to enforce that financial support or gain that recognition without the father's explicit knowledge and consent. The children, whose mother and father either intentionally or inadvertently lost touch with one another, lose any hopes of being legally declared a legitimate child if reconnecting with their biological fathers is off the table and lost to history.

Precarity and Citizenship in Global Borderlands

If the rape and murder of Filipina women by U.S. servicemen are about the stakes involved, and sex and romance among everyday people tell us about the contradictions that define global borderlands, then the plight of Amerasian children in the Philippines highlights the precarity of these places and of the families formed in their shadows—how citizenship, rights, and responsibilities are neither guaranteed by blood nor by contract, neither by desire nor by morality. Instead, they are highly contingent. They are based on place and whether the bases and the men stationed there were in direct combat and concern U.S. recognition, as well as legitimacy and competing legal interpretations in Philippine courts. But citizenship is not only a legal status. It is accompanied by imaginaries of belonging,[55] of who belongs where and why. And these imaginaries, whether positive or negative, and how they apply to Amerasian children are held by mothers, Amerasians themselves, and the people they encounter in their daily lives. They are also tied to how the relationships that produced these children are imagined and the use of the law—in this case, birth certificates—that provides proof of a loving relationship, not one defined by sex work, and of paternal rights fulfilled.

However, intimate encounters—whether marked by violence, sex, or progeny—are not the only things that blossom in global borderlands. Imaginaries related to cosmopolitanism and horror also take hold. They guide how people interact within this space and with each other and what it means to be of a particular nationality.

Labor and Imagined Identities 5

Juanita was born almost fifteen years after the Japanese occupation of the Philippines and stood witness to the rise of the former Subic Bay Naval Base, the U.S. military's subsequent withdrawal, and Subic Bay's transition to a Freeport Zone (FZ). Now in her fifties, she owns two small businesses, has five children—three adults and two school-aged children—and receives $500 a month in remittances from her husband, an overseas Filipino worker. She is also a former U.S. Subic Bay Naval Base employee. Over coffee one afternoon she tells me, "In comparison [to now], with the salary and their treatment, Americans are better. They gave us all the benefits and treat their employees right." Of course, she knows that not all Americans are kind or nice; she had an American supervisor who didn't "treat their workers well" and who "was biased against Filipinos." But she clarifies quickly that "it's not all of them. . . . The rest, they were all kind people." In fact, she explains that even though her supervisor was biased, he still gave her "an A or an outstanding rat[ing] for three years. . . . He appreciated [her] work." Working at the base also allowed her to earn a higher salary and an associate's degree. Back then, she tells me, "you can rely on Americans, that's why I miss those times."

In 1992, the U.S. military withdrew from Subic Bay. When they did, Juanita and her coworkers were sad. "We actually didn't want [them] to leave." Before the withdrawal, all the staff in her department gathered together to reminisce about working there. She tells me that she and her friends miss her coworkers that left and that once they returned to the Philippines and had a reunion. She holds a fondness for the base because comparatively higher wages allowed for chances to take care of her family, go to school, and save money. Now she says, "In comparison to those new workers, they're not satisfied with their salaries now. Their salaries are not enough for them. Not enough to feed their family. Unlike before, we had bonuses every December that were really high. Americans were good employers."[1]

In this chapter I use employment as a lens to examine how people on the ground experience Subic Bay. Focusing on the U.S. Subic Bay Naval Base as an employer and two businesses within the Subic Bay Freeport Zone (SBFZ)—the Filipino-owned, upscale Harbor Point mall and the South Korean company Hanjin Shipping—I show how people understand national identities and inequalities through *labor imaginaries*. According to Charles Taylor, imaginaries are the "ways people imagine their social existence, how they fit together with others, how things go on between them and their fellows, the expectations that are normally met, and the deeper normative notions and images that underlie these expectations."[2] We know from research by feminist labor scholars like Jennifer Bair, Patricia Fernandez-Kelly, Carla Freeman, Mary Beth Mills, Aihwa Ong, Leslie Salzinger, and Diane Wolfe that globalized labor and the international political economy are gendered and many of the women employed in factories and information sectors link their work to ideas of modernity and urbanity.[3] Uniting this stream of research, which documents the varied conditions of labor practices and associated meanings given to work, with that of Charles Taylor's understanding of imaginaries, I use the term *labor imaginaries* to describe how people understand nationalities through work experiences and labor conditions.[4] In and around each of these places of employment, what it means to be American, Korean, and Filipino is continually recreated and reinforced in everyday talk, interactions, and imaginations. People link their own and others' work experiences to understandings of what it means to be a particular nationality. These imaginaries are framed as either providing an opportunity to be a part of modernity and the "good life"[5] or showcasing the human rights violations, exploitation, and physical abuse that occurs within businesses' walls.

In comparing employment conditions and imaginaries related to the U.S. military, Harbor Point mall, and Hanjin Shipping, we also see the fluidity of power and identities, how situations become high- or low-stakes, and how these three things interact. For the United States and the Philippines, the rules outlining U.S. military employment benefits for Filipinos were a high-stakes matter. Although the decisions were often made privately and out of sight, and thus open to undue influence because of U.S. power, they were also part of the negotiated terms over the presence and maintenance of the base at Subic Bay, giving the Philippines some leverage. Yet, while the *creation* of said rules were high-stakes matters, neither the routinized, everyday work interaction nor work conflicts were. It is only when the media takes hold of a story, like that of an alleged strip search of Filipina workers, that these issues transform to a comparatively high-stakes situation for both governments. The media serves to frame our understanding of events and the world around us.[6] When it is used by activists and journalists to highlight perceived inequalities and injustices committed by Americans, the Philippine government can exert pressure on the U.S. military to better working conditions.

American workers also filed a lawsuit against the U.S. military. This time, however, they argued that preference for Filipinos was discrimination based on nationality against them. This, too, transformed the everyday workings of the base into a high-stakes matter for the U.S. military and government because of the unintended ripple effects of the court's ruling on U.S.-Philippine military agreements and U.S. military agreements with countries around the world. We see something similar occurring when Filipino base workers used their rights and pathways available to them to counter perceived wrongs and assert their rights, for example, to retirement benefits after the U.S. military withdrew. However, these claims were denied by U.S. courts. Here the question of whether Filipino former employees were entitled to certain benefits was high-stakes because the answer could have significant economic implications for the United States. In each of these legal cases, we see how arguments with potentially enormous economic consequences for the United States caught U.S. officials' attention and raised the stakes of what could initially be thought of as routine matters of little importance. Yet these lawsuits and failed claims to benefits did not erase nostalgia for the base. Former base workers continue to draw on understandings of working for the U.S. base as opportunities to lead "the good life" and obtain good benefits and training, all of which left a lasting impression of Americans as good employers and good people.

So, too, do Harbor Point mall employees see their jobs as an avenue to achieve the "good life" through better benefits than outside the SBFZ, and the everyday operations of Harbor Point are relatively low-stakes matters for Philippine and foreign governments.[7] This is not to suggest that the Philippine government does not care about the reputation of the SBFZ, who visits, or how much people buy from stores within it. Indeed, the Subic Bay Metropolitan Authority (SBMA), the SBFZ's government, includes officials and departments concerned with precisely this matter. It also purposefully exerts its power through controlling who enters the SBFZ by placing armed guards at its gated entrance. Yet what's at stake in these everyday decisions regarding working at Harbor Point mall are the identities of the SBFZ, the people who visit, and the businesses within.

What accounts for these differences in labor conditions and imaginaries? Leslie Salzinger suggests that gendered understandings of labor conditions are (re)produced and expressed differently across shop floors due to the particular ways in which "managerial decisions, worker responses, and resulting gendered subjectivities . . . are constituted in a specific context of domination and struggle,"[8] while Carla Freeman traces women's experience working in the information sector to Barbados's gendered and racialized colonial history.[9] In contrast, Shannon Blanton and Robert Blanton document how different sectors of foreign direct investment are differently correlated with human rights based on skill, integration with society, and whether the sector is resource-seeking, market-seeking, or efficiency-seeking.[10] We also know that labor conditions and workers' rights differ across context, and local governments can mediate the effects of global economic processes,[11] though much of the qualitative literature focuses on one sector, rather than multiple sectors, within a single special economic zone (SEZ) or compares sectors across different SEZs.[12] Here in Subic Bay, gender matters, as does class, nationality, empire, and its legacies. So, too, does the *visibility* of work matter for how labor conditions and imaginaries are reproduced. Harbor Point is a highly visible and marketed business within the FZ, one that attracts foreign and Filipino visitors alike. Other forms of work are hidden and not subject to scrutiny, and their daily operations are of relatively low importance to the government. Hanjin Shipping, for example, is known for violations of workers' rights, and while the local government has the resources to enforce certain regulations, they do so only when an issue becomes escalated to the courts and/or subject to public critique. Otherwise, the internal operations of hidden businesses are low-stakes for the Philippine national and local government, and thus are less regulated. In revealing the differences in labor conditions, imaginaries, and nationalities, this chapter challenges understandings of working conditions within a single special economic zone or military base as homogenous and uniformly negative or positive, and follows in the footsteps of scholars who focus on the contingent, local, and enacted ways that people understand work, gender, and nationality.[13] It does so by highlighting *variation* within the same place across time and industry, and tying these to the visibility of work and differences in how national identities are imagined.

Imagining Americans

Maria, a sixty-something Filipina who is married and has two children, and Eva, a fifty-something Filipina who is single and has one child, are friends and former U.S. Subic Bay Naval Base workers. Both women talk about their former base work with a sense of nostalgia, and both agreed that the standard of living was better when the base was in operation. Explaining the differences between working during the base's era and working in the contemporary FZ, Eva tells me, "It was better then, with the base, because, you know, higher wages. Because we were paid by the hour."[14] This is an important distinction, since Philippine businesses pay employees by the day, not the hour. Although their wages didn't meet U.S. minimum-wage standards, they met Philippine wage requirements and were higher than the salaries that could be found outside the base.[15] Additionally, they received, as Eva recounts, "actual training" from the military. She explains that they received a certificate from the U.S. Department of Labor and could take, in one quarter, three weeks of school, complete with exams and grades in English, science, math, and drawing. Furthermore, the military provided safety shoes and goggles and instituted five-day workweeks and eight-hour workdays. These work benefits and opportunities shape their understanding of Americans as a particular type of nationality and their imagined future interactions with them. Even now, Eva will use Americans greeting her with a "Hello!" "Have a nice day!" and "Good morning!" as evidence of their goodness as a people.

Juanita's, Eva's, Maria's, and others' understandings of Americans are also shaped by power. More specifically, they are shaped by the broader U.S.-Philippine "special relationship" that originated in U.S. colonialism and continues today through visiting U.S. military forces in the Philippines, unequal import and export markets, and the Philippines' continued dependence on the United States for millions of dollars in nonmilitary and military aid. The reputation of Americans as good employers is also shaped by the very visibility of working at the base, which meant, by definition, working for Americans. Subic Bay Naval Base employee passes signaled this visible connection to the United States. During the bases' era, the U.S. military was the second largest employer in the Philippines,[16] pumping an estimated $500 million each year into the Philippine economy. More than 80,000 people in Central Luzon made their living from the bases.[17]

Because of the large number of both American and Filipino veterans of the U.S. military living in the Philippines, the only U.S. Veterans Affairs office outside the United States is located in the Philippines. The naval base also had a four-year apprenticeship program for Filipino college graduates, and during the Vietnam War, the Aetas (one of the Philippines' indigenous peoples) of Subic trained troops in jungle survival skills.[18] Filipino employees had a five-day, eight-hour-per-day workweek and were unionized, and through the 1968 Base Labor Agreement (BLA) and the collective bargaining agreement between U.S. armed forces and the Federation of Filipino Civilian Employees, Filipino nationals employed at one of the bases were entitled to social security benefits and severance pay and had collective bargaining rights. However, their ability to organize was severely limited as "any action taken by a recognized labor organization which interrupts or disrupts the orderly and effective operation of the bases . . . may be considered just cause for withdrawal of recognition of that organization."[19]

Also written into this agreement were midyear, annual bonuses and assertions that employment conditions would meet local standards. These conditions would be regularly assessed by surveys of employees, which bargaining units would help develop. A 1985 BLA increased the annual bonus for Filipino nationals from P200 to P2,000, while a 1989 amendment increased it from P2,000 to P3,500. The 1985 BLA marked an important shift for Filipinos living in the shadow of the bases because it expanded employment benefits to an increasing number of locals. In addition to increasing the Filipino work force, the BLA and its amendments stipulated that when the U.S. military withdrew, Filipino civilian workers—excluding those privately contracted—were eligible to receive a lump sum separation allowance including "severance pay, a cash payment for accumulated sick and annual leave, and a pro rata portion of the calendar year-end bonus," which resulted in a total cost of about $71.3 million.[20]

Yet this nostalgia and goodwill regarding the former base as an employer does not suggest that Filipinos were wholly content with the U.S. military. Indeed, during the bases' era, Filipino base workers protested and organized against unfair treatment. In March 1976, twenty-five Filipina employees of the main navy exchange on the Subic Bay base, most of whom were salesclerks, were frisked and told to take off their blouses, bras, pants, and underwear to "check if the[re] are tax free items concealed in their body."[21] No such items were found. Afterward, the Federation of Filipino Civilian Employees Associations in U.S. Bases in the Philippines heavily criticized U.S. personnel involved in the incident, saying, "the procedure resorted to by the base authorities was most unkind, degrading, and uncalled for. It bespeaks a contempt for human dignity and a wanton disregard for basic values. Certainly, a civilized and humane approach could have been used to achieve the same end."[22]

U.S. Department of State telegrams show that this case, like similar conflicts, was tried in an Olongapo City court, an important point that often gets lost in writings about U.S.-Philippine military relations. Being tried in a Philippine court suggests some semblance of power and leverage that the Philippines could use to hold U.S. military personnel accountable. The incident was also investigated by the U.S. Navy. In April, officials "conclude[d] that the charges are grossly exaggerated. Clothing was loosened but reportedly there was no stripping. The major error of the U.S. Security employees was in not having a Filipino supervisor present while the searches were conducted. Other than that, the search was little different from those routinely and regularly conducted without incident."[23]

The incident was also informally tried in the Philippine media, though they came to a much different conclusion than the United States and used the incident as evidence of the United States' continued unequal power in the Philippines. In contrast to previous discussions of Americans as a positive moral nationality, the Philippine media constructed Americans as a negative nationality by drawing on their colonial history, putting pressure on the Philippine government to act. One newspaper quoted Ruben Ocampo, the president of the Federation of Filipino Civilian Employees Associations, who "refuted Subic NB apologies to sales-girls and is demanding immediate dismissal and expulsion of Nex supervisor and security personnel"[24] and who stated that the association was "threatening 'drastic steps' against the bases if disciplinary action is taken against any of the girls who have protested the search," which included a "sit down strike."

Valencia, a *Daily Express* columnist, used this incident as an opportunity to criticize colonialism, U.S. power, and Filipino national identities, which Valencia asserted was still colonial in mentality since "Subic Bay Navy Authorities will apologize to the 25 Filipinas whom they subjected to indignities in a celebrated body search incident. Not before the Philippine government protested this ins[ul]t." But Valencia said, "I don't blame the U.S. Naval authorities. Like the Japanese occupation forces who made the mistake of slapping Filipinos, thinking that was proper, the U.S. Navy had always believed they are here to do us a great favor." Elaborating, Valencia suggested that "Filipinos have fanned this belief, thanks to our colonial-minded leaders who talk and act as if this were true." Differentiating Filipino elites and nonelites, Valencia declared, "The common man, however, has never understood the situation. All they see is how the American behave in and out of those bases. They are certain the American troops, like the Japanese occupation forces, are here as masters."[25] Despite an apology by the U.S. military, for Valencia the fact that this incident occurred in the first place and that the apology only occurred after protests provided clear proof that the U.S. continued to hold undue power in the Philippines. Politics between the U.S. and Filipino elite, according to Valencia, didn't match how Filipinos think or experience the U.S. military on the ground because Filipino elites had bought into being grateful for U.S. protection and power.

In August of that year, and in response to the Philippine media, William H. Sullivan, the U.S. ambassador to the Philippines from 1973 to 1977, wrote to the U.S. secretary of state, saying, "Press harassment of this sort is annoying, of course, but so far has had little observable impact on the [base] negotiations themselves."[26] This latter point was key to Sullivan. He described the Philippine press as "us[ing] these incidents 1) to echo the popular theme that the GOP [government of the Philippines] must take more control over the bases to protect the dignity and honor of the Filipino people and 2) to provide a not-so-subtle reminder that the Filipinos can make things very difficult for our military bases here if they choose."[27] Sullivan saw the incident as relatively unimportant for the U.S. government because it was not interfering with base negotiations, which would have transformed it into a high-stakes issue. However, he also recognized the *potential* reach of a critical Philippine press framing the issue around Filipino nationalism and identity and the leverage or power the press could provide to the Philippine government in base negotiations, if they so desired. This incident occurred in the midst of ongoing base negotiations, which heightened the possibility of interfering with U.S. plans for the bases, so keeping an eye on the situation and placating Filipinos would be important.

Once the U.S. military withdrew from the Philippines in 1992, problems did not disappear. Many Filipinos' livelihoods were stripped away and several sought to reclaim their rights by suing the U.S. Office of Personal Management (OPM) to receive retirement benefits in a U.S. court. The outcome of these cases would have enormous economic consequences for the United States, and thus were high-stakes matters. There have been at least 136 cases of Filipinos suing the OPM for retirement benefits and another 20 cases of Filipino widows petitioning for survivor benefits. One of the primary cases of that set case law involves Juanita A. Rosete.

Juanita Rosete is a Filipina citizen who worked for the U.S. Department of the Navy for nearly twenty-six years, from August 25, 1966, to July 3, 1992.[28] When the Philippine Senate rejected a treaty that would have renewed the United States' lease on the military bases on September 16, 1991, the U.S. military put into place plans for their withdrawal. In anticipation of losing her job, Rosete retired from the U.S. Navy, and she received severance pay and other benefits guaranteed to her by the BLAs. Eight months later, Rosete applied to the OPM for benefits under the U.S. Civil Service Retirement Act (CSRA). After they denied her application, she appealed to the U.S. Merit Systems Protection Board, who then affirmed her denial. Next, her case made its way to the U.S. Court of Appeals, Federal Circuit.

A former employee of the U.S. Navy, Rosete's case revolved around the question of who has access to retirement benefits and under what conditions. That she previously received severance pay and other benefits was not an issue at hand. According to the U.S. CSRA,[29] you must have at least five years of "creditable" service to be eligible for benefits and how much you receive is based both on your age and how long you've worked for the government. Rosete argued that because she worked continuously for twenty-six years for the U.S. Navy, she was covered under this law and entitled to benefits. In response, OPM officials said none of the various positions she worked in her twenty-six years and the indefinite (nonpermanent) appointment of them were not covered under the law. The U.S. Merit Systems Protection Board agreed with OPM's findings. When her case went before the court of appeals, she had to meet the burden of proof that the previous decisions were faulty and unfounded and that she was entitled to the benefits. Judge Archer[30] affirmed the previous findings and ruled against Rosete's petition, stating that none of her positions were ever covered by the CSRA and she never contributed to the Civil Service Retirement and Disability Fund.

The judge's ruling was also based on the president's ability to exclude particular executive branch positions from the CSRA's coverage, and the wording of various executive orders and updates to the CSRA, including whether the term *indefinite appointments* fell under the "temporary or intermittent" CSRA's exclusions, something Rosete claimed they did not. She argues that the congressional change of wording from "of uncertain duration" to "temporary or intermittent" meant "that Congress must have intended different, narrower exclusionary authority." Going over historical interpretation, alongside the CSRA's evolution, Judge Archer disagreed and found that the OPM's interpretation was reasonable and consistently applied and was in line with case law. Rosete also claimed her employment documents indicated she held a tenure appointment and thus was not an indefinite employee. However, Judge Archer agreed with the Merit Systems Protection Board since "other parts of the . . . forms specifically related to civil service" were marked as "none," "other," or "not applicable." As such Rosete's twenty-six years of continuous service was classified as temporary or nonentitled employment. She and all other Filipino former base employees were ineligible for CSRA-related benefits.

Another set of Filipinos made related claims after the U.S. military withdrawal from the Philippines. From February 13, 1973, until July 10, 1992, Manuel Licudine was employed by the U.S. Navy. In February 2008 he filed a Title VII claim[31] "alleging that Navy discriminated against him on basis of his national origin by failing to inform him of opportunity, available to him during two-year period, to participate in federal civil service retirement system."[32] In this case, however, Licudine argued that because he was born in 1945 while the Philippines was under U.S. colonial rule, he was born in the United States, and thus he held dual citizenship from both the United States and the Philippines. As such, he is entitled to Title VII protections and should have been notified of the opportunity to enroll in the federal civil service retirement system. The navy dismissed his complaint. In their ruling, they specifically stated that the case was dismissed not because of his claim to coverage under the civil service retirement system. Instead, it was dismissed because they ruled that Licudine was a non-U.S. citizen whose work was for an agency that was outside the United States. Thus, he was not entitled to Title VII protections.

The case went before the U.S. District Court in Washington, DC. The defendant, Donald C. Winter, the secretary of the navy, moved to have the case dismissed since Licudine was a Philippine citizen. District Judge James Robertson, in his finding, notes that at issue is whether Licudine is a U.S. or Philippine citizen. If he is a Philippine citizen, Title VII does not apply because Title VII "provisions do not apply to 'aliens employed in positions . . . located outside the limits of the United States.' . . . An 'alien' is 'any person not a citizen or national of the United States.'" In his ruling, Judge Robertson relied on an amicus brief detailing the U.S. history in the Philippines, which concluded that "from the time the United States obtained dominion over the Philippines in 1899 until it granted independence to the islands in 1946, Congress classified natives of the Philippines as Philippine citizens, as non-citizen United States nationals, and as aliens, but never as United States citizens." The Treaty of Paris, where Spain granted the United States control over the Philippines and other territories, gave Filipinos an option of retaining Spanish nationality. Under the U.S. Congress, Filipinos who did not opt for Spanish nationality were considered U.S. nationals, not U.S. citizens.[33]

Judge Robertson also relied on case law where Filipinos made similar claims to U.S. citizenship based on colonial history in deportation proceedings. These claims were denied because "the United States Courts of Appeals for the Second, Third, and Ninth Circuits hold that a person's birth in the Philippines during the territorial period is not birth in the United States for purposes of the Fourteenth Amendment." As such, Judge Robertson granted the defendant's motion and dismissed the suit, ruling that Licudine was neither a U.S. citizen nor U.S. national and that Title VII did not apply to him.[34] Here again, we see how legal ambiguity opens up space for nationality-based claims, though this pathway does not guarantee a particular outcome, especially one that would have lasting consequences for the U.S. government regarding their financial responsibilities to similarly positioned Filipinos.[35]

For activists, the search-and-frisk incident and denial of retirement benefits were and continue to be evidence of continuing U.S. power in the Philippines and U.S. exploitation of Filipinos. Today, however, many Filipino former base workers continue to hold an overall nostalgia for the base, what it represented, and what it allowed them to achieve. Both understandings surround Subic Bay and the U.S. military.

Understanding Koreans

Hanjin Shipping is a Korean-owned shipping and manufacturing company that is one of South Korea's biggest shipping companies, the seventh largest container line in the world,[36] and one of the largest SBFZ employers. In 2006, it began building its Subic Bay shipyard, and within two years it was fully operational. According to interviews, newspaper accounts, and court cases,[37] it is also known for violating workers' rights. These allegations are similar to ones about the shipping industry more generally, an industry that is highly segmented, masculinized, and racialized and where, according to Steven McKay, "nearly one in every three workers at sea is from the Philippines."[38]

Rogelio M. Bernal Jr. and Christine L. Baylon were two Filipino supervisors who worked inside the SBFZ.[39] They both completed three months of training at the Skills Development Center inside the SBFZ before beginning their work—Bernal at the Redondo shipyard facility at Hanjin Shipping and Baylon at the Subic Shipbuilder Corp (SushiCorp). After their six-month probation was over, they were both hired full-time, and Baylon was transferred to Redondo. On July 16, 2008, they were part of a group of employees that were transferred to the Skills Development Center to become trainers for new employees. According to SushiCorp and Redondo, after they were transferred and before their four-day orientation was complete, Bernal and Baylon complained to C. Y. Park, their Korean manager, about their assignment to a section outside their expertise. Park replied that their reassignment was due to production requirements. That day, they left work without informing their supervisor. Two days later, they received a notice for their disobedience in leaving without notice and were told to submit written explanations for why they left. Bernal and Baylon then went to the SBMA to file a complaint but did not get approval from their supervisor to do so. Later they sought counsel from the SBMA's legal department. Although Bernal and Baylon and their respective companies attempted mediation—and at least one other person was reinstated—it ultimately failed.

Bernal and Baylon petitioned the National Labor Relations Commission (NLRC) regarding unfair labor practices and their illegal dismissal. They argued, "Their dismissal is unlawful and unjust. . . . They were not afforded due process; there is no basis for the charge of willful disobedience [and] the transfer was merely a ploy to create a situation wherein management can fabricate a charge because of their union activities." They sought reinstatement, back wages, and damages. Officials from SushiCorp and Redondo replied, stating that Bernal and Baylon never sought internal ways to remedy the situation and that "the case was blown out of proportion" because they had the rights to discipline and/or terminate their employees as they saw fit. According to SushiCorp and Redondo officials, Bernal's and Baylon's "recalcitrant attitude constitutes an open defiance of management order."

Hanjin officials also filed a separate position paper on December 28, 2009, saying that because Redondo and Sushi Corp were subcontractors, Hanjin was not responsible for their employment, the conditions of their employment, nor their dismissal. On December 29, 2009, the labor arbiter, Leandro M. Jose, found that there was "no substantial evidence" that proves insubordination, only allegations, and that SushiCorp and Redondo did not give them sufficient notice before their termination, and as such he found in favor of Bernal and Baylon—that they were, indeed, illegally dismissed. They were to be reinstated to their previous, senior positions with back pay. Jose also dismissed Hanjin from the complaint, as there was no evidence of a relationship between Bernal, Baylon, and Hanjin.

Both sets of parties appealed: Bernal and Baylon, regarding Hanjin; SushiCorp and Redondo, regarding evidence of Bernal's and Baylon's insubordination. On December 3, 2010, the NLRC modified the original decision, ordering that Hanjin be held jointly responsible, but otherwise affirmed the labor arbiter's decision. However, on June 17, 2011, after another motion for reconsideration by Hanjin, accompanied by Bernal's and Baylon's responses, the NLRC reversed the previous ruling that affirmed Hanjin's role in the matter. On November 11, 2011, the case was put before the Philippine court of appeals; this time SushiCorp and Redondo sought to overturn the decision that found in favor of Bernal and Baylon. They did not want to reinstate Bernal and Baylon, who both showed "willful insubordination" and "lack of respect and loyalty towards respective management and . . . rules" and argued that they had adhered to all labor laws in their firing of them. At issue in the court of appeals was whether or not to uphold the previous decision(s), which centered on workers' rights, employment, and labor conditions.

Judge Celia C. Librea-Leagogo[40] denied SushiCorp's and Redondo's petition. Upholding Bernal's and Baylon's rights, she focused on the 1987 Philippine Constitution, which requires "just or authorized cause" for terminating employment. Workers' rights are written into the Philippine Constitution, and termination has to be for "just" reasons and follow particular procedures. The onus of proving these reasons and that procedures were followed rests on the company, not the individual workers. More specifically, Judge Libera-Leagogo found that there was no proof that Bernal and Baylon received notice of what their manager called an "internal hearing" and that they did not commit insubordination when they expressed their frustration at their job assignment not matching their skills and experience. Furthermore, even if these could be proven, termination would be "too harsh" a sentence. Additionally, workers' due process rights meant that employers have to provide two written notices, one regarding the reasons for termination and the other regarding the final decision, and a hearing, held at least five calendar days after the first notice, so workers could defend themselves. Bernal and Baylon received their first notice on July 21, 2008, and two undated memoranda said their termination would be effective on July 25, 2008. As such, SushiCorp and Redondo did not give them ample opportunity to prepare for a hearing to defend themselves. In her ruling, she cites Article 279 of the labor code, which states that "an employee who is unjustly dismissed from work shall be entitled to reinstatement without loss of seniority rights and other privileges; to his full backwages, inclusive of allowances; and to other benefits or their monetary equivalent."

Judge Libera-Leagogo also ruled that "willful insubordination" requires two conditions: first, conduct "characterized by a wrongful and perverse attitude," and second, "the order violated must have been reasonable, lawful, made known to the employee and must pertain to the duties which he had been engaged to discharge." She found there was no evidence for either. By denying SushiCorp's and Redondo's petition, she ruled that the workers' constitutional rights had been denied. As such, she and the other judges throughout the case matched what they saw were the workers' entitled rights and the damages due to them because of these violations and who was liable for them, whether Hanjin, SushiCorp, and/or Redondo. As we can see in the case of Bernal and Baylon, Hanjin is known for violating constitutionally protected workers' rights. However, these allegations go far beyond the unfair termination processes seen in the case of Bernal and Baylon.

On September 11, 2014, twenty-year-old Jerwin Labajan had been working a twenty-hour shift at Hanjin when "he was pinned by a mobile elevated platform." Although Hanjin officials blamed the accident on human error, Jerwin was wearing the required safety gear and was up-to-date with his qualifications of operating the machinery when he became the third person to die in Hanjin's shipyard that year. In the six years that Hanjin was in operation, thirty-seven workers died at the shipyard, and there were about six thousand work-related accidents.[41] Video recordings show incidents that went unreported, like physical abuse and "several workers with worn-out uniforms . . . [who] use adhesive tape to fix the uniforms to protect themselves from toxic materials. Orlando Alfonso was left blinded in one eye . . . [and while] the company shouldered Orlando's medical expenses . . . he . . . did not get any hazard or disability pay."[42] Hanjin's monthly accident report to the Department of Labor "consistently has numbers over 30, and workers are paid less than the minimum wage, fed what they call 'maggot-laden food' and are frequently abused by their superiors."[43]

On Labor Day, May 1, 2011, protests and rallies were staged throughout the Philippines. Workers from across sectors "demand[ed] higher wages amid rising prices and [gathered] to protest contractualization," and in Manila, in response to President Benigno Aquino III's failure to address worker concerns in his talks with labor leaders, they set fire to an "effigy of Mr. Aquino in his Porsche."[44] Meanwhile, in South Korea, thousands of people were protesting layoffs by Hanjin Heavy Industries and Construction. In January 2011, in South Korea, a former Hanjin employee, fifty-two-year-old Kim Jin-Suk, began a 309-day protest by climbing on top of a crane, where she went "without running water, having supporters hoist up her meals each day inside a bucket—[and by protesting, she] focused attention on what she claimed are the excesses of the country's corporate culture, in this instance the 400 job cuts announced . . . last year."[45] On July 9, 2011, "thousands of protesters from across the country marched through Busan in a show of support for the laid-off workers. Police fired water cannon laced with a diluted tear gas solution and arrested 50 people."[46]

Building on the momentum from the Hanjin-related protests in South Korea, the labor protests in the Philippines, and outrage from the April 2011 deaths of two Hanjin workers, activists organized rallies in Subic Bay to protest unsafe working conditions, maltreatment, unsanitary food, unlawfully dismissed workers, and the withholding of the right to unionize.[47] On July 3, 2011, the Caravan for Decent Work and Human Working Conditions started their journey from Manila to the SBFZ.[48] Organized by the Church-Labor Conference, participants included members of Manggagawa para sa Kalayaan ng Bayan (Makabayan, a coalition of parties in the House of Representatives), Kilusan para sa Pambansang Demokrasya (KPD, a leftist alliance of political organizations and grassroots individuals), Alliance of Progressive Labor (APL, a progressive labor organization), Samahan ng mga Manggagawa sa Hanjin Shipyard (SAMAHAN, a group of current Hanjin workers and former workers), Korean Workers Union, and Hanjin Korean Union.[49] An estimated five hundred workers protested in Subic Bay.[50] Gathered together, they held signs declaring:

"Di tuwid ang daan, dayuhan ang pinaboran" (No straight path,[51] foreigners are the favorite)

"Shipyard not graveyard!—APL"

Hanjin: Libingan ng mga manggagawa—PM (Tomb of workers)

Respect the Rights of Hanjin Workers—APL

Uphold Hanjin Workers Rights!!

Stop Labor Contractualization—Samahan

Sapat na Sahod; Pagkain sa Hanjin Ayusin Wag Babuyin (Living Wage; Fix
Hanjin Food so It's Not Dirty)

Stop Abusing Hanjin Workers!—PM Partido ng Manggagawa

A Safe & Humane Workplace is Every Worker's Rights!—SAASAHAN

Living Wage

The shipyard gate was blocked by a line of police officers,[52] who wore light-
blue helmets and held up blue-and-white riot shields with the word PULIS
(police) on them. Sometime later, the protestors—some holding flags or signs,
others with backpacks—pushed against the shields, trying to break through.[53]
Hanjin's illegal practices didn't stop after a 2009 high-profile investigation
from the Senate Labor Committee that Hanjin violated labor laws and safety
standards[54] nor after these 2011 protests. In September 2012, Tina Santos, a reporter for the *Philippine Daily Inquirer*, revealed that undercover agents from
the Philippine Overseas Employment Administration and the Philippine National Police posed as seafarer applicants, and Hanjin was one of three agencies
that had no authority to recruit or deploy Filipinos to work aboard one of their
many cargo ships around the world.[55] These Hanjin-related labor violations
and protests rose to national consciousness through news reporting,[56] and in
December 2012, the Philippines Department of Labor and Employment and
the SBMA signed a memorandum of agreement that stipulates that the Department of Labor and Employment will conduct regular inspections of SBFZ businesses in order to protect workers' rights and regulate working conditions.[57]
     The reputation of Hanjin and its identity as a Korean company extends be-
yond this particular company to influence Filipino perceptions of Koreans and
Korean identities more broadly. That is, they understand Korean identities—
and their accompanying interactions, transactions, and relationships with
them—from a framework based on Hanjin's reputation, regardless of any
actual or perceived affiliation. Although we know, for example, that "people
continuously evaluate their actions in relation to their [own] internal identity
standard . . . along various dimensions such as being (more or less) moral," and
how that is tied to the "framing of [associated] surrounding situations,"[58] we
can also see how Filipinos interpret others—in this case, South Korean employers, customers, friends, and everyday people—as embodying the reputation of
Hanjin through personal experience and/or hearsay and actively match this
reputation with the transactions and interactions they have with them. That is,

the Filipinos I spoke with, framed[59] or understood Koreans through Hanjin's reputation. There is what sociologists and psychologists call a "group schema," which classifies Koreans as a particular type of moral nationality.[60]

For example, Bea, a forty-something Filipina SBFZ visitor with two children, told me, "Yeah, they *kwan*, they treat Filipinos like, as slave. Sabi nila ha? Hindi kwan, hindi tao. Sabi ha? Like in Hanjin. 'Di ba totoo 'yun, 'di ba? Like in Hanjin" (Yeah, they treat Filipinos like slaves. What did they say? That we're not people. Like in Hanjin). Similarly, Rosa, a Filipino SBFZ visitor who used to work for a Korean company inside the FZ, shared with me her own story of how Koreans treated Filipinos like they were not *tao* (people), saying that it was not uncommon for the Koreans to physically hit or assault employees. There is a link between physical altercations, understandings of what it means to be a Korean employer, and what that means for Filipino employees who work for them. Within the factory walls, workers are not shielded by the accountability that is associated with employees interacting with comparatively rich customers, Filipino and foreign alike, and here we see how people, like Bea, understand people as particular nationalities through a labor lens.

Current Harbor Point workers I spoke with agree with this differentiation of their customers based on nationality, where Korean customers are "rude" and treat the workers "poorly." In contrast, Americans embody the reputation of the former U.S. military as an employer in seemingly mundane worker-customer interactions or in greetings among strangers and are seen as "friendly" and treating workers "good" and with "more respect" than even Filipino visitors who were "stuck up," reflecting the class-based workings of Philippine society. The same sense of goodwill toward Americans as military employers is also seen through Harbor Point mall employees' understandings of Americans as particular types of customers. Miguel, a twenty-something Harbor Point worker in sales, noted that his Korean friends weren't sociable and didn't seek his advice, like his American friends did; whereas Juanita, a fifty-something Filipino SBFZ visitor who owns a karaoke bar and formerly worked at the Subic Bay Naval Base, and whose husband is an overseas Filipino worker, doesn't have any Korean friends because she doesn't find them approachable, particularly in comparison to Americans. She attributes these differences to "mentalities" of different types of foreigners. Here, treatment by and of customers in Harbor Point work is framed through an understanding of customers' nationalities.

In a similar vein and in contrast to their relative goodwill toward Americans, Maria and Eva cannot understand Chinese and Korean businessmen, and note how these visitors ignore Filipino overtures of friendliness. Compared to their experiences with East Asians, they tell me, "it's easier to communicate then [during the operation of the base, with Americans], because most Filipinos speak both English and Tagalog. Now, very few [of us] could speak, let's say, Korean or Chinese." Maria and Eva cannot understand Koreans when they speak, who, in turn, do not understand Maria's and Eva's greetings when they pass each other on the street. Here we see how Filipinos imagine nationalities through their interactions, transactions, familiarity (in this case, of language), and relationships with foreigners.

It is also necessary to situate this Hanjin-based perception of Koreans by Filipinos in Subic that I spoke with in a broader Philippine-Korean relationship. By this I do not reduce microinteractions to state-to-state relationships nor reduce state-to-state relationships to microinteractions; rather, I show how they reinforce one another. Broadly speaking, the Philippines and South Korea have strong economic and social ties, and the Philippines is a popular and relatively cheap place for people from Asian countries to learn English.[61] Over the past several years, South Koreans have made up the largest share of tourists in the Philippines, accounting for almost one-fourth of all visitors in 2012 alone.[62]

On October 18, a South Korean national and former Hanjin executive, Jee Ick Joo, and his unnamed Filipina domestic worker were kidnapped by members of the Philippine National Police in Angeles City, Philippines. While the domestic worker was eventually freed, Jee Ick Joo was strangled to death in police custody. His kidnapping and death sparked even more international outrage at Philippine president Duterte's war on drugs, which has resulted in the judicial and extrajudicial killing of thousands of Filipinos,[63] though this time, because Joo was a South Korean businessman, Duterte called for a suspension of the police force and a slowing down of the war until the police officers who were guilty could be punished.[64]

Conversely, in South Korea, Filipinos often live in dire circumstances. South Korea continues to host U.S. military bases, and reports suggest that the U.S. military personnel there, as well as Korean businessmen, make up a large number of the clientele for Filipina women, many of whom are recruited to work in the entertainment industry.[65] In 2003, a Seoul district court ruled in favor of the Philippine embassy, which took three nightclub owners to court on behalf of eleven Filipinas; the court agreed that the women had been forced into sex work and ordered the club owners to compensate the women.[66] Filipina marriage migrants in Korea also face discrimination and domestic violence, and Filipino migrant workers writ large are often invisible to broader society vis-à-vis government rules and regulations.[67]

Dire working conditions, including but not limited to the human rights violations associated with Hanjin, are often the focus of research on SEZs.[68] Indeed, many employment conditions in global borderlands leave workers vulnerable to abuse. Yet that does not have to be the case. In the SBFZ, Hanjin is one business that exploits the vulnerable conditions for workers who are hidden from sight; however, we also know that elsewhere not all factory work that is hidden from the public violates workers' rights or has the same cultures and management strategies.[69] Furthermore, there are also service-sector businesses, like Harbor Point, that thrive on interactions between workers and consumers, Filipinos and foreigners, in the SBFZ, which influences not only perceptions of whether people embody nationalities but also how those nationalities are culturally understood.[70]

Being Filipino

Being a part of the former base and continuing its legacy are ways to assert claims to being a certain type of Filipino: one who is modern, who is global, and who is different than those other, lower-class Filipinos that live, work, and *be* outside the FZ. I've witnessed this "sense of place"[71] in action. One hot day, just a few feet away from me, a Filipina woman who was carrying trash passed by me and the garbage cans. As soon as she exited, near one of the food vendors selling snacks at the SBFZ's entrance, she threw the trash she held in her hand on the ground. She didn't stop but continued on to her destination, and I lost sight of her.

These continuing legacies of the U.S. military are something that Harbor Point mall workers echo as a reason why they sought work there in the first place. Angie, a twenty-something Filipina worker at Harbor Point whose role is customer-facing describes it as "new and *maraming* foreigners and Filipino *nanagco-come dito sa* Harbor Point because *mas maganda siya* compared to other malls, it's bigger . . . and *yung* facilities *mas maganda* [In Harbor Point, it's new and more Filipinos and foreigners come to Harbor Point because it's more beautiful than other malls, it's bigger, and their facilities are better]." This sentiment echoes those of other Filipino workers and visitors, who described Harbor Point in similar terms and the SBFZ more generally as "boutique," "*maganda*" (beautiful), "*maluwang*" (spacious), "safe," "*maayos*" (orderly), "*mas bago, mas maganda"* (newer, better), *"mas kumpleto sila"* (the complete pack-age), and "a big place and much attractive."[72]

Safety is one adjective often used to describe the SBFZ; for example, accord-ing to Arvin, a single, twenty-something Harbor Point worker in a customer-facing position, the SBMA also takes immediate action to stop crime and maintain the peace, and this is an additional benefit of working inside.[73] Other Filipino workers similarly explained why they preferred to work inside versus outside of it—because it is "more organized," "hospitable," "strict," "safer, better secured," and "civilized"; they "control the people," and it is a "good place to work" with "work [that is] more stable," and they note that the SBFZ is "spa-cious" and "clean." The underlying comparison is Olongapo City right outside the SBFZ's gate, which is presumably more cramped, dirty, less secure, and with unstable work.

These descriptions of Harbor Point, whose two stories dot the landscape of the Kalaklan drainage canal, evoke an image of the SBFZ as a regulated and controlled environment that is an overall good place to work.[74] Yet that is not the whole story. While workers do find Harbor Point a nice place to work, with relatively higher wages than outside the SBFZ in Olongapo City, Harbor Point employment—like all places—is limited, and prospective employees have to navigate the barriers put up by the red tape of the local government, in this case, the SBMA.[75]

Under the florescent lights of his store's backroom, I talked with Boy, a twenty-something manager who recently moved to Olongapo to open up a store in Harbor Point mall for the company he works for. In his white button-up shirt and silver-rimmed glasses, he tells me how excited he is for this op-portunity to build his reputation and be a part of the company's expansion. But he also laments the preemployment obstacles he faced in securing his ability to work inside the SBFZ, obstacles he hadn't encountered elsewhere: "Require-ments here are quite hard to get. They really ask for so many things. I'm work-ing here in behalf of the [head of the company]. When we opened this store, there's actually numbers of gate passes that I need to get." Comparing his previ-ous experiences, he explains, "I opened a lot of stores, but we're not that strict. All I can say is, it's OK. They'll ask you for the papers needed for processing, but it's worth it. Especially me, who's not originally from this place." He clarifies why it's worth it, when he says, "The most important for us is the security. Of course, I won't go to where I can't be at ease. So, it's OK. When it comes to the guards, they'll check your IDs. We have an ID. I have SBMA ID [that works as a gate pass], mall ID, and company ID. I need to have those three IDs in order to work. And it's also because of those why I feel very secured [inside the FZ]." In addition to these IDs, prospective Harbor Point employees must get a clearance from the National Bureau of Investigation and submit their medical records, transcripts, and a letter from their *barangay* (neighborhood) captain, the elected official who represents the *barangay* and who testifies to the candidates' "moral being," something that Kelly[76] finds is a way to exert informal control over workers since they have influence over families.[77]

Born to a housewife and a retired Philippine armed forces serviceman, Marisol is a twenty-one-year-old Harbor Point worker who is from Bataan and lives with her long-term partner. She describes the SBFZ as very secure, and like most of the people I spoke with, Marisol was referred to her Harbor Point position by a friend who worked there. Your social capital, or who you know (such as an existing employee) and how connected or well liked your family is, helps land you a job since they can navigate the process for you and recommend you for hiring.[78] For Aida, a twenty-three-year-old college graduate, not having anyone to help her navigate the bureaucracy caused delays in getting her IDs and, ultimately, starting working. Although she still lives with her parents, who are relatively well-off, since they plan to sell property they own to distribute money among their family members, even passing along her resume was difficult. She explains, "I tried to pass my resume [inside the FZ], but I don't know where it can be located. Each building has guards, so you can ask the guard on how to get to the company," which can also lead to confusion if guards each point you in a different direction. The reliance on social networks is something many workers mentioned as the main thing they disliked about the SBFZ and see as a form of corruption. This generalized form of networks as corruption permeates the SBFZ and is similar to the rest of the Philippines, where it helps to filter which workers get what jobs. Being a Filipino SBFZ worker means having the right social and cultural capital.

Similar to other types of Filipino migrants, whether internationally or domestically to large cities, many of the Filipino Harbor Point workers have family who send remittances home from abroad and commonly practice dividing their salaries, with as much as half or more allocated to their families, most commonly their mothers (if living with their family) or the head of the household (sending the remittances to the home in the province in which their family still lived).[79] We know that both of these practices are important ways in which relationships and care among families are continually reconstituted.[80] Being

Filipino means taking care of their families, and Harbor Point work provides a relatively good means to do so, even though their wages are not enough to buy food within their work.

For example, Analyn is in her early twenties and works at Harbor Point mall in a customer-facing position. She has a two-year college degree and lives with her family. She describes her mother as "just a plain housewife," and her father is a jeepney driver. Both parents are high school graduates. They live in a three-room home, with running water and a television, but with no air-conditioning (which is common), in Olongapo City. She got her job through a friend's referral and left her job at a fast food company because Harbor Point "is popular. Wherever you go, a lot of people can recognize its name." She appreciates the SBFZ's "clean environment [and that] everyone's abiding the law here, unlike in Olongapo . . . SBMA has surveillance cameras, unlike there in Olongapo, they have none. It's secured here." She also tells me, "If you're working here in Freeport Zone, you're rest assured that you'll be paid by their minimum rate. Unlike in Olongapo, they'll give you as low as one hundred fifty php per day." She works six days a week, eleven hours per day, with a one-hour break. Each day she makes P330 (or US$8.25), which is a total of P10,000 a month (US$244.00) and is the highest salary that workers mentioned.[81] Each time she gets paid, she gives half of her salary to her mother, and the rest of the money is for her allowance and personal needs, such as her daily jeepney ride to work. She packs her lunch every day because "it's cheaper that way unlike when you're going to buy it from the outside. I usually bring what my mom cooks for lunch to save money." Indeed, the average fast food meal in the mall costs upward of P79 to P99, almost one-third of her daily wage. This is in contrast to meals, including rice and drinks, offered at *palengke* stalls that range from P30 to P65. Eating out is a luxury she cannot afford.

Despite being one of the highest paid wages at Harbor Point, her salary stands in stark contrast with the kind of money that the rich Filipinos and foreigners who visit the mall have. For example, Tomas is a self-employed Filipino businessman, whom I saw nearly every day at a coffee shop inside Harbor Point. Sometimes he would read a paper and drink coffee, while at other times he conducted business meetings, treated colleagues to *merienda* (snacks), and used the coffee shop as a work space. His salary was P100,000 per month—ten times greater than Analyn's. Compared to many foreigners, Analyn's salary is also extremely low.[82] For example, self-reported U.S. military salaries range from $1,000 ($600 in cash, $400 toward bills through allotments) every two weeks to $80,000 per year, while Kevin, a foreign "sexpat" (a term used by Peace Corps volunteers to describe sex tourists) who regularly visits the Philippines and other Southeast Asian countries, claims an annual salary that ranged from $20,000 to $60,000 depending on the year, and another foreign businessman who did not want to disclose his salary said that his salary was "a range. Quite a lot."

Similar to Analyn, Ramon is a twenty-something salesperson. He lives in a room he shares with his three brothers in Olongapo City, all of whom work and send home money to their family in the province. He's been working in formal employment since he was seventeen years old, and getting his sales job at Harbor Point was difficult because of all the additional paperwork and requirements needed. Costs of living and prices are much higher in the FZ than back home, and his wage is based on the provincial—not Manila—rate. However, he still considers working inside the SBFZ as a "good opportunity" because it "has a lot of job offers and it is a civilized place." Similar to Maria, he makes P330 per day and sends half of each paycheck to his mother and brings food from home "because it's too expensive when you buy here at Harbor Point."

As we can see—and perhaps it is not surprising given their relatively low wages—household chores and bringing food to work for lunch are strategies used to reduce costs. It is part and parcel of their daily responsibilities, because they have to scrimp to save money for necessities. Otherwise, it is "wasteful," and as Layana, a twenty-year-old Harbor Point worker who lives in a one-room dwelling with her baby, her live-in partner, and her sister tells me, "Ako naman kasi, I usually play lang ng games sa laptop eh. Watch TV gano'n lang. I don't usually go out, lalo na 'yung kunwari fun na manood ng sine. Medyo gastos 'yun eh. Not now. [For me, I usually only play games on my laptop. I like watching TV. I don't usually go out, like watching movies? You'll be wasting money. Not now]." To her, spending money on bills, transportation, food, and savings for her baby are more important. Leisure activities, in comparison, are not important. Seeking better opportunities, many Harbor Point mall workers sought their employment there precisely because it offered a relatively good job with good pay, from which they can help support their families, whether living with or apart from them. Yet, even though wages at Harbor Point are higher and more stable than those in Olongapo City, wages are so low that eating at a fast food restaurant inside the mall takes up one-third of their daily pay.

Working at Harbor Point mall not only allows these employees to be a part of both a modern global *and* modern Filipino community. It also shapes how they understand being Filipino through their interactions with conational customers. For example, Juana, a twenty-year-old local Harbor Point worker and bed spacer (someone who rents a bed in a hostel) in Olongapo City, echoes a common sentiment expressed by other workers when she says: "Maybe because the foreigners sometimes have more money than Filipinos. But there are also rich Filipinos. Because foreigners here, if they see something they want, they grab it immediately. Unlike Filipinos, they have a lot of questions. The foreigners [are like,] 'I like this one!' Then they pay for it. Straight to the counter."[83]

So, too, does Arvin note this difference when he tells me, "There is a difference because Filipino customers tend to look at others and compare prices first, but foreign customers, they see something they like and want it immediately."[84] And Ramon, a twenty-six-year-old Harbor Point worker, points out that Filipino customers just want to look at items, not buy anything. What it means to *be* Filipino correlates to the act of questioning, bargaining, and making informed choices on whether to buy anything, whereas foreigners are spendthrift, buying sometimes at a whim. Filipino customers are also easier to understand, because they often speak Tagalog to the workers and there are shared norms or expectations. However, Layana tells me, "Of course, there are also nice Filipino customers. There are also Filipino customers who's a little bossy type, you know? They're sometimes rude. Filipinos are more intimidating. They'll make you feel like, 'I'm the customer, you have to be intimidated by me.'" Ramon agrees. He tells me, "The truth is there are some customers or Filipino customers, they are arrogant. Even though you have the same nationality. Some are arrogant, [though] some are very kind." Here, we see the class-based differences between upper-middle-class Filipinos who visit Harbor Point and can afford to purchase the goods within and the Harbor Point workers who, despite making relatively high wages, cannot afford to eat at a fast food restaurant inside the mall. Workers engage in class-based boundary-making and to them, to be a rich Filipino is to be a bit arrogant and rude.

Americans see Filipinos and what it means to "be Filipino" as suggesting something other than modern and cosmopolitan. For some Americans, Filipinos represented a threat to their livelihood. The 1985 BLA marked an important shift for Filipinos living in the shadow of the bases because of the benefits base employment would now provide to an increasing number of locals; however, some U.S. citizens were upset that Filipino nationals were given preferential employment. They saw this preferential employment as an affront to their own work and as based in discrimination against U.S. military personnel and their rights. For example, Anthony Rossi and three other U.S. citizens, Bumgarner, Perry, and Frierson, lived in the Philippines and worked as civilian game room managers within the Subic Bay Naval Base. On March 14, 1978, they were told that they were losing their jobs because their positions would be given to Filipino nationals per the 1968 BLA. They first filed an Equal Employment Opportunity Commission complaint to their superior officers at Subic Bay, but the complaints were rejected because none of the officers could change the BLA terms. They "were subsequently fired ahead of schedule pursuant to a Reduction in Force," after which they filed two legal claims: one regarding the retaliation they faced after they complained to superior officers and the second centering on the illegality of their positions being transitioned to Filipino workers. The latter case was heard before the United States District Court, District of Columbia, where the court had to determine *who* had *which* rights *under* what conditions.

Rossi, Bumgarner, Perry, and Frierson began legal proceedings based on two interrelated points: that their termination "constituted unlawful discrimination on the basis of citizenship, actionable under Title VII of the Civil Rights Act of 1964" and that it violated Public Law 92-129, section 106, which says: "Unless prohibited by treaty, no person shall be discriminated against by the Department of Defense . . . in any foreign country because such person is a citizen of the United States or is a dependent of a member of the Armed Forces of the United States."

Similar to its importance in the trial of Daniel Smith, who was accused and found guilty of raping Filipina Nicole, and the subsequent appeals regarding where he was detained, the central focus of the case was the meaning of the word *treaty*, which can take two forms. First, and derived from the 1969 Vienna Convention of the Law of Treaties,[85] it can mean any binding agreement between nation-states. However, the U.S. Constitution uses a second, more particular meaning when it requires two-thirds of the Senate to approve a treaty. That is, according to the U.S. Constitution, treaties are those agreements that are first subject to Senate recommendations and approval. Similar to Nicole's unsuccessful claims that the Visiting Forces Agreement should be revoked because it is unconstitutional as it was never ratified by the U.S. Senate, Rossi, Bumgarner, Perry, and Frierson argue that the BLA is not a treaty in the constitutional sense, because the Senate was never consulted "for 'advice and consent'" and thus, their termination based on their nationality, and the subsequent hiring of Filipino nationals, is illegal.

The defendants in this case are Harold Brown, the U.S. secretary of defense, and W. Graham Claytor Jr., the U.S. secretary of the navy. Their response is threefold. First, despite not having had Senate "advice and consent," and thus it not being a treaty per the U.S. Constitution, the BLA "is a valid and binding international obligation of the [United States], entered into pursuant to congressional authority, and thus is a 'treaty' within the meaning of Section 106" and refers to case law, which "have held agreements between the United States and another nation to be 'treaties' within the meaning of certain statutes, even without the Senate's advice and consent." Second, they point out that similar agreements were also in force when section 106 was passed and that there is very little legislative history regarding section 106, "and the wording so awkward, that it would be a serious mistake to conclude that Congress intended to upset numerous international agreements by a statute so hastily passed." Finally, they "stress the need for the court to employ sound principles of judicial deference when interpreting the term 'treaty' in order to avoid upsetting existing relations with foreign nations and to refrain from interfering with the executive branch's conduct of foreign affairs." This was a high-stakes matter for the U.S. military and government because of the unintended effects of the court's ruling on international relations.

In his ruling, District Judge Flannery calls the BLA not an executive agreement nor a treaty in the constitutional sense but a "Congressional-Executive Agreement," and notes that "neither Congresses nor Presidents nor courts have been troubled by these conceptual difficulties and differences. Whatever their theoretical merits, it is now widely accepted that the Congressional-Executive agreement is a complete alternative to a treaty." Detailing the legislative history and "plain language" of section 106, he says that in implementing the act, Congress was seeking to address the economic hardship of military families in overseas bases across Europe due to U.S. servicemembers' wives being unable to find work on a tourist visa, the only visa for which they could apply. Judge Flannery also acknowledged that twelve similar agreements to that of the BLA were in effect when section 106 was implemented, while an additional two were added in 1977, and agrees with the defendants that the courts should "act cautiously in an area fraught with sensitivity and affecting foreign affairs of the United States . . . [though] the impact on foreign affairs of such construction does not render the case nonjusticiable." In the end, he rules that Title VII of the 1964 Civil Rights Act is not applicable and concludes that the term *treaty* is used in the international law sense (binding agreement between nation-states) and denies Rossi, Bumgarner, Perry, and Frierson's claims.[86]

Foreigners also link the practices they witness outside the FZ to how they see Filipinos as a particular type of nationality. In a different manner, Gloria makes it a point to take her car to the SBFZ dealership for repairs because she knows they have authorized replacement parts. She told me that at a mechanic shop outside the SBFZ, she's found that Filipinos, when faced with ill-fitting or incorrect replacement parts, will physically enlarge the hole in the car to make it fit rather than order the correct parts or tell her that the correct part is out of stock. Doing so will effectively ruin her car. The SBFZ dealership, however, denotes trust. Compared to Filipino mechanics who work outside the SBFZ, those who work within it can be relied upon to do the work correctly. Yet trust is not something she unilaterally gives to anyone or all business within the SBFZ.

With two cats, Gloria's house is often covered in cat hair. She hires someone to come in, once a week, to clean the cat hair—and only the cat hair—lying around her house. The cleaner wipes down surfaces but doesn't clean or do laundry. Gloria cleans the rest of her house by herself because otherwise she feels like she has to "babysit" the Filipino cleaners to make certain they clean to her specifications and do not drop or break anything—she does not trust domestic workers to live up to her expectations of cleanliness. She compares cleaners in the Philippines with those in the United States: "Because in the U.S. I have people who come to clean the house or whatever . . . they come and clean. They're bonded. If they break anything, they fix it. They're all insured—that kind of thing. They're not the same with a Filipino worker. You're taking on a whole different responsibility and I just don't care to have to deal with that kind of thing." Although Gloria thinks that formal work within the SBFZ adheres to higher standards than those outside, Filipino cleaners whom she would theoretically employ, need supervision to ensure they meet her standards. Someone who is Filipino and privately employed needs watching over.

For William, a white, foreign SBFZ businessman married to a Filipina and with one child, working with Filipinos takes another avenue: familial connections and problems with debt. In addition to sponsoring some of their cousins' college, William and his wife employ members of his wife's family, becoming the center of financial support for the extended family. They also hire nonfamily Filipino workers; though here, what he encounters is debt. As he tells me: "People don't pay their debts. People just have lots of problems on it, and we eventually try to solve things with the Philippine legal side and that's terrible.

It's very frustrating. Even though we get all the way up to court cases, you can delay it forever by turning around and paying the right people just a little bit of money, and of course, it will get delayed." In the end, he's "not impressed with the Philippine legal side. I think my [Filipina] wife can agree as well." What we see with William is the perception that Filipinos are able to strategically use Philippine bureaucracies to avoid legal and monetary obligations by taking a person to court as a strategy of avoidance or delaying prosecution until the other person does not show up in court or gives up.[87]

In a different manner, others tell me about the corruption of the Philippine government and its Filipino officials. According to my interviewees, you are able to ship in anything you want—legal or illegal—for $450,000. For example, because of these illegal contracts (or understandings), Michelle now buys things from the Chinese who live in the Philippines rather than importing her needs because she has to pay "that" amount ($450,000) to customs for legitimate business expenses. She tells me, "The corruption . . . That's not going to be discussed. [*chuckles*]. Customs. Unfortunately, I have got to be polite about that but we have [one or more] businesses that we would have done very well developing had the customs not been corrupt." I ask, "Do you think you have problems with customs because of the type of business or because of your nationality or just because from their side?"

Replying, she says, "No, everyone. It's everyone. If you want to bring a container—you can bring a container of marijuana in here and they wouldn't give a shit as long as you pay $450,000 for the container. They don't care what it is. Now that's ridiculous. But if I want to bring something in and it's got a genuine reason, they still want $450,000." Giving an example, she says "So if I want to bring spare parts or if I want to bring hardware materials, plumbing, electrical, things like this by the container, $450,000. That's ridiculous. Totally ridiculous. Of course, that's what stops it. That's what's killing the industry and that's the same in Manila, by the way." How does she get around that since she owns businesses within the SBFZ? "We buy from the Chinese. I don't know how they get in. The Chinese run the harbor and construction business in this country as well as the rice." Being Filipino is associated with being corrupt.

For David, however, working alongside Filipinos on the naval ship and being in port in the Philippines provided both friendly and romantic opportunities. One hot and sunny Friday, David was approached by two Filipinos who had come onto the ship to work. Behind him, he heard them say, "Excuse me. Excuse me, sir." And they asked him, "Can you weld something for us real quick?" David asked, "Where is it?" He tells me that "they brought in a tool and I was like, 'Oh, shit.' They broke their tool, so I have to fix [it]. I was like, 'What kind of metal is it?' 'I don't know.'" David took the tool from their hands because "you've got to tell what kind of metal it is before you start working it. So [he] found out what metal it was and started welding it . . . just got down and everything, put it together and tested and all, it worked fine." Afterward, they thanked David and asked for one more welding favor. He responded, "I got shit to do, a lot." The two men responded, "I'm sorry if you don't have time." He tells me,

> I was like, "I'm just joking." He's like, "We need this thing upstairs . . . , welder." I was like, "Can you carry my welder?" They're like, "Yeah." I was like, "All right. Cool." Then I . . . went up to where they were working. When I got it done, he's like, "What are you going to do after work?" I was like, "I'm going to be weld-ing shit." Then they're like, "All right. If you want, you can go to this bar. I know the bar right there. You and your friends can have free drinks." Yeah. I was like, "Yeah, sure." So, we went to that bar, and I see the dude there that I welded it up for. He's like, "That's the one. Those two over there, free drinks on mine." I was like—we got smashed."

As a token of appreciation, later that night, they treated him and one of David's friends to free beers at a nearby bar. After that exchange, they "were cool" with one another.

A few days before we sat down for coffee, David proposed to his fiancée, Rose, whom he'd met while the ship was docked in Subic Bay. In spending time with his Filipino fiancée and her family, David, whose own family is ra-cially mixed, feels an affinity with Filipino people, because of similarities in supporting and caring for families—David sends $200 from every paycheck to his mother, despite her telling him that she doesn't need it, but he does "it just in case." He explains what he sees as the differences between Filipinos and Americans: "I think the Filipinos are nice, really good people. Some of them are greedy. Well, you're going to get that everywhere. It doesn't matter, even in the U.S., but I know their culture is—I like the Philippines culture more than I like American culture." He elaborates, "I see people here, they work their asses off, all their money goes to their family, and they don't even care about themselves. In America, you got people that are greedy as shit. They get all the money and they're like—because they got their own family . . . It sucks." Comparing the Philippines to "American culture, I get disgusted when I see people here that are actually struggling and they give everything they have to their families and you've got people in America that their family is struggling but they're making money . . . It sucks." Here, David sees "being Filipino" as related to caring about family and feels an affinity to the culture he encounters in port.

Variation in Labor Imaginaries

The Philippines racializes and genders its migrant workers for "export,"[88] and scholars have long documented how what I call "labor imaginaries" within factory and information sector work is shaped by gender, culture, particularized shop-floor dynamics, and history.[89] Similarly, within the SBFZ, we see how people understand nationalities, inequality, and global relations through their own experiences in working for employers of different nationalities and the rumors, imaginations, and histories of others' experiences. Here, we also see how laws, such as minimum wage, may differ or are differently enforced, as well as how these imaginaries extend beyond the SBFZ confines to influence how people imagine nationalities as a particular type of people.

Working on the former U.S. Subic Bay Naval Base necessarily depended on American-Filipino interactions; if you worked inside it, it was clear you worked for the Americans, and for those who worked there or had family members or knew friends who were employees, the former U.S. Subic Bay Naval Base offered status and economic opportunity. That doesn't mean that the fantasy of working for the base reflected reality—there were conflicts between Filipinos and Americans. For example, some Americans were angered that the base had preferential hiring for Filipinos, and after the U.S. military withdrew, many Filipinos sued to get retirement benefits that they were denied. Nevertheless, working for the base signified a chance to achieve a "good life" through the benefits received—whether higher wages, education, or the ability to purchase tax-free or foreign items inside—and shaped how they viewed Americans as a type of nationality. So, too, does work at the upscale Harbor Point mall signify a chance to achieve the "good life" because regulations regarding wages and benefits are more strictly adhered to than outside the SBFZ, though here again, the reality does not always match the fantasy of what work is like since meals inside the mall cost half a day's wage. Yet South Korean–owned Hanjin Shipping is known for violating human rights and withholding wages and is linked in people's minds to what it means to be Korean, revealing differences in regulation when work is visible or hidden from public view.

Extending Ching Kwan Lee's work, which shows how local gender politics shape the dynamics of factory work,[90] Leslie Salzinger's work on how gender is produced within shop-floor politics, emerging "through the intentions, understandings, and limitations of the actors struggling in and over a particular social space,"[91] and Steve McKay's[92] research on different working regimes of electronics factories located in four different Philippine SEZs, I show how even within the same geographic location, working conditions and meanings differ. That is, whether a business is within or outside a FZ does not tell us what their working conditions are, nor how people understand these businesses. In addition to examining particular shop-floor politics, we have to pay attention to intended and unintended consequences of structural (in)visibility to a given company's adherence to employment standards, the rights workers have, workers' relative vulnerability, and how these come together in people's imaginations.

Labor imaginaries is but one aspect of daily life that shapes how people understand one another. Imaginaries related to cosmopolitanism and modernity also take hold. They similarly guide how people interact within this space and how they consume their desires to be a part of a global world through choices of where to buy which goods and services.

Buying Inequality

6

It looks like an ocean oasis that was transported directly from a travel guide or magazine.

Tucked away at the far end of the Subic Bay Freeport Zone's (SBFZ) boardwalk along Waterfront Road, the Lighthouse Marina Resort is surrounded by palm trees and offers a beachfront to Subic Bay's clear waters and a view of the nearby mountains. Its signature, white 65.5-foot-tall lighthouse juts above the skyline and can be seen from almost eight miles away.[1] The top of the lighthouse is painted red, and pink lights shine from it at nightfall. Inside, their Mediterranean-style resort calls to mind touches of "austere Italianate architectonics"[2] because of its clean, modern lines. Outside, found among the scattered palm trees, is an adult pool, a children's pool, and a Jacuzzi, offering an alternative to the bay for swimming while you watch the waves, since the bay itself may be filled with oil from an accidental spill, too cold, or not clean enough to wade in.

This is the quintessential and cultivated image of the SBFZ: contemporary and modern, offering world-class facilities, comfort, and amenities not found elsewhere nearby. It's billed as an international and domestic destination for weddings, corporations, and tourists alike, providing sailing, hiking, spa services, nightlife, and all the comforts one desires. The SBFZ, a place where informal vendors are kept out,[3] is both marketed and marked as different from Olongapo City, and people entering and leaving the SBFZ are regulated by armed guards at its gated entrances.[4]

These images are also reflected in people's understandings of the SBFZ and its former history as a U.S. naval base. The child of two former U.S. Subic Bay Naval Base workers, Cyril grew up privileged. He stayed with a nanny while both his parents worked and would beg his mother to take him into the base with her. Now in his late twenties / early thirties and a manager at a sales company, Cyril maintains this visceral connection to the place and explained to me one afternoon, over coffee in a SBFZ café, how the legacies of the U.S. military are purposefully and formally and informally maintained in ways beyond the visual symbolism of the built environment. These legacies provide guidelines for what it means to be a part of the place and its people, as well as its past and future glory. This comes to a head particularly as he tells me his fears regarding the newly constructed Harbor Point mall and the way it threatens to change the SBFZ and the American culture that it had institutionalized: "Maybe what I generally fear is having Harbor Point [mall], [there are] a lot more people who aren't from here . . . ? Because if you're from Olongapo or Subic . . . everyone knows everyone basically if you're from here. But now, there's so many new faces. You don't know right away, who they are." He says, "First, you just think, 'Oh no, they're not from here!' So what I fear is overpopulation since there's a lot of visitors that don't know, in general, the rules and regulations here." This fear of overpopulation extends beyond the people who occupy the space; he tells me, "I fear that the discipline inside here will vanish. Because of course, some other people throw their waste or garbage in random places. But us, generally, we're not like that. We don't spit on the floor. Normally we don't do that. . . . We're not like [Filipinos, Olongapo people]." Referring to the legacies of the U.S. military, he explains that the culture within the SBFZ is different from Olongapo "because that's the culture we got from the Americans. Some people from Manila throw used bubble gum [on the ground]. I just want to maintain, hopefully, our culture [here, from] before. Which has been Americanized."

In this chapter I focus on the Filipino and foreign men and women who work in, live in, and visit the SBFZ. Contrary to social science research that emphasizes the negative consequences of special economic zones, tourism, and military bases,[5] I draw and build on research that documents how factory and information sector work are tied to global understandings of urbanity and mobility[6] to show how these men and women who are closely connected to such places also see the SBFZ as a continuation of the past and a symbol of the future, both of which provide ways to achieve and live the good life.[7] The SBFZ and the businesses and roads inside of it are not an example of what

Marc Auge[8] calls a supermodern "non-place" that is temporary and stripped from history and identities; nor are they a place that is devoid of personality, homogenous, one you'll find replicated in any country you visit. Rather, people draw on identities of these places, the things they offer, and what they choose to buy to (re)create their own statuses, dreams, and desires. For many who are included in this space,[9] the SBFZ allows for people to construct what Margaret Frye[10] calls aspirational identities or claims to a particular and present-day moralized self that is built on an idealized future. Here, living, visiting, and working in the SBFZ offers an opportunity to be a part of a modern, global community.[11]

One way to become a part of this utopia is through *consumption imaginaries*, buying into this world through everyday purchases.[12] According to Charles Taylor, imaginaries are "the ways people imagine their social existence, how they fit together with others, how things go on between them and their fellows, the expectations that are normally met, and the deeper normative notions and images that underlie these expectations."[13] I use the term *consumption imaginaries* to highlight how people tie their decisions concerning what foods they eat, what places they shop, the places they live and work, and the transportation they take to their identities and relationship to the broader world.[14] In doing so, they recreate symbolic and tangible stratification, or, in the words of Pierre Bourdieu,[15] distinction, between classes and nationalities.

Thorstein Veblen uses the term *conspicuous consumption* to describe how people purchase and partake in luxury goods and services to display their wealth and status,[16] and Bourdieu's[17] work highlights how choices around taste and consumption reflect power relations and signal differences between classes. In many ways consumption imaginaries are similar to Veblen's and Bourdieu's work as these imaginaries relate to status, wealth, identity, and the reproduction of inequality. Consumption imaginaries also highlight how inconspicuous purchases, those that are not meant to be on display to others, are not only the result of personal taste and symbolic and socioeconomic hierarchies but also one's imagination. This imagination does not necessarily have to be rooted in how you grew up or your cultural capital. It can be globally oriented, oriented toward local life, or a mix of the two. These imaginaries reflect how people see their place in their society, as well as their place in the broader world around them in the present, in an imagined future,[18] and in a remembered past.

The consumption imaginaries within and around Subic Bay do not exist in a vacuum. Instead they are shaped by power, but not a Weberian[19] definition of power, which relies on the ability to assert one's will despite resistance, nor what Joseph Nye[20] calls "hard power," based on military and economic force. This is because everyday consumption within Subic Bay, while of some concern to the SBFZ government because of the revenue it generates, matters comparatively little to either the Philippine or U.S. government, so there is no need to use economic or military force to dictate these decisions. Instead, power is exerted through ideology, preference shaping, and attraction.[21] Here, in the desires to buy branded food and goods, work and live in U.S. military-style and modern buildings, and ride in transportation that is stripped away of any Philippine traces, we see the continuing influence of fifty years of formal U.S. colonial rule in the Philippines and another twenty-six years of permanent U.S. military presence in Subic Bay. We see the desire to maintain ties to the United States, as well as attempts to reach beyond the United States and be a part of a global community.

The focus of this chapter on consumption imaginaries that see the SBFZ as some form of modern utopia is not to agree with scholars who view global borderlands as places that help strengthen domestic economies and countries' GDP; nor does it fully align with critics who highlight the illicit sex, labor violations, and inequalities, as well as what Aihwa Ong[22] calls the cultural struggles that accompany these places.[23] Indeed, the global and modern imaginations associated with the SBFZ do not always reflect reality on the ground. Corruption, crime, and intimidation also infiltrate the SBFZ and perpetuate inequality, though this time it unexpectedly benefits the Philippine government, Subic Bay Metropolitan Authority (SBMA) employees, and/or Filipinos, not foreigners.[24] These tensions are built into global borderlands' very foundation and are the reason why inequalities continue to be perpetuated on the ground.[25] People buy into inequalities precisely because the image of the SBFZ allows them to maintain a distinction[26] between who they want to be and who they are with others who aren't allowed inside its walls and who serve as the antithesis of the global community.

Buying

The grocery sections at Royal Subic or PureGold are familiar to anyone who has shopped at a large chain grocery store.[27] That is, they are filled with a sterile, air-conditioned smell. Once a week, Gloria, a foreign white woman living in the SBFZ, drives to Royal Subic for her groceries. She times her grocery runs to when it's raining and either before 5:00 P.M. or after dinner. Otherwise, it's too crowded, and she gets bombarded with questions about being an American from Filipinos and other foreigners alike. Running her errands while it's raining and before 5:00 P.M. allows her to have the physical and mental space she desires when she ventures out into the world.

Taking the cart provided by the store, she walks through orderly rows of packaged goods, prepackaged fruits, vegetables, fish, and meats, and stops at the selection of fruits and vegetables because "there haven't been a lot of people handling, that it's just safer on the food perspective." There's also meat and fish counters, offering presliced or precooked and cleaned meats and fish from behind the counters, but Gloria passes by them because she's a vegetarian.

She arrives at the pet section, eager to see if they've restocked Friskies cat food and is frustrated that they haven't. Over the years, she's built a relationship with the managers of Royal Subic, helping them understand quality of brands and stock and the benefit of purchasing items from Manila rather than importing. As she says, they used to "get a very expensive brand of something and then nobody would buy it because they had to mark it up so much and let you know. There's an equally good quality brand that's much cheaper that people will still buy, but they just didn't know. So, I did a lot of that at the beginning."

The lack of Friskies brand cat food is particularly frustrating for her because it signals the continued lack of consistency in stocking items, which she has tried to address with the managers. This seemingly small issue upsets her because the changing stock has very real health implications for her pets, and she doesn't understand why the managers won't listen to her. She tells me, "Their buyer will get a big deal on Whiskas and then they don't have that relationship and order like a certain amount and then the next time they'll get only Whiskas, no Friskies. Do you have a pet? Your pet is just going to throw up when you change cat foods. But the concept of why that's important to get a little bit of Whiskas and a little bit of Friskies each time is not there."

Yet she continues to shop at Royal Subic and PureGold Duty Free, precisely because of the availability of foreign foods and goods. Although certain foreign foods and drinks have permeated Filipino stores outside Freeport Zones (FZs), such as Coca-Cola products, which can be found at *sari-sari* stalls, *palengke* (local market) stalls, and the like, the SBFZ grocery stores have a much wider variety, and their stock can be negotiated. And while Gloria does occasionally shop at *mga palengke* (local markets) or go to stores in other cities to find the goods she desires, she often patronizes Royal Subic, Harbor Point mall, and the Freeport Exchange (for clothing) precisely because of the environment to which they belong—the SBFZ and ideals of modernity, standards, and quality, where the employees "are much nicer trained . . . [and] much more professional."[28]

One afternoon, she went to a seamstress in Olongapo City. There, the seamstress and another woman were speaking in Tagalog, gossiping that she has a "big butt for [Gloria's nationality]. Like you know, I know that's not nice. You know what I mean? And it's just that constant bombardment of those kinds of things that kind of, on the one hand, the person is very nice and friendly to me, but she sits down and talks about me in Tagalog," saying she has a big butt. The seamstress was "just being mean." She explains why these types of encounters make her shy away from non-SBFZ encounters if she can: "So, it's those things that, some of it is just the general harassment, shouting things at me or that kind of thing. There are people that are also nice, of course. But I'm not exposed to that, say, if I deal in the Freeport. That's because the employees have been trained to not be like that."

Gloria navigating Royal Subic stands in stark contrast to walking through a *palengke*, where the smells of the city envelop you. The *palengke* down the street from the SBFZ smelled of the days and nights that I associate with Olongapo City—heat, sweat, and food. One entrance to it is marked by the food stalls situated alongside the main entry at Gordon Avenue. Farther down there are other stores, for furniture, decoration, or clothes. Behind the food stalls and near another entrance alongside a smaller street are fruit stalls. The Philippine fruit rambutan are sold at one such stall; their red-pinkish color and dark spines lay out in the open air. Inside the *palengke*, aisles are small and stalls are comparatively squished together, where people and things surround anyone who enters.

Scholarship and popular perceptions of global borderlands would have us believe that places like the SBFZ replace these local markets and businesses and reproduce inequality because they siphon off funds and goods overseas.[29] According to such theories, they are "non-places"—like highways, airports, and supermarkets—that are temporary, stripped from history, and those visiting them are stripped down to anonymous identities based on their roles as consumers and transient beings.[30] Yet, as Gloria shows, people make strategic decisions about what, where, when, and why to shop and purchase goods in these places and use these decisions as a way to make claims about their own identities. These decisions and claims are also based on the SBFZ as a particular type of place—one that stands in stark contrast to Olongapo, the city surrounding it—and their own participation in this modern, global, and high-status community. They are part and parcel of the fabric of society and play a key part in the creation, maintenance, and claims to and about identities. Indeed, similar to what Mary Douglas shows in her book *Purity and Danger*,[31] within and outside the SBFZ, people, places, and things are symbolically stratified based on what is considered "dirty" or "fresh" and are used to (re)create consumption imaginaries.

Born to a nurse and an air force serviceman, Patrick was one of six children, many of whom have become scattered around the globe. A white foreigner, he's been living in the Philippines for a number of years and met his Filipina wife while he was fulfilling a contract in Subic Bay. Running their own businesses, he and his wife employ many of his in-laws, and he tells me that they "sponsor quite a lot of children in college, mostly in the family of course," though while some maintain good grades, others don't and return home to Subic. They don't shop at one particular place; rather, they strategize on where to buy clothes, skin care products, and particular foods. For example, they go to the Pure-Gold Duty Free to "buy some fruit juices and snacks for [his son] James . . . because we like some of the things that you can get in the States, cheese balls, and there are others you can't get outside in the market." Inside the PureGold at Harbor Point mall, they "get some of the other products. Some of the vegetables are quite nice because they prepare them and they look presentable. I'm one hundred percent for presentable. If it's cheaper in the market but there are things crawling all over it, I won't go there, cheap or not." For groceries, they shop at both SBFZ PureGold stores and Royal Subic precisely because the fruit and vegetables are considered fresher and of higher quality than those outside, deemed dirty because of the bugs they attract while lying out in the open air. Price doesn't matter to Patrick or his family. Perceived quality trumps all.[32] And quality cannot be found in so-called dirty foods in local markets but in the clean and sanitized sections of the SBFZ duty-free grocery sections.

But this difference in regulating foods from local markets as "dirty" and those from supermarkets as "clean" or "presentable" is not a dichotomy that only foreigners make. The son of an air force serviceman and a music teacher, Tim began vocational training after he received his high school diploma. Years later, he began his own manufacturing businesses and transferred the headquarters of one to the SBFZ because the labor costs were cheaper than those in his country of origin and the allure of a tax-free haven was enticing. Tim is a white foreigner married to a Filipina. With their two school-age children, they live in one of the SBFZ's residential communities. As he tells me, "I like the lifestyle. I like the people." Inside the FZ, it's "just normal." He elaborates, "It's safe in here. You live in the Philippines but you're not really in the Philippines. I mean, the moment you drive outside, there are no road rules. There is no distance. It's totally different." The allure of the SBFZ is that it is a familiar place to Tim, one that can be found in his home country. Although traces of the Philippines may be found, the lifestyle within its walls protects him from life outside of them.

Tim has taken his family everywhere inside—the tiger zoo Zoobic Safari, the waterpark Ocean Adventure, and Harbor Point Mall—and has found a bar where he can hang out and grab a beer with fellow compatriots, though "it's expensive to go there and it's just a really nice place. It's not a girly bar and that is not a lot of stuff there, so my wife doesn't mind me going there." He shops at the duty-free stores, particularly for Jim Beam bourbon and cigarettes, and fervently compares prices and goods across shops. He knows that the Harbor Point PureGold sells cigarettes, but the PureGold Duty Free does not. Otherwise, he goes to SM Mall, located outside the SBFZ, for general groceries "because it's cheaper than on the base"—the SBFZ continues to retain the mythic association with its former iteration as a U.S. military base. But for fish, meat, fruits, and vegetables, his wife shops at *mga palengke* because the quality is fresher, and "because if they see me, the price doubles. That comes back to that being ripped off all the time. Where I can, I'll let my wife buy" to get a fair price. Here, in addition to differentiations of goods and services based on price and perceived quality, Tim alludes to the common sentiment expressed by foreigners, of being ripped off—or charged an extra "skin tax"—precisely because they are non-Filipino.

With an aura of confidence, his wife, Sabrina, walks into his office, which is located inside his mechanics-based business in the Gateway District, as we're talking. She's matter-of-fact when she tells me that people who are "smart" shop at the local markets because they are so much cheaper and fresher: "Well, basically shopping-wise, I go to what I think is cheaper. That's how it is. I go to the night market where I can get a bulk buy. I go to the fish market." She has to "wake up at two o'clock in the morning or three o'clock in the morning to get that occasionally or that's it all the time." Additionally, she buys things in bulk and says, "If I go to buy a pig, a whole pig in a wholesale or whatever because we got a big freezer, I can afford to stock—store things in there for months and months." Tim concurs, saying only those who do not know the difference between fresh and old food—particularly fish—purchase their food at supermarkets like Royal and PureGold. There is a perceived trade-off between duty-free store foods that are clean and without flies but more expensive and of lower quality because they're "old stock" and dirty foods found in *mga palengke* that are cheaper and higher quality.

But these differentiations aren't just made by foreigners or foreigners married to Filipinas. They're also made by Filipinos who live, work, and visit the SBFZ. Juanita is an orphan. Now in her fifties, she is a small business owner of a videoke (a karaoke business that plays video with the karaoke songs) and also maintains a side business selling goods to canteens. Her husband is an overseas Filipino worker, who sends $500 in remittances a month to help her with their five children, two of whom are still in school and four of whom still live with her.

Juanita often visits Harbor Point with her friend Bea to window-shop and sometimes buy groceries. Her husband's short return to Olongapo from overseas coincided with her birthday last year, and it was a muggy August day when her husband took her to eat at the American restaurant TGI Fridays—located on the second floor of Harbor Point—as a treat. Afterward he took her to the Filipino clothing store Penshoppe, which often has Americans and other foreigners as spokesmodels, to buy her something to wear. It was a nice, relaxing day, coming to Harbor Point in order to unwind from daily life and spend time together.

Every day Juanita wakes up at 6:00 A.M. to get her two daughters ready for school. Afterward, she cleans the house and speaks with her husband over the phone. After lunch, she goes grocery shopping and runs errands before cooking dinner at 6:00 P.M. After dinner, she leaves to go to work, staying at her videoke until 1:00 A.M. She comes home to sleep before waking up at 6:00 A.M. to start the next day. Thus, every other time she visits Harbor Point, whether with or without her husband, it's for the same reason—to unwind from her busy life as a mother, caretaker, and businesswoman. It also "has a thrill of enjoying the view while shopping. They have a lot of places to go and see, there are choices."

Although Juanita relishes her free time at Harbor Point, she buys her groceries at the *mga palengke* because they're cheaper and fresher than the SBFZ grocery store, where food is often frozen. She also laments how far away Royal Subic is, since "it's too far when you don't have your own car. And I don't have a lot of free time. That's one of the problem." Yet what she does buy inside the

SBFZ are clothes and specialty goods. At Harbor Point, if she sees something she likes—and has the money for—she'll buy it, since "clothes that are locally made, especially cheap ones, don't last long. I tried to buy something that costs P100 [$2.50], it didn't last even a week. Unlike those who have prices like P400 [$10] and higher. . . . It has a long durability. . . . Branded goods are different. Their durability is really something." Still, she waits for sales to make it more affordable for her family. She also gets excited when she has the time and money to buy chocolate from Royal Subic because "some chocolates outside are fake. But you can be rest assured if it's from Royal. . . . You know which is genuine." Here we see how Juanita and others like her make shopping decisions. Duty-free stores are for imported, specialty goods. Branded clothes denote quality. Geography and convenience are also important factors to take into consideration when planning where to shop and what to buy, since *mga palengke* are closer to home.

Tomas followed in the footsteps of his father when he graduated college with a bachelor's degree, though his mother was only a high school graduate. In his sixties, Tomas is a successful businessman who works closely with local government officials. To Tomas, geography and class mark the boundaries between SBFZ's Harbor Point mall and Olongapo's SM mall. Sitting in a café, talking over coffee, he tells me, "I think because of the proximity, the shoppers here inside [Harbor Point] are . . . richer. They have more money. Because some of these people are from Binictican [a residential community within the SBFZ; many of the residents are retirees]." The proximity of the two malls are miniscule; they are only a few feet away from each other, just across the Kalaklan drainage canal. However, armed guards police the SBFZ's gated entrance. They exclude the poor and determine who is allowed to enter the SBFZ. Here, we see again the perception of Harbor Point and SM as categorically different and is related to a perceived sense of both social and geographic distance.

Married and with three children, Tomas comes to Harbor Point's coffee shops every day to work and meet with clients because it is within walking distance of where he lives and because he thinks that "as a consumer, I am influenced subconsciously by the brand [of Starbucks]." The SBFZ is orderly, and that is one of the "clear differences inside the Freeport": "the practice just continued from an orderly military base to an economic zone." Although he originally states that he shops at whatever store is closer to him at the time, when pressed, Tomas admits that although he thinks that *mga palengke* are "dirtier" and "cheaper," they also have higher quality—that is, fresher—fruits and vegetables than Royal or PureGold, so he buys those goods there. "It's something that has been established over time, like grapes costs more in the mall than in the local market. So I buy at the local market. Fruits are better and less expensive in the local market. Like pineapples. You can get good pineapples in the local market but not in the malls." However, Tomas also frets about how Harbor Point and the duty-free stores negatively impact the *mga palengke* and their workers. He is consciously aware of the social implications of shopping and maintains strategies on when to purchase what goods where. Although Tomas voices concerns about the displacement of *mga palengke*, my interviews suggest that the SBFZ stores supplement rather than displace their role in the market since shoppers differentiate what goods they purchase at each store, with duty-free stores having a specialty niche of imported goods.

Buying food is constitutive of social life. The political economy and cultures of food involve power and inequality between nation-states and the reimagining of nation-states and are also central to the construction of moral and cultural markets, sociocultural identities, the reproduction of inequality through taste and symbolism, and what Michaela DeSoucey calls "gastropolitics."[33] We also know that "feeding work"—the "planning, shopping, preparation and management of meals"[34]—is a key component of constructing families.[35] As we've seen, it's also central in constructing consumption imaginaries—the world around you and where and for whom the modern, longed-for utopias are available.

The daughter of a beautician without a high school diploma and a now retired former SBMA contractor who graduated elementary school, Rosa grew up to become a schoolteacher, valuing education and cultivating a love of knowledge in the next generation. In her thirties, Rosa is married, with three children. While she can't afford to buy anything at Harbor Point, she likes visiting it to window-shop or occasionally eat at a fast food restaurant inside. She tells me, "SM is for everyone. It has a lot more visitors. While at Harbor Point, visitors there don't usually shop. At SM, you can see shoppers in every corners. Unlike at Harbor Point, because the location is more spacious, there are portions that you can see empty." She elaborates, "There's a big difference in terms of the place. Like I said earlier, their amenities and facilities are all new. It's a chance for us to experience new things like those. They have censored doors for entrance and exit." She adds, "At the same time, it's cooler, it's relaxing, less snatching incidents because there are a lot of guards. Harbor Point has plants that is good to see. Unlike on the outside where the buildings are really tight . . . it is much safer here inside Freeport Zone. The security here is more rigid than on the outside. Which is true. But as what the saying goes, the safeness is in our own hands."

Harbor Point is the better, newer, and higher-quality mall, where you can find boutique-like shops, as well as facilities and amenities that are similar to what you find in malls in foreign countries. Even the "quality of the products at Harbor Point is different from what we can see outside. Their product quality is much better. So it's better to choose expensive things. The amenities are better." It follows a more international, cosmopolitan, or U.S. cultural model of consumption.[36] Shopping and visiting Harbor Point is not just about what you can buy but also the experience you get while being physically there—the ability to partake in modernity and a globally themed good life—and the perceived safety that comes with armed guards at its entrance.

Although she prefers Harbor Point, she is also critical of the role it and the SBFZ in general play in the broader Philippine context. She elaborates, "But on the contrary, it affects the other entrepreneurs, like local malls outside Freeport Zone. Local entrepreneurs don't gain such profits because of it. We also know that Filipinos have colonial mentality." What is this colonial mentality? According to her, it's when "they look for branded things. Like signature clothes, signature shoes, bags. They even save money for it instead of being practical that there are also native products, which is better for me, that is cheaper but has a long durability. If someone asked you, where did you bought something like that, some are shy to say that it was only from a market. There are misconception for the consumers." Rosa explicitly links consumption practices to a Filipino imagination, its roots in U.S. colonialism, and its continual influence on everyday life.

The language used by Filipino SBFZ visitors also shows how SM exemplifies the opposite of Harbor Point. It is the mall that is geared more for lower- or middle-class Filipinos and is "*maliit*" (smaller) and "[more] crowded." Growing up, Anthony was one of ten children born to his mother, a market vendor who couldn't read or write, and his father, who despite only finishing fourth grade was able to work inside the former U.S. Subic Bay Naval Base. Anthony dropped out of the University of the Philippines after three semesters because his father died and he had to help support the twelve members of his family. Following in his father's footsteps, he then began working as an administrative officer at the former U.S. Subic Bay Naval Base and did so for thirty-seven years. Now in his eighties, he runs a senior citizen program that meets in the Harbor Point mall every week.

When I ask him about the differences between SM and Harbor Point, or why his group meets at one over the other, he tells me, "Right now, I cannot say because [Harbor Point is] new. SM was built long time ago. I can say now that [Harbor Point's] beautiful there because it's near their places. They just have to walk there. They have the scenery. While SM is very crowded. It's a small place." In contrast, he says, "Here, it's a big place and much attractive. [I like that] they have programs here. In SM they don't have that kind of place because it's only small. That's why Harbor Point hold[s] programs like [for senior citizens] every first Monday from 1:00 P.M. to 5:00 P.M. here." How people distinguish the two malls from one another—whether factually correct or not since Harbor Point and SM opened within months of each another—extends to the characterizations of the customers each attracts and how these decisions and their accompanying status are embodied. For example, Harbor Point is seen as a place for rich Filipinos and foreigners. Daniel, a forty-something local schoolteacher who also likes to window-shop at Harbor Point, differentiates each mall's customers based on clothes when he tells me, "The visitors at Harbor Point usually wears signature clothes, miniskirts for the girls. Unlike on the outside, they usually wear simple clothes. Harbor Point is on a higher class." In contrast, SM is seen as attracting local Filipinos from lower socioeconomic classes, who wear "simple" clothes. The class and status that come along with who shops where is embodied through clothing choices and presentation of self.[37]

How people talk about the malls contributes to social stratification by differentiating what Marco Garrido calls the "sense of place"—where "certain types of places (enclaves or slums) or the people associated with those places elicit certain introspective states (mental states, including affect and motivation), which, in turn, predispose certain segregating practices."[38] Shopping at one mall or the other helps them embody the cultural models the malls signify. Here, we also see that people can be *both* critical of the impact the SBFZ and Harbor Point has in perpetuating Philippine inequalities and see them as status symbols and chances to become a part of modernity. In doing so, Filipinos differentiate which mall they shop at, why, and what that means about themselves, others, the places people frequent, and how these relate to status and identities, though these meanings may not be internally congruent. These two malls signify how the interaction among place, the built environment, history, and meanings (re)constitute sociocultural and spatial boundaries and in doing so make up part of people's consumption imaginaries, both locally and globally oriented ones.

Research has shown how shopping malls have led to an increasingly privatized public life, where private owners deliberately keep out unwanted populations through their location, policing, marketing strategies, and/or built environment, despite malls functioning as the "new" town spaces.[39] Yet we know that people also use and understand malls in varied ways, including resisting their rules and regulations and using them for activities other than shopping.[40] For example, Joel Stillerman and Rodrigo Salcedo's[41] work on Chilean malls show us that the borders separating malls from so-called unwanted populations can be porous, while Erez Aharon Marantz, Alexandra Kalev, and Noah Lewin-Epstein[42] show us how "globally themed" malls provide new labor markets and can help dissolve ethnogender boundaries between Israeli-Palestinian women and Jewish mall employers. Manila is known colloquially as a city of malls because there is a mall on almost every metro rail stop. Some of these malls cater to the rich, while others cater to the middle class; both sets are said to "have become the new parks"—places where people congregate and spend time. However, they also continue to exclude the relatively poor.[43] The malls in and around Subic Bay are no exception to reproducing and reflecting these sociocultural inequalities among places on the ground.

Staying

In addition to the idealized understanding of Harbor Point as a modern, global center of commerce, the built environment of other SBFZ buildings evokes this same imagery of modernity, power, and links to a global community. The Harbor Point mall is located in the SBFZ's Central Business District. Walking straight past the mall, up Aguinaldo Street, you'll begin to see the SBMA's government buildings. Maintaining their original facades of their former lives as U.S. military buildings, these buildings are long and stark white,[44] with green-reflecting windows and columns that divide the building every few feet. They are barrack-style and stand juxtaposed with the palm trees that surround them. These buildings continue to call to mind and evoke the U.S. military and what it stands for: modernity, U.S. power, and a U.S. lifestyle.

Yet, the first time I visited the SBMA main office building, located on Waterfront Road, to see the chairman, Roberto Garcia, and obtain his permission to interview government officials, I was struck by the indoor amenities. Unlike the bathrooms I found in upscale stores and malls, like the Starbucks at Harbor Point, which are geared toward rich Filipinos and foreigners, here, inside the

SBMA headquarters, the toilets were like those found elsewhere in the Philippines: with no toilet lid, since the norm is to squat, and no toilet paper, as you are expected to bring your own.

Like the SBMA offices, many of the homes in the SBFZ residential communities reflect this same U.S. military history and style. Indeed, more than 1,800 housing units were left behind by the U.S. military, and these were converted into three long-term residential communities for foreigners and rich Filipinos alike: Cubi, which is located near the Port District; Kalayaan, located past the Subic Bay Gateway Park and to the north; and Binictican, inland and in between the port district and the Central Business District.[45] These neighborhoods are ruled by guidelines that prohibit residents from changing the facades of their homes because the SBMA wants "to preserve the architectural features," which are military in nature.[46] These guidelines rule over residential communities and government buildings not only to avoid costs and maintain architectural integrity and infrastructure for utilities but also to strategically and symbolically link the SBFZ to the United States and distance it from Olongapo. These buildings signal the availability of up-to-date facilities and provides modernity and international imaginaries, while also serving as a tax-free haven for business. So, too, do regulations over practices, like trash removal, and prohibitions, such as antilittering,[47] evoke similar sentiments of modernity.[48]

John was born to a military family; his father served, while his mother took care of the children and the household. He went on to receive a business degree and works in banking. A perpetual foreigner as a white man, John has lived in Asia for many years. Currently he also lives and runs his own business inside the SBFZ, precisely because of the amenities and lifestyle found within. However, soon after moving into his neighborhood, he discovered that the rules separating the SBFZ from Olongapo are not always enforced. He describes a "major conflict" he had with an SBMA department manager after he reported his neighbors for not following the housing rules in their residential community. He tells me, "It got totally out of control, totally, and we're talking death threats and everything just because I was putting pressure on them to enforce the housing rules, which are fourteen pages long, and still nothing being done. It got real ugly and . . . my tires were slashed, my car was keyed." I ask, "And the community is gated, with security, but they didn't do anything?" He responds, "Yeah. It's really kind of silly; they check everybody walking in but don't check anybody in and out with cars. . . . You call that gated? Yeah, it got really ugly. How it was resolved? He moved, but in the meantime, I had to have police protection every day. . . . It's just so ridiculous." Elaborating, he says, "Yeah. Some people—I'm not saying Filipinos—just don't know when to quit. All I'm trying to do is my job. You have rules, enforce them. Anyway, he took it personally. Finally, he moved. That was like of couple of years from now."

SBFZ regulations also symbolize modernity for those who stay within its gates. The daughter of a social worker and a retired businessman, Gloria is an educated, wealthy white foreigner who does business overseas but lives inside the SBFZ with her husband. One of the reasons she lives within the SBFZ is the practices, or lack thereof, that differentiate it from Olongapo City, just outside its gates. She marks these boundaries by describing to me how every time she leaves the SBFZ, she's inundated with the sights and smells she'd rather not be subjected to. "It's hard to see my husband fish a bunch of dead—or bunch of kittens live out of the garbage can. I've to see yet a day where there's not some-one urinating in public or an animal being abused outside of the Freeport."

Cyril, the aforementioned child of former U.S. base workers, told me about how everyone is held accountable to the same degree inside the SBFZ. Re-counting a story about Amelita "Ming" Jara Martinez-Ramos, the wife of then-president Fidel Ramos, he says, "What I mean is, if you have to pay a hundred dollars for not wearing your seatbelt, you really need to pay for it. You ever heard her story? The wife of the former president of the Philippines was here. She didn't stop at the stop signs. So, she was stopped by the police. She said, 'I'm Mrs. Ramos. I'm the wife of the president.'" He says the police "responded, 'We don't care. You have to follow the rules here.' Right? Of all the people, you're the wife, you should know that you should follow. So they gave her a citation. And then you know what? The guy who gave it received an award from the president. Really!"

To Cyril and others, this encounter is mythologized, signifying the meritoc-racy and equality of the rule of law that can be found within the SBFZ, which implicitly contrasts with the nepotism and cronyism that are seen as ruling the rest of the land. Yet, if this story is true and the First Lady was ticketed, it likely had to do with a renowned feud between friends-turned-enemies Richard "Dick" Gordon and Fidel Ramos, at the time the SBFZ chairman and Philip-pine president respectively. Still, the image of the First Lady being ticketed, just like everyone else, is powerful. It helps Cyril imagine the SBFZ as the center of democracy and modernity.

Mary is a white foreign woman who has worked within the SBFZ from its inception. Moving to Subic Bay was exciting for her because it meant she could be a part of a social movement: the transformation from a foreign-run military base to a domestic-run FZ. Change, anticipation, and the feeling of being a part of something bigger than oneself was in the air because "in those days, going back to the early days, it was all brand new and it was keen and there were a lot of pep rallies and everybody was excited." The possibilities of an imagined future prompted her move and the nostalgia for the past serves as a comparison for the present.

Of course, up close and over time, the modern facade of the SBFZ crumbles. Seeing a decline in the modern utopia that the SBFZ was supposed to be, she says, "There isn't that same sort of community—I'll call it camaraderie—that there used to be." Linking this decline to changing priorities of subsequent SBMA administrators, their lack of care in maintaining a community here, and the influx of more people, she describes how the "[SBMA police] don't enforce [laws] anyway so it doesn't matter. Sorry. I know I sound really negative but it's just—where you get a bigger influx of people of course there's more crime, if you will, mostly petty crime but copper theft is a huge problem here." She explains, "Anything that's got copper in it, street lights, sometimes two kilometers of street lights will not be working, we find out because they're stealing the wires constantly, which is a shame." Elaborating, she describes how police officers are civil servants who don't care about maintaining the rules. Instead, they sleep, play Angry Birds, and will watch as people cut cable cords to steal wires. Furthermore, the fence surrounding the SBFZ is ill maintained, cut, with wide openings that allow people to walk through. Indeed, corroborating what Mary describes, news reports capture photos on September 27, 2013, that depict two SBMA police officers in uniform watching two young men, in flip-flops and white T-shirts, as they "burn[ed] plastic covers off wires and cables allegedly stolen from the unoccupied SBMA-owned building of the former Legenda Hotel, only several hundred meters away."[49] The officers did nothing to stop them and let the men continue on and take home their loot. The present doesn't live up to memories of a remembered past of safety and community.

For those staying in the SBFZ, whether to live, work, or visit the cosmopolitan images evoked by the built environment and associated practices differentiate it from Olongapo City and play a key role in fostering the SBFZ's image of modernity. Yet these images are not always reflective of how the SBFZ works on the ground, and there are differences based on audience (foreign or Filipino) and between rules on the books and their regulation in everyday life.

Getting Around

One of the most visible markers differentiating the SBFZ and Olongapo City involves transportation. After leaving the Harbor Point mall and walking up Aguinaldo, you'll walk past Julie's Bakeshop and then a Mini Stop convenience store, which mark the first two stores of a small strip mall. Across the street is another small strip mall in the blue and green painted building of the now de-funct Times Square Cinemas. Here, there are smaller stores, selling minutes for your phone, lottery, and the like. Another is a small, cafeteria-like restaurant, and the aromas of adobo, rice, and fish waft through the air, while another sells clothing and shoes. The sidewalk ends in a concrete parking lot.

In this lot, you'll find small white shuttles lined up, side by side. They ful-fill the same function as the jeepneys in Olongapo City and elsewhere in the Philippines, carrying passengers to and fro. However, they are devoid of what often characterizes a Philippine jeepney: their color and personality. In places like Manila, you'll find jeepneys decorated to the nines, painted as though they were murals and reflecting the personalities and resources of their drivers. However, in Olongapo City each jeepney is painted a solid color—whether red, orange, blue, or another color signifying one of Olongapo's eleven routes, each color denoting its prescribed paths and each driver wearing a prescribed uni-form, both legacies of the U.S. military.[50] Yet neither the displayed personalities of jeepneys in Manila nor the color-coded model of Olongapo are found inside the SBFZ, whose shuttles stand in stark contrast in their white paint.[51]

The SBFZ shuttles line up at this concrete parking lot terminal, each with their own driver, and you climb into the back and wait, sitting thigh to thigh in the heat and in their often plastic-covered bench seats, until the vehicle is at capacity to begin your journey. However, these jeepneys won't take you every-where in the SBFZ, only along certain routes. They won't take you to Zoobic Safari, the tiger zoo at the far end of the SBFZ; nor will they take you to Ocean Adventure, a waterpark. There are buses that will transport people to duty-free stores. The blue-and-white bus, with "Royal Subic" painted on the side, will only take you to and from its namesake, one of the SBFZ duty-free stores fifteen minutes away from this terminal. I hop on this bus weekly, hoping to catch it after it's sat in the terminal for a while, so I don't have to sit and wait for it to fill.

Yet these shuttles are not the only transportation that is regulated. Rachel is a white foreign businesswoman who moved her business overseas precisely because manufacturing was so much cheaper in the SBFZ than in her home country. Yet, upon arrival and in setting up her business and her life there, she encountered the differences between the imagined tax-free haven and the reality of navigating the SBMA bureaucracy—and its seemingly changing rules and the enforcement of said rules. Rachel secured approval to import a personal motorcycle, tax-free, per SBMA rules.

Yet, she describes how, when it arrived, she and her lawyer went back and forth with SBMA lawyers because they did not allow "secondhand" imports, which was how they classified her motorcycle. She says it was the worst experience she's faced: "We had our container of the machinery and it was about $170,000 worth of machinery and we were approved locater, OK, we had the form. On the form, it says that I can bring all my personal stuff, tax- and duty-free, no problem. I send my motorcycle from [foreign country], a Honda XR 350." She imported her motorcycle "because we didn't want to buy another vehicle. I thought I would just use that, on the base [SBFZ is commonly referred to as "the base" by foreigners and Filipinos alike], you know to go to and from work and that sort of stuff. They held up mine and the entire container for two weeks."

According to Rachel, when she and her lawyer asked government workers why it was held up, "they said, 'You can't bring this motor because it's a secondhand vehicle.' I said, 'But that's not in any of the documentation, it's not in the book.' 'Oh, we changed the rule.' Even my accountant, who set up the whole thing said, 'It's not in the rule book. We have the rule book. Show me in the rule book where it says she can't bring her motorcycle. It's in her name. It's registered in her name in [name of foreign country]. And owns it,' you know." SBMA officials replied, "'Now we've changed the rule. You're not allowed to bring secondhand vehicles in because there are too many secondhand vehicles coming in.' . . . So anyway, we have this huge argument and in the end, I had to sign an affidavit to say that I would re-export the motorcycle back to [name of foreign country] whenever I could."

The SBFZ handbook is part of the contract that Rachel agreed to when she moved her business there, which detailed the privileges afforded SBFZ investors. Both she and her accountant consulted it as she began to set up her life there. Yet, the initial rules and her understandings of them changed without notice. Despite filing what they saw as the appropriate paperwork, she was subject to the changing legal whims of the SBMA and was no longer allowed to import her motorcycle, which she planned to use to travel around.

The cultivated utopian image also relies on the tax-free incentives offered to businesses in order to attract them to Subic Bay's shores. One additional SBFZ incentive revolves around what's known as "blue plate" cars: tax-exempt luxury vehicles that are permitted to be used around the SBFZ. If they are taken out, they must be returned to the SBFZ after fifteen days.[52] In practice, these luxury cars are often smuggled out of the SBFZ and not returned. In 2010, a task force called Oplan Subic Blue Plates was created to seize an estimated 184 of these cars to bring them back to the SBFZ and collect the accompanying export taxes.[53] Yet the SBFZ is not a foreign playground where everyone can partake in these luxury goods. The SBMA can decide *who* gets privileges, *where* privileges can be enjoyed, and *when* people can take advantage of these privileges, the essence of this modern utopia.

On May 6, 2008, a used 2002 Jaguar that the company Westwood Unlimited Trading Corporation (Westwood) imported "under a blue plate" arrived in the SBFZ docks early. Nine days later, "SBMA granted Westwood an admission authority . . . with notation that it will issue a release clearance upon presentation of the bill of lading, certificate of ownership/sales invoice, and packing list of the subsequent importation of vehicles." The next day, "Westwood requested for the temporary warehousing of the motor vehicle, but SBMA refused because of its hold order policy disallowing imported used cars for blue plating."[54]

Westwood took the SBMA to the regional trial court in Olongapo, seeking to find out if they could import it as a blue plate car. While awaiting judgment, Westwood was charged P849 per day in fees to the SBMA and P820 per day to American President Lines, which shipped the car. In their petition, Westwood claimed "SBMA violated its right as an accredited investor" and asked the court to stop the imposed daily fees and release their car. The regional trial court agreed and ruled that the SBFZ investors had certain rights, and because they followed proper procedure by gaining permission from the SBMA to import the car, Westwood's rights would be violated by the accumulation of daily fees. SBMA filed a motion for reconsideration, which was denied. After that, they filed a petition with the court of appeals to review the decision. The court of appeals granted SBMA's petition. In doing so, Judge Mario V. Lopez[55] ruled that "Westwood's rights as an accredited investor under its certificate of registration are not absolute and unconditional as to constitute *rights in esse* [an essential right] or those clearly enforceable as a matter of law. In fact, the certificate granting Westwood a permit to operate business in the freeport zone is in the nature of a license." He clarifies in the ruling that this certificate "does not confer an unquestioned legal right and is subject to such conditions as the SBMA sees fit to impose, including its revocation at pleasure. In the same vein, the admission authority issued in favor of Westwood to import the subject motor vehicle does not amount to a *right in esse* but is only a mere privilege."

Judge Lopez found that the SBMA gave Westwood conditions by which the vehicle could be released but Westwood did not adhere or attempt to adhere to them. Furthermore, while the SBMA stated that Westwood could import the car blue plate, the court found that doing so did not take away SBMA's authority to go through the processing and registering of imports. In the course of doing so, SBMA found that the car did not adhere to the policy that prohibited used cars to be used for blue plates, and they were within their right to refuse a permit. Judge Lopez ruled that Westwood had *no essential right* to import the car. Neither were the accumulating fees "grave and irreparable as understood in law" because the fees were, by definition, quantifiable. Therefore, the previous court, which granted a writ of injunction to stop the daily fees, was mistaken, and Judge Lopez annulled and set aside the previous ruling.[56]

In this case, the main issue revolved around investor rights and whether they were conditional or absolute. Judge Lopez, in his finding, disentangles *rights* from *privileges*, where the former is a guarantee while the latter is something that can be given and taken away at the discretion of someone else. SBFZ businesses are not entitled to rights but are granted particular privileges at SBMA's discretion. Despite being a lure used to attract foreign business, consumption privileges like being able to import luxury cars, which are linked to imaginaries surrounding the SBFZ, can be taken away and are not guaranteed.

Consuming Global Borderlands

This chapter focuses on consumption imaginaries: how decisions concerning what to buy, where to live, and how to travel are constitutive of identity and status and help signify the type of life one wants to live. These consumption imaginaries are central to the persistence of global borderlands around the world. In Subic Bay, the imaginaries of people who frequent the SBFZ center on being a part of a modern, global community and the lasting ideological power of the United States.

The image of being able to participate in the global cosmopolitan world through consumption is visible through how people differentiate between what foods are "dirty" or "clean," "cheap" or "expensive," and is also cultivated through the SBFZ's built environment and practices that differentiate it from

Olongapo. So, too, is the image of a modern life promoted through the public transportation offered, which is stripped of any Filipino characteristics and the personalization that jeepneys often embody outside the FZ's walls. Promises of luxury also attract businesses and people, though these promises, like being able to import personal motorcycles or luxury cars tax-free, may fall through. Like the availability of food and the built environment, the reality of transportation does not always match up to expectations and the SBFZ's cultivated and idealized symbol as a modern utopia. Yet the opportunities the SBFZ symbolizes leave a lasting impression on those who enter its walls.

Conclusion

The 2016 Philippine presidential election saw the rise of Rodrigo Duterte, a former mayor of Davao City in Mindanao and an outspoken critic of the United States. A few months after his election, in November 2016, it was announced that U.S. and Philippine joint exercises would be reduced, and Duterte called off the purchase of U.S. rifles just as the United States was debating whether to pull the sale because of mass extrajudicial and judicial killings that have occurred during his administration.[1] These killings are part of Duterte's war on drugs, where low-level drug dealers and users have been targeted, though children as young as five years old, like Danica May, have been killed as part of the war's "collateral damage."[2]

In public speeches and in the press, Duterte has denounced the United States and its military and has threatened to reduce or eliminate its role in Philippine society. The Board of Millennium Challenge Corporation, a U.S. government foreign aid organization, said in December 2016 that it deferred a vote to reselect the Philippines for a $430 million aid grant because of concerns around the killings. In response, Duterte threatened the 2014 Enhanced Defense Cooperation Agreement with the United States, which allows the U.S. military to have a quasi-permanent presence in the Philippines through "agreed locations," saying, "I understand that we have been stricken out of the Millennium Challenge. Well, good, I welcome it. We can survive without American money. . . . But you know, America, you might also be put on notice. Prepare to leave the Philippines, prepare for the eventual repeal or abrogation of the Visiting Forces

Agreement." Elaborating, he declared, "You know, tit for tat . . . if you can do this, so (can) we. It ain't a one-way traffic. Bye-bye America."[3]

Duterte is not the only player on the international stage who has been elected to a high office because of his ethnonational populist stance. On January 23, 2017, as one of his first acts as U.S. president, Donald Trump signed the death certificate of the Trans-Pacific Partnership, a free trade agreement among twelve countries across the Pacific Ocean, by withdrawing from the deal, though many countries in East and Southeast Asia have signed a similar, alternative agreement. Trump often scoffs at U.S. trade agreements, declaring them as bad deals for the American public, and has villainized and dehumanized immigrants, their families, and people of color more generally, calling for a not-too-subtle return to pre–civil rights rhetoric and laws in the United States based on racist sentiments. In addition, the United Kingdom voted in 2017 to leave the European Union, a socioeconomic political agreement among European countries to promote trade between signatories. Does the rise of populist leaders around the world, a more general move toward more protectionist policies, and the return of racist and nativist sentiments toward immigrants and their families signal the beginning of a deglobalizing world and the end of global borderlands as we know them?

No. The politics we're currently seeing echo those of the recent past. They are not new.[4] What we see, however, is that global borderlands are increasingly the critical places where international tensions arise. They are simultaneously places that evoke a sense of a global modernity for those who enter into their walls and are the symbols of foreign powers' penetration into domestic societies. As such, they are the battlegrounds of international politics. It's not surprising that populist or ethnonationalist movements attack these spaces, even as the U.S. Republican Party has traditionally been the party advocating for free-market policies. Nor is it surprising that liberal democrats in the United States who were once among the harshest critics of neoliberalism and free trade for institutionalizing inequality have now embraced the ideals of global integration. While the positions of the players have shifted, the stakes at hand—power, sovereignty, and how people understand the relationship between the foreign and the domestic—remain unchanged.

Although U.S. and European Union politics often dominate world news and the attention of scholars and pundits alike, the battlegrounds of global borderlands are not limited to those countries traditionally counted as "the West," as we see with Philippine president Duterte. Indeed, the interwoven fantasies, violence, and local understandings of foreign people, places, goods, and services are likely even more sharply divided when global borderlands are located in African, Asian, Middle Eastern, and Latin American countries. Within these lands the socioeconomic and political stakes at hand are heightened due to their colonial histories and their lower and sometimes more precarious places in the hierarchy of global politics. What may change, however, is who the central powers in any given global borderland are. China, for example, is pursuing foreign direct investment throughout the world, most notably in African countries though also in other postcolonial states, and is responding to local demands around labor conditions with flexibility.[5] In doing so, they are challenging the United States and vying to be the next global superpower, with allies around the world to support their desired geopolitical position on the global stage.

Recent international politics show how the study of global borderlands has not become obsolete. Instead, it highlights how global borderlands are a central object of study for the twenty-first century, precisely because they are the landscapes in which these tensions play out.

Methodological Appendix

I grew up feeling like I was always the odd person out. Raised by my grandmother, I grew up alongside my aunts and uncles, who were only a few years older than me. Much of the time we lived with her white boyfriend and his two children, who visited on the weekends. Sometimes friends, other family members, and significant others lived with us as well. We also moved all the time, renting houses and apartments. Sometimes we moved because we were evicted; other times I didn't know the reason why. All this time, I never felt like I belonged. I wasn't my grandmother's child; the people with whom I was raised weren't my sisters and brothers. When I visited my mother or my half siblings, I continued to feel as though I did not belong. My mother was only fifteen when she had me, and we had a tumultuous relationship. She didn't raise me, nor did I have the same father as my siblings. I never felt as connected to them as they seemed to be to each other. I don't know my maternal grandfather, and my attempts to trace him from the little information I possess have been unfruitful. I do not have a father.

My identities are always in flux, never belonging—always an outsider looking in, trying to find a place but never really succeeding. This is true for my family experience as well as my experience within the broader social world. Although I did not grow up in a multiethnic neighborhood like his participants, Anthony C. Ocampo's findings on Filipino American identity as situational, racially ambiguous, and with varying affinities to panethnic Asian/Asian American and Latino/a groups[1] echoes much of my own racial identity and experiences since I was a young child. However, being a disconnected observer in my own life taught me to see the hierarchies and the "rules of the game" for different social groups, as growing up I went through several. All of this is likely why my grandmother's story, of her migration to the United States through marriage to a U.S. serviceman and nostalgia for the former U.S. Subic Bay Naval Base, sparked my sociological imagination. It began as a puzzle I was trying to unravel in this book regarding how and why there are so many competing understandings of overseas military bases. Everything I was reading in my college courses only discussed the negative consequences—of the sex work, the exploitation, and the United States' undue power. Stories like my grandmother's weren't showcased. They remained hidden, untold. My own experience of being an "outsider within" primed me to think about stories that went untold. It also taught me how social groups have their own rules and their own codes because figuring out how to get "in" or groups' internal hierarchies required knowing what to say and what not to say. I was trained not to see people as cartoonish villains in the story of Subic Bay and to instead approach everyone in a way where I sought to understand their humanity.[2] Admittedly, this was difficult at times. Ultimately, however, using this approach allowed me to more holistically understand how and why social life within and around Subic Bay operates the way it does. During the course of my fieldwork and in the writing of this book, I began seeing how I could apply my personal insights to my academic research: by developing and using what I call the ethnographic tool kit.[3]

The Ethnographic Tool Kit

Ann Swidler describes how culture is a tool kit that consists of the "symbols, stories, rituals and world-views, which people use in varying configurations to solve different kinds of problems" and from which people configure their "strategies of action," the "persistent ways of ordering action through time,"[4] and how these differ whether people are experiencing a "settled" or "unsettled" time. I have found that the tool kit metaphor applies to the method of ethnography and other types of qualitative research. We are not just passive observers in the field. Instead, we, as researchers, often strategically and actively draw on certain traits over others in a given situation in an effort to build rapport. This is particularly the case because fieldwork is often an "unsettled" time, one where we are constantly trying to understand the world around us and not take anything for granted. These traits and characteristics from which we draw can be visible, such as our presenting race/ethnicity or gender, or invisible, such as our family background or social capital.

My visible tools include, but are not limited to, my American nationality, gender, and Filipina heritage.[5] These characteristics often opened doors to some people, for example, when Rebecca, a white Peace Corps Volunteer, discussed how I was the only foreign woman she's seen around town who wasn't a missionary and seemed eager to connect. However, as Matthew Desmond notes, these same traits also closed doors to others.[6] When I was trying to interview U.S. military personnel, for example, many of them passed by me and refused to take a flyer or talk to me. I suspected this was because of a popular view, whether true or not, that academic researchers are anti–U.S. military. This fear was heightened after Rebecca revealed to me how she would purposefully and publicly try to shame U.S. military men and people she perceived as sex tourists by discussing the high rates of sexually transmitted infections.

However, if my visible tools either opened or closed doors, it was my invisible tools that kept doors open or even opened doors that were previously closed. My invisible tools include things like my social capital in the Philippines in the form of family members and the accompanying cultural capital they held. Take, for example, how I handled the aftermath when I inadvertently damaged my relationship with the Subic Bay Freeport Zone's (SBFZ) governmental body, the Subic Bay Metropolitan Authority (SBMA). I had gotten permission from the chairman to examine documents from the legal department. I was under the impression that the permission I received extended to scanning documents for later analysis. I was wrong. I did not understand the extent to which I overstepped my bounds until my Tita Linda pulled me aside. She brought me to the local mayor's office to get a signed letter from the mayor advocating on my behalf and explained that I needed to apologize and give the chairman the letter we had secured. My invisible tool related to my marriage to someone then employed by the Department of Defense also proved handy. One member of the U.S. military, Sophia, agreed to be interviewed only after I told her of my marriage.

We also must not forget how who talks to us is a selection process in and of itself from the participant's end. Sophia told me, for example, how she fact-checked some of my claims regarding who I was and what I studied, and also checked with her supervisor before agreeing to a more formal interview. She listened to me long enough to provide information about my spouse and thought about it afterward enough to fact-check my statements and seek guidance from her supervisor. Not everyone did.

Equally important to understanding the ethnographic tool kit is to recognize the ways in which our attempts to use said tools to build rapport may fail.[7] Take, for example, a Filipino visitor to the SBFZ. Tomas is a wealthy businessman, and when we began the interview, I spoke in Tagalog. Yet, at his request, we switched to English. My attempt at rapport was unsuccessful. Regardless of whether he wanted to speak in English to show his own knowledge of the English language or if it was an attempt to make me feel more comfortable, my use of language as a tool did not match his interest in speaking English.

The conceptual ethnographic tool kit switches focus from passive descriptions of how a few of our characteristics—whether our race, class, or gender, among others—may shape our interactions to the active and strategic ways we use our traits in the field. By doing so, the conceptual ethnographic tool kit recognizes that *everyone* has assorted tools that they use. None of us are true "insiders" or "outsiders" regarding the people we study because the ethnographic tool kit highlights how shared demographic characteristics do not necessarily correspond to other traits, and researchers often use invisible tools to build rapport. Instead, our level of "insider" or "outsider" status lies on a spectrum. Neither status is more useful or "true" than the other. Both are needed and provide important, and perhaps different, insights.

This insight also addresses an important conundrum in the social sciences. Like many other scholars have noted, there is often a double standard related to research if it is conducted by people of color and/or women who study communities of color or topics related to race/ethnicity, gender, and sexuality, among others.[8] One way this is expressed is by labeling this work as "me-search" and seeing it as somehow less scientific or more biased. However, as the ethnographic tool kit shows, allegations of "me-search" are based on a fallacy, one that reflects a homogenous understanding of groups of people based on a single shared trait.

Transparency

In the past few years, more explicit attention has been made to increasing transparency in social science research.[9] In sociology, and qualitative research in particular, this turn corresponds to the widespread attention given to Alice Goffman's book *On the Run* and the accompanying widespread critique over her ethics, methodology, and confidentiality. It also runs parallel to the push for open science, digital humanities, and the development of SocArXiv, a free, open-access site for social scientists to upload papers, both working papers and published articles. Its founding director, Philip N. Cohen, has been a vocal critic of Goffman's book and its methods.[10] Yet concerns about transparency and ethnography long predate *On the Run* or any controversies surrounding it.[11] What the controversy did, however, was bring again to the forefront discussion around whether qualitative research can be transparent, and if so, how.[12]

It's important to differentiate between transparency in two different stages of the research process: data analysis and data collection. First, there is transparency in the *data analysis* stage. This includes sharing codes, replicating models, and rerunning analyses. It's a transparent process that involves researchers disclosing what they did with the raw data that was collected. This comprises the bulk of the discussion around transparent policies and guidelines concerning quantitative research. Second, there is transparency in the *data collection* stage. This involves being open about the who, what, where, when, and why of data collection. Yet, qualitative data typically contains sensitive identifying details, which scholars have a harder time sharing. Because these identifying details are often not included, and others cannot easily run models to analyze raw qualitative data, transparency in data collection tends to be the primary focus when academics, journalists, and advocates for open science discuss qualitative research.

Why does this distinction between transparency in data collection versus data analysis matter? It's important because there are different standards, applications, guidelines, and foci with regard to each. They are talking about fundamentally different things. For example, quantitative scholars don't tend to interrogate the in-person or over-the-phone surveyor about what they were wearing, what their race/ethnicity, gender, and sexuality are, and how the surveyor's own characteristics intersect with their respondents'—the very questions about data collection that qualitative researchers are often asked. Additionally, and having worked in a survey research center myself, there are often not verbatim transcripts of what's being discussed, only the scripts and direct answers to the questions. Statistics are not created in a vacuum but are gathered by, from, and for people—something that can get lost in the discussion of data rigor and analysis.

This is not to say that one type of transparency matters more; both types matter. Questions regarding both types of transparency are important and need to be addressed. However, my point is that we are talking about very different things when we talk about transparency in data analysis versus data collection, and it's important to keep this distinction in mind. The first step toward being able to evaluate qualitative research should be understanding why and how researchers make the decisions they do.

Broadly speaking, we can think of three different types of transparency in ethnographic research: naming places, naming people, and sharing data.[13] Each of these is marked by distinct choices ethnographers make in the course of their research and differ in degree of transparency.

In this project, I've named the place of my study because its identity as a former U.S. military base and current Freeport Zone in the Philippines is central to my argument. Any researcher can enter its gates to see the social life I've depicted, evaluate my claims, or compare them to others. Additionally, its characteristics are so identifying that any attempts at masking it would be fruitless. I have also named people who are identified in documents because it is in the public record, like court documents. I've also named senior officials, like the SBMA's chairman, because I refer to him in his official capacity and he was speaking to me as such. Yet I've also given pseudonyms to the primary participants of my work. I do this because it was part of the conditions of the interview but also because I recognize that to name some people can have repercussions for those we do not name[14] and that we as scholars are held to a higher standard of ethics when we conduct our research. We have to think of the possible unintended consequences of being identified and how someone might be identified in what details we write, not only when it concerns behavior and thoughts that may be illegal but also when it may cause reputational harm.

What is often not discussed, however, is the care and concern needed in order to generate pseudonyms. Our names often tell others something about ourselves, whether it be our gender, race/ethnicity, or other aspects of our identities. Take, for example, my grandmother, whom I spoke about in the acknowledgments. I refer to her birth name as "Maria" and her chosen name as "Frances." In choosing each of these names, I had to think about whether her given name and its pseudonym were similarly popular, Filipino/a, and gendered. So, too, did I have to generate a pseudonym for her chosen name that shared similar characteristics, such as a popular white name for a woman at that time that is no longer popular today. I had to approach each participant in my research with similar care.

What if the very reason researchers and participants were able talk about a certain subject was because of the promise of confidentiality? In these scenarios, discussing demographic or other identifying information could prove to be highly detrimental because of the very real consequences they could face, consequences that could be lethal. One way to combat this is to change the traits of the person whose story you are telling. Yet this is a dilemma the qualitative researcher faces. If, for example, I told you that I changed the nationality or gender of someone and the reason why, that lets the reader follow up in the pages and guess who I am talking about. Doing so presents a facade of confidentiality and may nullify any attempt I've made to conceal the identities I've tried to mask and weaken any aspect of confidentiality promised or desired. Either disclosing that I have or admitting I have not changed gender, class, or any other demographic characteristic has repercussions. This may seem at odds with transparency in the decision-making process that I advocate and ethnography as a social scientific method. Yet that I've touched on how I've thought about this issue in the book aligns with my goal of transparency in the process. Furthermore, it also shows how there may always be necessary exceptions to the formal or informal rules we follow. A one-size-fits-all approach does not work when research involves people.

In the course of this research, I've also shared data in a number of ways, across different outlets. I've documented direct quotes from tape-recorded conversations using quotation marks. I've shared field notes with my students, hiring one undergraduate to transcribe the notes that I took in a physical journal and using it as a learning tool to teach methods. I also shared select field notes in a peer-reviewed article I published in *Ethnography*, as well as in slides of public talks I've given. As is the case in all data collection efforts researchers undertake, much of the data I have does not fit into this book.

The lack of complete transparency in qualitative research is not an issue of quality or scientific merit. Instead, ethical concerns and differences in data collection versus data analysis mean that not all rigorous scholarship can be equally transparent. It is precisely because scholars are rigorous in thinking about the very real and possible intended and unintended consequences our methodological decisions have for our participants that transparency is not always a given. It is this thinking about ethics that is at the heart of whether and when we name people, name places, and/or share data, and to what extent we do so. These decisions are not static, but change depending on the purpose of the study, the topic of our research, and our participants. Thinking through these decisions and consequences, and deciding when and whether to use pseudonyms, is a necessary part of this type of research. Transparency and masking both matter, and each is used for different reasons and purposes.

Given that not all qualitative research can be equally transparent, and that the ethnographic tool kit highlights how researchers strategically use their own traits during the course of fieldwork, which may mean that researchers might not observe or be privy to the same situations or emphasize the same activities, how can we ensure we are pursuing a social scientific endeavor? How can we reconcile transparency and its constraints? Seeking broad swaths of data and points of view, for example, is one way to make sure we are not succumbing to confirmation bias or only seeing data that support our beliefs. So, too, can we verify some of the arguments authors make by the *type* of transparency they undertake: whether, how, and why they name the places or people they do and how they share their data, and whether researchers are transparent in their research processes and decisions. Similarly, we need to be careful in detailing which claims we are and are not making. Being able to evaluate data, claims, and theory is particularly important since we cannot control the reception of our work: how it is used in policy debates or traditional or social media, or how often it is cited by academics. However, what we can do is be clear in our arguments to make certain our analyses and conclusions cannot be easily misconstrued. In evaluating other research, then, we can also focus on how a given author's arguments align with more general patterns and the ways in which they depart, and we can interrogate whether researchers' claims match their data, logic, and theory.

The reason ethnographic research cannot often be as transparent as some scholars call for[15] is precisely because we have to rigorously think through the ethical consequences and the aftermath we and our participants face when their names are attached to what we write.

Notes

Preface

1. Many scholars make similar claims (e.g., Gille 2007).

2. Or, as Stephen Vaisey (2014) puts it, "The explanation of behavior requires attention to persons, situations, and the interactions between them" (229).

3. Healy 2017. To some degree I empathize with this argument because my case study research has been rejected from the top general journals in sociology for not having more cases, for not being generalizable enough, or for not taking into account "X" field. Yet this seems to me to be a problem separate from nuance. The latter comments seem to occur when reviewers critique a paper they wish the author had written rather than the argument at hand. If sociology seeks originality, adding detail accomplishes this because it forces us to engage with what other people write, to be specific about our contributions, and to not reproduce the wheel or insights. To not engage in conversations others are having is to present one's thoughts as new without having to do all of the work to show you know how your thoughts fit into others'. Very little of what people say is new. That's true even for those who mind the details, but it is even more true, I find, than not when people fail to engage in nuance.

4. Burawoy 2017.

5. See Reyes (forthcoming) regarding the debate between the Chicago School of Sociology and the Manchester School of Anthropology, and its updated version seen in the Berkeley School of Sociology.

6. Here, I reject Burawoy's (2017) claim that transactional ethnography is "hostile to comparison and theory" (266). Instead, I focus on how structural and transactional ethnographies both offer useful tools, similar to my call to see both the Chicago and Manchester Schools as offering useful tools to analyze social life (Reyes, forthcoming).

7. Salzinger 2003.

8. Zelizer 2005, 2011.

9. Desmond 2014.

10. Her narration and choice between love and travel echoes those of Dominican Republic sex workers found in Brennan's (2004) work.

11. Per her request, I've given my grandmother a pseudonym for both her original and changed names, though she did grant me permission to identify her as my grandmother.

12. Here, I draw on Contreras's (2013) insight regarding how his background shaped the theoretical perspectives to which he was drawn, and I use it to similarly discuss how my background shaped the theoretical perspectives to which I am drawn.

Introduction

1. http://kabataanpartylist.ph/blog/2013/03/08/on-international-womens-day-youth-groups-march-against-the-rape-of-our-sovereignty-environment/ (accessed January 12, 2009).

2. Ibid.

3. I have field notes about this protest.

4. For a discussion of how social relations shape foreign direct investment at the macro level, see Bandelj (2008).

5. Calls for a Philippine nation free from foreign intervention have a long history. In 1896 Spanish colonial officials discovered the existence of Katipunan, a secret society aimed at Philippine independence from Spain through armed revolution, and in doing so, sparked the 1896–98 Philippine Revolution. Born to parents who were Chinese mestizos (of mixed ancestry), Emilio Aguinaldo was one of the key figures in the revolution and a military leader who led Philippine forces against Spain. In the fight against continued Spanish occupation, Aguinaldo allied with the United States. However, when he did so, he erroneously assumed that U.S. officials were helping the Philippine Revolutionary Army defeat Spain in Manila, and afterward, they would support and recognize an independent Philippines (Agoncillo 2012 [1990]:199; Karnow 1989:114–15). In June 1898, Aguinaldo copenned the Philippine Declaration of Independence, declaring Philippine sovereignty and the Philippines as a nation-state. However, neither Spanish nor U.S. officials recognized this declaration and proceeded to collude to end the Spanish-American War through a mock battle at Manila in an effort to transfer the Philippines from Spain to the United States and keep it out of the hands of the Filipino revolutionary government (Agoncillo 2012 [1990], chap. 11; Karnow 1989:123–25). Officials from the United States and Spain signed the 1898 Treaty of Paris, which transferred the Philippines to the United States for $20 million (for a copy of the 1898 Treaty of Paris, see http://avalon.law.yale.edu/19th_century/sp1898.asp [accessed April 24, 2017]). A month after its signing, in January 1899, Filipino revolutionaries signed the Malolos Constitution (for a copy, see http://www.gov.ph/constitutions/the-1899-malolos-constitution/ [accessed April 24, 2017]) creating the First Philippine Republic and declaring Aguinaldo its first leader. Just a few weeks later, the Philippine-American War erupted between the First Philippine Republic and the United States. It lasted for over three years and culminated in a U.S. victory over its colony. These fights against the United States and for Philippine independence continued even after the Philippines was recognized as a sovereign nation in 1946. After independence, however, the protests revolved around the continued role of the U.S. military and their power and influence in the Philippines. The protest

I witnessed in Olongapo in 2013 was just one of many that have filled the streets in recent decades. For example, in 1986, anti–U.S. base protests and rhetoric helped topple
the dictator Ferdinand Marcos through the nonviolent People Power Revolution and
chart the rise of Corazon "Cory" Aquino. The wife of the slain Philippine senator and
outspoken Marcos critic Benigno Aquino Jr., she would become the eleventh Philippine
president and first female president of an Asian country. Additional anti–U.S. base protests erupted during the 1992 negotiations over renewing the Military Bases Agreement,
which gave the U.S. rights to bases in the Philippines. These negotiations failed when
the Philippine Senate rejected the new treaty that renewed it and ousted the U.S. military bases from the country. Yet the U.S. military never really left the Philippines. They
continued to return vis-à-vis other military-related treaties. However, this time, they
returned on a "visiting," nonpermanent basis, as we will see in the following chapters.

6. A more formal definition of a global borderland is a foreign-controlled, semiautonomous place of international exchange.

7. I use the term *foreign-controlled* or *controlled by foreigners* to refer to either foreign ownership or heavy foreign influence, where this influence is one of the defining
characteristics of a space. For example, special economic zones are not foreign-owned
per se but are created to cultivate foreign direct investment, or businesses partially or
fully owned by foreigners. The Subic Bay Freeport Zone, for example, is locally governed
despite the foreign businesses located within it.

8. *Special economic zone* is a generic term that encapsulates a "geographically
delimited area administered by a single body, offering certain incentives (generally
duty-free importing and streamlined customs procedures) to businesses which physically locate within the zone" (Foreign Investment Advisory Service, the Multi-Donor
Investment Climate Advisory Service of the World Bank Group, *Special Economic
Zones: Performance, Lessons Learned and Implications for Zone Development* (Washington, DC: World Bank Group, 2008), 2, http://documents.worldbank.org/curated
/en/343901468330977533/pdf/458690WP0Box331soApril200801PUBLIC1.pdf (accessed
January 15, 2019). This includes free-trade zones, export processing zones, enterprise
zones, freeports, single-factory export processing zones, and specialized zones (e.g., science parks), each with functions varying from the processing of imports that are then
exported out from the country to duty-free shopping. Because they take different forms,
names, and sizes in countries and these types differ by region, there is no overarching
international governing body.

9. Roberts 2013.

10. Sassen 1991.

11. Although sometimes the words "frontiers" and "borderlands" are used inter-
changeably, because they both represent the meeting between different types of groups
and acknowledge the existence of "internal" (within a specified territory) and "exter-
nal" (across two territories) spaces (D'Argemir and Pujadas 1999; Donnan and Wilson
2010), frontier scholarship tends to have a one-sided, imperial focus on powers expanding into "borderless" lands (such as colonial expansion into the American South-
west) and is "outward-oriented" (for differences between frontiers and borders, see

also Stoddard [1991]). In contrast, borderland researchers tend to analyze how national ideologies and understandings of "belonging" are shaped by changing political and transportation boundaries; how individuals and states are culturally, socially, and financially linked; how borderlands are sites of informal and formal consumption, and cross-national organizational cooperation; how borderland or transnational identities and cosmopolitanism are created; and how borderlands are sites of contestation, negotiation, and meaning-making (Adelman and Aron 1999; Pisani 2013; Rippl et al. 2010; Rutherford 2011; Tirres 2008–10; Widdis 2010). Baud and van Schendel (1997) call for the need to examine the historical and comparative development of borderlands. They divide borderlands spatially (the border heartland, intermediate borderland, and the outer borderland) and temporally (infant, adolescent, adult, declining, and defunct borderlands), and call for the need to more clearly examine the overlapping political, economic, and cultural networks within and around borderlands. Other scholars take a less optimistic view, suggesting that both border patrols and residents on either side of the border can place people into wanted and unwanted categories based on nationality, race/ethnicity, and class (Casas-Cortes, Cobarrubias, and Pickles 2012; Helleiner 2012; Heyman 2009; Sundberg 2008). To these scholars, geopolitical borderlands are sites of institutionalized inequality, are rooted in national boundaries, or form the symbolic identities of people living in two cultures (Alvarez 1995; Anzaldua 1999). Still others focus on the legal ambiguity of, and forces that shape, borderlands (Dudziak and Volpp 2005; Fahmy 2013, Tirres 2008–10). However, precisely because these researchers focus on geopolitical borders or cities along these borders, they tend to ignore bounded sites within the state that share similar characteristics. I extend this research by documenting the very similar borderland dynamics occur *within* the confines of a nation-state. In analyzing global borderlands, I draw on literatures that emphasize how these borderlands act as sites where people of groups interact and how they maintain and reproduce inequalities through social and economic relations as well as cultural meanings.

12. In defining global borderlands as semiautonomous, foreign-controlled geographic locations geared toward international exchange, I also draw on Sassen's (2000, 2003 [2000], 2006) work on "analytic borderlands," which are a "formation of particular types of territoriality assembled out of 'national' and 'global' elements, each individual or aggregate instance evincing distinct spatio-temporal features" (Sassen 2006:386). Analytic borderlands are "assemblages" of both the national and the local. I similarly emphasize the need to identify places, to understand how they are rooted in historical localized processes, to examine their "social thickness," and to understand the interconnected (that is, not mutually exclusive) and partial nature of the global and the national, and the transformation of states' and people's territory, authority, and rights. However, my work deviates from Sassen's in important ways. First, I focus on foreign-controlled spaces within a sovereign nation-state. Global borderlands are specific places of semiautonomy based on nationality. Second, my emphasis on place is rooted in specific geographic locations and their ties to local context. Although the analytic borderlands of digitized finance are "inserted in the physical space of national territory, they may have little to do with the surrounding context" (Sassen 2006:394). Within global borderlands,

the country, city, and immediate community in which they are located, the local history, and the historic and contemporary relationship between the host nation-state and foreign visitors' countries of origin are all important. This grounding in history is necessary to understand the complex interactions that occur within these spaces and to understand the implications these interactions have for broader state-to-state relationships. For example, it is important that the SBFZ's buildings are former U.S. naval structures and that it is located in Olongapo City rather than in another Philippine city. The relationship between the U.S. Navy and Olongapo is distinct from the relationship between Subic Bay Naval Base's sister base, Clark Air Force Base, and its surrounding community, Angeles City. I argue that this is, in part, because of the greater integration of the U.S. Navy with Olongapo. The Subic Bay Naval Base employed almost four times as many people as did Clark, and the navy was integrated into the Olongapo City political dynasty of the Gordons—the first mayor of Olongapo City was the son of an American Marine (Bowen 1986). Finally, whereas Sassen (2006) emphasizes analytic borderlands' cross-national connections, the networked nature of global borderlands is an empirical question. In analyzing the spaces of "global borderlands," I follow previous work on how place, culture, and economy interact with global and national processes. However, I extend this literature by examining how these interactions and processes occur within foreign-controlled spaces that are geared toward international exchange.

13. Berman 2009; Griffiths 1986; Merry 1988; Michaels 2009; Tamanaha 2007.

14. See Auyero (2007) for a different understanding of what he calls the "gray zone of state power, . . . where the obscure and obscured actions of local politicos, grassroots brokers, and cops meet and mesh in seemingly coordinated ways," and how "the National Guard took special care when it came to protecting stores like the French-owned Carrefour or the American-owned Norte" (81)—likely because of how the businesses' foreign ownership relate to politics, the "geography of policing" (85), and the "size of markets, police (under) protection and community and political relations" (144).

15. See Swidler (1986) for settled versus unsettled lives and the role that culture plays in determining what she calls peoples' "strategies of action."

16. For examples of how this plays out in human rights laws, see Bunting (2005) and Merry (2003). For work on legal pluralism, jurisdictional politics, culture, and empire, see Benton (2002) and Benton and Ross (2013).

17. For example, see Stinchcombe (2005).

18. Weber 1978 [1922].

19. According to Mann (1984), infrastructural power of the state is "the capacity of the state to actually penetrate civil society, and to implement logistically political decisions throughout the realm" (189) or "the power of the state to penetrate and centrally co-ordinate the activities of civil society through its own infrastructure" (190).

20. According to Mann (1984), despotic power of the state is "the range of actions which the elite is empowered to undertake without routine, institutionalized negotiation with civil society groups" (188) or "the power by the state elite itself *over* civil society" (190).

21. Reed 2013.

22. For example, see Mann (2012 [1986]):1–33; see Nye (2004) for differences between hard and soft power; see Gramsci (1989 [1971]) and Lears (1985) on cultural hegemony; and see Gaventa (1982) and Lukes (2005 [1974]) on the three faces or dimensions of power.

23. Steinmetz 2014:79.

24. For example, see Go (2011), Johnson (2004), and Lutz (2005, 2006, 2009) for overseas U.S. military bases as arms of U.S. empire.

25. For example, see Babb and Carruthers (2008).

26. See Cooley (2008) for one example of why he thinks traditional understandings of U.S. bases as part of a U.S. empire miss key negotiations; instead, he refers to these negotiations as "base politics."

27. Schmitt's (1988 [1922]) work is on states of exception, where norms are suspended and who is sovereign is the one who decides what is exceptional and what is not; Subic is not a state of exception, per se. It is a site where a set of different norms and laws are enforced, though government officials did designate it as a place that is subject to different (not no) regulations. See also Agamben (2005).

28. Ong 2006:108–9; see Chen (1995) and Cross (2010), who contend that workers experience these zones as a continuation of the informal labor processes that occur outside them.

29. Similar to McMahon (1999), who discusses how "influence moved in a multidirectional rather than a unidirectional manner" in Southeast Asia between Western powers and indigenous, Southeast Asian ones (5).

30. Carruthers and Halliday 2006:573.

31. For example, see Halliday (2009).

32. Steinmetz 2014:84–85. In showing how sovereignty is contingent and a process, I draw on Adams and Steinmetz (2015), who examine sovereignty as a cultural process and focus on the complexity of agency.

33. Cooley 2008.

34. Holmes 2014.

35. Following, for example, Go (2008).

36. Ralph (2014) shows how dreams and aspirations similarly shape meaning in a Chicago neighborhood. Global borderlands are based on these competing images and are places where these negotiations and contested symbolism are most visible; see Benedicto (2008) for his description of Manila as a city of contradictions and sites where "dreams of being elsewhere come to life in myriad ways and are set against the intense differences that mark and cut the urban landscape" (47)—that is, as "desired elsewhere" or "dreaming of elsewhere" (58–59), where Manila (and people within it) is "determined to reconstitute itself as a 'global city' within the third-world city, sequestered from the city but open to the world" (55). See Tadiar (2004) on how "imagination, as culturally organized social practice, is an intrinsic, constitutive part of political economy" (4). See Burawoy et al. (2000) and Gille and Ó Riain (2002) for the call to conduct global ethnography, which consists of analyzing "global forces, connections, and imaginations" (28). See Tsing (2010) for what she describes as the "friction" that propels globalization forward.

37. See Freeman (2000), Mills (2001 [1999]), Ong (2010), Salzinger (2003), and Wolfe (1992) on gendered imaginations and labor.

38. See Aneesh (2015) as an example of how working in call centers in India that cater to people in the United States and the United Kingdom shapes the social lives of their employees.

39. Similar to Brennan (2004), Frye (2012), and Salzinger (2003), among others.

40. See Norton (2014) on his argument that social situations should be the unit of analysis when studying culture.

41. For example, see Gamson and Wolfsfeld (1993); Lester (1980).

42. Myers and Caniglia 2004; Oliver and Myers 1999.

43. Lester 1980.

44. Vasi et al. 2015.

45. Benson and Saguy 2005.

46. For example, see McCammon et al. (2007).

47. Andrews and Caren 2010.

48. Bail 2012.

49. Vanberg 2001.

50. Krehbiel 2016; Staton 2006.

51. Guzman 2002:1822.

52. For example, see Staton (2006).

53. White 2011 [1991]:96.

54. Fahmy 2013.

55. Cooley 2008; Evinger 1995; United States Department of Defense 2010, 2015.

56. Boyenge 2007.

57. For example, see Goldstone (2001:2); Rivera (2008); Wherry (2007).

58. See the RCI online resort directory, http://www.rci.com/resort-directory /landing (accessed September 15, 2014). Although this measure is problematic since it is a U.S.-based organization, it allows for some tangible measure of this phenomenon.

59. For example, see Chuck (2015); Kaphle (2014); Ryan (2012).

60. Redden 2015.

61. Redden 2017.

62. For example, see Parker and Ariosto (2013).

63. See Kraul and Sanchez (2016); this also occurred in 2011–13 because of cartel violence; see Casey and Berzon (2011); Flannery (2013); Woody (2016); see also NBC News (2014). When crimes are committed in similar Mexican tourist locations, officials and businesspeople also fear a decrease in tourism; see McDonnell and Sanchez (2016).

64. For example, see Anderson (2011).

65. A play on Benedict Anderson's (2006 [1983]) imagined communities.

66. Merton 1987.

67. See Kramer (2006).

68. Francia 2010; Karnow 1989; National Policy Paper on the Republic of the Philippines: Part One—US Policy 1966; Staff Report to the Senate Select Committee on Intelligence 1985.

69. Spanish rule started after their forces defeated the king of Cebu; Maurer and Iyer (2008).

70. The trade route was also known the Manila galleon trade, where merchants from China, Guam, and other areas in Asia and the Pacific came to Manila to trade their spices, crafts, cotton, silks, and other commodities for silver, wine, soap, ironware, and crops from the New World; the galleons also carried with them Spanish royal decree letters from Mexico, Spanish officials themselves, and their salaries (e.g., Bjork 1998; Flynn and Giraldez 1995; Schurz 1918; Tremml 2012).

71. The port's vulnerability was evidenced in two ways: (1) its mercantile dependence—as seen by the trade route's collapse due to the British invasion of Manila during the Seven Years' War—and (2) the focus on international trade derailed domestic development (Francia 2010; Karnow 1989).

72. Francia 2010:77; Karnow 1989:62; National Intelligence Survey 1965.

73. Cristobal and Gregor 1987.

74. Linn 1997.

75. For a history of colonial Philippines under Spanish and U.S. rule, see Kramer (2006).

76. For example, see Baldoz (2011); Isidro (1957); Karnow (1989); Margold (1995); McHale (1962). Other U.S. styles and institutions, such as roads and a new tax system, were readily adapted into Philippine life, and U.S. political, economic, and cultural influence continues today; for example, see Delmendo (1998); Maurer and Iyer (2008).

77. See Baldoz (2011) and Choy (2003) for an example related to nursing; Kramer (2006) for the role of Filipinos in Hawaii's agricultural system. The Philippines is also what Rodriguez (2010) calls a "labor brokerage" state that prepares and manages export labor. It does so, in part, because of the colonial legacies left by the United States.

78. For example, see Baldoz (2011); Rafael (2000).

79. Go 2008.

80. W Anderson 2006.

81. Kramer 2006:5.

82. Kramer 2006.

83. Ibid., 121; see also Goh (2007) for details regarding specific ethnographic official/ethnographer exchanges regarding the racial classification of different Filipino groups.

84. For example, Kramer (2006) discusses how evidence of self-rule was purposefully ambiguous so that U.S. officials could continually move the so-called goalposts that Filipinos needed to meet to attain independence.

85. For example, see Maurer and Iyer (2008).

86. Francia 2010.

87. Kramer (2006) suggests that the agricultural sector and its many players were key actors in the Philippines' eventual independence because they could not compete with the price of Philippine goods being imported.

88. Juan de Salcedo, the grandson of Miguel Lopez de Legazpi, who was the first governor of the Philippines and an explorer who helped establish the Manila galleon trade route, first scouted Subic Bay in 1572, a year after Manila was established. Al-

though he reported on the bay's natural defenses, Cavite—alongside Manila Bay—was chosen to host the Spanish naval fleet. Over three hundred years later, a royal decree declared a naval base be built at Subic Bay because the Cavite facilities suffered from Manila Bay's shallow waters.

89. During the Spanish-American War, the Spanish admiral Motojo sought to use the deep-water and narrow entrance advantages of Subic Bay but found the reality of the facilities inadequate. Dewey received a cable that the Spanish were going to convene at Subic Bay, so he sent two ships to investigate. They did not find anything and were not fired upon. The naval arsenal was abandoned in June, and the Spanish navy, clergy, and other civilians moved to Grande Island, located within Subic Bay, where a Filipino ship ordered their surrender. The German ship *Irene* appeared and ordered the Filipinos to yield. When Dewey was informed of the situation, he sent two ships—the USS *Raleigh* and the USS *Concord*—to Subic Bay and demanded the Spanish to surrender; *Irene* fled. For example, see Granger's (2011) discussion of Dewey's battle at Manila Bay; see also the self-published accounts by G. Anderson (2006) and Pagaduan (2007). I see these self-published accounts as not "accurate" recordings of historical events but as types of memoirs and historical understandings of Subic Bay on the ground.

90. Such as Iloilo, Guimaras, Basilan, Cavite (for Manila Bay), and Dumanquilas Bay.

91. Linn 1997:84. Although the stronghold of the U.S. Pacific fleet eventually moved to Pearl Harbor, the naval station in the Philippines stayed at Subic, in part, because of Admiral Dewey's opposition to relocating it to Manila Bay. He used the 1898 Spanish-American Battle at Manila Bay as evidence of its vulnerabilities. See Grenville (1961); Linn (1997).

92. Dewey served as president of the navy's general board. His reasoning was based on Subic Bay's deep and wide water, it being surrounded by steep hills on all three sides, and the location of Grande Island at the mouth of the bay, where the military could command the surrounding areas. Additionally, it already included heavy artillery batteries and minefields left over from the Spanish and was an ideal place to counter an attack by sea; see Linn (1997).

93. The use of the Subic Bay facilities by the U.S. military began the following year, and in 1902, the U.S. War Department confirmed it as the main naval location, and in 1903 the general board, followed by the joint board, confirmed and made its fortification a priority. It hosted the first U.S. naval exercise in Asian waters (Linn 1997:83). Grenville (1961) lists 1903 general board confirmation as the date the United States selected Subic Bay as the location, whereas Linn (1997) says it was 1902 when the War Department accepted "an all-navy board" decision to select Subic Bay as the base's location (83).

94. For the first five years it had no funds for maintenance or improvements. However, "spurred by the Russo-Japanese War, Congress appropriated $862,395 for the fortifications at Subic Bay and $700,000 for other bases in the Philippines" (Lin 1997:86). See also Suter (1986).

95. Its independence—scheduled for 1944 per the terms of the 1934 Tydings-McDuffie Act—was delayed because of the war. After World War II, however, U.S.-Philippine relations were strained. Americans gave more postwar aid to Japan than to the Philippines, a political and combat ally and where Filipinos and Americans alike

died during the Bataan Death March. This was seen as a slight by Philippine politicians regarding their contributions to the war effort; see Karnow (1989); Thompson (1975).

96. Linn 1997; Suter 1986.

97. The area became part of the naval reservation when President Roosevelt expanded its borders (U.S. Executive Order 1026:1909).

98. The United States relinquished the city to the Philippines in 1959. Only after an exchange of notes between the U.S. embassy in Manila and the Philippine Department of Foreign Affairs did the United States relinquish its rights to the area (Francia 2010; Rimmer 1997; R.P. Republic Act No. 4645, 1966; U.S. Department of State, "Arrangements for the Transfer of Portions of the United States Naval Base, Subic Bay, to the Philippine Authority: Agreement Between the United States and the Republic of the Philippines, Effected by Notes Exchanged at Manila," December 7, 1959 (Excerpts).

99. Duque 2009:49.

100. Using a 45 Philippine pesos to 1 U.S. dollar exchange rate.

101. Subic Bay Metropolitan Authority 2012, 2013.

102. This does not include the size of the company nor the number of employees; I have information only on the raw counts of SBFZ businesses.

103. See Benedicto (2014) for Manila as a site of contradictions; see Freeman (2000) and Ong (2010) for globalized labor as sites of contradictions; and see Tsing (2010) for what she calls "friction": "The awkward, unequal, unstable, and creative qualities of interconnection across difference" that propels global power and connections forward (4).

104. Many contemporary and classical scholars have similarly united ethnographic and historical/document methods (e.g., Auyero 2007; Du Bois 1996 [1899]; Gille 2007; Hunter 2015; Ong 2010; Thomas and Znaniecki 1996).

105. Thomas 1923.

106. For example, see Gans (1999).

107. Jerolmack and Khan (2014) argue that this is the foundation of ethnography and warn against the dangers of what they call the attitudinal fallacy—"the error of inferring situated behavior from verbal accounts" (179). However, they are not the first to propose this as a foundation of ethnographic methods as this difference between "what they say" and "what they do" was at the center of my ethnographic training. Their discussion of the different strengths of methods and how different methods answer different questions was also a core element of my own graduate training more generally.

108. For defense of why talking to people is important, both by itself and in combination with other methods, see Cerulo (2014); DiMaggio (2014); Maynard (2014); Vaisey (2014); Wuthnow (2011).

109. For example, see Duck (2015); Duneier (2001 [1999]); Rios (2011); Small (2015).

110. For different types of explicitly comparative historical work, see Skocpol, and Somers (1980).

111. For example, see Aminzade (1992) on "the use of four temporal concepts—duration, pace, trajectory and cycles" (458).

112. Griffin 1992:415; Sewell 1996. For path dependency, see Mahoney (2000).

113. Griffin 1992:405; for narrative methods, see also Abbot (1992).

114. Go 2008.

115. Merry 2006.

116. Simmons 1998, 2010.

117. For example, see Chayes and Chayes (1993).

118. Leeds 2003; Smith 1995.

119. Keohane 2005 [1984]; Gibler 2008.

120. Morrow 1994.

121. Martin 2005.

122. See quisumbing king (2016) for a similar discussion of pre-1946 sovereignty in the Philippines and ambiguity in law in U.S.-Philippine relations.

123. Abbott and Snidal 2000:422.

124. Weil 1983:442.

125. Abbott and Snidal 2000:422.

126. Ibid., 423.

127. Shaffer and Pollack 2010.

128. Hunter (2015) writes about the importance of historical ethnography.

129. See Tadiar (2004) on how "imagination, as culturally organized social practice, is an intrinsic, constitutive part of political economy" (4) and how "the dreams of Filipinos, rulers and ruled, cannot be understood apart from the global material imaginary . . . on which they play out" (6).

130. Brubaker et al. 2006.

131. Wimmer 2013.

132. Brubaker et al. 2006.

133. Indeed, the theoretical underpinnings of sovereignty emerged inductively in my data.

134. For example, see Lamont and Molnár (2002).

135. Thomas 1923.

136. For example, see Fourcade and Healy (2007).

Chapter 1

1. For media coverage and commemoration of this event, see Angsioco (2014); Gavilan (2018); Paredes (2009).

2. Ninoy then spent eleven years in prison, before he was temporarily allowed by Marcos to travel to the United States for a triple-bypass heart surgery. Aquino defied Marcos by staying and not returning to the Philippine jail; thus began Ninoy's three years of self-imposed exile.

3. For this information about his life and assassination, see Kashiwahara (1983); Romulo (2004); Salanga (2014).

4. Cory publicly claimed to be only a housewife. However, she had ties to national politics as she was born to political dynasties on both sides of her family.

5. The Philippine equivalent of the U.S. White House, the presidential residence.

6. For taxes as a social contract, see Martin, Mehrotra, and Prasad (2009:1).

7. See Tilly (1999) for his book *Durable Inequality*.

8. Cooley 2008:3.

9. Centeno 2002; Schumpter 1991 [1918]; Tilly 1992. For overviews of fiscal sociology, see Martin and Prasad (2014); Martin et al. (2009); Tilly (2009:xiii).

10. Cooley 2008.

11. Here I use a Weberian (1978 [1968]) understanding of sovereignty as territorially based, and depending on the monopoly on the means of violence I combine this Weberian definition with the call to see sovereignty as a cultural process (e.g., Adams and Steinmetz 2015). Although research on empire, human rights, and similar subjects have moved beyond this Weberian definition, much of sociological research has not. For example, nation-states as geographically bounded political entities and their accompanying cultural frames have been a central tenet to scholars of states, development, and war, among others (Centeno 2002; Evans, Rueschemeyer, and Skocpol 1985; Scott 1998; Tilly 1992; Wimmer 2014). In his influential 1984 article, Michael Mann argues that the "autonomous power of the state" is territorially based and derives from two sources. First, there is despotic power, where states' rulers exercise absolute authority over decisions. In Weberian terms, this power is an exercise of domination. There is also infrastructural power, the ability of the state to penetrate civil society in everyday life through social and logistical systems. Both exist in states but to varying degrees on a continuum. Yet, in these terms, sovereignty continues to be centered on the idea of control over a territory. But what about control over people once they leave a given territory?

12. I use the term *administrative sovereignty* instead of *extraterritorial* because administrative sovereignty refers to a particular set of rights, responsibilities, and control over people. It's a specific type of extraterritoriality, since extraterritoriality can cover orders from intergovernmental organizations like the United Nations or the International Criminal Court. It also allows us to see how rights and responsibilities over people and places tend to coincide when citizens are within their country of birth and are disentangled under particular circumstances. Rodriguez's (2010) understanding of what she calls migrant citizenship is similar. Migrant citizenship, according to her, is where "the Philippine state's migration regime has included provisions that are supposed to protect migrants from exploitative working conditions as well as entitlements reserved only for overseas workers. . . . The state pledges particular kinds of protections and entitlements to secure legitimacy for its migration program among its citizens— both those who leave as well as those who stay . . . offering migrants what is essentially a portable set of 'rights'" (xx). That is, the Philippine government offers or promises to offer protection of its citizens when they migrate abroad for work.

13. This distinction is an analytic one; however, they are not always empirically distinct. For example, modern nation-states' bureaucracies are organizations instilled with administrative powers (Weber 1978 [1968]), so when citizens stay within their country of citizenship, the territorial and administrative rights of the nation-state are bundled. This is not to suggest that these rights are administered similarly—nation-states can have a strong hand in maintaining the monopoly of the means of violence within a given territory but have a comparatively weaker ability to administer control over the

people and their rights, and vice versa, precisely because these responsibilities derive from different types of power and can lead to different internal conditions (e.g., see Mann [1984] for two sources of state power and Brubaker [1992] for conceptions of the state as both territorial and membership based). However, territorial and administrative rights and responsibilities become *decoupled* when citizens leave the borders of their nation-state. In these cases, administrative sovereignty is bound to citizens, and its reach is extraterritorial, extending beyond the geographic boundaries it covers, and countries seek to control and manage citizens' rights who are not in their homeland. This chapter focuses on how territorial and administrative sovereignty are decoupled in Subic Bay as a global borderland.

14. Research on empire focuses on the expansion of a political unit's formal and informal control over territories, infrastructures, and peoples—those of other nations, as well as the empire's own citizens outside the metropole (Cooper 2014; Go 2011; Steinmetz 2014; Stoler 2002; see also Adams [2005] for how sovereignty was disentangled as it related to merchant ships and how the organization of sovereignty and power can be based on gendered and familial politics). Colonial scholars coming from a law and society perspective, which sees law as meaning-making systems, focus on the ways in which interactions among colonizers and colonized produced multiple types of laws on the ground. The coexistence of two or more legal systems is known as legal pluralism (Berman 2009; Burke-White 2004; Griffiths 1986; Merry 1988, 2006; Michaels 2009; Moore 1973; Tamanaha 2007). Using this lens, we see that legal systems are not just state or colonial laws that govern people but also include customary, state, traditional, international, and religious laws, with an analytic focus on how these systems overlap, how they are mutually constitutive, and how they become redefined. In colonial and postcolonial spaces, the adaptation, rejection, and redefinition of law from both sides is the focal point, and disputes over religious, cultural, ethnic/racial, and political boundaries translate to nation-building efforts, legitimacy, rights, and political institutions (Benton 2001a, 2001b, 2008; de Sousa Santos 2006; Fahmy 2013; Snyder 1981). Here, we see how law has multiple meanings and control over people varies depending on the legal systems in which they are associated. The regulation of and rights over citizens and noncitizens of the metropole in the colony and who in the colony is able to obtain citizenship-related rights from the metropole are central concerns of empire research. Such concerns push our knowledge away from a dichotomous colonized/colonizer understanding of empire to one that acknowledges the complex and competing interests and social and political rights of multiple social actors within each group (Cooper 2014). Indeed, international law itself, Anghie (1996) argues, was created out of the colonial experience and the attempt to understand who was sovereign in encounters between American Indians and the Spanish. Scholars of informal empire suggest that U.S. rule continues to dominate politics in its former colonies and those countries where the United States exercises its military might or financial prowess (Go 2011). Military bases, SEZs, multinational corporations, and the like have been sites where scholars, such as Enloe (2000 [1990]) and Lutz (2009), show how foreigners are able to assert their will precisely because of their foreign status. This stance leads us to believe that nation-state

rulers are subservient to the United States. Yet it gives us little guidance on how to understand, for example, the conviction of overseas U.S. servicemembers by local courts.

15. One rich set of studies examines immigration to wealthy, more developed nation-states like the United States, Canada, and states in western Europe, and while they reference political and economic relationships among host and origin countries, the focus is on varied immigrant rights, the adaptation of the children of immigrants, migration-related ties across borders, and modes of incorporation within the receiving country (Levitt and Jaworsky 2007; Massey, Durand, and Malone 2003; Parreñas 2001; Portes and Rumbaut 2001; Portes, Fernandez-Kelly, and Haller 2009; Portes and Zhou 1993; Smith 2005; Zhou and Xiong 2005). However, what these studies miss is a connection to any protections the country of origin's government might provide, as well as the rights of rich foreigners abroad, precisely because research in this area tends to focus on origin countries that are poorer and less developed than host nation-states and therefore may not have political power or influence to intercede on their citizens' behalf. In this set of research, rights and control over people revolve around host country dynamics. We also know that there are differences in who is able to move among countries based on their passport (Torpey 2000), and deep inequalities continue to divide countries (Korzeniewicz and Moran 2009). Bloemraad, Korteweg, and Yurdakul's (2008) review offers an important link between work on migration and research on citizenship by describing how the conceptualizations of citizen and citizenship are used as proxies for one of four meanings: political participation, "sense of belonging," legal status, and human rights regardless of country of birth or residence. The 1948 UN Universal Declaration of Human Rights and the 1952 UN resolution to report on South African racial conditions under apartheid represent a watershed in international relations—from noninterference to monitoring the conditions in which people live—and there has been a recent explosion of socio-legal scholarship focusing on transnational human rights (Klug 2005; Somers and Roberts 2008; Tsutsui, Whitlinger, and Lim 2012). Many scholars see these rights as cultural models that should be guaranteed to all, regardless of nationality; however, the implementation of such laws and reasons for their violations differ based on local context (Bunting 2005; Merry 2003). While there can be a "radical decoupling" of policies and their implementation, nonstate actors can also use treaty commitments to compel nation-states to meet human rights standards (Hafner-Burton and Tsutsui 2005:1405).

16. See quisumbing king (2016) for a similar discussion of pre-1946 sovereignty in the Philippines.

17. B. Anderson 2006 [1983].

18. Scholars have focused on how shared and/or "disaggregated" sovereignty (Slaughter 1995) that recognizes the "many hands of the state" (Morgan and Orloff 2017) allows for a type of global governance that is decentralized and interconnected with one another (e.g., Chayes and Chayes 1995; Slaughter 2004). For example, we know that nation-states voluntarily consent to and ratify the rules related to international laws, alliances, and institutional membership and standing with global organizations, and these

rules are followed because of norms around reciprocity, concerns about reputational effects, and fear of associated sanctions for not signing or noncompliance (Chayes and Chayes 1995; Gibler 2008; Goldstein, Rivers, and Tomz 2007; Keohane 2005 [1984]; Simmons 2002, 2010; Simmons and Danner 2010). However, compliance to treaties falls along a continuum rather than a dichotomous outcome, based on "the type of treaty, the context, the exact behavior involved, and over time" (Chayes and Chayes 1993:198) and on the legitimacy of intergovernmental organizations (Brunnee and Toope 2004). Much of this work sees sovereignty as something that has been voluntarily and partially ceded in order to maintain order and share governance. Similarly, although they don't use the term *sovereignty*, what Esty and Geradin (2000) call "regulatory co-opetition" similarly focuses on both competition and collaboration among and between governmental and non- or extragovernmental actors.

19. See "Remembering Manuel A. 'Manoling' Roxas of Capiz," Province of Capiz, http://capiz.gov.ph/index.php?option=com_content&view=article&id=452:remembering -manuel-a-qmanolingq-roxas-of-capiz&catid=1:latest-news&Itemid=18 (accessed May 24, 2017).

20. See Kotlowski (2015).

21. See https://blog.history.in.gov/paul-v-mcnutt-the-man-who-would-be-king/ (accessed January 16, 2019).

22. The Tydings-McDuffie Act, or Philippine Independence Act, of 1934 put forth a ten-year timetable for the transition to Philippine independence. However, with World War II and the Japanese occupation of the Philippines, independence occurred in 1946, a year after the United States took back the Philippines from the Japanese and reoccupied it.

23. Treaty of General Relations, 1946.

24. Ibid.

25. Inequality between the United States and the Philippines was further institutionalized through additional agreements, such as the Bell Trade Act of 1946. The Bell Trade Act, among other things, granted U.S. citizens and corporations parity with Filipino citizens in access to Philippine materials and resources, pegged the Philippine peso to the U.S. dollar, and gave the United States preferential tariffs. So, while the Treaty of General Relations formally turned over sovereignty of the Philippines to Filipinos, other negotiated agreements severely limited Philippine sovereignty by tying the economic integrity of the Philippines to the United States and giving U.S. citizens similar rights and responsibilities as Filipino citizens. See also discussion in Go (2011).

26. For example, see Stinchcombe (2005).

27. Other U.S.-Philippine agreements that I do not cover include but are not limited to (1) the 1947 Military Assistance Act, which, among other things, created the Joint U.S. Military Advisory Group and declared that the United States would provide training and assistance to armed forces of the Philippines; (2) the 1951 Mutual Defense Treaty, which states that the United States and the Philippines will provide mutual aid and that "each Party recognizes that an armed attack in the Pacific area on either of the Parties would be dangerous to its own peace and safety and declares that it would act to meet

the common dangers in accordance with its constitutional processes"; and (3) the 2011 Manila Declaration, which reaffirmed the Philippine-U.S. relationship and celebrated the sixtieth anniversary of the Mutual Defense Treaty.

28. In contrast to Johnson (2004), who states that "America's foreign military enclaves, though structurally, legally, and conceptually different from colonies, are themselves something like micro-colonies in that they are completely beyond the jurisdiction of the occupied nation" (p. 35), I find that U.S. bases are *semiautonomous* and that the limits and boundaries of their semiautonomy are continually negotiated, contingent, and contested, not taken for granted.

29. 1947 MBA, Introduction.

30. See MBA's Annex A and B, respectively.

31. Following this is an important clause that states, "The United States shall pay just compensation for any injury to persons or damage to property that may result from action taken in connection with this Article."

32. As long as they are in some way connected to the base.

33. He would also become president of the Philippines after Manuel Roxas's death.

34. For his vice presidency term, see the "Presidents & VP's" section of the Philippine History website, http://www.philippine-history.org/presidents.htm (accessed May 24, 2017); for a timeline of all the positions he held, including his term as foreign affairs secretary, see http://malacanang.gov.ph/presidents/third-republic/elpidio-quirino/ (accessed January 16, 2019).

35. See "Oneal, Emmet (1887–1967)," Biographical Directory of the U.S. Congress, http://bioguide.congress.gov/scripts/biodisplay.pl?index=O000089 (accessed May 24, 2017).

36. In the July 2016 EDCA decision, Justice Sereno writes that these "diplomatic exchanges of notes are not treaties but rather formal communication tools on routine agreements, akin to private law contracts, for the executive branch. This cannot truly amend or change the terms of the treaty, but merely serve as private contracts between the executive branches of government. They cannot *ipso facto* amend treaty obligations between States, but may be treaty-authorized or treaty-implementing. Hence, it is correct to state that the MBA as the treaty did not give the Philippines jurisdiction over the bases because its provisions on U.S. jurisdiction were explicit. What the exchange of notes did provide was effectively a contractual waiver of the jurisdictional rights granted to the U.S. under the MBA, but did not amend the treaty itself." Endnote 36 reads, "An 'exchange of notes' is a record of a routine agreement, that has many similarities with the private law contract. The agreement consists of the exchange of two documents, each of the parties being in the possession of the one signed by the representative of the other. Under the usual procedure, the accepting State repeats the text of the offering State to record its assent. The signatories of the letters may be government Ministers, diplomats or departmental heads. The technique of exchange of notes is frequently resorted to, either because of its speedy procedure, or, sometimes, to avoid the process of legislative approval." See https://treaties.un.org/Pages/Overview.aspx?path=overview/glossary /page1_en.xml#exchange (accessed January 16, 2019). For the purposes of this chapter,

I call these *exchanges* and others that would occur later *amendments* for clarity because they either *changed* or *clarified* the way U.S.-Philippine military relations operated.

37. An area also known then as Nichols Field and currently known as Fort Bonifacio.

38. Embassy note, CITA No. 820.005, The American Ambassador to the Philippine Secretary of Foreign Affairs No. 559, Title: "Amendment to Agreement concerning military bases," December 23, 1947.

39. Ibid.

40. Ibid.

41. The United States would also be free from any related fees, would not be required to give advance notice regarding landing or take-off, and would have the right to "free access" to related areas by land, sea, or air routes, while the Philippines would "maintain flight operations and facilities . . . on the level of present standards." Ibid.

42. Embassy note, Response, The Philippine Secretary of Foreign Affairs to the American Ambassador, December 24, 1947.

43. 1947 MBA, Article 13: Jurisdiction, number 2.

44. It is also important to note that Philippine citizens were able to volunteer to be members of the U.S. armed forces and thus, according to the MBA, subject to U.S., not Philippine, jurisdiction in criminal incidents.

45. See also Cooley (2008).

46. Through the 1968 Base Labor Agreement and the Collective Bargaining Agreement and the 1979 Amendment to the MBA. See also U.S. District Court, District of Columbia, Anthony Rossi et al., Plaintiffs, v. Harold Brown, Secretary of Defense, et al., Defendants, Civ. A No 78-2346, March 20, 1979; U.S. Court of Appeals, District of Columbia Circuit, Anthony M. Rossi et al., Appellants, v. Harold Brown, Secretary of Defense et al., Appellees, No. 79-1485, Argued April 15, 1980, Decided September 15, 1980, Rehearing Denied December 18, 1980; Supreme Court of the United States, Caspar W. Weinberger, Secretary of Defense, et al., Petitioners v. Anthony M. Rossi et al., 456 U.S. 25 (1982), No. 80-1924, argued February 22, 1982; decided March 31, 1982.

47. I do not have information on whether and how long this arrangement with Kawasaki Heavy Industries lasted.

48. For example, see "Assessing America's Options in the Philippines," Monday, February 3, 1986.

49. The eruption began at 1:42 P.M. local time; see, for example, https://www.livescience.com/14590-pinatubo-flashback-june-15-largest-volcanic-eruption.html (accessed June 18, 2017).

50. See Newhall, Hendley, and Stauffer (1997); U.S. Geological Survey (2016).

51. See Rudolph and Guard (1991).

52. U.S. Geological Survey 2016.

53. Newhall, Hendley, and Stauffer 1997.

54. For example, see "The Philippine Bases Treaty," September 25, 1991.

55. 1991 Treaty of Friendship, Cooperation and Security, Preamble.

56. Ibid., Article 1.

57. See Supplementary Agreement Number Two to the Treaty of Friendship, Cooperation and Security: Agreement on Installations and Military Operating Procedures, Article 7.

58. See Article 3: Scientific and Technological Cooperation.

59. See Article 4: Cultural and Educational Cooperation; Supplementary Agreement Number One to the Treaty of Friendship, Cooperation and Security: Agreement on Cultural and Educational Cooperation.

60. See Article 5: Health Cooperation.

61. See Cabotaje (1999); for U.S. laws, see Rescission Act of 1946 (38 U.S.C. §107), which denied benefits; 1990 Public Law 101-649, section 405, for conditions related to the naturalization of Filipino World War II vets; and 2009 American Recovery and Reinvestment Act, section 1002, for lump sum payments for Filipino World War II vets; see also 1991 Treaty of Friendship, Cooperation and Security, Article 6: Veterans Issues Cooperation.

62. See Supplementary Agreement Number Two to the Treaty of Friendship, Cooperation and Security: Agreement on Installations and Military Operating Procedures, Article 8.

63. U.S. General Accounting Office (1992:30).

64. See Gaventa (1982) and Lukes (2005 [1974]) on the three faces or dimensions of power. (Most relevant to this discussion is the third dimension of power.)

65. Neither did the United States. The United States paid out upward of $7 to $8 million in severance pay and transportation costs, though many Filipino employees unsuccessfully sued them for retirement benefits; I found 135 legal cases on this issue alone. Judges on the U.S. Court of Appeals, Federal Circuit ruled in favor of the U.S. military because former Filipino base workers' employment was classified as temporary or nonentitled; therefore, they were not entitled to retirement benefits, thus delineating rights between U.S. citizens and Filipino civilian nationals (see chapter 5, "Labor and Imagined Identities," in this volume).

66. Despite how contentious the bases issue was, the rejection of the treaty surprised U.S. government officials, and although they were offered a three-year withdrawal plan, the United States left in 1992, within the one-year period originally negotiated in the MBA and its subsequent amendments (Cruz De Castro 2003). The loss of the permanent bases within the Philippines was a blow to the strategic agenda of the U.S. military, and the cost of their removal was upward of $7 to $8 million due to severance pay for Filipino employees and transportation costs ("Assessing America's Options in the Philippines," Monday, February 3, 1986; "The Philippine Bases Treaty," September 25, 1991). They did not make any moves to support Aqunio's push for a national referendum or to renegotiate, in part because the United States wanted to at least be *seen* as being respectful of the Philippine people's sovereignty ("Implications of the US Withdrawal from Clark and Subic Bases," March 5, 1992) and soften the image of the United States as an exploitative power. Additionally, budget cuts had already reduced the number of U.S. forces stationed in the Philippines, which hosted comparatively fewer troops than other bases in Southeast Asia, and U.S. military officials used this as evidence to suggest that the withdrawal could mostly be compensated for in other locations (Department of the Air Force, July 1, 1977; Department of the Navy, June 13, 1977; He 2010; "Implications of

the US Withdrawal from Clark and Subic Bases," March 5, 1992; "The Philippine Bases Treaty," September 25, 1991).

67. The MBA was just one of many agreements concerning U.S.-Philippine military relations. Others include, for example, the 1951 Mutual Defense Treaty and the 1947 Military Assistance Agreement. These non-MBA military agreements remained in effect after the MBA/TFCS was not renewed.

68. See ABS-CBN News (2016); Philippines Japan Society (2015).

69. For a list of all former Secretaries see https://dfa.gov.ph/about/history-of-dfa (accessed January 16, 2019).

70. See https://2001-2009.state.gov/outofdate/bios/h/4811.htm (accessed January 16, 2019) and the "Chiefs of Mission for Philippines" section of the Department of State Office of the Historian's website, https://history.state.gov/departmenthistory /people/chiefsofmission/philippines (accessed May 25, 2017).

71. The VFA refers to two agreements: one that governs U.S. forces visiting the Philippines and another that governs Philippine forces visiting the United States. For the purposes of this section, the VFA will refer to the former, except when specified.

72. For example, the VFA still includes stipulations on jurisdiction when crimes are against U.S. or Philippine property, persons, or security, as well as articles governing entry and departure, vehicles and registration, importation and exportation, and the movement of military vessels. It remains in effect until 180 days after either the United States or the Philippines gives written notice to the other regarding their desire to terminate it.

73. In contrast, the criminal jurisdiction article in the October 1998 agreement that governs Philippine military forces in the United States has a similar caveat regarding waiving jurisdiction, though the wording is much more ambiguous and less detailed (1998 VFA [governing Philippine military personnel visiting the United States], Article 8: Criminal Jurisdiction, point 2). Rather than agree to waive their right to jurisdiction, except in special cases, like the Philippine government agreed to do in the February 1998 agreement, the U.S. government only agreed that the Department of State or Department of Defense would *ask* the relevant U.S. authority to waive their jurisdiction. There is no firm commitment—"real" or symbolic—to waiving jurisdiction regarding Philippine military personnel in the United States who are charged with or found committing crimes. Neither are there clauses regarding when, where, and under what circumstances the Philippine versus the U.S. governments have jurisdiction. Instead, in the 1998 October VFA, there is a single paragraph that leaves criminal jurisdiction— specifically how it relates to negotiations on who has what rights over people, location, property, and content (e.g., related to national security)—in the hands of government officials and their abilities to negotiate and exert power.

74. See 1998 VFA, Article 5: Criminal Jurisdiction, points 1 and 2.

75. Ibid., point 3, 2.d; emphasis added.

76. Ibid.

77. There are also time limits on trials of U.S. personnel in the Philippines—one year—and prohibition of U.S. personnel being tried in Philippine military or religious courts.

78. Republic of the Philippines Supreme Court, G.R. No. 138570, BAYAN (Bagong Alyansang Makabayan), a Junk VFA Movement, Bishop Tomas Millamena (Iglesia Filipina Independiente), Bishop Elmer Bolocan (United Church of Christ of the Phil.), Dr. Reynaldo Legasca, MD, Kilusang Mambubukid Ng Pilipinas, Kilusang Mayo Uno, GABRIELA, Prolabor, and the Public Interest Law Center, petitioners, vs. Executive Secretary Ronaldo Zamora, Foreign Affairs Secretary Domingo Siazon, Defense Secretary Orlando Mercado, Brig. Gen. Alexander Aguirre, Senate President Marcelo Fernan, Senator Franklin Drilon, Senator Blas Ople, Senator Rodolfo Biazon, and Senator Francisco Tatad, respondents, October 10, 2000; Republic of the Philippines Supreme Court, G.R. No. 138572, Philippine Constitution Association, Inc. (PHILCONSA), Exequiel B. Garcia, Amadogat Inciong, Camilo L. Sabio, and Ramon A. Gonzales, petitioners, vs. Hon. Ronaldo B. Zamora, as Executive Secretary, Hon. Orlando Mercado, as Secretary of National Defense, and Hon. Domingo L. Siazon, Jr., as Secretary of Foreign Affairs, respondents, October 10, 2000; Republic of the Philippines Supreme Court, G.R. No. 138587, Teofisto T. Guingona, Jr., Raul S. Roco, and Sergio R. Osmea Iii, petitioners, vs. Joseph E. Estrada, Ronaldo B. Zamora, Domingo L. Siazon, Jr., Orlando B. Mercado, Marcelo B. Fernan, Franklin M. Drilon, Blas F. Ople and Rodolfo G. Biazon, respondents; G.R. No. 138680, Integrated Bar Of The Philippines, Represented by its National President, Jose Aguila Grapilon, petitioners, vs. Joseph Ejercito Estrada, in his capacity as President, Republic of the Philippines, and Hon. Domingo Siazon, in his capacity as Secretary of Foreign Affairs, respondents, October 10, 2000; Republic of the Philippines Supreme Court, G.R. No. 138698, Jovito R. Salonga, Wigberto Taada, Zenaida Quezon-Avencea, Rolando Simbulan, Pablito V. Sanidad, Ma. Socorro I. Diokno, Agapito A. Aquino, Joker P. Arroyo, Francisco C. Rivera Jr., Rene A. V. Saguisag, Kilosbayan, Movement of Attorneys for Brotherhood, Integrity And Nationalism, Inc. (Mabini), petitioners, vs. The Executive Secretary, The Secretary of Foreign Affairs, The Secretary Of National Defense, Senate President Marcelo B. Fernan, Senator Blas F. Ople, Senator Rodolfo G. Biazon, and All Other Persons Acting Their Control, Supervision, Direction, And Instruction In Relation To The Visiting Forces Agreement (VFA), respondents, October 10, 2000.

79. Section 25, Article 18.

80. Section 21, Article 7.

81. With Davide, Jr., C. J., Bellosillo, Kapunan, Quisumbing, Purisima, Pardo, Gonzaga-Reyes, Ynares-Santiago, and De Leon, Jr., concurring; Melo, and Vitug, join the dissent of J. Puno. Puno, J., see dissenting opinion. Mendoza, J., in the result; Panganiban, J., no part due to close personal and former professional relations with a petitioner, Sen. J. R. Salonga.

82. See also Republic of the Philippines Supreme Court, G.R. No. 151445, April 11, 2002, Arthur D. Lim and Paulino R. Ersando, petitioners, vs. Honorable Executive Secretary as alter ego of Her Excellency Gloria Macapagal-Arroyo, and Honorable Angelo Reyes in his capacity as Secretary of National Defense, respondents; Sanlakas and Partido Ng Manggagwa, petitioners-intervenors, vs. Gloria Macapagal-Arroyo, Alberto Romulo, Angelo Reyes, respondents, for a similar case regarding the constitutionality of Balikatan joint exercises between the United States and the Philippines, and chapter 2, "Rape and

Murder," in this volume for an analysis of additional legal cases regarding the constitutionality of the VFA.

83. See http://www.dnd.gov.ph/voltaire-t-gazmin.html (accessed May 25, 2017).

84. See his "Biography" on the Philippines main country page of the *Washington Diplomat,* http://www.washdiplomat.com/index.php?option=com_content&view=article&id=11972&Itemid=175 (accessed May 25, 2017); the "People" section of the Department of State Office of the Historian's website, https://history.state.gov/departmenthistory/people/goldberg-philip-s (accessed May 25, 2017); and the "Embassy" section of the U.S. Embassy in the Philippines website, https://ph.usembassy.gov/our-relationship/ambassador/ (accessed May 25, 2017).

85. This is a marked change from the previous agreements, which were signed by the U.S. ambassador and the Philippine secretary of foreign affairs.

86. See Section 25.

87. 2014 EDCA, Article 1: Purpose and Scope, point 1b.

88. Ibid., point 3. "United States forces" refers to not only U.S. military and civilian personnel but also "all property, equipment, and materiel of the United States Armed Forces present in the territory of the Philippines" (2014 EDCA, Article 2: Definitions, point 2).

89. 2014 EDCA, Article 3: Agreed Locations, point 5.

90. 2014 EDCA, Article 5: Ownership, point 3.

91. 2014 EDCA, Article 8: Contracting Procedures, point 2.

92. 2014 EDCA, Article 9: Environment, Human Health, and Safety, point 3.

93. The EDCA does not have an article on criminal jurisdiction since criminal jurisdiction continues to be covered under the VFA.

94. One included the organizations Bayan and party-list representatives from Gabriela, Alliance of Concerned Teachers (ACT), Anakpawis, Kabataan, and Makabayan, while the other included prominent individuals like Roland Simbulan, a University of the Philippines professor.

95. PS Res No. 1414, Republic of the Philippines, Congress of the Philippines, Senate, 16th Congress, 3rd regular session, resolution No. 105: Resolution Expressing the Strong Sense of the Senate that any Treaty Ratified by the President of the Philippines Should be Concurred in by the Senate, Otherwise the Treaty Becomes Invalid and Ineffective, November 10, 2015. However, the Office of Solicitor General disagreed and "maintains that there is no actual case or controversy that exists, since the Senators have not been deprived of the opportunity to invoke the privileges of the institution they are representing. It contends that the nonparticipation of the Senators in the present petitions only confirms that even they believe that EDCA is a binding executive agreement that does not require their concurrence." See EDCA January 2016 decision.

96. And who intensely debated the legality, use, and presence of the U.S. military in the Philippines during the commission.

97. The Honorable Justices Leonardo-De Castro, Brion, Perlas-Bernabe, and Leonen dissented the opinion, and in their dissent, they also conducted close readings of U.S.-Philippine military agreements, though they argued that the EDCA was unconstitutional, or "constitutionally deficient," and couched their opinions in upholding

the constitution and maintaining Philippine sovereignty—to show how and why they deemed the EDCA to be constitutional.

98. With Judges Velasco, Del Castillo, Villarama, Perez, Mendoza, and Reyes concurring. Judge Carpio wrote a separate concurring opinion that Peralta and Bersamin joined. Judge Jardeleza took "no part."

99. It also included a dissection of whether these parties were the appropriate ones to bring forth the suit. The judges found that they weren't but decided to hear the suit because "they nonetheless raise issues involving matters of transcendental importance." See section 25 of the 1987 Constitution.

100. They do find that contractors are not covered in the VFA, so the Philippines can expel them, though they also note that previous case law has shown how Philippine officials have known contractors have been a part of the personnel the U.S. military has brought in.

101. 2014 EDCA. She ends the July 2016 legal opinion with an epilogue on the 2016 United Nations Permanent Court of Arbitration tribunal's decision in *Republic of the Philippines v. People's Republic of China*, which concerned Chinese encroachment on Philippine islands in the South China Sea and was ruled in favor to the Philippines and against China. Noting that China rejected the ruling, Sereno claims that the EDCA, which "fully conforms to the government's continued policy to enhance our military capability in the face of various military and humanitarian issues that may arise," will help bolster Philippine sovereignty in this contentious area. This is because under Benigno Aquino III, the Philippines, with legal assistance from a U.S. lawyer, filed the complaint with Permanent Court of Arbitration in The Hague over Chinese interference in the South China Sea (see the "Arbitration on the South China Sea: Rulings from The Hague" section of the Asia Maritime Transparency Initiative website, https://amti.csis .org/ArbitrationTL/ [accessed May 30, 2017]). When The Hague ruled against China and in favor of the Philippines (see Denyer and Rauhala [2016]), it marked a Philippine victory over these long-disputed islands and served as an international and symbolic reproach to China (see Tharoor [2016]). However, the ruling came about under the newly elected president of the Philippines, Rodrigo Duterte, who has not capitalized on this ruling. Instead, Duterte has opted to direct South China Sea negotiations through conversations with China (see Perlez [2016]) rather than through legal means (see Hernández [2017]), in another effort to cultivate ties with Chinese leader Xi Jinping (see https://web.archive.org/web/20170502051102/http://www.philstar.com/headlines /2017/05/02/1695983/duterte-hesitant-us-visit-warm-china [accessed January 16, 2019]).

Yet this was not the end of the EDCA controversy. In July 2016, the cases were again jointly heard before the Philippine Supreme Court because the petitioners filed a motion for reconsideration. The petitioners sought to reverse the January 2016 decision and called for the Court to declare the EDCA "UNCONSTITUTIONAL AND INVALID and to permanently enjoin its implementation" (capitalization in court document). Justice Sereno denied the motion and claimed that the "petitioners do not present new arguments to buttress their claims of error on the part of this Court. They have rehashed their prior arguments." She also addressed "certain claims made by the petitioners [that] must be addressed," including the interpretation of the wording of "allowed in" in the Constitution (*verba legis* interpretation), "on strict construction of an exception," "on EDCA as a treaty," "on EDCA as basing agreement," and "on policy matters." See Republic of the Philippines Supreme Court, G.R. No. 212426, Rene A. V. Saguisag, Wigberto E. Tañada, Francisco "Dodong" Nemenzo, Jr., Sr. Mary John Mananzan, Pacifico A. Agabin, Esteban "Steve" Salonga, H. Harry L. Roque, Jr., Evalyn G. Ursua, Edre U. Olalia, Dr. Carol Pagaduan-Araullo, Dr. Roland Simbulan, and Teddy Casiño, petitioners, v. Executive Secretary Paquito N. Ochoa, Jr., Department of National Defense Secretary Voltaire Gazmin, Department of Foreign Affairs Secretary Albert Del Rosario, Jr., Department of Budget and Management Secretary Florencio Abad, and Armed Forces of the Philippines Chief of Staff General Emmanuel T. Bautista, respondents, July 26, 2016; Republic of the Philippines Supreme Court, G.R. No. 212444, Bagong Alyansang Makabayan (BAYAN), represented by its Secretary General Renato M. Reyes, Jr., BAYAN Muna Party-List Representatives Neri J. Colmenares and Carlos Zarate, GABRIELA Women's Party-List Representatives Luz Ilagan and Emerenciana de Jesus, ACT Teachers Party-List Representative Antonio L. Tinio, Anakpawis Party-List Representative Fernando Hicap, Kabataan Party-List Representative Terry Ridon, Makabayang Koalisyon Ng Mamamayan (MAKABAYAN), represented by Saturnino Ocampo, and Liza Maza, Bienvenido Lumbera, Joel C. Lamangan, Rafael Mariano, Salvador France, Rogelio M. Soluta, and Clemente G. Bautista, petitioners, vs. Department of National Defense (DND) Secretary Voltaire Gazmin, Department of Foreign Affairs Secretary Albert Del Rosario, Executive Secretary Paquito N. Ochoa, Jr., Armed Forces of the Philippines Chief of Staff General Emmanuel T. Bautista, Defense Undersecretary Pio Lorenzo Batino, Ambassador Lourdes Yparraguirre, Ambassador J. Eduardo Malaya, Department of Justice Undersecretary Francisco Baraan III, and DND Assistant Secretary for Strategic Assessments Raymund Jose Quilop as Chairperson and Members, respectively, of The Negotiating Panel for the Philippines on EDCA, respondents; Kilusang Mayo Uno, represented by its Chairperson, Elmer Labog, Confederation for Unity, Recognition and Advancement of Government Employees (COURAGE), represented by its National President Ferdinand Gaite, National Federation of Labor Unions-Kilusang Mayo Uno, represented by its National President Joselito Ustarez, Nenita Gonzaga, Violeta Espiritu, Virginia Flores, and Armando Teodoro, Jr., petitioners-in-intervention, Rene A. Q. Saguisag, Jr., petitioner-in-intervention, July 26, 2016.

    102. RA 7227 originally said it would be 3 percent, but a 2007 amendment, RA 9400, changed it to 5 percent of gross income earned.

    103. See Centeno (2002); Schumpter (1991 [1918]); Tilly (1992); for overviews of fiscal sociology, see Martin and Prasad (2014); Martin et al. (2009); Tilly (2009: xiii).

    104. Martin et al. 2009:1.

    105. For an example of how taxes shape U.S. inequality, see Newman and O'Brien (2011).

    106. Foreign retirees who have a pension or who work less than 750 hours during the year but make at least $50,000 can also be granted one of these special visas (Subic Bay Metropolitan Authority 2014:11).

    107. C.T.A. Case No. 6267, Jaime A. Cotero v. Commissioner of Internal Revenue.

    108. With Judge Juanito C. Castañeda concurring.

109. For another example, see CA-G.R. SP No. 78075, Donald L. Smith v. Commissioner of Internal Revenue.

110. At the time of my fieldwork, it was not duty-free.

111. The court case classifies it as a domestic corporation, but according to a 2011 list of SBFZ businesses and their nationalities that was given to me by SBFZ officials, the company's nationality is Taiwanese.

112. Using a 45 Philippine pesos to 1 U.S. dollar exchange rate.

113. C.T.A. Case No. 5895, Contex Corporation v. the Honorable Commissioner of Internal Revenue.

114. With Judges de Veyra and Saga concurring.

115. See summary of CA's case in Supreme Court Case G.R. No. 151135, Contex Corporation v. Hon. Commissioner of Internal Revenue, July 2, 2004.

116. With Judges Puno (Chairman), Callejo, Sr., and Tinga, JJ., concurring.

117. For a similar case, see C.T.A. Case No. 7575, Diageo Philippines Freeport, Inc. v. Commissioner of Internal Revenue and the Commissioner of Customs.

118. C.T.A. Case No. 6314, Taian (Subic) Electric, Inc. v. Commissioner of Internal Revenue.

119. With Judges Erlinda P. Uy and Olga Palanca-Enriquez concurring.

120. Lieberman 2009; see also Martin et al. (2009).

121. For example, see Ong (2006).

122. Goffman 1967.

Chapter 2

1. Nicole was the pseudonym used in the media and initial court documents to protect her identity, which was eventually released.

2. Republic of the Philippines, Court of Appeals, CA-G.R. CR HC No. 02587, People of the Philippines v. L/Cpl Daniel J. Smith, R.P. Court of Appeals, 2009, p. 7.

3. For example, see Republic of the Philippines, Court of Appeals, CA-G.R. CR HC No. 02587, p. 8.

4. Ibid.

5. Ibid., p. 9.

6. Republic of the Philippines, Criminal case number 865-14, Olongapo City Regional Trial Court, Branch 74, Prosecutor's memorandum, Testimony of Elias Gallamos, p. 9.

7. Ibid., Testimony of Barbie Galviro, p. 10.

8. Ibid., Testimony of LCpl Jairn Michael Rose, p. 14.

9. Ibid.

10. Criminal case number 865-14, Olongapo City Regional Trial Court, Branch 74, Defendant's memorandum, p. 12.

11. See Macatuno (2015); *Philippine Daily Inquirer* (2015).

12. B. Anderson 2006 [1983]:6.

13. B. Anderson 2006 [1983]; W. Anderson 2006; Enloe 2000 [1990]; Stoler 2002.

14. Baxi 2014; Das 2008.

15. Kanaaneh 2002.

16. Stoler 2002.

17. See Appadurai (1990) for his idea of a "mediascape."

18. For example, see Kramer (2006).

19. See Armstrong and Bernstein (2008) for what they call the "multi-institutional politics" approach to the study of social movements. This cultural and historical approach emphasizes multiple sources of power, the many institutions that compose the state, how social movement struggles are often over both systems of classification (as reflecting cultural meanings) and the accompanying allocation of resources (as material resources), since these are entwined, and the varied strategies activists use to address their central issues; see Krehbiel (2016) and Staton (2006) for how courts selectively use the media to promote awareness of cases.

20. Myers and Caniglia 2004; Oliver and Myers 1999. See Lester (1980) for the role that journalists and news organizations play in determining what is worthy of coverage.

21. For example, see Gamson and Wolfsfeld (1993); Lester (1980).

22. Gamson and Wolfsfeld 1993:116.

23. For example, see McCammon et al. (2007); see Benson and Saguy (2005) for how problems are framed differently across countries.

24. Bail 2012.

25. That his trial would be held in a Philippine court was not something that sparked controversy. The VFA specifies which court has jurisdiction over what crimes. For example, Filipino personnel cannot be tried by a U.S. military court nor detained by one; rather, they must be turned over to a U.S. civilian court or a Philippine authority. Similarly, U.S. military personnel cannot be tried under Philippine military or religious courts, only civil ones. Although these specifications are identified with two sentences, the bulk of the agreement related to criminal jurisdiction involves crimes committed by U.S. personnel and whether and when to try them under Filipino civil courts, echoing the importance of how custody and jurisdiction are perceived by each country. However, oftentimes, these authorities and rights run concurrent. When this occurs, Philippine authorities have primary jurisdiction except if the crime is committed solely against U.S. property or personnel or committed while in the "performance of official duty." Additionally, each government can request a waiver, and the Philippines will waive their right if the crime relates to the United States maintaining good order and discipline among its forces, unless Philippine officials think that the case is of particular importance. Each government also agrees to assist the other concerning arrest of criminals and to notify the other when an arrest has been made. In the Subic rape case, Lance Corporal Smith was tried under Philippine law and in Philippine courts. Once he was convicted, the agreement allows for the U.S. military to try him if he violated military laws while committing the offense, circumventing double jeopardy; however, the U.S. military did not proceed with any charges.

26. Republic of the Philippines, Court of Appeals, CA-G.R. CR HC No. 02587, p. 19.

27. Ibid., p. 36.

28. See Republic of the Philippines, Court of Appeals, CA-G.R. SP. No. 97212, Lance Corporal Daniel J. Smith, Petitioner v. Hon. Benjamin T. Pozon, in his capacity as Pre-

siding Judge of RTC, Makati, Br. 139, Jail Warden of the Makati City Jail, and People of
the Philippines, Respondents. Republic of the Philippines, Court of Appeals, for copies
of embassy notes discussing this issue.

29. Zerubavel 1987:345.

30. See Republic of the Philippines, Court of Appeals, CA-G.R. SP No. 97212, p. 18.

31. For the difference between "hard" and "soft" laws, where "soft" laws are ambiguously worded, see Abbott and Snidal (2000); see also Weil (1983) regarding how
ambiguous wording can lead to decisions subject to power and influence.

32. "'Nicole' Leads Protest in Subic, One Year after Rape," *Olongapo SubicBay
BatangGapo Newscenter*, November 3, 2006, http://subicbaynews.blogspot.com/2006/11
/nicole-leads-protest-in-subic-one-year.html (accessed January 17, 2019).

33. "Gabriela Holds Rally Near US Embassy Ahead of Nicole Verdict," Philstar
Global, November 22, 2006, https://www.philstar.com/headlines/2006/11/22/370558
/gabriela-holds-rally-near-us-embassy-ahead-nicole-verdict (accessed January 17, 2019).

34. Associated Press 2015.

35. Jennifer had a German fiancé named Marc Suseselbeck. Suseselbeck and Marilou Laude, one of Jennifer's sisters, participated in protests at Camp Aguinaldo when
Pemberton was transferred there. On October 22, 2014, they climbed over the gated entrance to the camp. Suseselbeck was caught on tape shoving one of the Filipino soldiers.
He was set to return home on October 27, 2014, but was stopped because the Philippine
Bureau of Immigration declared him an "undesirable alien," and he was under investigation for his behavior. Suseselbeck, as a white German citizen not associated with the
U.S. military, was voluntarily deported on November 1, 2014, and placed on a Philippine
blacklist, barred from entering the country. See Avendaño and Brizuela (2014); Esguerra
(2014); Fonbuena (2014); Rappler.com (2014); Santos (2014).

36. Republic of the Philippines, Criminal case number 865-14, Olongapo City Regional Trial Court, Branch 74, Prosecutor's memorandum, p. 11.

37. Larter 2015b; see also Larter 2015a.

38. Republic of the Philippines, Criminal case number 865-14, Olongapo City Regional Trial Court, Branch 74, Decision, p. 3.

39. Carcamo 2014.

40. Republic of the Philippines, Executive Order No. 199, s. 2000. It was renamed
and expanded in November 2014; see the Lawphil Project's website, https://www.lawphil
.net/executive/execord/eo2014/eo_175_2014.html (accessed May 24, 2018).

41. Ibid.

42. As previously mentioned, court documents suggested this occurred on October 19, 2014. However, newspaper articles say the transfer occurred on October 22, 2014.
See Esguerra (2014).

43. Esguerra 2014.

44. Ibid.

45. Ibid.

46. Ibid.

47. Ibid.

48. Ibid.

49. Ibid.

50. Ibid.

51. See Lee-Brago (2014).

52. Ibid.; Esguerra 2014.

53. VFA, Article 5: Criminal Jurisdiction, point 6.

54. Ibid.

55. Although I do not have access to contemporary embassy exchanges, we can make an educated hypothesis that similar debates occurred over custody of Pemberton.

56. Lee-Brago 2014.

57. VFA, Article 5: Criminal Jurisdiction, point 6.

58. Republic of the Philippines, Court of Appeals, CA-G.R. SP No. 97212, p. 2.

59. This echoes Weber's (1978) definition of power as "the probability that one actor within a social relationship will be in a position to carry out his own will despite resistance" (53) and the state as an actor who "successful upholds the claim to the *monopoly* of the *legitimate* use of physical force in the enforcement of order" (54).

60. Republic of the Philippines, Court of Appeals, CA-G.R. SP No. 97212; for draft version, see pp. 20–21; final opinion, see p. 22.

61. See U.S. embassy spokesman Matthew Lussenhop's quote in Cerojano (2006).

62. Republic of the Philippines, Court of Appeals, CA-G.R. SP No. 97212; for draft version, see p. 31; final opinion, see pp. 35–36.

63. Veronica Uy, "Smith Returned to Custody of US Embassy," *Philippine Daily Inquirer*, 2006, http://www.inquirer.net/specialreports/subicrapecase/view.php?db =1&article=20061230-40832 (accessed June 7, 2014, but no longer available on the site).

64. The president's residence, comparable to the U.S. White House.

65. Uy, "Smith Returned to Custody of US Embassy."

66. Republic of the Philippines Supreme Court, G.R. No. 175888, Suzette Nicolas y Sombilon v. Alberto Romulo, Raul Gonzalez, Eduardo Ermita, Ronaldo Puno and L/Cpl Daniel Smith, February 11, 2009.

67. Republic of the Philippines Supreme Court, G.R. 176051, Jovito R. Salonga, Wigberto E. Tanada, Jose de la Rama, Emilio C. Capulong, H. Harry L. Roque Jr., Florin Hilbay, and Benjamin Pozon v. Daniel Smith, Raul Gonzalez, Sergio Apostol, Ronaldo Puno, Alberto Romulo and all persons acting in the capacity, February 11, 2009; G.R. 176222, Bagong Alyansang Makabayan, represented by Dr. Carol Araullo, GABRIELA, represented by Emerenciana de Jesus, Bayan Muna, GABRIELA Women's Party, represented by Rep Liza Maza, Kilusang Mayo Uno (KMU), represented by El-mer Labog, Kilusang Magbubukid ng Pilipinas (KMP), represented by Willy Marbella; League of Filipino Students (LFS), represented by Vencer Crisostomo, and the Public Interest Law Center, represented by Atty Rachel Pastores v. President Gloria Macapagal-Arroyo, Eduardo Ermita, Alberto Romulo, Raul Gonzalez, and Ronaldo Puno, February 11, 2009.

68. Republic of the Philippines Supreme Court, G.R. No. 175888, G.R. No. 176051, G.R. No. 176222.

69. Republic of the Philippines Supreme Court, G.R. No. 175888, G.R. No. 176051, G.R. No. 176222, Dissenting Opinion by Chief Justice Reynato S. Puno.

70. Republic of the Philippines Supreme Court, G.R. No. 175888, G.R. No. 176051, G.R. No. 176222, Dissenting Opinion by Associate Justice Antonio T. Carpio.

71. GMA News 2009.

72. Preda Foundation 2011.

73. The 1987 Philippine Constitution states, "The State values the dignity of every person and guarantees full respect for human rights" (Article 2, Section 11); see https://www.lawphil.net/consti/cons1987.html (accessed January 17, 2019). RA 9710, the Magna Carta of Women, states, "The State affirms women's rights as human rights and shall intensify its efforts to fulfill its duties under international and domestic law to recognize, respect, protect, fulfill, and promote all human rights and fundamental freedoms of women, especially marginalized women, in the economic, social, political, cultural, and other fields without distinction or discrimination on account of class, age, sex, gender, language, ethnicity, religion, ideology, disability, education, and status"; see the Lawphil Project's website, https://www.lawphil.net/statutes/repacts/ra2009/ra_9710_2009.html (accessed February 5, 2019). Similar language is used in RA 9432, the Magna Carta for Public Social Workers; see the Lawphil Project's website, http://www.lawphil.net/statutes/repacts/ra2007/ra_9433_2007.html accessed (April 25, 2017); see also https://www.pcw.gov.ph/wpla/enacting-anti-discrimination-based-sexual-orientation-and-gender-identity-law (accessed January 22, 2019). However, there is no specific LGBTQ national law.

There have been efforts to introduce anti–hate crime and anti-discrimination laws concerning LGBT rights in the Philippines. For example, the Honorable Sol Aragones introduced a bill in 2013 (see the Philippine Congress website, http://www.congress.gov.ph/legisdocs/basic_16/HB02572.pdf [accessed April 25, 2017]); Senator Sonny Angara introduced a bill in 2014 (see the Philippine Senate website, http://www.senate.gov.ph/lisdata/2016217272!.pdf [accessed April 25, 2017]); and Representative Geraldine Roman, the first transgender representative, introduced a bill in 2016 (see the Philippine Congress website, http://www.congress.gov.ph/legisdocs/basic_17/HB00267.pdf [accessed April 25, 2017]). Although previous bills failed to move forward, there is hope "that Roman—who has been recently included in a global list of inspiring women for 2016—will finally set the bill firmly as part of the law of the land" (see Bueno [2016]). Additionally, the Philippines does not recognize same sex marriage (see the Family Code, on the Chan Robles Virtual Law Library website, http://www.chanrobles.com/executiveorderno209.htm#.WP-AG2nyuUk [accessed April 25, 2017]). As recently as 2011, Representative Rene Relampagos introduced a bill that would prohibit recognition of same sex marriage, even if the couple was married elsewhere (Erik 2011), though there is a current, 2016 bill being considered that would legalize civil unions—but not marriage (Dizon 2016). The Communist Party of the Philippines, however, does recognize same sex marriage (Manlupig 2016). The Philippines also has a long history of recognizing the role of *bakla* ("effeminate and/or cross-dressing male") in society, from precolonial Philippines to the present (Garcia 2009 [1996]: xxi). See Benedicto (2014) for a discussion of "gay Manila" and chapter 3 in particular for a discussion of contemporary *bakla*.

74. See the "LGBT Archives Project" section of Eric Julian Manalastas's website, http://pages.upd.edu.ph/ejmanalastas/policies-ordinances (accessed April 25, 2017).

75. Talusan 2016.

76. For example, see Republic of the Philippines, Criminal case number 865-14, Olongapo City Regional Trial Court, Branch 74, Defendant's memorandum, p. 49.

77. Here, the judge engaged in relational work—the matching of media, transactions, boundaries, and relationships—in her ruling by deciding that Jennifer's family was entitled to monies from Pemberton because of her death and his U.S. citizenship; see Zelizer (2005).

78. Republic of the Philippines, Criminal case number 865-14, Olongapo City Regional Trial Court, Branch 74, Decision, p. 57.

79. Using a 45 Philippine pesos to 1 U.S. dollar exchange rate.

80. See Republic of the Philippines, Criminal case number 865-14, Olongapo City Regional Trial Court, Branch 74, Decision, p. 59.

81. See Macatuno (2015); *Philippine Daily Inquirer* (2015).

82. *Philippine Daily Inquirer* 2015.

83. Cahiles 2015.

84. De Jesus 2015.

85. Ayroso 2015.

86. De Jesus 2015.

87. Dizon 2015.

88. Cruz 2016.

89. "Walden Bello Statement on the March 30 Pemberton Ruling, Balikatan 2016, EDCA and VFA," April 5, 2016, https://www.facebook.com/notes/walden-bello-for-senator-movement/walden-bello-statement-on-the-march-30-pemberton-ruling-balikatan-2016-edca-and-/10154017672570610/ (accessed January 17, 2019).

90. UCANews.com 2016.

91. Gomez 2016b.

92. Talusan 2016.

93. Ibid. Talusan recounted the ambivalent conversations she witnessed while in the SBFZ: "Ronald Troops Jr., a light-skinned taxi driver a head taller than the rest . . . [said,] 'If it were me, I would have killed her too. . . . [The Laude family] should take their money and stab it down their throats. There are so many families that have gone hungry because of their greed.' Troops says that he is half American, but he has never been able to locate his father, Ronald Sr., who was a servicemember based in Olongapo. He recounts his struggles trying to make a living as a taxi driver when servicemembers are not allowed to leave the area. Suddenly, his mood turns calmer. 'I was only joking when I said I would have killed Jennifer,' Troops says, balking. 'Transgenders are also Filipinos like us.'"

94. Talusan 2016.

95. Republic of the Philippines Supreme Court, G.R. No. L-50276, The People of the Philippines vs. Michael J. Butler, January 27, 1983.

Chapter 3

1. For Susan's story, see Moselina (1987:59–62, Open Forum subsection) and Añonuevo (1987:91–97). Here, I use Rhacel Parreñas's (2011) understanding of sex work as a way to describe "a wide array of sexual provisions that include flirtation, stripping, escort service, and prostitution" (5).

2. See Miralao, Carlos, and Santos (1990).

3. Constable 2003:30.

4. Estimates are from the 1986 National Consultation on Prostitution in the Philippines conference (Puno 1987:10; Mananzan 1987:17).

5. Brennan 2004:15–16.

6. David 2015.

7. For example, see Choo (2016b); Enloe (2000 [1990]).

8. Whether called "cultural wealth" (Bandelj and Wherry 2011), "global imaginaries" (Constable 2003:30), or "metroimperial fantasies" (Mendoza 2015).

9. See also Choo (2016a) for how South Korean feminist advocacy groups' portrayals of Filipina migrant hostesses and migrant wives in South Korea reinforces their place at the bottom of a "moral hierarchy" and for a discussion regarding each group's different "material and moral costs associated with the status of victim" (464) and how they, in response, framed their lives; see Moselina (1987:62, Open Forum subsection) for a brief mention that activists realize "that not all relationships are exploitative. There are some who are only looking for conversation. But you could count those on your fingers. There is almost always intercourse."

10. Swidler 2001:82.

11. See Armstrong and Bernstein (2008) on their multi-institutional politics perspective, which emphasizes the role of culture in social movements and how political activity is about changing both symbolic (such as categories of classification) and material resources.

12. Swidler 2001. In her book, Swidler presents two types of love myths: a prosaic-realistic love myth that describes love as a choice that required commitment and work and the bourgeois love myth where love is romantic, unique, and all encompassing.

13. The Roman Catholic Church played a key role in these demonstrations, and GABRIELA was founded in response to Marcos's rule. For a brief overview of the early, evolving stance of the Roman Catholic Church and the NCCP regarding martial law under Marcos, see Rigos (1975).

14. Mananzan 1987:19.

15. Ibid., 23.

16. For example, see Enloe (2000 [1990]. Parreñas shows how entertainer migrants are also seen as a fundamentally moral problem, despite their own creation of alternative moralities and moral orders and their adherence to societal understandings thereof; Parreñas also links the wide-reaching and unsubstantiated claims of human trafficking as

it relates to migrant entertainers to "the moralistic norm of antiprostitution . . . resulting in the mistaken basis of their identification as trafficked persons and as a result, the near elimination of their migrant community. . . . [It] flatten[s] our perspective on their experiences as well as diverting our attention from the need to closely examine the conditions of their labor and migration" (8).

17. Bulawan 2003:97.

18. Ibid., 98.

19. Ibid., 99.

20. Kanlungan Ministry and Bagwis 1987:156–58.

21. Ibid., 157.

22. Ibid., 158.

23. Ibid.

24. In contrast, see Constable (2003) for a virtual ethnography of "mail-order" or correspondence marriages.

25. See Violy's story in Caagusan 2001 [1998]:160–78.

26. Caagusan 2001 [1998]:163.

27. Ibid.

28. Ibid., 164.

29. Ibid.

30. Ibid.

31. Ibid.

32. Ibid, 169.

33. Ibid.

34. Ibid., 171.

35. Stoltzfus 1987a:171.

36. Marasigan 1987:106.

37. This moral framing of sexual intimacies and militaries is also commonly seen in social scientific and humanistic research within and outside the United States and the Philippines. For example, see Enloe (2000 [1990]); Lee (2010); Sturdevant and Stoltzfus (1992); Tadiar (2004).

38. According to Preda, Cullen won the 2000 Human Rights Award from the city of Weimar (Germany) for his work. See https://www.preda.org/main/work/weimar /pressrelease.html (accessed January 17, 2019). Preda also claims that he has been nominated four times for the Nobel Peace Prize (see the "About Us" section of the Preda Foundation's website, http://www.preda.org/biography-of-fr-shay-cullen/ [accessed October 17, 2016]). Neither Cullen's name nor the Preda organization's name are listed in the Nobel Prize nominations archive (see the Nobel Prize searchable archives, https:// www.nobelprize.org/nomination/archive/search_people.php [accessed October 17, 2016]). However, this is likely due to the policy of the Norwegian Nobel Committee (which chooses Nobel Peace Prize candidates), which states that they do not disclose the names of nominees for fifty years. See: https://www.nobelprize.org/nomination/peace/ (accessed January 17, 2019).

39. Cullen 2003b:164.

40. Cullen 2003a:146.

41. Ibid., 146–47.

42. Cullen 2003c:167.

43. Noticeably absent in his speech are black or other Americans of different races, despite the existence of the "jungle" in Olongapo City, which was the entertainment part of the city that catered to black servicemembers.

44. For example, see Enloe (2000 [1990]); Go (2011); Lutz (2009).

45. For example, see Menez (1986–87:136).

46. Añonuevo 1987:64.

47. Ibid., 70–73.

48. Ordinance No. 4, series of 1963, as cited in Añonuevo (1987:84).

49. Ordinance No. 22, series of 1975, as cited in Añonuevo (1987:85).

50. Olongapo City Ordinance No. 56, series of 1969, section 6.3, as cited in Añonuevo (1987:84).

51. Sturdevant and Stoltzfus 1992:46.

52. U.S. servicemembers were also tested, given medicine for treatment, and re-stricted to being inside the base if they tested positive. However, it's speculated that men would seek treatment outside the base to avoid the restrictions accompanying a positive test. For information on the organization of sex work and the accompanying processes, see Añonuevo (1987); Stoltzfus (1987a, 1987b); Sturdevant and Stoltzfus (1992).

53. Moselina 1987:54, Open Forum subsection.

54. And contemporarily, the military police.

55. Stoltzfus 1987a:173. It is important to note that they stopped bar fights and other types of physical altercations. Women were also able to complain to the shore patrol to investigate charges of violence and/or abuse by servicemembers, and during the base's era, if he were found guilty, he could have been ordered to pay a fine to the complainant directly. It allowed an institutionalized path for Filipino/as to direct their complaints about U.S. servicemembers and provided oversight of said members. However, whether and how often Filipino/as used this avenue and how many fights were stopped remains unknown (see Stoltzfus [1987b: 168]).

56. Tan and de la Paz 1987:40.

57. They also interviewed 150 women in Angeles but focus here on the Olongapo City women they interviewed.

58. Miralao et al. 1990:36.

59. Ibid., 31.

60. Ibid., 33.

61. See the "Who We Are" section of WeDpro's website, http://wedprophils.org /about-us/history/ (accessed October 7, 2016).

62. From their report, the Olongapo data comes from "125 registered women en-tertainers contacted at the Social Hygiene Clinic work mostly in the bars, clubs, or massage clinics along Olongapo's Magsaysay Drive, and in Barrio Barreto and nearby Subic. Representing the city's unregistered entertainers were another 25 streetwalkers, most of whom were interviewed while temporarily detained at the Police Substation in

Olongapo. These women were in jail for failure to produce their Identification Cards as registered entertainers in the city" (Miralao, Carlos, and Santos 1990:4).

63. See Parreñas (2011).

64. Ibid.

65. Ibid., 147.

66. Zelizer 2005.

67. Moselina 1987:59, Open Forum subsection.

68. Parreñas 2011.

69. Hoang 2015.

70. Moselina 1987:59–60, Open Forum subsection.

71. See "Madelin" and "Lita" chapters in Sturdevant and Stoltzfus (1992) for additional stories of women standing up for themselves and even using threats of calling the military on men who take—or want to take—advantage of them.

72. Moselina 1987:61–62, Open Forum subsection.

73. Parreñas (2011) finds that the entertainers are conditioned to not say no and instead find other ways around stopping unwanted behavior.

74. The report does not include direct quotations; rather, it includes the number of women and their reported answers to particular survey questions.

75. Miralao et al. 1990:39.

76. Ibid., 47.

77. Ibid., 41.

78. Stoltzfus 1987a:172.

79. This is in contrast to Brennan's (2004) findings that there is not exclusive commitment between sex workers and foreign clients or husbands.

80. The other being Vatican City.

81. See the Philippine Family Code on the Chan Robles Virtual Law Library website, http://www.chanrobles.com/executiveordreno209.htm#.WrFFI-jwaUk (accessed March 20, 2018), and news articles and opinions, such as De Mesa Laranas (2016) and BBC News (2018).

82. Swidler 2001.

83. Constable 2003.

84. Brennan 2004:20.

85. This included $1.436 billion in removable property (which the military was able to take with them when they withdrew) and $763 million in buildings and structures; the navy itself invested $772 million in property at the Naval Supply Depot and $164 million in removable property, such as floating cranes or dry dock generators (United States General Accounting Office 1992).

86. "The Philippine Bases Treaty," Hearing before the Subcommittee on Asian and Pacific Affairs of the Committee on Foreign Affairs, House of Representatives, 102nd Cong., 1st Sess., September 25, 1991, p. 26.

87. Declassified/Released former confidential Department of State telegrams, Subject: U.S.-Philippines Military Bases Agreement, January 1979, From: SecState WashDC to AmEmbassy Lisbon.

88. Brennan 2004.

89. Caagusan 2001 [1998]:176; emphasis added.

90. Ibid., 177.

91. Zelizer 2005.

92. The Amerasian mothers, like Maria and Danielle, that I interviewed were in Clark/Angeles City. Although Subic and Clark were very similar in some ways, in other ways they were very different—for example, the aftermath of the U.S. military's withdrawal, where Clark was looted and Subic was taken over by volunteers to keep it from being looted. I include these stories here because of the similarities echoed in the WeDpro's survey on Olongapo City women entertainers. These women were affiliates of a nonprofit organization with ties to an international headquarters and mothers of Amerasian children (those with U.S. servicemen as fathers). As such, they could have held more critical views of sex work than those without such ties. Yet, even here, lines are blurred between what constitutes sex work and what is a romantic partnership, as the Amerasian mothers I spoke with in the Philippines conceptualized their relationships with these men as a type of marriage, regardless of whether they were legally married, while also simultaneously hoping to legally marry an American. Even self-confessed sex workers described these relationships in similar terms and actively constructed moral boundaries about them.

93. She had thought that with her Japanese husband, she found someone who accepted her for who she was and who was the epitome of the all-consuming love and acceptance seen in movies. However, her marriage to her Japanese husband did not work out due to, she said, communication and cultural issues.

94. The concept of women "being saved" by foreign men is not new; see Spivak (1994).

95. See also "Madelin," "Lita," and "Glenda" in Sturdevant and Stoltzfus (1992) regarding discussions of both constructions of "marriage," hopes, and love, as well as the anger and betrayal felt toward Americans who fail to live up to these love myths and/or hurt them.

96. Lamont and Molnar 2002.

97. See Cunneen and Stubbs (1997:41) for these fears from Filipina marriage migrants in Australia. Cahill (1990) found that approximately 62 percent (twenty-three of the thirty-seven) Filipinas married to Australians in their survey, approximately 63 percent (forty-one of the sixty-five) Filipinas married to Japanese in their survey, and only approximately 35 percent (eighteen of the fifty-one) Filipinas married to Swiss men in their survey report that a Filipina wife will experience discrimination in their neighborhood by other women (98); see also Choo (2016b) for how this plays out in "Basetown," a U.S. overseas military base in South Korea, and how, in contrast, the Filipina hostesses seek to "produce and suppress feelings of true love, depending on the conditions of their relationships because they hoped to use their romantic relationships with US GIs to accomplish two important goals. First, they aimed to lay a material foundation for upward mobility by securing financial support and the ability to migrate to the United States. Second, they sought moral affirmation that their romantic feelings were sincere, not instrumental" (197).

98. See Brennan (2004) for similar moral boundary work that sex workers engage in to differentiate themselves from one another.

99. U.S. Navy Board of Review, WC NCM 60-00615, August 8, 1960. Although this case does not explicitly say that Hernandez is a Philippine citizen, the decision and arguments laid out by the judges do not indicate that Hernandez is a U.S. servicemember nor a U.S. citizen. Hernandez is also a common Spanish surname in the Philippines. The case law cited in the decision—on both sides—also includes a U.S. servicemember marrying a Filipina national without a commander's permission. Thus, for this legal case, I assume that Hernandez is a Filipina citizen, though the ban on marriages in the Philippines—regardless of the spouse's nationality—without the commander's permission is a blanket rule that covers any marriage that takes place in the Philippines and involves U.S. servicemembers, with the exception of retired personnel and reservists on inactive duty.

100. He ended up serving three months and one week, and his salary forfeiture was delayed until six months after his release.

101. For violating Article 92 of the Uniform Code of Military Justice, failing "to obey any lawful general order or regulation." This continues to be in place; see the "Military Naturalization" section of the U.S. Navy Judge Advocate General's website, http://www.jag.navy.mil/organization/code_16_immigration_info.htm#foreignmarriage (accessed May 27, 2014).

102. Though "normally, permission to marry will be granted, except in those instances where the prospective alien spouse would certainly or probably be barred from entry into the United States or territory of residence of the applicant for permanent residence or naturalization"; see Public Law 414, in June 27, 1952, chap. 8—General Penalty Provisions (pp. 226–30), which outlines restrictions on immigration. For example, fines were to be paid if someone brought an immigrant who was "(1) feeble-minded, (2) insane, (3) an epileptic, (4) afflicted with psychopathic personality, (5) a chronic alcoholic, (6) afflicted with tuberculosis in any form, (7) afflicted with leprosy or any dangerous contagious disease, or (8) a narcotic drug addict, shall pay to the collector of customs of the customs district in which the place of arrival is located for each and every alien so afflicted (226)" and unless they have the proper documentation, which was approved within 120 days of their application, and if not, that the existence of such disease or disability could not have been detected by the exercise of due diligence prior to the alien's embarkation" (227). Contemporary immigration laws have similar mental and physical health restrictions. See, for example, the U.S. Citizenship and Immigration Service's website, https://www.uscis.gov/ilink/docView/SLB/HTML/SLB/0-0-0-1/0-0-0-29/0-0-0-2006.html#0-0-0-2301 (accessed October 6, 2016).

103. "Or alternatively, an explanation why entrance into the United States is not contemplated."

104. For example, he agreed that he examined whether "his prospective spouse and children" were eligible to migrate; he understood that migration eligibility is only determined when they apply for a visa and that the United States "is in no way obligated to transport the spouse or dependents to the United States except as provided for in current directives." See U.S. Navy Board of Review, WC NCM 60-00615, August 8, 1960.

105. 9 USCMA 724, 26 CMR 504.

106. Ibid., p. 506.

107. Though his sentence was later lessened by superior officers, see ibid., p. 505.

108. And received the same sentence and subsequent reduction of sentence.

109. 9 USCMA 724, 26 CMR 504, p. 505.

110. Ibid., p. 506.

111. Ibid., p. 507.

112. Ibid.

113. See Wu (2002) for a history of the racialization of Asians and Asian Americans in the United States and Shimizu (2007) for how Asian/American women are hypersexualized.

114. See Bonilla-Silva (2006) for a discussion of what he calls color-blind racism.

115. Brandt 1987.

116. For example, see Baldoz (2011, chap. 3).

117. Ibid. for a discussion related to interracial marriages and relations between Filipino men and white women during the 1920s and 1930s.

118. See the entry for "Mildred Loving" in the "People" section of Biography.com, http://www.biography.com/people/mildred-loving-5884 (accessed April 27, 2017).

119. W. Anderson 2006; Choy 2003; Espiritu 2003; Go 2008; Mendoza 2015.

120. David 2015.

121. Even today there are currently two types of visas for which spouses or intended spouses of U.S. citizens can apply. One is the IR1 (Immediate Relative) or CR1 (Conditional Residence) immigrant visa for the spouse—meaning that the two people are already wed, where the IR1 is for those married over two years or more, while a CR1 is issued for those couples married under two years (see the "U.S. Visas" section of the U.S. Department of State's website, https://travel.state.gov/content/visas/en /immigrate/family/immediate-relative.html [accessed October 14, 2016]). The other type of visa is a K-1 nonimmigrant visa for intended spouses or fiancé(e)s of U.S. citizens, which requires the marriage to take place within ninety days of entering the United States and—with exceptions—requires the prospective spouses to have physically met one another within the past two years (see the "U.S. Visas" section of the U.S. Department of State's website, https://travel.state.gov/content/visas/en/immigrate /family/fiance-k-1.html [accessed October 14, 2016]). The K-1 visa was established in 1970, during the Vietnam War, under Public Law 91-225 [An Act to amend the Immigration and Nationality Act to facilitate the entry of certain nonimmigrants into the United States, and for other purposes, April 1970]). According to retired foreign service officer Lange Schermerhorn (2015), after approximately one hundred Vietnamese fiancées of U.S. servicemen were ineligible for visas since they were not yet married, Congress debated what to do, until "one day the head of the Consular Affairs Bureau's Visa Office called from Washington, D.C., to order the issuance of a visitor's visa to one of these cases, citing the interest of a very senior U.S. senator. The consul general responded that on the grounds of equity and fairness, the consulate would take that as an instruction to issue visitor's visas to all of the fiancées in limbo. The Visa Office backed off the request, but that situation eventually led to the establishment of the 'K' (fiancée) visa category" (n.p.).

Chapter 4

1. Bondoc 2017. The Pearl S. Buck Foundation is now called Pearl S. Buck International. The writer and philanthropist Pearl S. Buck founded this foundation to help Amerasian children, because, as she wrote, "after fifteen years in the field of lost and needy children I am convinced that the most needy in the world are the children born in Asia whose mothers are Asian but whose fathers are American," as cited in Conn (1998:355).

2. Amerasians were a specific concern of Pearl S. Buck because of the many Amerasian children she saw abandoned by U.S. servicemen after World War II. See, for example, "Pearl S. Buck's Biography," Pearl S. Buck International, https://www.pearlsbuck .org/wp-content/uploads/2018/02/2018-1-Jan-Biography.pdf (accessed June 28, 2018).

3. See the "About" section of his website, http://www.apldeap.com/ (accessed April 27, 2017).

4. For example, see Huang-Teves (2015).

5. Fernandez 2015:4.

6. See the "About" section of his website, http://www.apldeap.com/ (accessed April 27, 2017).

7. Fernandez 2015:8.

8. Ibid.

9. See the "About" section of his website, http://www.apldeap.com/ (accessed April 27, 2017).

10. For information on his biography, see the "About" section of his website, http:// www.apldeap.com/ (accessed September 27, 2016). Details about his Amerasian childhood background and blindness are also often mentioned in news articles about him; see, for example, Lacorte (2015); Pimentel (2005); http://newsinfo.inquirer.net/733481 /apl-de-ap-donates-retinal-camera-to-davao-city-hospital (accessed September 29, 2016).

11. Starting with the first album they released after Stacy "Fergie" Ferguson joined the group, there have been Tagalog songs on each of their three major studio albums. For example, the album *Elephunk* has "The Apl Song," *Monkey Business* has "Bebot," and *The E.N.D.* has "Mare," which was released first as an international bonus track and then added onto the deluxe two-disc version of the album. apl.de.ap has released Tagalog singles as a solo artist.

12. apl.de.ap comes from the initials of his name (Allan Pineda Lindo), "de" is from, and "ap" stands for where he is from, Angeles, Philippines. apl.de.ap maintains not only family but also philanthropic ties to his former homeland. He created a foundation that centers on the arts, technology, and health (particularly eye care) (see, for example, Lo [2011] and the "About" section of his website, http://apldeapfoundation [accessed September 29, 2016]) and partners with the Children's Hospital Los Angeles for children's eye care in the Philippines (Business Wire 2014) and Philippine national philanthropic organizations, such as the Ninoy and Cory Aquino Foundation, the Ayala Foundation, and the Philippine Development Foundation, among others, to help build classrooms (Ignacio 2011). He is also a National Peace Ambassador for Malacañang,

the name of the presidential residence and workplace (it is also used as a shorthand for the Philippine government) (https://www.officialgazette.gov.ph/2012/09/12/apl-de-ap-anne-curtis-gerald-anderson-among-celebs-named-peace-ambassadors/ and https://www.officialgazette.gov.ph/2012/10/12/peace-ambassador-apl-de-ap-pledges-books-classrooms-for-bangsamoro-children/ last [accessed January 17, 2019]); an official endorser of Clark Green City, part of the Bases Conversion and Development Authority, which transforms the former U.S. military bases into places that benefit the Philippines (*Philippine Daily Inquirer* 2014); and was honored for his charity work by Children's Hospital Los Angeles in 2016 (Rueda 2016; https://globalnation.inquirer.net/138103/apl-de-ap-honored-for-saving-babies-from-blindness (accessed January 17, 2019) and by Philippine president Aquino in 2012 (Arcayan 2012). He also owns a Jollibee restaurant, a popular Philippine fast food chain (Inquirer.net. 2015); developed a music label, Jeepney Music, for Filipino artists (see Estoista-Koo [2010]); and has a children's book written about him, although it doesn't mention his Amerasian heritage (Fernandez 2015; Macas 2015).

13. To my knowledge, there is no global database that estimates the number of Amerasian children born throughout Southeast Asia during this time.

14. For example, see Ahern (1992); Gastardo-Conaco and Israel-Sobritchea (1999); Kutschera, Pelayo, and Talamera-Sandico (2012); Kolby (1995); Montes (1995).

15. See Bloemraad, Korteweg, and Yurdakul (2008).

16. Gieryn 2000.

17. Gastardo-Conaco and Israel-Sobritchea 1999:38.

18. Ibid., 39.

19. Ibid., 45.

20. For example, see Gastardo-Conaco and Israel-Sobritchea (1999); Kutschera et al. (2012).

21. Gastardo-Conaco and Israel-Sobritchea 1999. For this focus group, they were accompanied by two additional members of their research team.

22. Ibid., 53.

23. Ibid., 54.

24. For example, see ibid.

25. See "Amerasian Immigration Proposals," Serial No J-97-121, June 21, 1982.

26. A similar act is the 1987 Amerasian Homecoming Act, which was aimed to financially assist Vietnamese Amerasian children, who would be classified as refugees.

27. "Amerasian Immigration Proposals," Serial No J-97-121, June 21, 1982.

28. For example, see Baldoz (2011).

29. For example, see 1987 H.R. 2265; 1983 H.R. 1990.

30. I focus on the Southeast Asian rather than the East Asian (Japan, Taiwan, Korea) countries in the acts. Note, however, that Korean Amerasians are included because of the Korean War.

31. For example, see 1987 U.S. Homecoming Act.

32. Christopher Acebedo, Ruby Acebedo, Tyson David, and Brenda David v. United States, No. 93-124C, U.S. Court of Federal Claims, 1993 (unpublished opinion).

33. Abortion is illegal in the Philippines, and the Revised Penal Code of the Philippines describes women's abortions as attempts to "conceal her dishonor" and disregards the structural factors that often shape women's decisions, such as lack of contraception, poverty, and lack of sexual education; see Revised Penal Code of the Philippines, Book 2, Section 2—Infanticide and Abortion, and in particular, articles 258 and 259, on the Chan Robles Virtual Law Library website, http://www.chanrobles.com/revisedpenal codeofthephilippinesbook2.htm#.WQc9d2nyuUk (accessed May 1, 2017).

34. See Crimmins (2007).

35. United States Claims Court, Case No. 93-124C, Christopher Acebedo, an individual; Ruby Acebedo, an individual; Tyson David, an individual; Brenda David, an individual, and those similarly situated, Plaintiffs v. United States of America, Defendant, p. 12.

36. Ibid.

37. Ibid., p. 13.

38. Ibid., Attorneys for Plaintiff Class, p. 10.

39. United States Claims Court, Case No. 93-124C, p. 16. See Ahern (1992); Collins (2000); Kolby (1995); Levi (1992); Mermelstein (1983); and Montes (1995) for further analysis of this case and other laws/legal cases dealing with Filipino Amerasians.

40. United States Claims Court, Case No. 93-124C, p. 4.

41. Ibid., p. 3.

42. Ibid., Defendant's Motion to Dismiss, pp. 29–30.

43. When countries and nationalities are named, Vietnamese Amerasians are the group that is specified.

44. See Title 8 of the Philippine Civil Code, on the Chan Robles Virtual Law Library website, http://www.chanrobles.com/civilcodeofthephilippinesbook1.htm (accessed July 6, 2018), and chapter 6 of the Philippine Family Code, on the Chan Robles Virtual Law Library website, http://www.chanrobles.com/executiveordeno209.htm# .VOt1TC7Ygrg (accessed July 6, 2018).

45. Republic of the Philippines Supreme Court, G.R. No. L-18566, In the matter of the adoption of Elizabeth Mira, Gilbert R. Brehm and Ester Mira Brehm, petitioners-appellees, vs. Republic of the Philippines, oppositor-appellant, September 30, 1963.

46. With Judges Bengzon, Padilla, Bautista Angelo, Concepcion, Barrera, Dizon, Regala, and Makalintal, JJ., concurring, and Labrador and Reyes, J.B.L., JJ., took no part.

47. Republic of the Philippines Supreme Court, G.R. Nos. 77737-38, Christina Marie Dempsey, a Minor and Represented by Her Mother, Janalita Rapada, and the People of the Philippines v. Regional Trial Court, Branch LXXV, Third Judicial Region, Olongapo City, and Joel Dempsey, R.P. Supreme Court, August 15, 1988.

48. Using a 39.23 Philippine pesos to 1 U.S. dollar exchange rate.

49. With Judges Fernan, C.J., Feliciano, Bidin, and Cortes, JJ., concurring.

50. See "Largest U.S. Immigrant Groups over Time, 1960–Present" of the Migration Policy Institute's website, http://www.migrationpolicy.org/programs/data-hub/charts /largest-immigrant-groups-over-time (accessed May 1, 2017); they've fluctuated between third and fourth place (see the "Hispanics" section of the Pew Research Center Hispanic

Trends website, http://www.pewhispanic.org/2015/09/28/chapter-5-u-s-foreign-born
-population-trends/ [accessed May 1, 2017]).

51. See McKinley (1900:193).

52. See Bonus (2000); Espiritu (2003); Filipino American National Historical Society (2011); New York Theater Wire (n.d.).

53. We would get to know each other throughout my stay, and two nights after our
initial conversation, we saw the movie *John Tucker Must Die* at the local SM's theater.

54. For example, see Title 8 of the Philippine Civil Code, on the Chan Robles Virtual
Law Library website, http://www.chanrobles.com/civilcodeofthephilippinesbook1.htm
(accessed February 22, 2015), and chapter 6 of the Philippine Family Code, on the Chan
Robles Virtual Law Library website, http://www.chanrobles.com/executiveorderno209
.htm#.VOt1TC7Ygrg (accessed February 22, 2015).

55. See Bloemraad et al. (2008).

Chapter 5

1. This is my English translation of a Tagalog quote.

2. Taylor 2004:23.

3. Bair 2010; Fernandez-Kelly 1983; Freeman 2000; Mills 2001 [1999]; Ong 2010;
Salzinger 2003; Wolfe 1992.

4. I follow in the footsteps of the feminist scholarship I cite. However, in my reading
none of the authors I cite above provide an analytic category or concept in which to refer, think about, and compare these images, such as that which I call "labor imaginaries."

5. For an overview of sociological understandings of morals, see Hitlin and Vaisey
(2013).

6. For example, see Gamson and Wolfsfeld (1993); Lester (1980).

7. Similar to Freeman's (2000) research on Caribbean women employed in the information sector.

8. Salzinger 2003:29.

9. Freeman 2000.

10. Blanton and Blanton 2009.

11. See Mosley and Singer (2015) for an overview.

12. See McKay (2006) for variation in four electronics factories, each located in one
of four SEZs in the Philippines, as well as each factory's different working regime—
despotic, panoptic, peripheral human resource, or collectively negotiated—and how different workers understood their employment (similar to Harbor Point mall, as "clean"
and "modern"); see Lee (1998), Mills (2001 [1999]), Salzinger (2003), and Wolf (1991) for
differences in gender regimes and place in factory work.

13. Bair 2010; Fernandez-Kelly 1983; Freeman 2000; Mills 2001 [1999]; Ong 2010;
Salzinger 2003; Wolfe 1992.

14. This is my English translation of a Tagalog quote.

15. Many scholars document how factory and/or work inside SEZs often adhere to
labor laws and minimum wage standards and that their wages are often higher than what
is found outside of these factories and zones, e.g., Freeman (2000) and Mills (2001).

16. This is in contrast to Johnson (2004), who suggests, "Once on their bases, America's modern proconsuls and their sous-warriors never have to mix with either 'natives' or American civilians. Just as they did for young nineteenth-century Englishmen and Frenchmen these military city-states teach American youths arrogance and racism, instilling in them the basic ingredients of racial superiority" (25). Although I would agree with the latter claim regarding racialization, the former claim regarding never having to mix with "natives" or American civilian workers is not true. Both Filipinos and American civilians worked within the base.

17. U.S. 102nd Congress, "Implications of the US Withdrawal from Clark and Subic Bases," Hearing before the Subcommittee on Asian and Pacific Affairs of the Committee on Foreign Affairs, House of Representatives (Washington, DC: U.S. Government Printing Office, 1992).

18. For example, see "Assessing America's Options in the Philippines," House of Representatives, Committee on Foreign Affairs, Subcommittee on Asian and Pacific Affairs, the Woodrow Wilson International Center for Scholars and the Congressional Research Service, February 3, 1986.

19. Military Bases in the Philippines: Employment of Philippine Nationals Agreement signed at Manila, May 27, 1968.

20. U.S. General Accounting Office 1992:11–12.

21. Declassified message from the American Embassy in Manila to the Secretary of State, Washington DC, April 1976.

22. Ibid.

23. Declassified/Released former confidential Department of State telegrams, Subject: Possible Press Play on Search of BX Employees at Subic, April 1976. Soon after the incident, U.S. officials found out that the Philippine press got wind of the situation and brainstormed ways to answer anticipated questions from reporters.

24. Ibid.

25. Ibid.

26. Declassified/Released former confidential Department of State telegrams, Subject: Nex Search at Subic: Recent Developments, August 1976.

27. Ibid.

28. 48 F.3d 514, Juanita A. Rosete, petitioner, v. Office of Personnel Management, respondent, No. 94-3342, U.S. Court of Appeals, Federal Circuit, February 3, 1995, rehearing denied April 3, 1995.

29. See both *Rosete v. Office of Personnel Management* and the "Retirement" section of the U.S. Office of Personnel Management's website, https://www.opm.gov/retirement-services/csrs-information/ (accessed November 16, 2016).

30. With Judges Newman and Clevenger concurring.

31. Title VII is also known as the Civil Rights Act of 1964, which prohibits discrimination based on an "individual's race, color, religion, sex, or national origin"; see Title VII, Unlawful Employment Practices, SEC 2000e-2 [Section 703]a, of the "Laws, Regulations, & Guidance" section of the U.S. Equal Employment Opportunity Commission's website, https://www.eeoc.gov/laws/statutes/titlevii.cfm (accessed December 26, 2016).

32. U.S. District Court, District of Columbia, Manuel Licudine, Plaintiff v. Donald C. Winter, Secretary of the Navy, Defendant, Civil Action No. 08-1086 (JR), March 26, 2009.

33. The amicus brief includes language from the 1902 Philippine Government Act, 1916 Philippine Autonomy Act, and 1934 Tydings-McDuffie Act/Philippine Independence Act as evidence that the U.S. Congress considered Filipinos to be Philippine, not U.S., citizens.

34. See also U.S. District Court, District of Columbia, Gualberto Alver, Plaintiff vs. Donald C. Winter, Secretary of the Navy, Defendant, Civil Action No. 08-1384 (JR), June 29, 2009; Miguel Abaigar, Plaintiff vs. Donald C. Winter, Secretary of the Navy, Defendant. Civil Action No. 08-1466 (JR), June 29, 2009; Menandro Cipriano, Plaintiff vs. Donald C. Winter, Secretary of the Navy, Defendant. Civil Action No. 08-2035 (JR), June 29, 2009; Hortencio Arcelo, Plaintiff vs. Donald C. Winter, Secretary of the Navy, Defendant. Civil Action No. 08-1247 (JR), June 29, 2009; Alfredo R. Alipio, Plaintiff vs. Donald C. Winter, Secretary of the Navy, Defendant. Civil Action No. 08-1251 (JR), June 29, 2009; and Rogelio Acosta, Plaintiff vs. Donald C. Winter, Secretary of the Navy, Defendant. Civil Action No. 08-1318 (JR), June 29, 2009, for similar claims that Judge Robertson denied based on his *Licudine v. Winter* ruling.

35. For a discussion of the liminal legal space Filipinos occupy as it relates to the early twentieth century, race, and citizenship, see Baldoz (2011, chap. 3).

36. Port Technology 2016.

37. For example, see Torres (2012).

38. McKay 2007:617–18; see also McKay and Lucero-Prisno (2012).

39. For details, see Republic of the Philippines, Court of Appeals, CA-G.R. SP No. 121186, Subic Shipbuilder Corp. and Redondo I-Tech Corp. v. National Labor Relations Commission (Fourth Division) [Formerly 7th Division], Rogelio Bernal and Christine Baylon, November 11, 2011.

40. With Judges Andres B. Reyes Jr. and Michael P. Elbinias concurring.

41. Ramos 2016.

42. ABS-CBN News 2012.

43. Santolan 2011.

44. Gamil 2011.

45. *Los Angeles Times* 2011; see also Seol (2011).

46. Mysinchew.com 2011; see also Robinson (2011).

47. For example, see Bacani (2011); *Olongapo SubicBay BatangGapo Newscenter* (2010).

48. See press release, http://la.indymedia.org/news/2011/06/246678.php and http://partidongmanggagawa2001.blogspot.com/2011/07/protest-caravan-presses-hanjin-to.html (accessed January 22, 2019).

49. Ibid.; and see Anthony Bayarong's blog, https://abayarong.wordpress.com/2011/09/24/slideshow-workers-protest-against-hanjin-shipyard-subic/amp/ (accessed June 14, 2017).

50. Anthony Bayarong's blog.

51. "No straight path" is a reference to former Benigno Aquino III's "tuwid ang daan" (the straight path) slogan, which is about anticorruption, reform, and good governance; see, for example, http://newsinfo.inquirer.net/729614/palace-straight path-better -than-fast-path (accessed June 14, 2017).

52. Anthony Bayarong's blog.

53. For images see ibid. or his photos on www.subictimes.com's Vimeo account, https://vimeo.com/25933940 (accessed June 14, 2017).

54. See https://www.senate.gov.ph/press_release/2009/0207_cayetano1.asp, https://www.senate.gov.ph/press_release/2009/0207_estradaj1.asp, and https://www.senate.gov .ph/press_release/2009/0124_cayetano1.asp (accessed January 22, 2019).

55. Sixteen other companies had valid licenses to recruit but were violating regulations (T. Santos, 2012). See Zhao and Amante (2005) for a comparison of Filipino and Chinese seafarers, including their recruitment.

56. See also Han (2012).

57. Torres 2012. Note that recently, Hanjin has collapsed due to bankruptcy, and the South Korean government has been unwilling to bail them out; this has had a worldwide impact on the global shipping industry. See, for example, Carey (2016); Christie, Richwine, and Hals (2016); Hals (2016a, 2016b); Lee (2016a, 2016b); Reuters (2016a, 2016b).

58. Stets and Carter 2012:121.

59. Or "schemata of interpretation" (Goffman 1974:21) or the "organization of experience" (13).

60. See Howard (2000) for an overview of multiple types of identity formation and symbolic interaction.

61. In 2011, South Korea was the fifth largest major trading partner for the Philippines, comprising 6.1 percent (US$6.67 billion) of total trade, 4.6 percent (US$2.24 billion) of exports, and 7.3 percent (US$4.42 billion) of imports (see National Statistics Office [2011a:13]; National Statistics Office [2011b:13]), while in 2009, there were 497,936 Korean visitors to the Philippines ("Arrivals by Region," Department of Tourism Philippines, http://www.visitmyphilippines.com/index.php?title=VisitorStatistics&func=all&pid =39&tbl=1 [accessed July 15, 2013]). In 2011 and 2012, South Korea was the Philippines' largest visitor market, with 1,031,155 arrivals (24.13 percent of total arrivals) in 2012, which was up 11.45 percent from the 925,204 visitors from Korea who arrived in 2011 (Philippines Department of Tourism 2011, 2012). In 2012, there were 337,268 Filipino visitors to South Korea, which accounts for 3.4 percent of all total visitors and the seventh largest market for visitors, while in 2012, there were 331,346 Filipino visitors to South Korea, which accounted for 3 percent of all total tourists and the ninth largest market for visitors. See https://kto.visitkorea.or.kr/eng/tourismStatics/keyFacts/KoreaMonthlyStatistics /eng/inout/inout.kto and https://kto.visitkorea.or.kr/eng/tourismStatics/keyFacts /KoreaMonthlyStatistics/eng/inout/inout.kto (accessed January 22, 2019).

62. In 2012, over 1,031,155 South Koreans visitors (24.13 percent of all visitors) traveled to the Philippines ("Visitor Arrivals to the Philippines Reached Record-High 4.3 Million in 2012," Department of Tourism Philippines, http://www.visitmyphilippines .com/images/ads/681e231e0a5d37d2e5b7090b7db5d8c1.pdf [accessed July 15, 2013]).

63. See, for example, Berehulak (2016).

64. See, for example, Carvajal (2017), and Lema and Petty (2017).

65. As seen in Rhacel Parreñas's 2011 work, using the term *trafficking* can be misleading and is not appropriate for all the Filipina migrant entertainment workers.

66. "Court Rules in Favor of Filipina Prostitutes" 2003; Kim 2002.

67. For example, see Lee (2008).

68. For example, see Ong (2006); Nash and Fernandez-Kelly (1983).

69. For example, see Lee (1998); McKay (2006); Salzinger (2003).

70. See Freeman (2000) for an account of Caribbean women working in the information sector.

71. Garrido 2013b.

72. This discursive stratification extends to other goods and services found inside the SBFZ. For example, a handful of the Filipino Harbor Point workers visit the mall on their day off to window-shop or go to the beach. Inside the SBFZ, going to the beach along the main boardwalk is free, although there are some located outside the Central Business District that charge admission. This is in contrast to the beach alongside the main highway connecting various *barangays* to Olongapo City, where hotels and other stores set admission prices to enter. For Filipino visitors, window-shopping at Harbor Point was also a highlight of their trips to the SBFZ. Most Filipinos also mentioned that the strictness of the FZ meant that you are able to do more or engage in more activities (such as drinking or smoking) outside of the area and that the strict, regulated behavior expected within the SBFZ extended to everyone, including foreigners.

73. How does that compare to actual crime statistics, and is the regulation of crime similarly blurred? According to SBMA Authority Law Enforcement Department statistics there were 295 crime incidents in 2007, 195 in 2008, 116 in 2009, 128 in 2010, and 106 in 2011. In 2012, from January to June there were 23 incidents; 11 of them were related to theft. The Law Enforcement Department does not keep track of the nationalities of perpetrators or victims. In comparison, the Olongapo City Police Department reported 2,195 crime incidents in 2011, which represents a crime rate of 898 incidents per 100,000 people, higher than the national figure; 80 percent (1,094 of the index crimes) were related to robbery and theft (http://www.olongapocity.gov.ph/ProtectiveService3 .html, accessed February 5, 2014). The SBFZ covers more land—262 square miles compared to Olongapo City's approximate 71.4 square miles—and is less densely populated; it is home to 6,124 residents, whereas Olongapo City contains 247,842 residents (for land in Subic Bay, see the "Major Districts" section of the SBMA's website, http://invest .mysubicbay.com.ph/major-districts (accessed February 5, 2014); for residents and land in Olongapo City, see the "Residents" section of the same, http://live.mysubicbay.com .ph/residents/residents-profile (accessed February 5, 2014). Although these figures do suggest that the SBFZ has less crime across more area than Olongapo City, they do not take into account the number of visitors to the SBFZ—an estimated 4 million in 2011— or unreported crimes.

74. Similar to factory and information sector work around the world. See Freeman (2000), Mills (2001 [1999]), Salzinger (2003), and Wolfe (1992) for accounts of gendered

labor in these sectors and how labor conditions differ across sectors, place, and by managers.

75. This type of bureaucratic red tape is common throughout the Philippines. See Rodriguez (2010) on "document processing" for labor migrants. Employment in the SBFZ, like the rest of the Philippines and in many places around the world, also takes on a particular gendered form, with advertisements for jobs that specify particular demographic characteristics like gender, age, and the like. While this would be illegal in the United States, it is legal in the Philippines. See Rodriguez (2010) for discussion of how Filipinos are racialized and gendered in marketing their labor force.

76. Kelly 2001.

77. Although this is not the primary focus of this chapter and applies to employment outside of Harbor Point, many jobs within the SBFZ, like those in the rest of the Philippines, place advertisements for workers that specify gender, age, and other characteristics, shaping who applies and gets hired within; see also McKay (2006) for demographics of workers of Philippine SEZs and advertisements.

78. See Granovetter (1973) for his foundational work on the "strength of weak ties"—what I describe here is slightly different and more akin to crony capitalism or what Kang (2002) calls money politics (corruption and cronyism).

79. This is similar to many accounts of rural-urban migrants (e.g., Ong 2010), though see Wolfe (1992) for an account of how Javanese women's salaries don't always go to supporting their families and may often cost families money.

80. See Parreñas (2001); Zelizer (2005).

81. Wages of Harbor Point employees that I interviewed ranged from P230 to P330 per day (or $5.75 to $8.25 per day, using a 40 Philippine pesos to 1 U.S. dollar exchange rate).

82. However, Peace Corps Volunteers' salaries are comparable at P150 per day, and missionaries raise their own money before they embark on their trip.

83. This is my English translation of a Tagalog quote.

84. Ibid.

85. See https://treaties.un.org/doc/Publication/UNTS/Volume%201155/volume-1155 -I-18232-English.pdf (accessed November 21, 2016).

86. See U.S. District Court, District of Columbia, Anthony Rossi et al., Plaintiffs, v. Harold Brown, Secretary of Defense, et al., Defendants, Civ. A. No. 78-2346, March 20, 1979. Yet Judge Flannery's ruling was reversed when the case was heard by the U.S. Court of Appeals, District of Columbia. In his ruling, Circuit Judge Wilkey disagrees with the previous court's interpretation of the case and says that because the Senate was not consulted, nor did they approve it by two-thirds vote, the BLA was not a treaty per the U.S. Constitution; rather it is an executive agreement. As such, Rossi, Bumgarner, Perry, and Frierson were illegally discriminated against because of their nationality, and the BLA's employment preference for Filipino nationals is invalid. See U.S. Court of Appeals, District of Columbia Circuit, Anthony M. Rossi et al., Appellants, v. Harold Brown, Secretary of Defense et al., Appellees, No. 79-1485, argued April 15, 1980; decided September 15, 1980; rehearing denied December 18, 1980. However, when the case

was brought again to the courts, this time the U.S. Supreme Court, Justice Rehnquist, using essentially the same arguments and evidence as Judge Flannery, ruled that the "treaty exception" clause applies to the BLA, thus reversing the court of appeals decision and validating the preferential employment of Filipino nationals. See Supreme Court of the United States, Caspar W. Weinberger, Secretary of Defense, et al., Petitioners v. Anthony M. Rossi et al., 456 U.S. 25 (1982), No. 80-1924, argued February 22, 1982; decided March 31, 1982.

87. This banality of corruption is also seen in legal cases, where the same set of parties file multiple grievances and appeals over the years.

88. Rodriguez 2010.

89. Freeman 2000; Lee 1998; Mills 2001 [1999]; Ong 2010; Salzinger 2003. Mills 2001 [1999];

90. Lee 1998.

91. Salzinger 2003:23.

92. McKay 2006.

Chapter 6

1. If the view is not blocked by other buildings. I calculated this using the formula: distance to horizon (miles) = sqrt [(7 × h [feet])/4].

2. See their LinkedIn description at https://www.linkedin.com/company/lighthouse-marina-resort and their photo gallery at http://www.lighthousesubic.com/gallery.php (both accessed May 4, 2017).

3. Another exception is when U.S. military ships—or other types of ships, such as evangelical ones—are docked and informal vendors line the boardwalk; see Reyes (2018a).

4. During the holiday season, however, there is an official exception to these rules. The Night Market and Subic Bay Fiesta Carnival spring to life, and anyone and everyone may cross through the SBFZ's gates. Lining Aguinaldo Street, white, red, and green pop-up tents suddenly appear, filled with clothing, toys, purses, accessories, and almost any goods you may desire. Come nightfall, it's often difficult to navigate the crowds of people it attracts. Smoke emanates from the food cooking in the streets, and the following morning, what is left behind are mounds of trash scattered along the street, some of it blowing in the wind. People come inside the SBFZ not only for the Night Market but also the other holiday attraction open to the public: the Subic Fiesta Carnival. The entrance looks like a medieval castle, with faux-painted bricks lining the outer gate. Two towers, each with a red cone that lights up at night and topped with yellow flags, anchor the entrance. On top of this entrance, keeping with the medieval theme, is the facade of a pink and purple keep with a white window, surrounded by five more towers: two shorter yellow towers with blue cones in front, slightly higher red and green towers to the left-hand side, and a taller pink tower with a blue cone to the right rear of it. The colorful, light-filled words SUBIC FIESTA CARNIVAL beckon visitors to come inside. Although this entrance is permanent, seen year-round, come November, it comes alive at night as people flock to the sweet, sticky smells of popcorn

and candy and the chance to play games and climb into amusement park rides that twist and twirl in the sky and on the ground. It becomes a symbol of the good life whose doors are open to all. Yet the limited open access to the SBFZ has not stopped SBFZ visitors and workers, as well as those who have never stepped foot inside of it, from imagining it as a different world. It may even contribute to the SBFZ's reputation as an exclusive, global community because the Night Market and Carnival offer a taste of what life could be.

5. For example, see Enloe (2000 [1990]); Go (2011).

6. For example, see Freeman (2000) and Mills (2001 [1999]), among others.

7. For an overview of sociological understandings of morals, see Hitlin and Vaisey (2013). For an overview of the sociological approach to morals and markets, see Fourcade and Healy (2007).

8. Auge 1995. Although many of the nonplaces Auge specifies are transient, such as airports or motoways, he also describes supermarkets as nonplaces. Here, I show how a supermarket in a mall and a duty-free store, which can be considered a megasupermarket, are in fact places.

9. This chapter does not focus on those excluded from the SBFZ—whether voluntarily (activists) or involuntarily (the poor). Instead, it highlights those who are included to counter the narrative that these are capitalist spaces that only bring negative consequences and are perceived as such by local communities.

10. Frye 2012.

11. Research shows how geographic boundaries carry symbolic meanings that enforce social boundaries (Lamont and Molnar 2002). Places' imageries, characters, and cultures also have implications for policy and symbolize "who belongs," thus implying who does not belong (e.g., see Molotch, Freudenberg, and Paulsen [2000]; Zukin [1995]). The meanings that people assign to cultural objects are not static; rather, they are malleable and depend on context (Griswold 1987; Milligan 1998). In the transformation from colonial to postcolonial, these meanings and practices become particularly important and are continually negotiated, contested, and manipulated to promote certain ideologies and distinctions, such as national and cultural identities and myths, as well as economic advancement (Clarke 2007; Kusno 1998; Low 1993; Yeoh 1996, 2000). For example, Manila's segregation derives not only from the city's socio-spatial organization but from people's "sense of place," where "certain types of places (enclaves or slums) or the people associated with those places elicit certain introspective states (mental states, including affect and motivation), which, in turn, predispose certain segregating practices" (Garrido 2013b:1344). The enclosed spaces of special economic zones, including Philippine economic zones, are tax-free areas within countries that are meant to attract foreign businesses and investment and call to mind similar research on the privatization and segregation of cities. These spaces are also differentiated by practices. For example, Bach (2010) and Sklair (1992) show how the Shenzhen special economic zone and its surrounding villages maintain distinct appearances through practices related to order and disorder, and these differences create a symbolic story—"if Shenzhen is a narrative about speed, progress and civilization, its villages serve as the narrative's other" (Bach 2010:422). In

the Philippine FZs, through the practice of requiring *barangay* (neighborhood) clearance passes and using employment agencies, corporations can avoid "unwanted" workers who may be pro-union "troublemakers" and cultivate a compliant workforce (Kelly 2001). Another type of differentiation involves moral ordering around dirt and pollution. Mary Douglas (2008 [1966]) argues that categorizations of "dirty" and "clean" are products of systemic ordering and classification. Societies use different definitions of acceptability and prohibitions, and these reflect symbolic patterns that maintain status and social order by enacting social relations. U.S. colonialism in the Philippines also provides an example of how these boundaries are constructed, because it was rooted in efforts to "civilize" Filipinos through practices related to hygiene and the construction of "healthy" versus "diseased" (W. Anderson 2006). In modern metro Manila, gated communities and other policed and exclusionary zones are similarly linked to notions of order as "good." These communities provide a respite from the disorder of the rest of the city (Murphy and Hogan [2012]). Indeed, Garrido (2013a) specifies that the elites' exclusive spaces—upscale shopping malls, residential communities, and business centers—are seen as "modern" and "rational," a "model" that serves as a direct contrast to the "disorder" of the rest of Manila. This differentiation of space by morality and order also extends to Manila's public parks (Yotsumoto 2013). Many researchers have also examined bases' symbolic representations, linking them to disparities in class structure, material goods, national identity, and crimes in such places as Okinawa, Korea, Vietnam, and the Philippines (Cooley and Marten 2006; Inoue 2003; Morris and Dunkelberger 1998; Ralston and Keeble 2009).

12. For related looks at how waste and hygiene are socially imagined and produced see W. Anderson (2006), Douglas (2002 [1966]), and Gille (2007).

13. Taylor 2004:23; see also Arjun Appadurai's (1996) definition: "the imagination has become an organized field of social practices, a form of work (in the sense of both labor and culturally organized practice), and a form of negotiation between sites of agency (individuals) and globally defined fields of possibility . . . [it] is the key component of the new global order" (31).

14. Scholars have long recognized how consumption relates to identity; for overviews of consumption, both conspicuous and otherwise, see Ward (2015); Zukin and Maguire (2004).

15. Bourdieu 1984.

16. Veblen 1994 [1899]: chap. 4.

17. Bourdieu 1984.

18. For a call to study a sociology of the future, see Mische (2009).

19. Weber 1978 [1922].

20. Nye 1990, 2004.

21. See Nye (1990, 2004) on America's "soft power," which is asserted through attraction rather than force; Gramsci (1989 [1971]) and Lears (1985) on cultural hegemony; and Gaventa (1982) and Lukes (2005 [1974]) on the three faces or dimensions of power (most relevant to this discussion is the third dimension of power).

22. Ong 1991.

23. See Mosley and Singer (2015) for an overview of the complex processes regarding labor and globalization, how multinational corporations and foreign aid may have positive or negative consequences for workers depending on context, and how governments mediate global economic processes.

24. Human rights violations and labor are addressed in chapter 5, "Labor and Imagined Identities," in this volume.

25. See also Mills (2003) for an overview of research that focuses on the gendered inequalities associated with global borderlands and other forms of global labor, as well as research that highlights how these gendered forms of labor can create new identities and opportunities. See Tsing (2005) for what she calls the "friction" produced by global connections.

26. In the Bourdieuan sense, see Bourdieu (1984).

27. Small (non-*palengke*) grocery stores in the Philippines are also similarly laid out with rows of packaged goods.

28. Also, Gloria only goes to the authorized Ford dealership inside the SBFZ because of the assurance of quality she'll receive there. They can be "assure[d] that their worker won't make the hole bigger to make it fit. So, you can imagine if you start to put in, it doesn't quite fit for whatever reason, [non-SBFZ employees will] make the hole bigger, put it on there, and that is really how much you have to pay attention. So, that kind of thing, it just takes a lot of time. You can't do that."

29. See Mosley and Singer (2015) for an overview of positive and negative consequences.

30. Auge 1995.

31. Douglas 2002 [1966].

32. The *mga palengke* do provide opportunities for customized clothing, which they buy for their son's required school uniform. However, not all clothes are bought there. It's specifically limited to customized uniforms for his son, as Patrick's wife tends to buy clothes at SM—particularly one in San Fernando, not the one in Olongapo—instead of Harbor Point because it's cheaper and "she's not a fashion victim." Nevertheless, the SBFZ grocery stores and the *mga palengke* are differentiated on perceived quality.

33. Bourdieu 1984; DeSoucey 2016; Phillips 2006.

34. Carrington 1999:31.

35. Carrington 1999; DeVault 1991.

36. However, it is not a "cosmopolitan canopy" (Anderson 2011) where racial differences are suspended, precisely because the stratification of these two malls rely on the stratification of people by nationality and class, among others.

37. See Goffman (1959).

38. Garrido 2013b:1344.

39. For an example in the United States, see Cohen (1996); in Australia, see Voyce (2003); for a description of Egyptian malls, see Abaza (2001); for a comparison of U.S. and non-U.S. malls, see Salcedo (2003).

40. Stillerman and Salcedo 2012.

41. Ibid.

42. Marantz, Kalev, and Lewin-Epstein 2014.

43. Connell 1999:433.

44. Though some, including the Maintenance Division (ironically enough), have rust and dirt embedded in their outdoor walls.

45. Interview with SBMA Law Enforcement Department staff member, September 14, 2012; see also "Residents' Profile: Subic Bay's Residents' Population Count by Nationality," on the SBMA's website, http://live.mysubicbay.com.ph/residents/residents -profile (accessed May 10, 2017).

46. Subic Bay Metropolitan Authority 2011:14.

47. Ibid. See also Subic Bay Metropolitan Authority 1992, 2014.

48. While the Philippines has healthy or anti-littering laws more generally (see Philippine Presidential Decree No. 825 and Philippines Administrative Order 341), they are not as strictly enforced as similar rules within the Subic Bay Freeport Zones.

49. "SBMA Police Watch Thieves Burn Plastic Off Cables (SBN Exclusive!)," *Subic Bay News*, September 30, 2012, http://subicbaynews.net/?p=2940 (accessed January 30, 2013).

50. See "The Colorful Jeepneys of Olongapo City," Official Site of Alongapo City, http://www.olongapocity.gov.ph/jeepneys (accessed May 8, 2017).

51. There may be exceptions if someone is driving a noncommercial-use jeepney through the SBFZ highways on their way to another destination.

52. For example, see *Olongapo SubicBay BatangGapo Newscenter* (2010); Philippines News Agency (2010).

53. Republic of the Philippines, Court of Appeals, CA-G.R. SP No. 111627, Philippine Court of Appeals, Manila, Fifteenth Division, Subic Bay Metropolitan Authority, petitioner v. Hon. Richard Paradeza in his capacity as the Presiding Judge of Olongapo City Regional Trial Court, Branch 72, and Westwood Unlimited Trading Corporation, respondents, June 27, 2011.

54. Ibid.

55. With Judges Magdangal M. De Leon and Socorro B. Inting concurring.

56. Republic of the Philippines, Court of Appeals, CA-GR SP No. 111627.

Conclusion

1. CNBC 2016; Reuters 2016b.

2. Berehulak 2016; Paddock 2016.

3. Gomez 2016a.

4. For example, see Baldoz (2011) for U.S. nativist sentiments regarding the Philippines and Filipino migration.

5. Lee 2017. For a discussion of Chinese foreign direct investment in the Philippines see Camba 2017.

Methodological Appendix

1. Ocampo 2016.

2. Following in the footsteps of many urban scholars, such as Contreras (2013); Duck (2015); Ralph (2014); and Rios (2011).

3. For more in-depth discussion of the ethnographic tool kit and examples from my fieldwork, see Reyes (2018a).

4. Swidler 1986:273.

5. I am multiracial, not biracial, but I focus on my Filipina and white heritage here because it directly relates to the research.

6. Desmond 2016.

7. See Lichterman (2017).

8. For example, see Contreras (2013); Hoang (2015).

9. For example, Abramson and Dohan (2015); Abramson et al. (2018); Guenther (2009); Jerolmack and Murphy (2017).

10. Cohen 2015, 2017.

11. For example, Humphrey (1970) and Scheper-Highes (1979) also generated controversy regarding ethics and confidentiality.

12. For example, Jerolmack and Murphy (2017).

13. Reyes 2018c.

14. Similar to Ralph (2014).

15. For example, see Jerolmack and Murphy (2017).

References

I collected a wide array of documents from the U.S. National Archives, the U.S. Digital National Security Archives, Access to Archival Databases (AAD) from the National Archives and Records Administration (http://aad.archives.gov/aad/), the Chan Robles Virtual Law Library, Lawphil.net, Philippine government websites, U.S. government websites, and Philippine and U.S. court system archives. All are available upon request. Writings, memoirs, oral histories, news articles, and research by Filipino authors, activists, and writers are included in the "Secondary Sources" list.

Primary Sources

"Amerasian Immigration Proposals." Hearing before the Subcommittee on Immigration and Refugee Policy of the Committee on the Judiciary, United States Senate, 97th Congress, second session on S. 1698, A Bill to Amend the Immigration and Nationality Act to Provide Preferential Treatment in the Admission of Certain Children of United States Armed Forces Personnel, Serial No. J-97-121, June 21, 1982.

"Assessing America's Options in the Philippines." House of Representatives, Committee on Foreign Affairs, Subcommittee on Asian and Pacific Affairs, the Woodrow Wilson International Center for Scholars and the Congressional Research Service, February 3, 1986.

Base Labor Agreement and the Collective Bargaining Agreement. 1968.

Bell Trade Act. 1946.

Christopher Acebedo, Ruby Acebedo, Tyson David, and Brenda David v. United States, No. 93-124C, U.S. Court of Federal Claims, 1993 (unpublished opinion).

C.T.A. Case No. 5895. Contex Corporation v. the Honorable Commissioner of Internal Revenue.

C.T.A. Case No. 6267. Jaime A. Cotero v. Commissioner of Internal Revenue.

C.T.A. Case No. 6314. Taian (Subic) Electric, Inc. v. Commissioner of Internal Revenue.

C.T.A. Case No. 7575. Diageo Philippines Freeport, Inc. v. Commissioner of Internal Revenue and the Commissioner of Customs.

Declassified message from the American Embassy in Manila to SecState Washington DC, April 1976. Subject: GOP Protest on Subic Search Incident.

Declassified/Released former confidential Department of State telegrams, Subject: Nex Search at Subic: Recent Developments, August 1976. From: AmEmbassy Manila, To: SecState WashDC Priority 9187.

Declassified/Released former confidential Department of State telegrams, Subject: Possible Press Play on Search of BX Employees at Subic, April 1976. From: AmEmbassy Manila, To: SecState WashDC 3790.

Declassified/Released former confidential Department of State telegrams, Subject: Press Play on Nex Search at Subic, April 1976. From: AmEmbassy Manila, To: SecState WashDC Priority 3963.

Declassified/Released former confidential Department of State telegrams, Subject: U.S.-Philippines Military Bases Agreement, January 1979, From: SecState WashDC to AmEmbassy Lisbon.

Department of the Navy. Memorandum for the Deputy Secretary of Defense, June 13, 1977. Subj: Reductions in Our Philippine Military Presence (S)—Information Memorandum; Department of the Air Force, July 1, 1977. Memorandum for the Deputy Secretary of Defense; Subject: Reductions in our Philippine Military Presence—Information Memorandum (U); Signed: John C Stetson, Sec of Air Force; "Implications of the US Withdrawal from Clark and Subic Bases," Hearing before the Subcommittee on Asian and Pacific Affairs of the Committee on Foreign Affairs, House of Representatives. March 5, 1992; "The Philippine Bases Treaty," Hearing before the Subcommittee on Asian and Pacific Affairs of the Committee on Foreign Affairs, House of Representatives, September 25, 1991.

Embassy note, CITA No. 820.005. The American Ambassador to the Philippine Secretary of Foreign Affairs No. 559, Title: "Amendment to Agreement concerning military bases," December 23, 1947.

Embassy note, Response. The Philippine Secretary of Foreign Affairs to the American Ambassador, December 24, 1947.

Enhanced Defense Cooperation Agreement. 2014.

48 F.3d 514. Juanita A. Rosete, petitioner, v. Office of Personnel Management, respondent, No. 94-3342, U.S. Court of Appeals, Federal Circuit, February 3, 1995, rehearing denied April 3, 1995.

"Implications of the US Withdrawal from Clark and Subic Bases." Hearing before the Subcommittee on Asian and Pacific Affairs of the Committee on Foreign Affairs, House of Representatives, March 5, 1992.

Laurel-Langley Agreement. 1955.

Military Assistance Act. 1947.

Military Bases Agreement. 1947.

Military Bases in the Philippines: Employment of Philippine Nationals Agreement signed at Manila May 27, 1968; Entered into force May 27, 1968. With agreed minutes. Agreement between the government of the United States of America and the government of the republic of the Philippines relating to the employment of Philippine nationals in the United States military bases in the Philippines.

Mutual Defense Treaty. 1951.

National Policy Paper on the Republic of the Philippines: Part One—US Policy: 1966.

Philippine Autonomy Act. 1916.

"The Philippine Bases Treaty." Hearing before the Subcommittee on Asian and Pacific Affairs of the Committee on Foreign Affairs, House of Representatives, 102nd Cong., 1st Sess., September 25, 1991.

Philippine Government Act. 1902.

Philippine Presidential Decree No. 825, Providing penalty for improper disposal of garbage and other forms of uncleanliness and for other purposes. November 7, 1975.

Philippine Republic Act 9003, An act providing for an ecological solid waste management program, creating the necessary institutional mechanisms and incentives, declaring certain acts prohibited and providing penalties, appropriating funds therefor, and for other purposes. January 26, 2001.

"The Philippines: A Situation Report." Staff Report to the Senate Select Committee on Intelligence, United States Senate, November 1, 1985.

"Philippines: General Survey." National Intelligence Survey, 1965.

Philippines Administrative Order 341. Implementing the Philippine health promotion program through healthy places. 1997.

PS Res No. 1414. Republic of the Philippines, Congress of the Philippines, Senate, 16th Congress, 3rd regular session, resolution No. 105: Resolution Expressing the Strong Sense of the Senate that any Treaty Ratified by the President of the Philippines Should be Concurred in by the Senate, Otherwise the Treaty Becomes Invalid and Ineffective, November 10, 2015.

Public Law 91-225. An Act to amend the Immigration and Nationality Act to facilitate the entry of certain nonimmigrants into the United States, and for other purposes, April 1970.

Public Law 414, Chapter 8—General Penalty Provisions. June 27, 1952.

Republic Act No. 7227—An act accelerating the conversion of military reservations into other productive uses, creating the bases conversion and development authority for the purpose, providing funds therefore and for other purposes. March 13, 1992.

Republic of the Philippines. Criminal case number 865-14. Olongapo City Regional Trial Court, Branch 74.

———. Executive Order No. 199, s. 2000. Creating a presidential commission to monitor compliance with the provisions of the "agreement between the government of the republic of the Philippines and the government of the United States of America regarding the treatment of United States armed forces visiting the Philippines," prescribing its authority and functions, January 17, 2000.

———. Republic Act No. 4645. An act creating the city of Olongapo. June 1, 1966.

Republic of the Philippines, Court of Appeals. CA-G.R. CR HC No. 02587. People of the Philippines v. L/Cpl Daniel J. Smith, R.P. Court of Appeals, 2009.

———. CA-G.R. SP No. 78075. Donald L. Smith v. Commissioner of Internal Revenue, n.d.

———. CA-G.R. SP No. 97212. Lance Corporal Daniel J. Smith, Petitioner v. Hon. Benjamin T. Pozon, in his capacity as Presiding Judge of RTC, Makati, Br. 139, Jail Warden of the Makati City Jail, and People of the Philippines, Respondents. Republic of the Philippines, Court of Appeals, n.d.

———. CA-G.R. SP. No. 97212. Lance Corporal Daniel J. Smith v. Hon. Benjamin T Pozon and the People of the Philippines, R.P. Court of Appeals Special 16th Division, 2006.

———. CA-G.R. SP No. 111627, Philippine Court of Appeals, Manila, Fifteenth Division, Subic Bay Metropolitan Authority, petitioner v. Hon Richard Paradeza in his capacity as the Presiding Judge of Olongapo City Regional Trial Court, Branch 72, and Westwood Unlimited Trading Corporation, respondents, June 27, 2011.

———. CA-G.R. SP No. 121186, Subic Shipbuilder Corp. and Redondo I-Tech Corp. v. National Labor Relations Commission (Forth Division) [Formerly 7th Division], Rogelio Bernal and Christine Baylon, November 11, 2011.

Republic of the Philippines Supreme Court. G.R. No. 138570, BAYAN (Bagong Alyansang Makabayan), a Junk VFA Movement, Bishop Tomas Millamena (Iglesia Filipina Independiente), Bishop Elmer Bolocan (United Church of Christ of the Phil.), Dr. Reynaldo Legasca, MD, Kilusang Mambubukid Ng Pilipinas, Kilusang Mayo Uno, GABRIELA, Prolabor, and the Public Interest Law Center, petitioners, vs. Executive Secretary Ronaldo Zamora, Foreign Affairs Secretary Domingo Siazon, Defense Secretary Orlando Mercado, Brig. Gen. Alexander Aguirre, Senate President Marcelo Fernan, Senator Franklin Drilon, Senator Blas Ople, Senator Rodolfo Biazon, and Senator Francisco Tatad, respondents, October 10, 2000.

———. G.R. No. 138572, Philippine Constitution Association, Inc. (PHILCONSA), Exequiel B. Garcia, Amadogat Inciong, Camilo L. Sabio, and Ramon A. Gonzales, petitioners, vs. Hon. Ronaldo B. Zamora, as Executive Secretary, Hon. Orlando Mercado, as Secretary of National Defense, and Hon. Domingo L. Siazon, Jr., as Secretary of Foreign Affairs, respondents, October 10, 2000.

———. G.R. No. 138587, Teofisto T. Guingona, Jr., Raul S. Roco, and Sergio R. Osmea III, petitioners, vs. Joseph E. Estrada, Ronaldo B. Zamora, Domingo L. Siazon, Jr., Orlando B. Mercado, Marcelo B. Fernan, Franklin M. Drilon, Blas F. Ople and Rodolfo G. Biazon, respondents, October 10, 2000.

———. G.R. No. 138680, Integrated Bar of the Philippines, Represented by its National President, Jose Aguila Grapilon, petitioners, vs. Joseph Ejercito Estrada, in his capacity as President, Republic of the Philippines, and Hon. Domingo Siazon, in his capacity as Secretary of Foreign Affairs, respondents, October 10, 2000.

———. G.R. No. 138698, Jovito R. Salonga, Wigberto Taada, Zenaida Quezon-Avencea, Rolando Simbulan, Pablito V. Sanidad, Ma. Socorro I. Diokno, Agapito A. Aquino, Joker P. Arroyo, Francisco C. Rivera Jr., Rene A. V. Saguisag, Kilosbayan, Movement of Attorneys for Brotherhood, Integrity and Nationalism, Inc. (MABINI), petitioners, vs. The Executive Secretary, The Secretary of Foreign Affairs, The Secretary of National Defense, Senate President Marcelo B. Fernan, Senator Blas F. Ople, Senator Rodolfo G. Biazon, and All Other Persons Acting Their Control, Supervision, Direction, and Instruction in Relation to the Visiting Forces Agreement (VFA), respondents, October 10, 2000.

———. G.R. No. 151135, Contex Corporation v. Hon. Commissioner of Internal Revenue, July 2, 2004.

———. G.R. No. 151445, Arthur D. Lim and Paulino R. Ersando, petitioners, vs. Honorable Executive Secretary as alter ego of Her Excellency Gloria Macapagal-Arroyo, and Honorable Angelo Reyes in his capacity as Secretary of National Defense, respondents; Sanlakas and Partido Ng Manggagawa, petitioners-intervenors, vs. Gloria Macapaga-Arroyo, Alberto Romulo, Angelo Reyes, respondents April 11, 2002.

———. G.R. No. 175888, Suzette Nicolas y Sombilon v. Alberto Romulo, Raul Gonzalez, Eduardo Ermita, Ronaldo Puno and L/Cpl Daniel Smith, February 11, 2009.

———. G.R. No. 176051, Jovito R. Salonga, Wigberto E. Tanada, Jose de la Rama, Emilio C. Capulong, H. Harry L. Roque Jr., Florin Hilbay, and Benjamin Pozon v. Daniel Smith, Raul Gonzalez, Sergio Apostol, Ronaldo Puno, Alberto Romulo and all persons acting in the capacity, February 11, 2009.

———. G.R. No. 176222, Bagong Alyansang Makabayan, represented by Dr. Carol Araullo, GABRIELA, represented by Emerenciana de Jesus, Bayan Muna, GABRIELA Women's Party, represented by Rep Liza Maza, Kilusang Mayo Uno (KMU), represented by Elmer Labog, Kilusang Magbubukid ng Pilipinas (KMP), represented by Willy Marbella; League of Filipino Students (LFS), represented by Vencer Crisostomo, and the Public Interest Law Center, represented by Atty Rachel Pastores v. President Gloria Macapagal-Arroyo, Eduardo Ermita, Alberto Romulo, Raul Gonzalez, and Ronaldo Puno, February 11, 2009.

———. G.R. No. 212426, Rene A. V. Saguisag, Wigberto E. Tañada, Francisco "Dodong" Nemenzo, Jr., Sr. Mary John Mananzan, Pacifico A. Agabin, Esteban "Steve" Salonga, H. Harry L. Roque, Jr., Evalyn G. Ursua, Edre U. Olalia, Dr. Carol Pagaduan-Araullo, Dr. Roland Simbulan, and Teddy Casiño, petitioners, v. Executive Secretary Paquito N. Ochoa, Jr., Department of National Defense Secretary Voltaire Gazmin, Department of Foreign Affairs Secretary Albert Del Rosario, Jr., Department of Budget and Management Secretary Florencio Abad, and Armed Forces of the Philippines Chief of Staff General Emmanuel T. Bautista, respondents, July 26, 2016.

———. G.R. No. 212444, Bagong Alyansang Makabayan (BAYAN), represented by its Secretary General Renato M. Reyes, Jr., BAYAN Muna Party-List Representatives Neri J. Colmenares and Carlos Zarate, GABRIELA Women's Party-List Representatives Luz Ilagan and Emerenciana de Jesus, ACT Teachers Party-List Representative Antonio L. Tinio, Anakpawis Party-List Representative Fernando Hicap, Kabataan Party-List Representative Terry Ridon, Makabayang Koalisyon Ng Mamamayan (MAKABAYAN), represented by Saturnino Ocampo, and Liza Maza, Bienvenido Lumbera, Joel C. Lamangan, Rafael Mariano, Salvador France, Rogelio M. Soluta, and Clemente G. Bautista, petitioners, vs. Department of National Defense (DND) Secretary Voltaire Gazmin, Department of Foreign Affairs Secretary Albert Del Rosario, Executive Secretary Paquito N. Ochoa, Jr., Armed Forces of the Philippines Chief of Staff General Emmanuel T. Bautista, Defense Undersecretary Pio Lorenzo Batino, Ambassador Lourdes Yparraguirre, Ambassador J. Eduardo Malaya, Department of Justice Undersecretary Francisco Baraan III, and DND Assistant Secretary for Strategic

Assessments Raymund Jose Quilop as Chairperson and Members, respectively, of the Negotiating Panel for the Philippines on EDCA, respondents; Kilusang Mayo Uno, represented by its Chairperson, Elmer Labog, Confederation for Unity, Recognition and Advancement of Government Employees (COURAGE), represented by Its National President Ferdinand Gaite, National Federation of Labor Unions-Kilusang Mayo Uno, represented by Its National President Joselito Ustarez, Nenita Gonzaga, Violeta Espiritu, Virginia Flores, and Armando Teodoro, Jr., petitioners-in-intervention, Rene A. Q. Saguisag, Jr., petitioner-in-intervention, July 26, 2016.

———. G.R. No. L-18566, In the matter of the adoption of Elizabeth Mira, Gilbert R. Brehm and Ester Mira Brehm, petitioners-appellees, vs. Republic of the Philippines, oppositor-appellant, September 30, 1963.

———. G.R. No. L-50276, The People of the Philippines vs. Michael J. Butler, January 27, 1983.

———. G.R. Nos. 77737-38, Christina Marie Dempsey, a Minor and Represented by Her Mother, Janalita Rapada, and the People of the Philippines v. Regional Trial Court, Branch LXXV, Third Judicial Region, Olongapo City, and Joel Dempsey, R.P. Supreme Court, August 15, 1988.

Rescission Act of 1946 (38 U.S.C. §107), which denied benefits; 1990 Public Law 101-649, section 405 for conditions related to the naturalization of Filipino World War II vets; and 2009 American Recovery and Reinvestment Act, section 1002, for lump sum payments for Filipino World War II vets.

Revised Penal Code of the Philippines. December 8, 1930.

Supreme Court of the United States. Caspar W. Weinberger, Secretary of Defense, et al., Petitioners v. Anthony M. Rossi et al., 456 U.S. 25 (1982), No. 80-1924. Argued February 22, 1982. Decided March 31, 1982.

Treaty of Friendship, Cooperation and Security. 1991.

Treaty of General Relations. 1946.

Tydings-McDuffie Act/Philippine Independence Act. 1934.

United Nations Permanent Court of Arbitration tribunal's decision in Republic of the Philippines v. People's Republic of China. 2016.

United States, Appellant v. Paul S. Nation Jr., Seaman Apprentice, U.S. Navy, Appellee, 9 USCMA 724, 26 CMR 504. October 3, 1958.

United States Claims Court, Case No. 93-124C, Christopher Acebedo, an individual; Ruby Acebedo, an individual; Tyson David, an individual; Brenda David, an individual; and those similarly situated, Plaintiffs v. United States of America, Defendant, November 5, 1993.

U.S. Court of Appeals, District of Columbia Circuit. Anthony M. Rossi et al., Appellants, v. Harold Brown, Secretary of Defense et al., Appellees. No. 79-1485. Argued April 15, 1980. Decided September 15, 1980. Rehearing Denied December 18, 1980.

U.S. Department of State. "Arrangements for the Transfer of Portions of the United States Naval Base, Subic Bay, to the Philippine Authority: Agreement between the United States and the Republic of the Philippines, Effected by Notes Exchanged at Manila," December 7, 1959 (Excerpts).

U.S. District Court, District of Columbia. Alfredo R. Alipio, Plaintiff vs. Donald C. Winter, Secretary of the Navy, Defendant. Civil Action No. 08-1251 (JR), June 29, 2009.
———. Anthony Rossi et al., Plaintiffs vs. Harold Brown, Secretary of Defense, et al., Defendants. Civ. A. No. 78-2346, March 20, 1979.
———. Gualberto Alver, Plaintiff vs. Donald C. Winter, Secretary of the Navy, Defendant. Civil Action No. 08-1384 (JR), June 29, 2009.
———. Hortencio Arcelo, Plaintiff vs. Donald C. Winter, Secretary of the Navy, Defendant. Civil Action No. 08-1247 (JR), June 29, 2009.
———. Manuel Licudine, Plaintiff vs. Donald C. Winter, Secretary of the Navy, Defendant. Civil Action No. 08-1086 (JR), March 26, 2009.
———. Menandro Cipriano, Plaintiff vs. Donald C. Winter, Secretary of the Navy, Defendant. Civil Action No. 08-2035 (JR), June 29, 2009.
———. Miguel Abaigar, Plaintiff vs. Donald C. Winter, Secretary of the Navy, Defendant. Civil Action No. 08-1466 (JR), June 29, 2009.
———. Rogelio Acosta, Plaintiff vs. Donald C. Winter, Secretary of the Navy, Defendant. Civil Action No. 08-1318 (JR), June 29, 2009.
U.S. Executive Order 1026. Enlarging Naval Reservation on Subic Bay, Olongapo, Philippine Islands, February 13, 1909.
U.S. Homecoming Act, a.k.a. Indochinese Refugee Resettlement and Protection Act, Pub. L. No. 100-202, 1982 Amerasian Act, a.k.a. Public Law 97-359; for failed Amerasian bills that also exclude Filipino Amerasians, see 2003 H.R. 3360 1987 S. 1601, 2005 H.R. 2687, 1985 H.R. 1684. 1987.
U.S. H.R. 1990—A bill to amend the Immigration and Nationality Act to provide special preference treatment for certain children born in the Philippines and fathered by American servicemen. 1983.
U.S. H.R. 2265—Amerasian Immigration Amendments. 1987.
U.S. Navy Board of Review. United States v. Herbert Levinsky, 1633120, Private First Class (E-2) U. S. Marine Corps. WC NCM 60-00615. August 8, 1960.
U.S. 102nd Congress. "Implications of the US Withdrawal from Clark and Subic Bases." Hearing before the Subcommittee on Asian and Pacific Affairs of the Committee on Foreign Affairs, House of Representatives. Washington, DC: U.S. Government Printing Office, 1992.
Visiting Forces Agreement between the United States and the Philippines. 1998.

Secondary Sources

Abaza, Mona. 2001. "Shopping Malls, Consumer Culture and the Reshaping of Public Space in Egypt." *Theory, Culture & Society* 18(5):97–122.
Abbot, Andrew. 1992. "From Causes to Events: Notes on Narrative Positivism." *Sociological Methods & Research* 20(4):428–55.
Abbott, Kenneth W. and Duncan Snidal. 2000. "Hard and Soft Law in International Governance." *International Organization* 54(3):421–56.
Abramson, Corey M. and Daniel Dohan. 2015. "Beyond Text: Using Arrays to Represent and Analyze Ethnographic Data." *Sociological Methodology* 45(1):272–319.

Abramson, Corey M., Jacqueline Joslyn, Katharine A. Rendle, Sarah B. Garrett, and Daniel Dohan. 2018. "The Promises of Computation Ethnography: Improving Transparency, Replicability, and Validity for Realist Approaches to Ethnographic Analysis." *Ethnography* 19(2): 254–84.

ABS-CBN News. 2012. "Hanjin Labor 'Abuse' Caught on Cam." March 19. http://news.abs -cbn.com/-depth/03/19/12/hanjin-labor-abuse-caught-cam (accessed June 14, 2017).

———. 2016. "Former DFA Chief Domingo Siazon Passes Away." May 4. https://news .abs-cbn.com/global-filipino/05/04/16/former-dfa-chief-domingo-siazon-passes -away (accessed May 25, 2017).

Adams, Julia. 2005. *The Familial State: Ruling Families and Merchant Capitalism in Early Modern Europe*. Ithaca, NY: Cornell University Press.

Adams, Julia and George Steinmetz. 2015. "Sovereignty and Sociology: From State Theory to Theories of Empire." Pp. 269–85 in *Patrimonial Capitalism and Empire*, edited by Mounira M. Charrad and Julia Adams. Bingley, UK: Emerald Books.

Adelman, Jeremy and Stephen Aron. 1999. "From Borderlands to Borders: Empires, Nation-States, and the Peoples in between in North American History." *American Historical Review* 104(3):814–41.

Agamben, Giorgio. 2005. *State of Exception*. Chicago, IL: University of Chicago Press.

Agoncillo, Teodoro A. 2012 [1990]. *History of the Filipino People*. 8th ed. Quezon City, Philippines: C&E Publishing.

Ahern, Joseph M. 1992. "Out of Sight, Out of Mind: United States Immigration Law and Policy as Applied to Filipino-Amerasians." *Pacific Rim Law & Policy Journal* 1(1):105–26.

Alvarez, Robert R. 1995. "The Mexican-US Border: The Making of an Anthropology of Borderlands." *Annual Review of Anthropology* 24:447–70.

Aminzade, Ronald. 1992. "Historical Sociology and Time." *Sociological Methods & Research* 20(4):456–80.

Anderson, Benedict. 2006 [1983]. *Imagined Communities: Reflections on the Origin and Spread of Nationalism*. London, UK: Verso.

Anderson, Elijah. 2011. *Cosmopolitan Canopy: Race and Civility in Everyday Life*. New York, NY: W. W. Norton & Company.

Anderson, Gerald R. 2006. *Subic Bay: From Magellan to Pinatubo; The History of the U.S. Naval Station, Subic Bay*. Lexington, KY: CreateSpace Independent Publishing Platform.

Anderson, Warwick. 2006. *Colonial Pathologies: American Tropical Medicine, Race, and Hygiene in the Philippines*. Durham, NC: Duke University Press.

Andrews, Kenneth T. and Neal Caren. 2010. "Making the News: Movement Organizations, Media Attention, and the Public Agenda." *American Sociological Review* 75(6):841–66.

Aneesh, Aneesh. 2015. *Neutral Accent: How Language, Labor and Life Become Global*. Durham, NC: Duke University Press.

Anghie, Antony. 1996. "Francisco de Vitoria and the Colonial Origins of International Law." *Social & Legal Studies* 5(3):321–36.

Angsioco, Elizabeth. 2014. "Politics of the Color Yellow." Manilastandard.net, July 19. http://manilastandard.net/opinion/columns/power-point-by-elizabeth-angsioco /152715/politics-of-the-color-yellow.html (accessed May 17, 2017).

Añonuevo, Carol. 1987. "Prostitution in the Philippines." Pp. 64–97 in *Cast the First Stone*. Quezon City, Philippines: A Joint Publication of the World Council of Churches, Women's Desk and the National Council of Churches, Division of Family Ministries.

Anzaldúa, Gloria. 1999. *Borderlands/La Frontera: The New Mestiza*. San Francisco, CA: Aunt Lute Books.

Appadurai, Arjun. 1990. "Disjuncture and Difference in the Global Cultural Economy." *Theory, Culture, and Society* 7:295–310.

———. 1996. *Modernity at Large: Cultural Dimensions of Globalization*. Minneapolis, MN: University of Minnesota Press.

Arcayan, Benhur. 2012. "Apl.de.ap Receives Award from PNoy." GMA Network, December 6. http://www.gmanetwork.com/news/photo/29126/showbiz/apldeap-receives -award-from-pnoy- (accessed September 29, 2016).

Armstrong, Elizabeth A. and Mary Bernstein. 2008. "Culture, Power, and Institutions: A Multi-Institutional Politics Approach to Social Movements." *Sociological Theory* 26(1):74–99.

Associated Press. 2015. "Joseph Pemberton, a U.S. Marine, Doesn't Enter Plea in Transgender Murder Trial." CBC News, February 23. http://www.cbc.ca/news/world /joseph-pemberton-u-s-marine-doesn-t-enter-plea-in-transgender-murder-trial-1 .2967043 (accessed April 23, 2016).

Auge, Marc. 1995. *Non-Places: An Introduction to Supermodernity*. London, UK: Verso.

Auyero, Javier. 2007. *Routine Politics and Violence in Argentina: The Gray Zone of State Power*. New York, NY: Cambridge University Press.

Avendaño, Christine O. and Maricar Brizuela. 2014. "Laude Fiancé Sueselbeck Stopped from Leaving Philippines." *Philippine Daily Inquirer*, October 27. http://globalnation .inquirer.net/113466/sueselbeck-pemberton-tagged-undesirable-aliens-doj (accessed April 21, 2016).

Ayroso, Dee. 2015. "'Under Aquino, the LGBT Have No Rights.'" Bulatlat.com, December 11. http://bulatlat.com/main/2015/12/11/under-aquino-the-lgbt-have-no-rights/ (accessed April 26, 2016).

Babb, Sarah L. and Bruce G. Carruthers. 2008. "Conditionality: Forms, Function, and History." *Annual Review of Law and Social Science* 4:13–29.

Bacani, Teodoro C. 2011. "Hanjin Workers Cannot Take It Anymore, They Are Going on a Protest Caravan This Sunday, July 3." *Olongapo SubicBay BatangGapo Newscenter*, June 29. http://subicbaynews.blogspot.com/2011/06/hanjin-workers-cannot-take-it -anymore.html?m=0 (accessed June 14, 2017).

Bach, Jonathan. 2010. "'They Come in Peasants and Leave Citizens': Urban Villages and the Making of Shenzhen, China." *Cultural Anthropology* 25:421–58.

Bail, Christopher A. 2012. "The Fringe Effect: Civil Society Organizations and the Evolution of Media Discourse about Islam since the September 11th Attacks." *American Sociological Review* 77(6):855–79.

Baldoz, Rick. 2011. *The Third Asiatic Invasion: Empire and Migration in Filipino America, 1898–1946*. New York, NY: New York University Press.

Bandelj, Nina. 2008. *From Communists to Foreign Capitalists: The Social Foundations of Foreign Direct Investment in Postsocialist Europe*. Princeton, NJ: Princeton University Press.

Bandelj, Nina and Frederick F. Wherry, eds. 2011. *The Cultural Wealth of Nations*. Stanford, CA: Stanford University Press.

Baxi, Pratiksha. 2014. "Sexual Violence and Its Discontents." *Annual Review of Anthropology* 43:139–54.

BBC News. 2018. "Philippines Moves Closer to Allowing Divorce." March 19. https://www.bbc.com/news/world-asia-43457117 (accessed March 20, 2018).

Benedicto, Bobby. 2008. *Under Bright Lights: Gay Manila and the Global Scene*. Minneapolis, MN: University of Minnesota Press.

Benson, Rodney and Abigail C. Saguy. 2005. "Constructing Social Problems in an Age of Globalization: A French-American Comparison." *American Sociological Review* 70:233–59.

Benton, Lauren. 2001a. "'The Laws of This Country': Foreigners and the Legal Construction of Sovereignty in Uruguay, 1830–1875." *Law and History Review* 19(3):479–511.

———. 2001b. "Making Order Out of Trouble: Jurisdictional Politics in the Spanish Colonial Borderlands." *Law & Social Inquiry* 26(2):373–401.

———. 2002. *Law and Colonial Cultures: Legal Regimes in World History: 1400–1900*. Cambridge, UK: Cambridge University Press.

———. 2008. "From International Law to Imperial Constitutions: The Problem of Quasi-Sovereignty, 1870–1900." *Law and History* 26(3):595–619.

Benton, Laura and Richard J Ross. 2013. *Legal Pluralism and Empires, 1500–1850*. New York, NY: New York University Press.

Berehulak, Daniel. 2016. "'They Are Slaughtering Us Like Animals.'" *New York Times*, December 7. https://www.nytimes.com/interactive/2016/12/07/world/asia/rodrigo-duterte-philippines-drugs-killings.html?_r=0 (accessed June 13, 2017).

Berman, Paul Schiff. 2009. "The New Legal Pluralism." *Annual Review of Law and Social Science* 5:225–42.

Bjork, Katharine. 1998. "The Link That Kept the Philippines Spanish: Mexican Merchant Interests and the Manila Trade, 1571–1815." *Journal of World History* 9(1):25–50.

Blanton, Shannon Lindsey and Robert G. Blanton. 2009. "A Sectoral Analysis of Human Rights and FDI: Does Industry Type Matter?" *International Studies Quarterly* 53:469–93.

Bloemraad, Irene, Anna Korteweg, and Gökçe Yurdakul. 2008. "Citizenship and Immigration: Multiculturalism, Assimilation, and Challenges to the Nation-State." *Annual Review of Sociology* 34:153–79.

Bondoc, Marlly Rome C. 2017. "Transform a Life for as Little as P20 through the Pearl S. Buck Foundation." GMA News, March 3. http://www.gmanetwork.com/news/lifestyle/content/601757/transform-a-life-for-as-little-as-p20-through-the-pearl-s-buck-foundation/story (accessed April 27, 2017).

Bonilla-Silva, Eduardo. 2006. *Racism without Racists: Color-Blind Racism and the Persistence of Racial Inequality in the United States.* Lanham, MD: Rowman & Littlefield.

Bonus, Rick. 2000. *Locating Filipino Americans: Ethnicity and the Cultural Politics of Space.* Philadelphia, PA: Temple University Press.

Bourdieu, Pierre. 1984. *Distinction: A Social Critique of the Judgement of Taste.* Cambridge, MA: Harvard University Press.

Boyenge, Jean-Pierre Singa. 2007. "ILO Database on Export Processing Zones (Revised)." Working Paper No. 251. Geneva, Switzerland: International Labour Organization.

Brandt, Allan M. 1987. *No Magic Bullet: A Social History of Venereal Disease in the United States since 1880.* New York, NY: Oxford University Press.

Brennan, Denise. 2004. *What's Love Got to Do with It? Transnational Desires and Sex Tourism in the Dominican Republic.* Durham, NC: Duke University Press.

Brubaker, Rogers. 1992. *Citizenship and Nationhood in France and Germany.* Cambridge, MA: Harvard University Press.

Brubaker, Rogers, Margit Feischmidt, Jon Fox, and Liana Grancea. 2006. *Nationalist Politics and Everyday Ethnicity in a Transylvania Town.* Princeton, NJ: Princeton University Press.

Brunnee, Jutta and Stephen J. Toope. 2004. "The Use of Force: International Law after Iraq." *International & Comparative Law Quarterly* 53:785–806.

Bueno, Anna. 2016. "5 Things You Should Know about the Anti-Discrimination Bill." CNN Philippines, October 17. http://cnnphilippines.com/life/culture/politics/2016/10/17/adbprimer.html (accessed January 22, 2019).

Bulawan, Alma. "The Filipino Experience by Alma Bulawan." Pp. 97–101 in *The Olongapo Colonial Experience: History, Politics, and Memories,* edited by Herman Tiu Laurel. Quezon City, Philippines: Independent Media.

Bunting, Annie. 2005. "Stages of Development: Marriage of Girls and Teens as an International Human Rights Issue." *Social & Legal Studies* 14(1):17–38.

Burawoy, Michael. 2017. "On Desmond: The Limits of Spontaneous Sociology." *Theory and Society* 46:261–84.

Burawoy, Michael, Joseph A. Blum, Sheba George, Zsuzsa Gille, Teresa Gowan, Lynne Haney, Maren Klawiter, Steven H. Lopez, Seán Ó Riain, and Millie Thayer. 2000. *Global Ethnography: Forces, Connections, and Imaginations in a Postmodern World.* Berkeley, CA: University of California Press.

Burke-White, William W. 2004. "Human Rights and National Security: The Strategic Correlation." *Harvard Human Rights Journal* 17:249.

Business Wire. 2014. "Apl.de.ap Foundation International Joins with Children's Hospital Los Angeles to Combat Blindness in Filipino Babies." Press release, June 6. http://www.businesswire.com/news/home/20140605006541/en/Apl.de.ap-Foundation-International-Joins-Children%E2%80%99s-Hospital-Los (accessed September 29, 2016).

Caagusan, Flor, ed. 2001 [1998]. *Halfway through the Circle: The Lives of 8 Filipino Survivors of Prostitution & Sex Trafficking.* Quezon City, Philippines: WeDpro.

Cabotaje, Michael A. 1999. "Equity Denied: Historical and Legal Analyses in Support of the Extension of U.S. Veterans' Benefits to Filipino World War II Veterans." *Asian Law Journal* 6:67–97.

Cahiles, Gerg. 2015. "PH, U.S. Agree on Pemberton Detention." CNN Philippines, December 8. http://cnnphilippines.com/news/2015/12/08/Philippines-U.S.-agree-on -Marine-Lance-Corporal-Pemberton-detention.html (accessed April 26, 2016).

Cahill, Desmond. 1990. *Intermarriages in International Contexts.* Quezon City, Philippines: Scalabrini Migration Center.

Camba, Alvin. 2017. "Inter-state Relations and State Capacity: The Rise and Fall of Chinese Foreign Direct Investment in the Philippines." *Palgrave Communications* 3(41):1–19.

Carcamo, Dennis. 2014. "Groups to Storm US Embassy for Pemberton's Turnover." *Philippine Star*, October 16. http://www.philstar.com/headlines/2014/10/16 /1380851/groups-storm-us-embassy-pembertons-turnover (accessed April 25, 2016).

Carey, Nick. 2016. "Hanjin's Fall Will Not Fix the Global Shipping Industry's Ills." Reuters, September 12. http://www.reuters.com/article/us-hanjin-shipping-debt -capacity-idUSKCN11I2GP (accessed June 14, 2017).

Carrington, Christopher. 1999. *No Place like Home: Relationships and Family Life among Lesbians and Gay Men.* Chicago, IL: University of Chicago Press.

Carruthers, Bruce G. and Terence C Halliday. 2006. "Negotiating Globalization: Global Scripts and Intermediation in the Construction of Asian Insolvency Regimes." *Law & Social Inquiry* 31(3):521–84.

Casas-Cortes, Maribel, Sebastian Cobarrubias, and John Pickles. 2012. "Re-Bordering the Neighbourhood: Europe's Emerging Geographies of Non-Accession Integration." *European Urban and Regional Studies* 20(1):37–58.

Carvajal, Nancy. 2017. "The Kidnap-Slay of Jee Ick Joo: May an Accused Arrest a Suspect?" ABS-CBN News, January 24. http://news.abs-cbn.com/focus/01/24/17/the-kidnap -slay-of-jee-ick-joo-may-an-accused-arrest-a-suspect (accessed June 13, 2017).

Casey, Nicholas and Alexandra Berzon. 2011. "Mexico Tourism Feels Chill of Ongoing Drug Violence." *Wall Street Journal*, June 8. https://www.wsj.com/articles/SB100014 24052702304432304576367710290674534 (accessed January 16, 2017).

Centeno, Miguel Angel. 2002. *Blood and Debt: War and the Nation-State in Latin America.* University Park, PA: Pennsylvania State University Press.

Cerojano, Teresa. 2006. "U.S. Cancels Philippines Military Exercise." Associated Press, December 22. http://www.washingtonpost.com/wp-dyn/content/article/2006/12/22 /AR2006122200159_pf.html (accessed May 24, 2018).

Cerulo, Karen A. 2014. "Reassessing the Problem: Response to Jerolmack and Khan." *Sociological Methods & Research* 43(2):219–26.

Chayes, Abram and Antonia Handler Chayes. 1993. "On Compliance." *International Organization* 47(2):175–205.

———. 1995. *The New Sovereignty: Compliance with International Regulatory Agreements.* Cambridge, MA: Harvard University Press.

Chen, Xiangming. 1995. "The Evolution of Free Economic Zones and the Recent Development of Cross-National Growth Zones." *International Journal of Urban and Regional Research* 19:593–621.

Choo, Hae Yeon. 2016a. "The Costs of Rights: Migrant Women, Feminist Advocacy, and Gendered Morality in South Korea." *Gender & Society* 27(4):445–68.

———. 2016b. "Selling Fantasies of Rescue: Intimate Labor, Filipina Migrant Hostesses, and US GIs in a Shifting Global Order." *Positions: East Asia Cultures Critique* 24(1):179–203.

Choy, Catherine Ceniza. 2003. *Empire of Care: Nursing and Migration in Filipino American History.* Durham, NC: Duke University Press.

Christie, Jim, Lisa Richwine, and Tom Hals. 2016. "Hanjin Crisis Brings New Headache to U.S. Importers; Trailer Shortage Looms." Reuters, September 13. http://www.reuters.com/article/us-hanjin-shipping-debt-containers-idUSKCN11J2U8?il=0 (accessed June 14, 2017).

Chuck, Elizabeth. 2015. "Benghazi 101: What You Need to Know ahead of Clinton's Testimony." NBCNews.com, October 22. http://www.nbcnews.com/news/world/benghazi-101-what-you-need-know-ahead-clintons-testimony-n447996 (accessed January 16, 2017).

Clarke, David. 2007. "Contested Sites: Hong Kong's Built Environment in the Post-Colonial Era." *Postcolonial Studies* 10:357–77.

CNBC. 2016. "Philippine's [*sic*] Duterte Cancels Police Rifle Deal with U.S." November 7. http://www.cnbc.com/2016/11/07/philippines-duterte-cancels-police-rifle-deal-with-us.html (accessed April 17, 2017).

Cohen, Lizabeth. 1996. "From Town Center to Shopping Center: The Reconfiguration of Community Marketplaces in Postwar America." *American Historical Review* 101(4):1050–81.

Cohen, Philip N. 2015. "Survey and Ethnography: Comment on Goffman's *On the Run.*" June 22. http://www.terpconnect.umd.edu/~pnc/working/GoffmanComment-06-22-15.pdf (accessed August 2, 2018).

———. 2017. *On the Run: Fugitive Life in an American City* by Alice Goffman (review). *Social Forces* 95(4):e5.

Collins, Kristin. 2000. "When Fathers' Rights Are Mothers' Duties: The Failure of Equal Protection in Miller v Albright." *The Yale Law Journal* 109(7):1669–708.

Connell, J. 1999. "Beyond Manila: Walls, Malls, and Private Spaces." *Environment and Planning A* 31:417–39.

Constable, Nicole. 2003. *Romance on a Global Stage: Pen Pals, Virtual Ethnography, and "Mail-Order" Marriages.* Berkeley, CA: University of California Press.

Contreras, Randol. 2013. *The Stickup Kids: Race, Drugs, Violence and the American Dream.* Berkeley, CA: University of California Press.

Cooley, Alexander. 2008. *Base Politics: Democratic Change and the U.S. Military Overseas.* Ithaca, NY: Cornell University Press.

Cooley, Alexander and Kimberly Marten. 2006. "Base Motives: The Political Economy of Okinawa's Antimilitarism." *Armed Forces & Society* 32:566–83.

Cooper, Frederick. 2014. *Citizenship between Empire and Nation: Remaking France and French Africa, 1945–1960*. Princeton, NJ: Princeton University Press.

"Court Rules in Favor of Filipina Prostitutes." 2003. *Korea JoongAng Daily*, May 31. https://web.archive.org/web/20130619001522/http://koreajoongangdaily.joinsmsn .com/news/article/article.aspx?aid=1987730 (accessed February 5, 2019).

Crimmins, Carmel. 2007. "Abortion in the Philippines: A National Secret." Reuters, September 5. http://www.reuters.com/article/us-philippines-abortion-idUSMAN 29804620070905 (accessed May 1, 2017).

Cristobal, Adrian E. and James Gregor. 1987. "The Philippines and the United States: A Short History of the Security Connection." *Comparative Strategy* 6(1):61–89.

Cross, Jamie. 2010. "Neoliberalism as Unexceptional: Economic Zones and the Everyday Precariousness of Working Life in South India." *Critique of Anthropology* 30:355–73.

Cruz, Maricel. 2016. "Pemberton Most Favored Convict, Says Lawmaker." *Manila Standard*, April 6. http://thestandard.com.ph/news/-main-stories/202996/pemberton -most-favored-convict-says-lawmaker.html (accessed April 26, 2016).

Cruz De Castro, Renato. 2003. "The Revitalized Philippine-U.S. Security Relations: A Ghost from the Cold War or an Alliance for the 21st Century?" *Asian Survey* 43(6):971–88.

Cullen, Shay. 2003a. "Bringing Back the US Navy to Subic?" Pp. 145–47 in *The Olongapo Colonial Experience: History, Politics, and Memories*, edited by Herman Tiu Laurel. Quezon City, Philippines: Independent Media.

———. 2003b. "Holy Mary! Still Violence against Women Continues." Pp. 162–66 in *The Olongapo Colonial Experience: History, Politics, and Memories*, edited by Herman Tiu Laurel. Quezon City, Philippines: Independent Media.

———. 2003c. "Return of U.S. Troops with Immunity 1997." Pp. 166–68 in *The Olongapo Colonial Experience: History, Politics, and Memories*, edited by Herman Tiu Laurel. Quezon City, Philippines: Independent Media.

Cunneen, Chris and Julie Stubbs. 1997. *Gender, "Race" and International Relations: Violence against Filipino Women in Australia*. Institute of Criminology Monograph Series No. 9. Sydney: Australia: Institute of Criminology.

D'Argemir, Dolors Comas and Joan J. Pujadas. 1999 "Living in/on the Frontier: Migration, Identities, and Citizenship in Andorra." *Social Anthropology* 7(3):253–64.

Das, Veena. 2008. "Violence, Gender, and Subjectivity." *Annual Review of Anthropology* 37:283–99.

David, Emmanuel. 2015. "The Sexual Fields of Empire: On the Ethnosexual Frontiers of Global Outsourcing." *Radical History Review* 123:115–43.

De Jesus, Julliane Love. 2015. "Protesters Demand Transfer of Pemberton to Bilibid." In-quirer.net, December 4. http://globalnation.inquirer.net/133370/protesters-demand -transfer-of-pemberton-to-bilibid (accessed April 26, 2016).

Delmendo, Sharon. 1998. "The Star Entangled Banner: Commemorating 100 Years of Philippine (In)dependence and Philippine-American Relations." *Journal of Asian American Studies* 1(3):211–44.

De Mesa Laranas, Gin. 2016. "Will the Philippines Finally Legalize Divorce?" *New York Times*, Opinion, July 28. https://www.nytimes.com/2016/07/29/opinion/will-the-philippines-finally-legalize-divorce.html (accessed March 20, 2018).

Denyer, Simon and Emily Rauhala. 2016. "Beijing's Claims to South China Sea Rejected by International Tribunal." *Washington Post*, July 12. https://www.washingtonpost.com/world/beijing-remains-angry-defiant-and-defensive-as-key-south-china-sea-tribunal-ruling-looms/2016/07/12/11100f48-4771-11e6-8dac-0c6e4accc5b1_story.html?hpid=hp_hp-top-table-main_southchina-1240 a.m.%3Ahomepage%2Fstory&utm_term=.125bef1ae6ea (accessed May 30, 2017).

Desmond, Matthew. 2014. "Relational Ethnography." *Theory and Society* 43(5):547–79.

———. 2016. *Evicted: Poverty and Profit in the American City*. New York, NY: Crown Publishers.

DeSoucey, Michaela. 2016. *Contested Tastes: Foie Gras and the Politics of Food*. Princeton, NJ: Princeton University Press.

De Sousa Santos, Boaventura. 2006. "The Heterogeneous State and Legal Pluralism in Mozambique." *Law & Society Review* 40(1):39–76.

DeVault, Marjorie L. 1991. *Feeding the Family: The Social Organization of Caring as Gendered Work*. Chicago, IL: University of Chicago Press.

DiMaggio, Paul. 2014. "Comment on Jerolmack and Khan, 'Talk Is Cheap': Ethnography and the Attitudinal Fallacy." *Sociological Methods & Research* 43(2):232–35.

Dizon, Nikko. 2015. "Aquino: Pemberton 'in a Facility Controlled by the Philippines.'" *Philippine Daily Inquirer*, December 5. http://globalnation.inquirer.net/133424/aquino-pemberton-in-a-facility-controlled-by-the-philippines (accessed April 26, 2016).

———. 2016. "'It's Civil Union, Not Marriage.'" *Philippine Daily Inquirer*, October 5. http://newsinfo.inquirer.net/821825/its-civil-union-not-marriage (accessed January 22, 2019).

Donnan, Hastings and Thomas M. Wilson. 2010. "Ethnography, Security, and the 'Frontier Effect' in Borderlands." Pp. 1–20 in *Borderlands: Ethnographic Approaches to Security, Power, and Identity*, edited by Hastings Donnan and Thomas M. Wilson. Lanham, MD: University Press of America.

Douglas, Mary. 2002 [1966]. *Purity and Danger*. London, UK: Routledge.

Du Bois, W. E. B. 1996 [1899]. *The Philadelphia Negro: A Social Study*. Philadelphia: University of Pennsylvania Press.

Duck, Waverly. 2015. *No Way Out: Precarious Living in the Shadow of Poverty and Drug Dealing*. Chicago, IL: University of Chicago Press.

Duneier, Mitchell. 2001 [1999]. *Sidewalk*. New York, NY: Farrar, Straus, and Giroux.

Duque, Estela. 2009. "Militarization of the City: Implementing Burnham's 1905 Plan of Manila." *Fabrications: The Journal of the Society of Architectural Historians, Australia, and New Zealand* 19(1):48–67.

Economist. 2015. "Special Economic Zones: Not So Special." April 4. https://www.economist.com/leaders/2015/04/04/not-so-special (accessed November 24, 2016).

Enloe, Cynthia. 2000 [1990]. *Bananas, Beaches, and Bases: Making Feminist Sense of International Politics*. Berkeley, CA: University of California Press.

Erik. 2011. "Discriminatory Amendment Proposed by Bohol Representative." *There's a Cure for That* (blog), June 22. http://progressph.blogspot.com/2011/06/discrim inatory-amendment-proposed-by.html (accessed April 25, 2017).

Esguerra, Christian V. 2014. "Aquino: Pemberton Getting Special Negative Treatment." *Philippine Daily Inquirer*, October 23. http://globalnation.inquirer.net/113169/aquino -pemberton-getting-special-negative-treatment-in-laude-slay-probe (accessed April 23, 2016).

Espiritu, Yen Lee. 2003. *Home Bound: Filipino American Lives across Cultures, Communities, and Countries*. Berkeley, CA: University of California Press.

Estoista-Koo, Kaye. 2010. "Black Eyed Peas' Apl.de.Ap Gives Back to His Kababayans through Charity Club Tour." *Pep.ph*, December 23. http://www.pep.ph/news/27749 /black-eyed-peas39-apldeap-gives-back-to-his-kababayans-through-charity-club -tour (accessed September 29, 2016).

Esty, Daniel C. and Damien Geradin. 2000. "Regulatory Co-Opetition." *Journal of International Economic Law* 3(2):235–55.

Evans, Peter B., Dietrich Rueschemeyer, and Theda Skocpol. 1985. *Bringing the State Back In*. Cambridge, UK: Cambridge University Press.

Evinger, William R. 1995. *Directory of U.S. Military Bases Worldwide*. Phoenix, AZ: Oryx Press.

Fahmy, Ziad. 2013. "Jurisdictional Borderlands: Extraterritoriality and 'Legal Chameleons' in Precolonial Alexandria, 1840–1870." *Comparative Studies in Society and History* 55(2):316.

Fernandez, Yvette. 2015. *What's Ap? The Life Story of apl.de.ap*. Manadaluyong City, Philippines: Dream Big Books.

Fernandez-Kelly, Maria Patricia. 1983. *For We Are Sold, I and My People: Women and Industry in Mexico's Frontier*. Albany, NY: State University of New York Press.

Flannery, Nathaniel Parish. 2013. "Is Drug War Violence Scaring Away Mexico's Spring Break Tourists?" *Forbes*, March 18. https://www.forbes.com/sites/nathanielparishflannery /2013/03/18/is-drugwar-violence-scaring-away-mexicos-spring-break-tourists /#4b284ea572db (accessed January 16, 2017).

Flynn, Dennis O. and Arturo Giraldez. 1995. "Born with a 'Silver Spoon': The Origin of World Trade in 1571." *Journal of World History* 6(2):201–21.

Fonbuena, Carmela. 2014. "WATCH: Jennifer Laude's Fiancé, Sister Climb Military Gate." Rappler.com, October 22. http://www.rappler.com/nation/72780-jennifer-laude -fiance-sister-climb-protest (accessed May 16, 2016).

Fourcade, Marion and Kieran Healy. 2007. "Moral Views of Market Society." *Annual Review of Sociology* 33:285–311.

Francia, Luis H. 2010. *A History of the Philippines: From Indios Bravos to Filipinos*. New York, NY: Overlook Press.

Freeman, Carla. 2000. *High Tech and High Heels in the Global Economy: Women, Work, and Pink-Collar Identities in the Caribbean*. Durham, NC: Duke University Press.

Frye, Margaret. 2012. "Bright Futures in Malawi's New Dawn: Educational Aspirations as Assertions of Identity." *American Journal of Sociology* 117(6):1565–624.

Gamil, Jaymee T. 2011. "Militants Stage Rallies Nationwide." *Philippine Daily Inquirer*, May 2. http://newsinfo.inquirer.net/4382/militants-stage-rallies-nationwide (accessed June 13, 2017).

Gamson, William A. and Gadi Wolfsfeld. 1993. "Movements and Media as Interacting Systems." *Annals of the American Academy of Political and Social Science* 528:114–25.

Gans, Herbert. 1999. "Participant Observation in the Era of 'Ethnography.'" *Journal of Contemporary Ethnography* 28(5):540–48.

Garcia, J. Neil C. 2009 [1996]. *Philippine Gay Culture: Binabae to Bakla, Silahis to MSM.* Aberdeen, Hongkong: Hongkong University Press.

Garrido, Marco. 2013a. "The Ideology of the Dual City: The Modernist Ethic in the Corporate Development of Makati City, Metro Manila." *International Journal of Urban and Regional Research* 37:165–85.

———. 2013b. "The Sense of Place behind Segregating Practices: An Ethnographic Approach to the Symbolic Partitioning of Metro Manila." *Social Forces* 91:1343–82.

Gastardo-Conaco, Cecilia and Carolyn Israel-Sobritchea. 1999. *Filipino-Amerasians: Living in the Margins.* Quezon City, Philippines: University Center for Women's Studies Foundation.

Gaventa, John. 1982. *Power and Powerlessness: Quiescence and Rebellion in an Appalachian Valley.* Urbana, IL: University of Illinois Press.

Gavilan, Jodesz. 2018. "Look Back: The Aquino Assassination." Rappler, July 19. http://www.rappler.com/newsbreak/iq/143594-look-back-ninoy-aquino-assassination (accessed January 22, 2019).

Gibler, Douglas M. 2008. "The Costs of Reneging: Reputation and Alliance Formation." *Journal of Conflict Resolution* 52(3):426–54.

Gieryn, Thomas F. 2000. "A Space for Place in Sociology." *Annual Review of Sociology* 26:463–96.

Gille, Zsuzsa. 2007. *From the Cult of Waste to the Trash Heap of History: The Politics of Waste in Socialist and Postsocialist Hungary.* Bloomington, IN: Indiana University Press.

Gille, Zsuzsa and Seán Ó Riain. 2002. "Global Ethnography." *Annual Review of Sociology* 28:271–95.

GMA News. 2009. "Pag-absuwelto kay Smith inasahan na raw ng mga mambabatas." April 24. http://www.gmanetwork.com/news/news/ulatfilipino/158488/pag-absuwelto-kay-smith-inasahan-na-raw-ng-mga-mambabatas/story/ (accessed May 24, 2018).

Go, Julian. 2008. "Global Fields and Imperial Forms: Field Theory and the British and American Empires." *Sociological Theory* 26(3):201–29.

———. 2011. *Patterns of Empire: The British and American Empires, 1688 to the Present.* Cambridge, UK: Cambridge University Press.

Goffman, Erving. 1959. *The Presentation of Self in Everyday Life.* New York, NY: Anchor Books.

———. 1967. *Interaction Ritual: Essays on Face-to-Face Behavior*. New York, NY: Anchor Books.

———. 1974. *Frame Analysis: An Essay on the Organization of Experience*. Cambridge, MA: Harvard University Press.

Goh, Daniel P. S. 2007. "States of Ethnography: Colonialism, Resistance and Cultural Transcription in Malaya and the Philippines, 1890s–1930s." *Comparative Studies in Society and History* 49(1):109–42.

Goldstein, Judith L., Douglas Rivers, and Michael Tomz. 2007. "Institutions in International Relations: Understanding the Effects of the GATT and the WTO on World Trade." *International Organization* 61:37–67.

Goldstone, Patricia. 2001. *Making the World Safe for Tourism*. New Haven, CT: Yale University Press.

Gomez, Jim. 2016a. "Philippines' Duterte to US over Aid Issue: 'Bye-Bye America,'" AP News, December 16. https://apnews.com/b0265f897aed46f283cce413b6a22c39 (accessed April 17, 2017).

———. 2016b. "US Marine Asked Philippine Court to Reverse Conviction in Killing of Transgender Filipino." *GlobalNews.ca*, January 6. http://globalnews.ca/news/2436129 /us-marine-asked-philippine-court-to-reverse-conviction-in-killing-of-transgender -filipino/ (accessed April 26, 2016).

Gramsci, Antonio. 1989 [1971]. *Selections from the Prison Notebooks*. New York, NY: International Publishers.

Granger, Derek. 2011. "Dewey at Manila Bay: Lessons in Operational Art and Operational Leadership from America's First Fleet Admiral." *Naval War College Review* 64(4):127–41.

Granovetter, Mark. 1973. "The Strength of Weak Ties." *American Journal of Sociology* 78(6):1360–80.

Grenville, J. A. S. 1961. "Diplomacy and War Plans in the US, 1890–1917." *Transactions of the Royal Historical Society* 11:1–21.

Griffin, Larry J. 1992. "Temporality, Events, and Explanation in Historical Sociology: An Introduction." *Sociological Methods & Research* 20(4):403–27.

Griffiths, John. 1986. "What Is Legal Pluralism?" *Journal of Legal Pluralism and Unofficial Law* 24:1.

Griswold, Wendy. 1987. "The Fabrication of Meaning: Literary Interpretation in the United States, Great Britain, and the West Indies." *American Journal of Sociology* 92:1077–117.

Guenther, Katja M. 2009. "The Politics of Names: Rethinking the Methodological and Ethical Significance of Naming People, Organizations, and Places." *Qualitative Research* 9(4):411–21.

Guzman, Andrew. 2002. "A Compliance-Based Theory of International Law." *California Law Review* 90(6):1823–87.

Hafner-Burton, Emilie and Kiyoteru Tsutsui. 2005. "Human Rights in a Globalizing World: The Paradox of Empty Promises." *American Journal of Sociology* 110(5):1373–411.

Halliday, Terence C. 2009. "Recursivity of Global Normmaking: A Sociolegal Agenda." *Annual Review of Law and Social Science* 5:263–89.

Hals, Tom. 2016a. "Hanjin Says U.S.-Bound Ship Is Being Held 'Hostage.'" Reuters, September 15. http://www.reuters.com/article/us-hanjin-shipping-debt-usa-bankruptcy -idUSKCN11L2NL (accessed June 14, 2017).

———. 2016b. "Samsung Seeks Court Order to Remove Goods from Hanjin Vessels." Reuters, September 8. http://uk.reuters.com/article/us-hanjin-shipping-debt -samsung-elec-idUKKCN11E2ZH (accessed June 14, 2017).

Han, Kirsten. 2012. "A Union under Construction at Philippine Shipyard." *Waging Nonviolence*, July 6. https://wagingnonviolence.org/feature/a-union-under-construction -at-philippine-shipyard/ (accessed June 14, 2017).

He, Kai. 2010. "The Hegemon's Choice between Power and Security: Explaining US Policy toward Asia after the Cold War." *Review of International Studies* 36:1121–43.

Healy, Kieran. 2017. "Fuck Nuance." *Sociological Theory* 35(2):118–27.

Helleiner, Jane. 2012. "Whiteness and Narratives of a Racialized Canada-US Border at Niagara." *Canadian Journal of Sociology/Cahiers Canadiens de Sociologie* 37(2):109–35.

Hernández, Javier C. 2017. "After Trump's Phone Call to Philippines Leader, China's President Calls Him." *New York Times*, May 3. https://www.nytimes.com/2017/05/03 /world/asia/trump-duterte-xi-south-china-sea.html (accessed May 30, 2017).

Heyman, Josiah McC. 2009. "Trust, Privilege, and Discretion in the Governance of US Borderlands with Mexico." *Canadian Journal of Law and Society* 24(3):367–90.

Hitlin, Steven and Stephen Vaisey. 2013. "The New Sociology of Morality." *Annual Review of Sociology* 39:51–68.

Hoang, Kimberly Kay. 2015. *Dealing in Desire: Asian Ascendancy, Western Decline, and the Hidden Currencies of Global Sex Work.* Berkeley, CA: University of California Press.

Holmes, Amy Austin. 2014. *Social Unrest and American Military Bases in Turkey and Germany since 1945.* New York, NY: Cambridge University Press.

Howard, Judith A. 2000. "Social Psychology of Identities." *Annual Review of Sociology* 26:367–93.

Huang-Teves, Janette. 2015. "Apl of Their Eyes." *Sun Star Philippines*, November 6. http:// www.sunstar.com.ph/davao/lifestyle/2015/11/06/apl-their-eyes-440076 (accessed September 27, 2016).

Humphrey, Laude. 1970. *Tearoom Trade: Impersonal Sex in Public Places.* New Brunswick, NJ: Aldine Transaction.

Hunter, Marcus Anthony. 2015. *Black Citymakers: How "The Philadelphia Negro" Changed Urban America.* Oxford, UK: Oxford University Press.

Ignacio, Angela V. 2011. "Apl.de.ap Helps Build Pinoy Classroom." *Philippine Daily Inquirer*, October 28. http://lifestyle.inquirer.net/19945/apl-de-ap-helps-build-pinoy -classroom (accessed September 29, 2016).

Inoue, Masamichi S. 2004. "'We Are Okinawans but of a Different Kind': New/Old Social Movements and the U.S. Military in Okinawa." *Current Anthropology* 45:85–104.

Inquirer.net. 2015. "Apl.de.ap on Owning a Jollibee Store: 'A Dream Come True.'" February 9. http://entertainment.inquirer.net/162630/apl-de-ap-on-owning-a-jollibee -store-a-dream-come-true (accessed September 29, 2016).

Isidro, Antonio. 1957. "Problems and Promise of Secondary Education in the Philippines." *Clearing House* 31(9):527–30.

Jerolmack, Colin and Shamus Khan. 2014. "Talk Is Cheap: Ethnography and the Attitudinal Fallacy." *Sociological Methods & Research* 43(2):178–209.

Jerolmack, Colin and Alexandra Murphy. 2017. "The Ethical Dilemmas and Social Scientific Trade-offs of Masking in Ethnography." *Sociological Methods & Research*, first published online March 30. https://doi.org/10.1177/0049124117701483 (accessed January 22, 2019).

Johnson, Chalmers. 2004. *The Sorrows of Empire: Militarism, Secrecy and the End of the Republic*. New York, NY: Metropolitan Books.

Kanaaneh, Rhoda Ann. 2002. *Birthing the Nation: Strategies of Palestinian Women in Israel*. Berkeley, CA: University of California Press.

Kang, David C. 2002. *Crony Capitalism: Corruption and Development in South Korea and the Philippines*. Cambridge, UK: Cambridge University Press.

Kanlungan Ministry and Bagwis. 1987. "Case Studies." Pp. 152–62 in *Cast the First Stone*. Quezon City, Philippines: A Joint Publication of the World Council of Churches, Women's Desk and the National Council of Churches, Division of Family Ministries.

Kaphle, Anup. 2014. "Timeline: How the Benghazi Attacks Played Out." *Washington Post*, June 17. https://www.washingtonpost.com/world/national-security/timeline -how-the-benghazi-attack-played-out/2014/06/17/a5c34e90-f62c-11e3-a3a5 -42be35962a52_story.html?noredirect=on&utm_term=.b86f60047f83 (accessed January 16, 2017).

Karnow, Stanley. 1989. *In Our Image: America's Empire in the Philippines*. New York, NY: Ballantine Books.

Kashiwahara, Ken. 1983. "Aquino's Final Journey." *New York Times*, October 16. http:// www.nytimes.com/1983/10/16/magazine/aquino-s-final-journey.html?pagewanted =all (accessed January 22, 2019).

Kelly, Philip F. 2001. "The Political Economy of Local Labor Control in the Philippines." *Economic Geography* 77:1–22.

Keohane, Robert O. 2005 [1984]. *After Hegemony: Cooperation and Discord in the World Political Economy*. Princeton, NJ: Princeton University Press.

Kim, Seung-hyun. 2002. "11 Filipinas Sue Owners of Club." *Korea JoongAng Daily*, October 17. https://web.archive.org/web/20130619004659/http://koreajoongangdaily .joinsmsn.com/news/article/article.aspx?aid=1909907 (accessed February 5, 2019).

Klug, Heinz. 2005. "Transnational Human Rights: Exploring the Persistence and Globalization of Human Rights." *Annual Review of Law and Social Science* 1:85–103.

Kolby, Elizabeth. 1995. "Moral Responsibility to Amerasians: Potential Immigration and Child Support Alternatives." *Asian Law Journal* 2:61–85.

Korzeniewicz, Roberto and Timothy Moran. 2009. *Unveiling Inequality: A World-Historical Perspective*. New York, NY: Russell Sage Foundation.

Kotlowski, Dean J. 2015. "Introduction." Pp. 13–37 in *Paul V. McNutt and the Age of FDR*. Bloomington, IN: Indiana University Press.

Kramer, Paul A. 2006. *The Blood of Government: Race, Empire, the United States, & the Philippines*. Chapel Hill, NC: University of North Carolina Press.

Kraul, Chris and Cecilia Sanchez. 2016. "Acapulco Paralyzed by Fear after Gunfights between Police and Gang Members." *Los Angeles Times*, April 27. http://www.latimes .com/world/mexico-americas/la-fg-mexico-violence-20160427-story.html (accessed January 16, 2017).

Krehbiel, Jay N. 2016. "The Politics of Judicial Procedures: The Role of Public Oral Hearings in the German Constitutional Court." *American Journal of Political Science* 60(4):990–1005.

Kusno, Abidin. 1998. "Beyond the Postcolonial: Architecture and Political Cultures in Indonesia." *Public Culture* 10:549–75.

Kutschera, P. C., Jose Maria G. Pelayo III, and Mary Grace Talamera-Sandico. 2012. "The Continuing Conundrum of Southeast Asia's 50,000 Filipino Military 'Amerasians.'" *International Proceedings of Economics Development and Research Journal (IPEDR)* 48(14):62–67.

Lacorte, Germelina. 2015. "Apl de Ap Donates Retinal Camera to Davao City Hospital." *Inquirer Mindanao*, October 21. http://newsinfo.inquirer.net/733481/apl-de-ap -donates-retinal-camera-to-davao-city-hospital (accessed September 29, 2016).

Lamont, Michèle and Virág Molnár. 2002. "The Study of Boundaries in the Social Sciences." *Annual Review of Sociology* 28:167–95.

Larter, David B. 2015a. "Limited Liberty for Troops in Philippine Exercise." *Navy Times*, April 10. http://www.navytimes.com/story/military/2015/04/10/balikatan-exercise -philippines-jennifer-laude-pemberton/25586185/ (accessed April 22, 2016).

———. 2015b. "Philippines Liberty Policy Was Decades in the Making." *Navy Times*, April 25. https://www.navytimes.com/news/your-navy/2015/04/22/philippines -liberty-policy-was-decades-in-the-making/ (accessed May 24, 2017).

Lears, T. J. Jackson. 1985. "The Concept of Cultural Hegemony: Problems and Possibilities." *American Historical Review* 90(3):567.

Lee, Ching Kwan. 1998. *Gender and the South China Miracle: Two Worlds of Factory Women*. Berkeley, CA: University of California Press.

———. 2017. *The Spector of Global China: Politics, Labor, and Foreign Investment in Africa*. Chicago, IL: University of Chicago Press.

Lee, Hye-Kyung. 2008. "International Marriage and the State in South Korea: Focusing on Governmental Policy." *Citizenship Studies* 12(1):107–23.

Lee, Jin-Kyung. 2010. *Service Economies: Militarism, Sex Work and Migrant Labor in South Korea*. Minneapolis, MN: University of Minnesota Press.

Lee, Joyce. 2016a. "Hanjin Lost 'Game of Chicken' among Global Shippers, Chairman Says." Reuters, October 4. http://www.reuters.com/article/us-hanjin-shipping-debt -idUSKCN1240JC?il=0 (accessed June 14, 2017).

———. 2016b. "Hanjin Shipping Gets $54 Million Loan to Unload Stranded Cargo." Reuters, September 20. http://uk.reuters.com/article/uk-hanjin-shipping-debt -idUKKCN11R061 (accessed June 14, 2017).

Lee-Brago, Pia. 2014. "Phl Bows to US on Pemberton Custody." *Philippine Star*, December 19. http://www.philstar.com/headlines/2014/12/19/1404277/phl-bows-us -pemberton-custody (accessed April 23, 2016).

Leeds, Brett Ashley. 2003. "Do Alliances Deter Aggression? The Influence of Military Alliances on the Initiation of Militarized Interstate Disputes." *American Journal of Political Science* 47(3):427–39.

Lema, Karen and Martin Petty. 2017. "Death of a Businessman: How the Philippines Drugs War Was Slowed." Reuters, February 12. http://www.reuters.com/article/us -philippines-drugs-southkorea-idUSKBN15R121 (accessed June 13, 2017).

Lester, Marilyn. 1980. "Generating Newsworthiness: The Interpretive Construction of Public Events." *American Sociological Review* 45(6):984–94.

Levi, Robin S. 1992. "Legacies of War: The United States' Obligation toward Ameriasians." *Stanford Journal of International Law* 29:459–502.

Levitt, Peggy and B. Nadya Jaworsky. 2007. "Transnational Migration Studies: Past Developments and Future Trends." *Annual Review of Sociology* 33:129–56.

Lichterman, Paul. 2017. "Interpretive Reflexivity in Ethnography." *Ethnography* 18(1):35–45.

Lieberman, Evan S. 2009. "The Politics of Demanding Sacrifice: Applying Insights from Fiscal Sociology to the Study of AIDS Policy and State Capacity." Pp. 101–18 in *The New Fiscal Sociology: Taxation in Comparative and Historical Perspective*, edited by Isaac William Martin, Ajay K. Mehrotra, and Monica Prasad. Cambridge, UK: Cambridge University Press.

Linn, Brian McAllister. 1997. *Guardians of Empire: The U.S. Army and the Pacific, 1902–1940*. Chapel Hill, NC: University of North Carolina Press.

Lo, Ricky. 2011. "Apl.de.ap Is Legally Blind." *Philippine Star*, January 24. http://www .philstar.com/entertainment/650429/apldeap-legally-blind (accessed September 27, 2016).

Los Angeles Times. 2011. "South Korean Activist Returns to Earth after Almost a Year atop Crane." November 10. http://latimesblogs.latimes.com/world_now/2011/11/south -korean-labor-protestor-spends-a-year-in-crane-hanin-heavy-industries-and -construction.html (accessed June 14, 2017).

Low, Setha. 1993. "Cultural Meaning of the Plaza: The History of the Spanish-American Gridplan-Plaza Urban Design." Pp. 75–94 in *The Cultural Meaning of Urban Space*, edited by Robert Rotenberg and Gary McDonogh. Westport, CT: Bergin & Garvey.

Lukes, Steven. 2005 [1974]. *Power: A Radical View*. Basingstoke, UK: Palgrave Macmillan.

Lutz, Catherine. 2005. "Military Bases and Ethnographies of the New Militarization." *Anthropology News* 46(1):11.

———. 2006. "Empire Is in the Details." *American Ethnologist* 33(4):593–611.

———, ed. 2009. *The Bases of Empire: The Global Struggle against U.S. Military Posts*. Washington Square, NY: New York University Press.

Macas, Trisha. 2015. "Apl.de.ap Shares Life Story in Children's Book 'What's Ap?'" GMA News, December 15. http://www.gmanetwork.com/news/story/548022/lifestyle

/artandculture/apl-de-ap-shares-life-story-in-children-s-book-what-s-ap (accessed September 29, 2016).

Macatuno, Allan. 2015. "Pemberton to Serve Sentence in Camp Aguinaldo." *Inquirer Central Luzon*, December 10. http://globalnation.inquirer.net/133616/pemberton-to -serve-sentence-in-camp-aguinaldo (accessed April 22, 2016).

Mahoney, James. 2000. "Path Dependence in Historical Sociology." *Theory and Society* 29(4):507–48.

Mananzan, Sr. Mary John. 1987. "Tourism and Prostitution." Pp. 13–31 in *Cast the First Stone*. Quezon City, Philippines: A Joint Publication of the World Council of Churches, Women's Desk and the National Council of Churches, Division of Family Ministries.

Manlupig, Karlos. 2016. "Love Is Love in Communist Movement." *Inquirer Mindanao*, July 18. http://newsinfo.inquirer.net/796671/love-is-love-in-communist-movement (accessed January 22, 2019).

Mann, Michael. 1984. "The Autonomous Power of the State: Its Origins, Mechanisms and Results." *European Journal of Sociology* 25(2):185–213.

———. 2012 [1986]. *The Sources of Social Power*, vol. 1, *A History of Power from the Beginning to AD 1760*. Cambridge, UK: Cambridge University Press.

Marantz, Erez Aharon, Alexandra Kalev, and Noah Lewin-Epstein. 2014. "Globally Themed Organizations as Labor Market Intermediaries: The Rise of Israeli-Palestinian Women's Employment in Retail." *Social Forces* 93(2):595–622.

Marasigan, Violeta A. 1987. "Closing Remarks." Pp. 105–12 in *Cast the First Stone*. Quezon City, Philippines: A Joint Publication of the World Council of Churches, Women's Desk and the National Council of Churches, Division of Family Ministries.

Margold, Jane A. 1995. "Egalitarian Ideals and Exclusionary Practices: U.S. Pedagogy in the Colonial Philippines." *Journal of Historical Sociology* 8(4):375–94.

Martin, Isaac William, Ajay K. Mehrotra, and Monica Prasad, eds. 2009. *The New Fiscal Sociology: Taxation in Comparative and Historical Perspective*. Cambridge, UK: Cambridge University Press.

Martin, Isaac William and Monica Prasad. 2014. "Taxes and Fiscal Sociology." *Annual Review of Sociology* 40:331–45.

Martin, Lisa L. 2005. "The President and International Commitments: Treaties as Signaling Devices." *Presidential Studies Quarterly* 35(3):440–65.

Massey, Douglas S., Jorge Durand, and Nolan J. Malone. 2003. *Beyond Smoke and Mirrors: Mexican Immigration in an Era of Economic Integration*. New York, NY: Russell Sage Foundation.

Maurer, Noel and Lakshmi Iyer. 2008. "The Cost of Property Rights: Establishing Institutions on the Philippine Frontier under American Rule, 1898–1918." Working Paper 14298. Cambridge, MA: National Bureau of Economic Research.

Maynard, Douglas W. 2014. "News from *Somewhere*, News from *Nowhere*: On the Study of Interaction in Ethnographic Inquiry." *Sociological Methods & Research* 43(2):210–18.

McCammon, Holly J., Harmony D. Newman, Courtney Sanders Muse, and Teresa M. Terrell. 2007. "Movement Framing and Discursive Opportunity Structures: The Political Successes of the U.S. Women's Jury Movements." *American Sociological Review* 72:725–49.

McDonnell, Patrick J. and Cecilia Sanchez. 2016. "Wary of Losing Tourists, Mexico Says Mass Abduction in Puerto Vallarta Was Likely a Gang-on-Gang Crime." *Los Angeles Times*, August 15. https://www.latimes.com/world/la-fg-puerto-vallarta-abduction -20160815-snap-story.html (accessed January 16, 2017).

McHale, Thomas R. 1962. "American Colonial Policy towards the Philippines." *Journal of Southeast Asian History* 3(1):24–43.

McKay, Steven and Don Eliseo Lucero-Prisno III. 2012. "Masculinities Afloat: Filipino Seafarers and the Situational Performance of Manhood." Pp. 20–37 in *Men and Masculinities in Southeast Asia*, edited by Michele Ford and Lenore Lyons. London, UK: Routledge.

McKay, Steven C. 2006. *Satanic Mills or Silicon Islands? The Politics of High-Tech Production in the Philippines*. Ithaca, NY: Cornell University Press.

———. 2007. "Filipino Sea Men: Constructing Masculinities in an Ethnic Labour Niche." *Journal of Ethnic and Migration Studies* 33(4):617–33.

McKinley, William. 1900. *Speeches and Addresses of William McKinley: From March 1, 1897 to May 30, 1900*. New York, NY: Doubleday & McClure Co.

McMahon, Robert J. 1999. *The Limits of Empire: The United States and Southeast Asia since World War II*. New York, NY: Columbia University Press.

Mendoza, Victor. 2015. *Metroimperial Intimacies: Fantasy, Racial-Sexual Governance, and the Philippines in U.S. Imperialism, 1899–1913*. Durham, NC: Duke University Press.

Menez, Herminia Q. 1986–87. "Agyu and the Skyworld: The Philippine Folk Epic and Multicultural Education." *Amerasia* 13(1):135–49.

Mermelstein, Richard T. 1983. "Welcoming Home Our Children: An Analysis of New Amerasian Immigration Law." *Boston University International Law Journal* 2:299–316.

Merry, Sally Engle. 1988. "Legal Pluralism." *Law & Society Review* 22(5):869–96.

———. 2003. "Constructing a Global Law—Violence against Women and the Human Rights System." *Law & Social Inquiry* 28(4):941–77.

———. 2006. "Anthropology and International Law." *Annual Review of Anthropology* 35:99–116.

Merton, Robert K. 1987. "Three Fragments from a Sociologist's Notebooks: Establishing the Phenomenon, Specified Ignorance, and Strategic Research Materials." *Annual Review of Sociology* 13:1–28.

Michaels, Ralf. 2009. "Global Legal Pluralism." *Annual Review of Law and Social Sciences* 5:243–62.

Milligan, Melinda J. 1998. "Interactional Past and Potential: The Social Construction of Place Attachment." *Symbolic Interaction* 21:1–33.

Mills, Mary Beth. 2001 [1999]. *Thai Women in the Global Labor Force: Consuming Desires, Contested Selves.* New Brunswick, NJ: Rutgers University Press.

———. 2003. "Gender and Inequality in the Global Labor Force." *Annual Review of Anthropology* 32:41–62.

Miralao, V. A., C. O. Carlos, and A. F. Santos. 1990. *Women Entertainers in Angeles and Olongap: A Survey Report.* Quezon City, Philippines: Women's Education, Development, Productivity and Research Organization (WeDpro).

Mische, Ann. 2009. "Projects and Possibilities: Researching Futures in Action." *Sociological Forum* 24(3):694–704.

Molotch, Harvey, William Freudenburg, and Krista E. Paulsen. 2000. "History Repeats Itself, but How? City Character, Urban Tradition, and the Accomplishment of Place." *American Sociological Review* 65:791–823.

Montes, Maria B. 1995. "U.S. Recognition of Its Obligation to Filipino Amerasian Children under International Law." *Hastings Law Journal* 46:1621–41.

Moore, Sally Falk. 1973. "The Semi-Autonomous Social Field as an Appropriate Subject of Study." *Law & Society Review* 7(4):719–46.

Morgan, Kimberly and Ann Shola Orloff. 2017. *The Many Hands of the State: Theorizing Political Authority and Social Control.* New York, NY: Cambridge University Press.

Morris, George Hoey and John E. Dunkelberger. 1998. "Duc Hoa Villagers' Opinions about the U.S., Americans and Vietnamese Affairs, 1992: A Study of Then and Now." *Contemporary Sociology* 35:91–105.

Morrow, James D. 1994. "Alliances, Credibility, and Peacetime Costs." *Journal of Conflict Resolution* 38(2):270–97.

Moselina, Leopoldo. 1987. "Prostitution and Militarization." Pp. 49–64 in *Cast the First Stone*, edited by the World Council of Churches and the National Council of Churches. Quezon City, Philippines: A Joint Publication of the World Council of Churches, Women's Desk and the National Council of Churches, Division of Family Ministries.

Mosley, Layna and David A. Singer. 2015. "Migration, Labor, and the International Political Economy." *Annual Review of Political Science* 18:283–301.

Murphy, Peter and Trevor Hogan. 2012. "Discordant Order: Manila's Neo-Patrimonial Urbanism." *Thesis Eleven* 112(1):10–34.

Myers, Daniel J. and Beth Schaefer Caniglia. 2004. "All the Rioting That's Fit to Print: Selection Effects in National Newspaper Coverage of Civil Disorders, 1968–1969." *American Sociological Review* 69:519–43.

Mysinchew.com. 2011. "Female S. Korea Activist on 188th Day of Crane Protest." July 12. http://www.mysinchew.com/node/60405 (accessed June 14, 2017).

Nash, June C. and Maria Patricia Fernandez-Kelly, eds. 1983. *Women, Men, and the International Division of Labor.* Albany, NY: State University of New York Press.

National Statistics Office. 2011a. *Foreign Trade Statistics of the Philippines*, vol. 1, *Imports.* https://psa.gov.ph/sites/default/files/2011%20Foreign%20Trade%20Statistics%20of%20the%20Philippines%20VOLUME%20I-IMPORTS.pdf (accessed January 22, 2019).

———. 2011b. *Foreign Trade Statistics of the Philippines*, vol. 2, *Exports*. https://psa.gov.ph /sites/default/files/2011%20Foreign%20Trade%20Statistics%20of%20the%20Phili- pines%20VOLUME%20II-EXPORTS.pdf (accessed January 22, 2019).

NBC News. 2014. "Summer Like No Other: Mexico Tourism Hits Record Levels." September 2. http://www.nbcnews.com/news/latino/summer-no-other-mexico -tourism-hits-record-levels-n193706 (accessed January 16, 2017).

Newhall, Chris, James W. Hendley II, and Peter H. Stauffer. 1997. "The Cataclys- mic 1991 Eruption of Mount Pinatubo, Philippines." U.S. Geological Survey Fact Sheet 113-97. Last modified February 28, 2005. https://www.usgs.gov/news /remembering-mount-pinatubo-25-years-ago-mitigating-crisis (accessed May 31, 2017).

Newman, Katherine S. and Rourke O'Brien. 2011. *Taxing the Poor: Doing Damage to the Truly Disadvantaged*. Berkeley, CA: University of California Press.

New York Theater Wire. n.d. "'Positively No Filipinos Allowed." http://www.nytheatre -wire.com/c007051t.htm (accessed May 1, 2017).

Norton, Matthew. 2014. "Mechanisms and Meaning Structures." *Sociological Theory* 32(2):162–87.

Nye, Joseph S. 1990. "Soft Power." *Foreign Policy* 80:153–71.

———. 2004. *Soft Power: The Means to Success in World Politics*. New York, NY: PublicAffairs.

Ocampo, Anthony Christian. 2016. *The Latinos of Asia: How Filipino Americans Break the Rules of Race*. Stanford, CA: Stanford University Press.

Olongapo SubicBay BatangGapo Newscenter. 2010. "Owners of Subic Blue Plates Warned." February 27. http://subicbaynews.blogspot.com/2010/02/owners-of-subic -blue-plates-warned.html (accessed November 23, 2016).

———. 2011. "Hanjin Workers Gaining Support." June 30. http://subicbaynews.blogspot .com/2011/06/hanjin-workers-gaining-support.html (accessed June 14, 2017).

Oliver, Pamela E. and Daniel J Myers. 1999. "How Events Enter the Public Sphere: Con- flict, Location, and Sponsorship in Local Newspaper Coverage of Public Events." *American Journal of Sociology* 105(1):38–87.

Ong, Aihwa. 1991. "The Gender and Labor Politics of Postmodernity." *Annual Review of Anthropology* 20:279–309.

———. 2006. *Neoliberalism as Exception: Mutations in Citizenship and Sovereignty*. Dur- ham, NC: Duke University Press.

———. 2010. *Spirits of Resistance and Capitalist Discipline: Factory Women in Malaysia*. 2nd ed. Albany, NY: State University of New York Press.

Paddock, Richard C. 2016. "In Philippine Drug War, Little Help for Those Who Sur- render." *New York Times*, September 5. https://www.nytimes.com/2016/09/06/world /asia/in-philippine-drug-war-little-help-for-those-who-surrender.html (accessed April 19, 2017).

Pagaduan, Angel N. 2007. *Subic: An Epochal Philippine Town the U.S. Navy Helped Shape*. Baltimore: PublishAmerica.

Paredes, Joel C. 2009. "A Million Came for Ninoy as Reporters Battled Censors." Philippine Center for Investigative Journalism, August–September. http://pcij.org/stories/a-million-came-for-ninoy-as-reporters-battled-censors/ (accessed January 22, 2019).

Parker, Nick and David Ariosto. 2013. "Gunmen Rape 6 Tourists near Acapulco, Mexico." CNN.com, February 5. http://www.cnn.com/2013/02/05/world/americas/mexico-tourists-raped/ (accessed September 15, 2014).

Parreñas, Rhacel Salazar. 2001. *Servants of Globalization: Women, Migration, and Domestic Work*. Stanford, CA: Stanford University Press.

———. 2011. *Illicit Flirtations: Labor, Migration and Sex Trafficking in Tokyo*. Stanford, CA: Stanford University Press.

Perlez, Jane. 2016. "Rodrigo Duterte and Xi Jinping Agree to Reopen South China Sea Talks." *New York Times*, October 20. https://www.nytimes.com/2016/10/21/world/asia/rodrigo-duterte-philippines-china-xi-jinping.html?_r=1 (accessed May 30, 2017).

Philippine Daily Inquirer. 2014. "Apl.de.ap Is Clark Green City Endorser." September 9. http://newsinfo.inquirer.net/636304/apl-de-ap-is-clark-green-city-endorser (accessed September 29, 2016).

———. 2015. "Laudes Sue VFA Exec, 11 Pemberton Guards for Contempt." December 15. http://newsinfo.inquirer.net/747688/laudes-sue-vfa-exec-11-pemberton-guards-for-contempt (accessed April 22, 2016).

Philippines Department of Tourism. 2011. "A Strong Philippine Tourism in 2011: Department of Tourism Year-End Report." http://www.tourism.gov.ph/files/2011%20DOT%20Year%20End%20Report.pdf (accessed January 22, 2019).

———. 2012. "Philippine Tourism 2012: Gearing for More Fun and Progress." http://www.tourism.gov.ph/files/2012%20DOT%20Year%20End%20Report.pdf (accessed January 22, 2109).

Philippines Japan Society. 2015. "Domingo L. Siazon, Jr." Philippines Japan Society Medal of Merit Award (website), January 9. https://pjsmedalofmerit.wordpress.com/2015/01/09/domingo-l-siazon-jr/ (accessed May 25, 2017).

Philippines News Agency. 2010. "Customs Orders Crackdown on Blue-Plated Cars." February 18. http://balita.ph/2010/02/18/customs-orders-crackdown-on-blue-plated-cars/ (accessed November 23, 2016).

Phillips, Lynne. 2006. "Food and Globalization." *Annual Review of Anthropology* 35:37–57.

Pimentel, Benjamin. 2005. "No Matter How Successful He Gets, Black Eyed Peas' Apl Never Forgets His Roots in a Filipino Barrio, and His All-Tagalog Hip-Hop Hit Proves It." *SF Gate*, August 8. http://www.sfgate.com/entertainment/article/No-matter-how-succesful-he-gets-Black-Eyed-Peas-2617906.php (accessed September 29, 2016).

Pisani, Michael J. 2013. "Cross-Border Consumption of Informal and Underground Goods: A Case Study of Alternative Consumerism in South Texas." *Social Science Quarterly* 94(1):242–62.

Portes, Alejandro, Patricia Fernández-Kelly, and William Haller. 2009. "The Adaptation of the Immigrant Second Generation in America: A Theoretical Overview and Recent Evidence." *Journal of Ethnic and Migration Studies* 35(7):1077–104.

Portes, Alejandro and Ruben G. Rumbaut. 2001. *Legacies: The Story of the Immigrant Second Generation.* Berkeley, CA: University of California Press.

Portes, Alejandro and Min Zhou. 1993. "The New Second Generation: Segmented Assimilation and Its Variants." *Annals of the American Academy of Political and Social Science* 530(1):74–96.

Port Technology. 2016. "Infographic: Hanjin in Numbers." September 14. https://www.porttechnology.org/news/infographic_hanjin_in_numbers (accessed June 12, 2017).

Preda Foundation. 2011. "Subic Rape Victim 'Nicole' Recanted Her Earlier Statements That Lance Corporal Daniel Smith, Who Was Convicted in 2007, Raped Her." May 11. http://www.preda.org/world/subic-rape-victim-nicole-recanted-her-earlier-statements-that-lance-corporal-daniel-smith-who-was-convicted-in-2007-raped-her/ (accessed May 24, 2018).

Puno, Reynato S. 1987. "Keynote Address: Perspective on Prostitution." Pp. 5–12 in *Cast the First Stone.* Quezon City, Philippines: A Joint Publication of the World Council of Churches, Women's Desk and the National Council of Churches, Division of Family Ministries.

quisumbing king, katrina. 2016. "Between Sovereignty and Suzerainty: Filipino Elites and Negotiated Independence." Working paper.

Rafael, Vicente L. 2000. *White Love and Other Events in Filipino History.* Durham, NC: Duke University Press.

Ralph, Laurence. 2014. *Renegade Dreams: Living through Injury in Gangland Chicago.* Chicago, IL: University of Chicago Press.

Ralston, Meredith and Edna Keeble. 2009. *Reluctant Bedfellows: Feminism, Activism, and Prostitution in the Philippines.* Sterling, VA: Kumarian Press.

Ramos, Marlon. 2016. "12 Agencies to Lead Gov't Antipoverty Programs." *Philippine Daily Inquirer*, July 5. http://newsinfo.inquirer.net/639624/extended-work-hours-cited-in-death-in-hanjin (accessed June 12, 2017).

Rappler.com. 2014. "Laude Fiancé Sueselbeck Leaves Manila." November 1. http://www.rappler.com/nation/73733-laude-fiance-sueselbeck-leaves-manila (accessed May 16, 2016).

Redden, Elizabeth. 2015. "Persona Non Grata." InsiderHigherEd.com, March 18. https://www.insidehighered.com/news/2015/03/18/nyu-professor-denied-entry-uae-where-university-has-campus (accessed January 16, 2017).

———. 2017. "Visa Denied." InsiderHigherEd.com, January 9. https://www.insidehighered.com/news/2017/01/09/georgetown-student-denied-visa-study-universitys-qatar-campus (accessed January 16, 2017).

Reed, Isaac Ariail. 2013. "Power: Relational, Discursive, and Performative Dimensions." *Sociological Theory* 31(3): 193–218.

Reuters. 2016a. "Hanjin Shipping Sells Part of Container Ship Business for \$31 Million." November 21. http://uk.reuters.com/article/uk-hanjin-shipping-debt-idUKKBN13G2I0 (accessed June 14, 2017).

———. 2016b. "Philippines, U.S. Agree to Reduce Joint Military Drills: Philippine General." November 22. http://www.reuters.com/article/us-philippines-usa-defence-idUSKBN13H0UW (accessed April 17, 2017).

———. 2016c. "UPDATE 1—S. Korea's Hanjin Shipping to Seek Bank-Debt Restructuring." April 22. http://in.reuters.com/article/hanjin-shipping-restructuring-idINL3N17P2KY (accessed June 14, 2017).

Reyes, Victoria. 2018a. "Ethnographic Toolkit: Strategic Positionality and Researchers' Visible and Invisible Tools in Field Research." *Ethnography*, first published online October 25. https://doi.org/10.1177/1466138118805121.

———. 2018b. "Port of Call: How Ships Shape Foreign-Local Encounters." *Social Forces* 96(3):1097–118.

———. 2018c. "Three Models of Transparency in Ethnographic Research: Naming Places, Naming People, and Sharing Data." *Ethnography* (Special issue on innovations in ethnographic research) 19(2):204–26.

———. Forthcoming. "Global Ethnography: Lessons from the Chicago School." *Research in Urban Sociology, Volume 16: Urban Ethnography.*

Rigos, Cirilo A. 1975. "The Posture of the Church in the Philippines under Martial Law." *Southeast Asian Affairs*: 127–32.

Rimmer, Peter J. 1997. "US Western Pacific Geostrategy: Subic Bay before and after Withdrawal." *Marine Policy* 21(4):325–44.

Rios, Victor M. 2011. *Punished: Policing the Lives of Black and Latino Boys*. New York, NY: New York University Press.

Rippl, Susanne, Nicola Bucker, Anke Petrat, and Klaus Boehnke. 2010. "Crossing the Frontier: Transnational Social Integration in the EU's Border Regions." *International Journal of Comparative Sociology* 5(1–2):5–31.

Rivera, Lauren. 2008. "Managing 'Spoiled' National Identity: War, Tourism and Memory in Croatia." *American Sociological Review* 73:613–34.

Roberts, Amy. 2013. "By the Numbers: U.S. Diplomatic Presence." CNN, May 9. http://www.cnn.com/2013/05/09/politics/btn-diplomatic-presence/index.html (accessed June 20, 2017).

Robinson, Tammy Ko. 2011. "The Plight of Precarious Workers in Korea and the Philippines." *Global Research*, November 10. http://www.globalresearch.ca/the-plight-of-precarious-workers-in-korea-and-the-philippines/27576 (accessed June 14, 2017).

Rodriguez, Robyn Magalit. 2010. *Migrants for Export: How the Philippine State Brokers Labor to the World*. Minneapolis, MN: University of Minnesota Press.

Romulo, Mons. 2004. "What Are Your Memories of the Day Ninoy Was Killed?" *Philippine Star*, August 15. http://www.philstar.com/sunday-life/261347/what-are-your-memories-day-ninoy-was-killed (accessed July 5, 2017).

Rudolph, Dieter K. and Charles P. Guard. 1991. *Annual Tropical Cyclone Report*. U.S. Naval Oceanography Command Center, Joint Typhoon Warning Center. FPO AP 96540-0051. http://www.usno.navy.mil/NOOC/nmfc-ph/RSS/jtwc/atcr/1991atcr.pdf (accessed May 31, 2017).

Rueda, Nimfa U. 2016. "Apl.de.ap Honored for Saving Babies from Blindness." *Philippine Daily Inquirer*, March 27. http://globalnation.inquirer.net/138103/apl-de-ap-honored -for-saving-babies-from-blindness (accessed September 29, 2016).

Rutherford, Blair. 2011. "The Uneasy Ties of Working and Belonging: The Changing Situation for Undocumented Zimbabwean Migrants in Northern South Africa." *Ethnic and Racial Studies* 34(8):1303–19.

Ryan, Erica. 2012. "Chronology: The Benghazi Attack and the Fallout." NPR.org, December 19. http://www.npr.org/2012/11/30/166243318/chronology-the-benghazi-attack -and-the-fallout (accessed January 16, 2017).

Salanga, Elyas. 2014. "A Look Back at Ninoy Aquino's Murder." *Philippine Star*, August 20. http://www.philstar.com/news-feature/2014/08/20/1359731/look-back-ninoy -aquinos-murder (accessed January 22, 2019).

Salcedo, Rodrigo. 2003. "When the Global Meets the Local at the Mall." *American Behavioral Scientist* 46(8):1084–103.

Salzinger, Leslie. 2003. *Genders in Production: Making Workers in Mexico's Global Factories*. Berkeley, CA: University of California Press.

Santolan, Joseph. 2011. "Six Workers Die in Subic Shipyard in the Philippines." *World Socialist Web Site*, October 10. https://www.wsws.org/en/articles/2011/10/phil-o10 .html (accessed June 12, 2017).

Santos, Matikas. 2014. "Marc Sueselbeck: A 'Big Price to Pay' for 'Losing Control' over Pemberton." Inquirer.net, October 28. http://globalnation.inquirer.net/113601 /marc-sueselbeck-a-big-price-to-pay-for-losing-control-over-pemberton (accessed May 16, 2014).

Santos, Tina G. 2012. "Illegal Recruiters at Luneta Charged." *Philippine Daily Inquirer*, September 22. http://globalnation.inquirer.net/50908/illegal-recruiters-at-luneta -charged (accessed June 12, 2017).

Sassen, Saskia. 1991. *The Global City: New York, London, Tokyo*. Princeton, NJ: Princeton University Press.

———. 2000. "Spatialities and Temporalities of the Global: Elements for a Theorization." *Public Culture* 12(1):215–32.

———. 2003 [2000]. "Analytic Borderlands: Economy and Culture in the Global City." Pp. 168–80 in *A Companion to the City*, edited by Gary Bridge and Sophie Watson (Blackwell Companions to Geography). Malden, MA: Wiley-Blackwell.

———. 2006. *Territory, Authority, and Rights: From Medieval to Global Assemblages*. Princeton, NJ: Princeton University Press.

Scheper Hughes, Nancy. 1979. *Saints, Scholars, and Schizophrenics: Mental Illness in Rural Ireland*. Berkeley, CA: University of California Press.

Schermerhorn, Lange. 2015. "Serving in Embassy Saigon's Consular Section Meant Dealing with the Social Consequences—Marriages, Births, Adoptions—of More Than Three Million Americans Coming through a Country of 26 Million." *Foreign Service Journal*, April. http://www.afsa.org/doing-social-work-southeast-asia (accessed October 14, 2016).

Schmitt, Carl. 1988 [1922]. *Political Theology: Four Chapters on the Concept of Sovereignty.* Translated by George Schwab. Chicago, IL: University of Chicago Press.

Schumpeter, Joseph A. 1991 [1918]. "The Crisis of the Tax State." Pp. 99–149 in *The Economics and Sociology of Capitalism,* edited by Richard Swedberg. Princeton, NJ: Princeton University Press.

Schurz, William Lytle. 1918. "Mexico, Peru, and the Manila Galleon." *Hispanic American Historical Review* 1(4):389–402.

Scott, James C. 1998. *Seeing like a State: How Certain Schemes to Improve the Human Condition Have Failed.* New Haven, CT: Yale University Press.

Seol, Kap Su. 2011. "Video: Woman Welder Sits In atop Crane to Protest Job Cuts." *Labor Notes,* July 14. http://labornotes.org/blogs/2011/07/video-woman-welder-sits-atop -crane-protest-job-cuts (accessed June 14, 2017).

Sewell, William H. 1996. "Three Temporalities: Toward an Eventful Sociology." Pp. 245–80 in *The Historic Turn in the Human Sciences,* edited by Terrence J. McDonald. Ann Arbor, MI: University of Michigan Press.

Shaffer, Gregory C. and Mark A. Pollack. 2010. "Hard vs Soft Law: Alternatives, Complements, and Antagonists in International Governance." *Minnesota Law Review* 94:706–99.

Shimizu, Celine Parreñas. 2007. *The Hypersexuality of Race: Performing Asian/American Women on Screen and Scene.* Durham, NC: Duke University Press.

Simmons, Beth A. 1998. "Compliance with International Agreements." *Annual Review of Political Science* 1:75–93.

———. 2002. "Capacity, Commitment, and Compliance: International Institutions and Territorial Disputes." *Journal of Conflict Resolution* 46(6):829–56.

———. 2010. "Treaty Compliance and Violation." *Annual Review of Political Science* 13:273–96.

Simmons, Beth A. and Allison Danner. 2010. "Credible Commitments and the International Criminal Court." *International Organization* 64:225–56.

Sklair, Leslie. 1991. "Problems of Socialist Development: The Significance of Shenzhen Special Economic Zone for China's Open Door Development Strategy." *International Journal of Urban and Regional Research* 15:197–215.

Skocpol, Theda and Margaret Somers. 1980. "The Uses of Comparative History in Macrosocial Inquiry." *Comparative Studies in Society and History* 22(2):174–97.

Slaughter, Anne-Marie. 1995. "International Law in a World of Liberal States." *European Journal of International Law* 6(1):503–38.

———. 2004. *A New World Order.* Princeton, NJ: Princeton University Press.

Small, Mario L. 2015. "De-Exoticizing Ghetto Poverty: On the Ethics of Representation in Urban Ethnography." *City & Community* 14(4):352–58.

Smith, Alastair. 1995. "Alliance Formation and War." *International Studies Quarterly* 39(4):405–25.

Smith, Robert. 2005. *Mexican New York: Transnational Lives of New Immigrants.* Berkeley, CA: University of California Press.

Snyder, Francis G. 1981. "Colonialism and Legal Form: The Creation of 'Customary Law' in Senegal." *Journal of Legal Pluralism* 19:49–90.

Somers, Margaret R. and Christopher N. J. Roberts. 2008. "Toward a New Sociology of Rights: A Genealogy of 'Buried Bodies' of Citizenship and Human Rights." *Annual Review of Law and Social Science* 4:385–425.

Spivak, Gayatri Chakravorty. 1994. "Can the Subaltern Speak?" Pp. 66–111 in *Colonial Discourse and Postcolonial Theory: A Reader*, edited by Patrick Williams and Laura Chrisman. New York, NY: Columbia University Press.

Staton, Jeffery K. 2006. "Constitutional Review and the Selective Promotion of Case Results." *American Journal of Political Science* 50(1):98–112.

Steinmetz, George. 2014. "The Sociology of Empires, Colonies, and Postcolonialism." *Annual Review of Sociology* 40:77–103.

Stets, Jan E. and Michael J. Carter. 2012. "A Theory of Self for the Sociology of Morality." *American Sociological Review* 77(1):120–40.

Stillerman, Joel and Rodrigo Salcedo. 2012. "Transposing the Urban to the Mall: Routes, Relationships, and Resistance in Two Santiago, Chile, Shopping Centers." *Journal of Contemporary Ethnography* 41(3):309–36.

Stinchcombe, Arthus. 2005. "Law Facts." *Annual Review of Law and Social Science* 1:233–54.

Stoler, Ann Laura. 2002. *Carnal Knowledge and Imperial Power: Race and the Intimate in Colonial Rule*. Berkeley, CA: University of California Press.

Stoltzfus, Brenda. 1987a. "Olongapo's Trap." Pp. 169–73 in *Cast the First Stone*. Quezon City, Philippines: A Joint Publication of the World Council of Churches, Women's Desk and the National Council of Churches, Division of Family Ministries.

———. 1987b. "Situationer on Prostitution in Olongapo." Pp. 162–68 in *Cast the First Stone*. Quezon City, Philippines: A Joint Publication of the World Council of Churches, Women's Desk and the National Council of Churches, Division of Family Ministries.

Sturdevant, Saundra Pollock and Brenda Stoltzfus. 1992. *Let the Good Times Roll: Prostitution and the U.S. Military in Asia*. New York, NY: New Press.

Subic Bay Metropolitan Authority. 1992. "Implementing Rules and Regulations of the Subic Special Economic and Freeport Zone and the Subic Bay Metropolitan Authority under Republic Act No. 7227." Subic Bay Freeport Zone, Philippines: Subic Bay Metropolitan Authority. http://www.mysubicbay.com.ph/files/general/20160830-115756-485.pdf (accessed February 5, 2019).

———. 2011. "Subic Bay Freeport: Residents' Handbook." Subic Bay Freeport Zone, Philippines: Subic Bay Metropolitan Authority.

———. 2012. "SBMA Signs MOU with Korea's Silicon Valley." Subic Bay Freeport Zone, Philippines: Subic Bay Metropolitan Authority, August 15. http://www.mysubicbay.com.ph/news/2012/08/15/sbma-signs-mou-with-koreas-silicon-valley (accessed January 15, 2019).

———. 2013. "SBMA, Resom Sign P20-Billion Tourism Project." Subic Bay Freeport Zone, Philippines: Subic Bay Metropolitan Authority, June 17. http://www.sbma

.com/news/2013/06/17/sbma-resom-sign-p20-billion-tourism-project (accessed January 15, 2019).

———. 2014. "Investor's Guide." Subic Bay Freeport Zone, Philippines: Subic Bay Metropolitan Authority. http://invest.mysubicbay.com.ph/investors-guide (accessed January 22, 2019).

Sundberg, Juanita. 2008. "'Trash-Talk' and the Production of Quotidian Geopolitical Boundaries in the USA-Mexico Borderlands." *Social & Cultural Geography* 9(8):871–90.

Suter, Keith. 1986. "The Current Military Situation in the Philippines." *RUSI Journal* 131(3):43–48.

Swidler, Ann. 1986. "Culture in Action: Symbols and Strategies." *American Sociological Review* 51(2):273–86.

———. 2001. *Talk of Love: How Culture Matters*. Chicago, IL: University of Chicago Press.

Tadiar, Neferti Xina M. 2004. *Fantasy-Production: Sexual Economies and Other Philippine Consequences for the New World Order*. Aberdeen, Hong Kong: Hong Kong University Press.

Talusan, Meredith. 2016. "The Aftermath of a U.S. Marine's Conviction in the Death of a Philippine Trans Woman." *BuzzFeed News*, January 3. http://www.buzzfeed.com/meredithtalusan/the-aftermath-of-jennifer-laude-and-joseph-scott-pemberton?utm_term=.hn6OLD2LJ (accessed April 26, 2016).

Tamanaha, Brian. 2007. "Understanding Legal Pluralism: Past to Present, Local to Global." *Sydney Law Review* 30:375.

Tan, Michael L. and Adelina de la Paz. 1987. "Preliminary Report on the Health Situation of Child and Youth Prostitutes in Pansanjan." Pp. 35–48 in *Cast the First Stone*. Quezon City, Philippines: A Joint Publication of the World Council of Churches, Women's Desk and the National Council of Churches, Division of Family Ministries.

Taylor, Charles. 2004. *Modern Social Imaginaries*. Durham, NC: Duke University Press.

Tharoor, Ishaan. 2016. "What the South China Sea Ruling Means for the World." *Washington Post*, July 13. https://www.washingtonpost.com/news/worldviews/wp/2016/07/13/what-the-south-china-sea-ruling-means-for-the-world/?utm_term=.d1b28f6c22dc (accessed May 30, 2017).

Thomas, W. I. 1923. *The Unadjusted Girl*. Boston, MA: Little, Brown and Co.

Thomas, William I. and Florian Znaniecki. 1996. *The Polish Peasant in Europe and America*. Edited by Eli Zaretsky. Champaign, IL: University of Illinois Press.

Thompson, Willard Scott. 1975. *Unequal Partners: Philippine and Thai Relations with the United States, 1965–75*. Lexington, MA: Lexington Books.

Tilly, Charles. 1992. *Coercion, Capital, and European States, AD 990–1992*. Oxford, UK: Blackwell.

———. 2009. "Foreword." Pp. xi–xiii in *The New Fiscal Sociology: Taxation in Comparative and Historical Perspective*, edited by Isaac William Martin, Ajay K. Mehrotra, and Monica Prasad. Cambridge, UK: Cambridge University Press.

Tirres, Allison Brownell. 2008–10. "Lawyers and Legal Borderlands." *American Journal of Legal History* 50(2):157–99.

Tremml, Birgit M. 2012. "The Global and the Local: Problematic Dynamics of the Triangular Trade in Early Modern Manila." *Journal of World History* 23(3):555–86.

Tsing, Anna Lowenhaupt. 2005. *Friction: An Ethnography of Global Connection*. Princeton, NJ: Princeton University Press.

Tsutsui, Kiyoteru, Claire Whitlinger, and Alwyn Lim. 2012. "International Human Rights Law and Social Movements: States' Resistance and Civil Society's Insistence." *Annual Review of Law and Social Science* 8:367–96.

UCANews.com. 2016. "Philippine Activists Slam Reduced Sentence for US Marine." April 5. http://www.ucanews.com/news/philippine-activists-slam-reduced-sentence -for-us-marine/75665 (accessed April 26, 2016).

United States Department of Defense. 2010. *Base Structure Report: Fiscal Year 2010 Baseline, A Summary of DoD's Real Property Inventory*. Washington, DC: Office of the Deputy Under Secretary of Defense (Installations & Environment).

———. 2015. *Base Structure Report: Fiscal Year 2015 Baseline, A Summary of DoD's Real Property Inventory*. Washington, DC: Office of the Deputy Under Secretary of Defense (Installations & Environment).

U.S. General Accounting Office. 1992. *Report to Congressional Requesters: Military Base Closures: U.S. Financial Obligations in the Philippines*. Washington, DC: U.S. General Accounting Office.

U.S. Geological Survey. 2016. "Remembering Mount Pinatubo 25 Years Ago: Mitigating a Crisis." June 13. https://www.usgs.gov/news/remembering-mount-pinatubo-25 -years-ago-mitigating-crisis (accessed May 31, 2017).

Vaisey, Stephen. 2014. "The 'Attitudinal Fallacy' Is a Fallacy: Why We Need Many Methods to Study Culture." *Sociological Methods & Research* 43(2):227–31.

Vanberg, Georg. 2001. "Legislative-Judicial Relations: A Game-Theoretic Approach to Constitutional Review." *American Journal of Political Science* 45(2):346–61.

Vasi, Ion Bogdan, Edward T. Walker, John S. Johnson, and Hui Fen Tan. 2015. "'No Fracking Way!' Documentary Film, Discursive Opportunity, and Local Opposition against Hydraulic Fracturing in the United States, 2010 to 2013." *American Sociological Review* 80(5):934–59.

Veblen, Thorstein. 1994 [1899]. *The Theory of the Leisure Class*. New York, NY: Penguin Books.

Voyce, Malcolm. 2003. "The Privatisation of Public Property: The Development of a Shopping Mall in Sydney and Its Implications for Governance through Spatial Practices." *Urban Policy and Research* 21(3):249–62.

Ward, Alan. 2015. "The Sociology of Consumption: Its Recent Development." *Annual Review of Sociology* 41:117–34.

Weber, Max. 1978 [1968]. *Economy and Society*. Edited by Guenther Roth and Claus Wittich. Berkeley, CA: University of California Press.

Weil, Prosper. 1983. "Towards Relative Normativity in International Law?" *American Journal of International Law* 77(3):413–42.

Wherry, Fredrick. 2007. "Trading Impressions: Evidence from Costa Rica." *Annals of the American Academy of Political and Social Science* 610(1):217–31.

White, Richard. 2011 [1991]. *The Middle Ground: Indians, Empires, and Republics in the Great Lakes Region, 1650–1815*. Cambridge, UK: Cambridge University Press.

Widdis, Randy William. 2010. "Crossing an Intellectual and Geographic Border: The Importance of Migration in Shaping the Canadian-American Borderlands at the Turn of the Twentieth Century." *Social Science History* 34(4):445–97.

Wimmer, Andreas. 2013. *Ethnic Boundary Making: Institutions, Power, Networks*. Oxford, UK: Oxford University Press.

———. 2014. "War." *Annual Review of Sociology* 40:173–97.

Wolfe, Diane Lauren. 1992. *Factory Daughters: Gender, Household Dynamics, and Rural Industrialization in Java*. Berkeley, CA: University of California Press.

Woody, Christopher. 2016. "Mexico's Drug Cartels Have Turned a Tourist Mecca into 'Guerrero's Iraq.'" BusinessInsider.com, June 2. https://www.businessinsider.com/acapulco-growing-violence-as-cartels-battle-2016-6 (accessed January 16, 2017).

Wu, Frank. 2002. *Yellow: Race in America beyond Black and White*. New York, NY: Basic Books.

Wuthnow, Robert. 2011. "Taking Talk Seriously: Religious Discourse as Social Practice." *Journal for the Scientific Study of Religion* 50(1):1–21.

Yeoh, Brenda. 1996. "Street-Naming and Nation-Building: Toponymic Inscriptions of Nationhood in Singapore." *Area* 28:298–307.

———. 2000. "From Colonial Neglect to Post-Independence Heritage: The Housing Landscape in the Central Area of Singapore." *City & Society* 12:103–24.

Yotsumoto, Yukio. 2013. "Formalization of Urban Poor Vendors and Their Contribution to Tourism Development in Manila, Philippines." *International Journal of Japanese Sociology* 22:128–42.

Zelizer, Viviana. 2005. *The Purchase of Intimacy*. Princeton, NJ: Princeton University Press.

———. 2011. *Economic Lives: How Culture Shapes the Economy*. Princeton, NJ: Princeton University Press.

Zerubavel, Eviatar. 1987. "The Language of Time: Toward a Semiotics of Temporality." *Sociological Quarterly* 28(3):343–56.

Zhao, Minghua and Maragtas S. V. Amante. 2005. "Chinese and Filipino Seafarers: A Race to the Top or the Bottom?" *Modern Asian Studies* 39(3):535–57.

Zhou, Min and Yang Sao Xiong. 2005. "The Multifaceted American Experiences of the Children of Asian Immigrants: Lessons for Segmented Assimilation." *Ethnic and Racial Studies* 28(6):1119–152.

Zukin, Sharon. 1995. *The Cultures of Cities*. Malden, MA: Blackwell.

Zukin, Sharon and Jennifer Smith Maguire. 2004. "Consumers and Consumption." *Annual Review of Sociology* 30:173–97.

Index

Culture and Economic Life

Diverse sets of actors create meaning in markets: consumers and socially engaged actors from below; producers, suppliers, and distributors from above; and the gatekeepers and intermediaries that span these levels. Scholars have studied the interactions of people, objects, and technology; charted networks of innovation and diffusion among producers and consumers; and explored the categories that constrain and enable economic action. This series captures the many angles in which these phenomena have been investigated and serves as a high-profile forum for discussing the evolution, creation, and consequences of commerce and culture.

The Moral Power of Money: Morality and Economy in the Life of the Poor
Ariel Wilkis
2018

The Work of Art: Value in Creative Careers
Alison Gerber
2017

Behind the Laughs: Community and Inequality in Comedy
Michael P. Jeffries
2017

Freedom from Work: Embracing Financial Self-Help in the United States and Argentina
Daniel Fridman
2016